7TH EDITION • 2004-2008

THE BOOK OF
U.S. POSTAL
EXAMS

HOW TO SCORE 95-100% ON 473/473-C/460 TESTS AND OTHER EXAMS

VELTISEZAR B. BAUTISTA

BOOKHAUS PUBLISHERS

International Standard Book Number 0-931613-19-1

Publisher's Cataloging-in-Publication
(Provided by Quality Books, Inc.)

Bautista, Veltisezar B., 1933-
   The book of U.S. postal exams : how to score 95-100%
on 470 battery/460 RCA tests and other exams /
Veltisezar B. Bautista. -- 7th ed., 2004-2008.
   p. cm.
   ISBN 0-931613-19-1

   1. Postal service--United States--Examinations,
questions, etc. 2. Civil service--United States--
Examinations--Study guides. 3. Postal service--United
States--Employees.   I. Title.

HE6499.B38 2004   383'.145'076
                         QBI04-200170

Printed in the United States of America

Bookhaus Publishers
P.O. Box 836
Warren, Michigan 48090-0836
U.S.A.

Dedication

I dedicate this book to the light of my life,
Genoveva Abes-Bautista;
to my beloved children,
Hubert, Lester, Melvin, Ronald, and Janet;
to my daughter-in-law,
Maria Cecilia Asi-Bautista;
and to all job seekers who will read this book.

A Special Reminder: You now have in your possession a complete guide to scoring 95-100% on Post Office exams. The book covers exams for clerk-carrier, rural carrier, rural carrier associate, mail handler, mail processor, clerk-typist, clerk-stenographer, mark-up clerk, distribution clerk, flat sorting machine, operator, stationary engineer, electronics technician, garageman, and many more, making it the only book of its kind in the world.

The book is written in simple, easy-to-understand English. It covers in detail all the Postal exams and goings-on in the U.S. Postal Service. The book gives straight-to-the-point instructions that you can easily follow.

You can use this book as a reference not only for postal exams but also for civil service exams, so let it be a useful tool for you in this land of the survival of the fittest.

With this book, you'll know my test-taking secrets. Keep the secrets to yourself, and you and your family will always have the edge in competing for high-paying Postal jobs.

Similarities between characters in this book and persons living or dead are intentional, and not coincidental, for they are Real People like you!

Good luck!—The Author

Contents

Foreword

You Can Pass ANY Post Office Exam with Flying Colors—and Get a High-Paying Job!

I know the above is a **bold statement.**

But it's 100% true.

You *can* get that job with the Post Office and make $25,000 a year. But first you have to pass the required examination, and this is what stops most people.

Here's why:

> Although 70% is a passing score, you want to make 90 to 100% because the Post Office usually hires people who score in that range. To make a high score, you need to know certain tricks of the trade.

First, let me emphasize one point:

I'm not basing my knowledge on hearsay. I'm basing it on my own practical experience in taking these exams. I don't want to brag, but I've been among the top scorers on postal exams. As a result of my hands-on experience, I've put all the tricks of the trade, ins and outs, tips and secrets into one power-packed book called **The Book of U.S. Postal Exams: How to Score 95-100% and Get a Job.**

But before you read the book from cover to cover, let's see what life is like for a Postal Service employee.

One word describes it: *tremendous!* Did you know that postal jobs are recession-proof? As inflation rises, your cost-of-living allowance rises too. It's automatically added to your salary. (How many jobs in business give you this benefit?)

But that's not all — far from it.

The pay is high (the average postal employee makes $23,000 a year). The fringe benefits are sensational. Retirement income is great. You have freedom from layoffs. In short, *you've got lifetime financial security.*

What's more, there's no age limit. As long as you're at least 18, you can take any exam and compete with people in their 40s and 50s. It's not your age or experience or education that counts. The only thing that matters is *the score you make on the exam. Period.*

Take education, for example.

I've known college-educated people who made low scores on the exam. Were they selected? No, indeed. The jobs went to high school graduates who managed a score between 90% and 100%. I can't emphasize enough how important that score is.

The book I want to send you on a trial basis covers all the exams.

- Clerk and Carrier
- Mail Handler
- Clerk-Typist
- Clerk-Stenographer
- Mark-Up Clerk Automated
- Maintenance Mechanic (MPE)
- Rural Carrier

- Distribution Clerk, Machine (LSM Operator)
- Stationary Engineer
- Electronics Technician
- Garageman
- Mail Processor
- Assistant Engineman
- and many more!

If you've done any checking around, you've no doubt found that most books and courses cover only *one* exam. But my book covers them all — in plain, easy-to-read English.

Making a good grade on the exam is as easy as falling off a log backwards — *if you know how.*

Now, I know the word "exam" is enough to scare you. If you're like most people, you automatically think about high school and all those tests you had to take. And how scared you were. And how your mouth got full of cotton and your palms got sweaty.

Let me assure you that with my book, you'll go into any exam with all the confidence in the world. You'll already know beforehand what to expect. You'll know how to take the test. You'll know how to make that 95 to 100%.

Start flipping through this compact book and you'll discover how easy it is to read. And the beauty is, it covers *everything* you need:

- Sample test questions with answers
- Where and how to apply for examinations
- How to mark the answer sheets
- How to compare 95 pairs of names and addresses in five minutes
- How my memory code enables you to memorize 25 names and addresses in five minutes
- How to get 95-100% on a *scheme* exam
- Instant math, vocabulary, and spelling
- How to transfer from one job to another
- How to transfer from one state to another without losing your seniority

— and much more.

Employment hinges on one thing and one thing only: *how well you do on the exam.*

This rule is strictly enforced with no ifs, ands, or buts. You could have a Ph.D. and still not be hired if you didn't come through on the exam. It doesn't matter whether you're a United States citizen or an immigrant, man or woman, black or white, brown or yellow, you name it. *It's your exam score that counts.*

People are happy with their Post Office exam scores, thanks to this book.

People who've benefited from this new book write me all the time. (See the excerpts from their letters on the back cover of this book.) If you're ever in Farmington Hills, (MI), stop by and I'll show you file cabinets full of letters I've received.

I'm thrilled with what this book is doing for others, but my main concern today is with *you*. I want to help *you* pass the exam and get a high-paying postal job. Will you let me?

Yes, just think what a secure, high-paying job with the Postal Service will mean to you. No more worrying about being laid off. No more politics on the job. No more have to apple-polish the boss. You'll have it made.

But, as I've said so many times, making a high score is essential.

This new book is based on my success and on the systems I've worked out.

In fact, Susan L. Lindeman, Notary Public, Wayne County, Michigan, certifies that my scores on postal exams have been 78.5%, 88.5%, 95.8%, 99%, and 100%.

Notice how the scores have gone up and up—because I worked out sure-fire, can't-fail systems; the very systems I want to share with you now. Use them and you can't fail!

Veltisezar B. Bautista
Author

About the Author:

The author, **Veltisezar B. Bautista,** is a
multi-award winning author and entrepreneur.
Named the Small Press Publisher of the Year in 1990
by Quality Books, Inc., he is the recipient of six other
book awards, (including two Benjamin Franklin
Awards from Publishers Marketing Association).
A former journalist and the author of five books,
Bautista lives in Farmington Hills, Michigan.

Who Is Qualified to Apply for Exams?

1

Age Requirement

"The general minimum age requirement for positions in the Postal Service is 18 at the time of employment. For high school graduates or for persons certified by local authorities as having terminated formal education for adequate reasons, the minimum age is 16. Applicants who are less than 18 years of age, who are not high school graduates, and have not terminated formal education may participate in the examination if they will reach 18 within two years from the date of examination. For carrier positions which require driving, applicants must be 18 years of age or over. There is no maximum age limit."

If you are 18 years old and if you're really ambitious, you might already be a supervisor or a postmaster when you reach 30 or 35.

Citizenship

"All applicants must be citizens of or owe allegiance to the United States of America or have been granted permanent resident alien status in the United States."

Whether you are from the Philippines, Haiti, or Nicaragua, provided you are an immigrant, you are eligible to take a postal exam and to be employed in the USPS.

Qualification Requirements

Many positions, such as clerk and carrier, require passing an entrance exam; but some do not. To be a plumber, a machinist, or a maintenance mechanic, you have to pass a written exam. Your rating will be based both on the written test and on your qualifications. But you don't need to pass a written exam, for example, if you're a physician, a nurse, a psychologist, or a computer programmer. Your rating on these jobs will be based on your education, training, and experience. In the written tests, the passing score is 70 (excluding the extra five or 10 points for applicants entitled to veteran preference.)

Educational Requirements

The Postal Service does not indicate that you must be a high school graduate to be eligible for any position. So unless it is stated specifically that you need a college degree to be qualified for a certain position, such as doctor, nurse, or engineer, you will be considered for any position if you meet the the requirements and win over other competitors.

Physical Requirements

Applicants must be physically able to perform efficiently the arduous duties of any position. For instance, the physical requirements for a carrier are different from those for a maintenance electrician. The carrier must be able to carry a load of 70 lbs. and must be on the road in all conditions. The electrician must be able to perform the duties of the position, which may involve standing, walking, climbing, bending, reaching, and stooping for prolonged periods of time as well as intermittent lifting and carrying of heavy tools, tool boxes, and equipment on level surfaces and up ladders and stairways.

Physical examination. All applicants who will be called for employment must undergo a thorough physical examination, including eye and ear tests. The Post Office does not care whether you're the size of Tinker Belle or Mr. T.

Like your car, you should always be in top condition. No matter how cold or how hot it is, your car engine must turn over as soon as you turn the ignition key. Your own engine should also be in good condition to withstand the conditions of the roads and the climate. Whether you are a carrier or clerk, you must be healthy enough to carry a load of mail weighing up to 70 pounds.

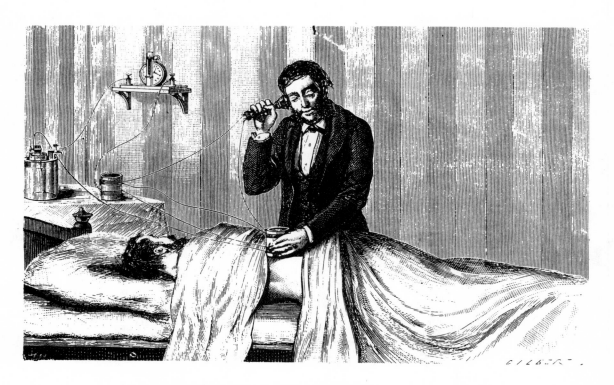

Thorough Physical Exam

It's a Test of Strength

As for the lifting or carrying a sack of mail up to seventy pounds, don't worry. Although, it's a test of strength, it's not for the championship of the world. You don't need the help of **The Incredible Hulk,** either. Even a thin woman can lift a seventy-pound sack of paper. If you lift weights, then you can lift it with one hand. (Look Ma, only one hand!)

Eye Examination. As regards the eye examination, the Post Office says that the requirement for distance vision is 20/40 (Snellen) in the better eye and at least 20/100 (Snellen) in the other eye. However, you are allowed to wear eyeglasses. Don't ask me what these figures mean; frankly, I don't know. I do know that in the eye test, you are asked to read some letters a few yards away, just as when you are taking eye examinations to be fitted for a new pair of glasses.

The person who gives your eye test will also determine whether you can read printing as small as Jaeger's test, type No 4 (whatever it is) at 14 inches with the better eye. I don't know how small this is, but as long as you can read letters and figures ordinarily written on envelopes, you'll pass the eye test.

Hearing test. Like other applicants for any postal job, you must also have good hearing. For this reason, your ears will also be tested; you'll be wearing a headset and you'll be asked which ear hears a certain sound produced by a testing machine. Your ears must be keen enough to hear ordinary conversation; if you are an applicant for a letter carrier or a rural carrier position, you must be able to hear shouts from a distance, such as *"The dogs are coming, the dogs are coming!"*

According to USPS announcement sheets, Post Office jobs offer paid vacations, on-the-job training, liberal retirement, sick leave with pay, life insurance, low-cost health insurance, cash for suggestions, promotion opportunities, and paid holidays. Employees are paid ten percent extra for work performed between 6:00 p.m. and 6 a.m.

"The Dogs are Coming!
The Dogs are Coming!"

Training Requirements

Applicants for some positions may be required to complete satisfactorily a prescribed training course or courses before assignment, reassignment, or promotion.

Operator's Permit

Some positions may require driving a government vehicle. Such positions include city carrier, rural carrier, garageman, and electronics technician.

Before you are hired for one of these jobs, you must hold a valid driver's license from the state in which the post office is located. After that you must obtain the appropriate government operator's permit.

Road Test

As an applicant for carrier or any other position requiring that you drive a government vehicle, you must demonstrate a safe driving record and pass a postal road test. If you fail the road test the first time, you cannot be hired, but you may be given a second chance later. Some people who have taken this test complain that it is more difficult than the state road test. That's because safety is the name of the game in the Postal Service; to pass this road test, you must show that you follow traffic rules, drive safely, and deliver letters, magazines, and parcels to the addressees without damage.

Pay Raise Under the Contract Effective September 7, 2002

Under the Agreement effective September 7, 2002, providing with automatic pay increases, the pay scales depending on grade levels are as follows:

```
L-1: $23,548 — $39,545
L-2: $24,534 — $40,;290
L-3: $25,681 — $41,100
L-4: $29,116 — $41,911
L-5: $30,693 — $42,798
L-6: $32,369 — $43,799
L-7: $33,144 — $44,919
L-8: $38,890 — $46,521
L-9: $39,805 — $47,878
L-10: $40,769 — $49,336
```

The above salaries are for regular postal employees. Part-time flexible employees at grade Level 1 receive from $11.77 — $19.77 per hour. Part-time regular rates (Level 1) are from $11.32 — $19.01 per hour. Transitional employee rates are from $10.43 — $13.49 per hour.

Postal examinations are held in testing centers throughout the United States. (See Supplement B: **National Directory of U.S. Postal Service Examination Centers.**) How often tests are held depends on the need for new or additional personnel. Examinations are not usually announced in the newspapers, over the radio, or on television.

Call the testing center in your area at least once a week so you won't miss an examination. The personnel department will not say whether there will be an exam any week in the future; an exam is usually announced only during the week when it accepts applications for tests. Postal exams are announced only by posting announcement sheets on postal bulletin boards; it is usually posted only for the week when it is announced. After that, it's gone with the wind!

Eligibility is Transferable

You must file an application for examinations, even if the test is for a city far from your home. In that way, you'll gain test experience. Furthermore, if you make a high score, you can request the transfer of your "eligibility" to the city where you live or to any city of your choice. The best time to transfer your eligibility is when there are "openings" in the city where you intend to move. In other words, you can take postal exams in any city of any state and if you make a high score, you request the transfer of your eligibility to the city where you want to live and work. If your eligibility is transferred, you'll lose your eligibility in the city where you took the exam. When you are an *eligible*, you can postpone your employment in the Post Office for a certain period of time and still remain an eligible. (See **Canvassing of Eligibles,** page 23.)

How to Fill Out the Application Form

When a Post Office testing center tells you that it is accepting applications for examinations, go to that office, get the application form, and fill it out — it's easy to do. Complete it there and turn it in. If you mail it, the Post Office may not receive it that week. Who knows? Your application may be put by mistake into a pouch bound for Maine, instead of one bound for a city in California. Filled-out application forms are accepted only Monday through Friday.

The U.S. Postal Service   2

More than three hundred years ago, in 1657 to be exact, the Post Office of England was established as a government entity. In the same year, the Colonial Court of Virginia required every tobacco planter to convey official mail dispatches to the next plantation. This action became the first move in the colonies to transport mail from one locality to another. This service, however, was intended only for official mail. Another four years passed before the Virginia assembly required planters to forward "all letters superscribed for the service of His Majesty or publique," or to pay a fine of 350 pounds of tobacco. This step opened the service to all people in the colony.

Today, the U.S. Postal Service, a semiprivate corporation but still considered a federal agency, remains the giant in US civilian employment. Compared to previous years' employment of more than 660,000, the USPS now employs more than 900,000. The number of employees rose to this number with the hiring of a variety of categories of temporary employees. These temporary workers, many of whom are considered as not temps, number more than 186,000. They include the part-time flexible, part-time regular, and transitional employees. The new employees are replacements of those who die or retire or workers who fill new positions created by expansion.

Scheduled Postal Service

Way back in 1672, the first serious attempt was made to establish scheduled postal service between several of the northern colonies. Francis Lovelace, the governor of New York, directed a man to carry letters monthly on horseback between New York and Boston. Then in 1692 Great Britain established the first national postal system for the American colonies. In 1753, Britain appointed Benjamin Franklin, then postmaster of Philadelphia, as a deputy postmaster general for all the colonies. In 1774, however, Franklin was removed from his post because of his questionable allegiance to the Crown.

New U.S. Postal System

After the colonies severed their ties to England in 1775, the Continental Congress established its own postal system and appointed Franklin as its head. On February 20, 1792, the U.S. Congress authorized the Post Office as a permanent government agency. By 1794 Congress had authorized the hiring of letter carriers and paid them a two-cent fee for every letter delivered to a business firm.

Then in 1825 the name *Post Office Department* acquired official sanction. In that year, Congress also authorized the delivery of mail to private homes. The carriers, however, were paid not by the government but by the addressees.

Pony Express

The famous Pony Express was established on April 3, 1860. A private postal and express system, the service ran between St. Joseph, Missouri and San Francisco, via Sacramento. Horses, running in relays at 190 stations along the 2,000-mile route, took eight to ten days to complete the delivery route. The Pony Express met its demise when telegraph lines were established between the east and the west.

By 1861 President Abraham Lincoln's postmaster general, Montgomery Blair, had introduced free city delivery, postal money orders, and railway post offices. In 1862 the first railway post office began to operate in the United States. In the 1880's the government added more postal services and established more railroad post offices.

New Services

In 1953 air mail service was begun; in 1955 the certified mail service was established. On June 30, 1971 the name *U.S. Post Office Department* was changed to *U.S. Postal Service.* The Service became independent and is no longer supervised by the Office of Personnel Management (OPM), formerly the Civil Service Commission. Its head is still called the Postmaster General, but he is not a member of the President's Cabinet. Over 25 percent of all federal employees are paid under the coordinated Federal Wage Board System, but postal workers are paid according to wage schedules set under the Postal Pay Act.

Pay Rates

At present, the Postal Service pay scale consists of several rate schedules. These schedules cover different types and levels of postal employees such as technical, clerical, production, supervisory, mail carriers, and executive management. Pay schedules provide periodic increases for fixed numbers of years of service, and postal workers are paid cost-of-living adjustments (COLA). When inflation rises, postal COLA rises too.

When a man or woman is hired as a postal employee, he or she may join the American Postal Workers Union (APWU), the largest postal union in the world, the National Association of Letter Carriers, or one of other post office unions.

USPS Automation and Computerization   3

The U.S. Postal Service, like other businesses and government agencies, is undergoing automation and computerization. Computers, flat-sorting machines, and optical character reader (OCR) machines are invading post offices premises. Do these machines steal jobs from humans?

In mid-1982, positions of mark-up clerks in central mark-up units (CMU's) were abolished in about 21 offices in the Royal Oak (MI) management sectional center (MSC). Two to four positions were eliminated in every post office, but the former mark-up clerks were transferred to other jobs within the service. They were not laid off. Then over 30 new mark-up clerks, automated, were hired and assigned to the new Royal Oak computerized forwarding system (CFS) unit.

Thus, the transformation of the mark-up clerks into mark-up clerks, automated, took place throughout the country.

The Postal Service needs employees to operate the new flat-sorting machines, which process magazines and other "flat" mail, such as manila envelopes. It also needs operators for OCR machines, which read the ZIP codes on machinable mail (letters that can run through the machines). These positions are offered first to those already in the Postal Service. If the service cannot recruit the required crew, the jobs are offered to "outsiders." In this way, new positions are created.

How's the volume of mail? Unemployment is going down in every state. Many babies are born and people are living longer, so there are many people to send messages through the mail (even if there are already the so-called E-mail, which means electronic mail, and fax machines). Such messages say, *"I love you! Long time, no see. I miss you so much"* or *"It's great to be in Florida! The weather is so good. I've forgotten to say hello to you. I wish you were here!"*

Transitional Employes and Retirees

Sometime ago, the Postal Service adopted the policy of hiring so-called transitional employees, such as transitional carriers. In connection with the automation of letter sorting, the Postal Service hired transitional carriers with the contract that they would be working for only three years. The management expected to automate the sorting of mail now done in the offices by carriers themselves before they go out to deliver mail. So the Postal Service would need only a handful of carriers in each office because all they would have to do is deliver letters, magazines, and packages.

It is the hope of the management to phase out the LSMs (letter-sorting machines) that process machinable mail. In other words, the positions of LSM operators were scheduled to be abolished; thus, the former LSM operators would be moved to other clerical positions. It's because the mail processed by LSMs was expected to be handled by multiline OCRs.

At the same time, the Postal Service offered early retirement packages to career employees, offering them a six-month lump sum payments in addition to retirement benefits. Bingo! Thousands of employees accepted the offer. In one post office district in the Detroit area, 200 employees retired! All of a sudden, the Postal Service awoke to learn that it lacked enough personnel to handle the mountains of mail.

The Good News!

As a result, post offices throughout the country hired and are still hiring thousands of employees, (as career, part-time flexible, part-time regular, and transitional employees).

The priority projects of the Postal Service for its continuous automation as contained in a report are discussed in the following paragraphs.

Multiline Optical Character Reader

This project is a two-phase operation. Part A is the conversion of existing phase II single-line OCRs to multiline OCRs (MLOCRs). Part B is the awarding of single-source contracts to UNISYS (Burroughs) and Pitney-Bowes to develop conversion kits for the single-line OCRs they manufactured under the Phase I program.

This program, combined with other advancements in the application of bar codes to letters, is expected to reduce the time that letter carriers spend sorting mail. Mail is fed to the MLOCR at a rate of 32,000 to 40,000 pieces of mail per hour. The machine reads as many as five lines of address information, sends this information to the computer that holds the national and local directories, verifies it, returns nine-digit ZIP code information, and applies it in bar/half-bar format. The piece of mail is then distributed to one of 44 machine stackers.

Remote Video Encoding

Even with the Multiline OCR, a significant percentage of letter mail is rejected because the address cannot be machine read sufficiently to apply a nine-digit bar code. With the remote video encoding (RVE), the nine-digit bar code can be applied on virtually all letter mail. This remote video encoding program has been implemented.

Computer Forwarding System II

This is a new address mark-up system that replaced the Computerized Forwarding System I in 197 facilities and to be deployed in 28 additional sites. (The CFS II involves more automation. For instance, the change-of-address labels (meaning the new address labels) that used to be stuck on mail matters by mark-up clerks, automated, are now automatically done by computerized machines.

Integrated Mail Handling System

This project involves the development of a "universal mail container" to replace the so-called GPMG and the ERMC. An attempt will be made to eliminate bedloading between bulk mail centers (MBCs) by the use of a new type of container.

The Postal Service will also test new "long-life" plastic pallets to see if they can replace the Litco pallets currently in use. In addition, the Postal Service will test the possible use of automated staging retrieval systems—one for letter/flat trays and one for pallets.

One-Bundle Sliding Shelf

This project will evaluate the benefits of the one-bundle sliding shelf on 240 city delivery routes.

Shrinkwrap Technology Applications Program

Shrink wrapping eliminates the fiberboard sleeve and strapping on the MM tray and the lids and straps on the flats tray.

Integrated Logistics Support System

This system will manage the stocking and handling of supplies throughout the Postal Service.

Small Parcel and Bundle Sorter

This new machine will sort bundled letters, bundled flats, or small parcels to 100 sort destinations.

Prediction Planning and Control Systems

This system will help managers determine how many employees with the necessary skills will be required to ensure the timely and efficient processing and delivery of mail.

Multipositional Flat Sorting Machines

This is a two-part project. Part A is involved with improving the operation's environment. Part B will rearrange the induction stations.

Facer-Canceller Update

The Micro Mark Retrofit will enable the Mark II to identify machinable mail. The Alhambra retrofit enables the Mark II to separate machinable/bar-coded mail. The FC200 is a new-generation facer-canceler.

ACDCS Maintenance Transition

Maintenance of the ACDCS is being turned over to the USPS maintenance personnel.

In spite of the above projects, the Postal Service does not yet plan to replace letter carriers with robots. Nobody knows yet whether robots can walk over snow and ice, delivering mail from door to door. But if the Postal Service uses robots to carry mail, a nationwide strike may be staged (even if it's illegal)—by dogs!

Computer and other equipment break down and need to be fixed, so the Postal Service is hiring more technicians and other people to meet the demand of new technologies. It would seem, therefore, that while computers and other machines are eliminating many jobs, they are creating many others. People are sending more letters than ever before, too, and businesses are sending more junk mail!

And here's the truth! When you "get in," you are in. You won't be laid off without cause. Have you ever heard of any lay-offs in the Postal Service? (Of course, you've heard of some workers who might have said, "I'll kill and be killed!")

How to Get a Job in the Postal Service 4

It doesn't matter whether you're an electrician, a professional person or just a high school graduate. It doesn't matter where you were born or where you grew up. If you're a U.S. citizen or an immigrant, you can get a job in the U.S. Postal Service by one of two routes — either by getting high scores on postal entrance examinations or (if you're a doctor, nurse, or other professional) by getting a job without any examinations.

Civil Service Eligibles

You cannot apply for a job with the USPS without being a civil service eligible (except for technical positions). To be an eligible you must pass the postal exams. The Post Service gives different exams for different positions, such as clerk and carrier, mail handler, mark-up clerk, automated, distribution clerk (machine), rural carrier, and other positions (See Part II of this book for positions that require passing entrance examinations and Part III for technical positions that don't require passing written exams.)

You can't apply for an exam if there is no opening. It's best if you have a friend or relative working in the Post Office who can tell you when an exam is forthcoming, but if you don't, you must call the personnel department of the local management sectional center.

Post offices throughout the country give exams to compile a *register of eligibles* from which they can take people, according to their ranking, to fill current and future vacancies. Tests are given by management sectional centers, general mail facilities, and bulk mail centers. For instance, the Pittsburgh MSC gives examinations for its associate offices within the area covered by 150, 151, 153, 154, 156, and 260 (West Virginia) zip codes.

Although the Postal Service says that 70 is the passing score, your hair will turn gray while you wait to be called for employment if you score only in the 70's. The records show that only those who score from 90 to 100% are called by the Post Office, because hundreds and even thousands of people take and pass the exams and the Post Office can afford to be selective. Also, if you wish, you may request for the transfer of eligibility to the city where you live or to any city of your choice. The best time to transfer your eligibility is when there are openings in the city where you intend to move. You can take postal exams in any city. If you make a high score, request that your eligibility be transferred to the city where you want to live and work. If your eligibility is transferred, you'll lose your eligibility in the city where you took the exam. When you are an eligible, you can postpone your employment in the Post Office for a certain period of time and still remain an eligible.

Route to Other Positions

When you are already employed by the Post Office, as a clerk, for instance and you have gained enough seniority, you can submit bids for other positions. You may also take in-service examinations for other positions. The most qualified of course, gets the job on the basis of seniority, rating, and experience. The opportunities for promotion are unlimited; it's up to you. You can be the master of your fate and the captain of your soul!

Flexible Employees

Before you obtain any of these positions, however, you start as a part-time flexible clerk or carrier. You are not yet a regular employee, but this does not mean that you are employed temporarily; your employment is permanent. You receive benefits similar to those given to regular employees.

"Part-time" does not mean you work only part time. Usually you work five or six days a week. In many cases you work six days as a part-time flexible. You are not guaranteed 40 hours' work a week, but you may sometimes work about 50 hours a week. Sometimes you may work less than 40 hours a week, sometimes more. The major difference between a part-time flexible employee and a regular is that the former does not receive any holiday pay.

All employees of the U.S. Postal Service (except those who occupy technical positions) start as part-time flexibles. From that position one moves up to a regular position with a monthly salary after six months' to one or two years' employment, depending on the post office where one is employed. Positions become available through promotion, retirement, death, transfer, employees' leaving, and expansion of postal facilities.

Hiring Through Interviews

You can get some positions in the Postal Service without taking written examinations; these include jobs as doctors, nurses, computer analysts, psychologists, and forensic chemists. However, these jobs have to be offered first to current postal employees. For instance, if there is a vacancy for a medical officer in a certain area, the job will be offered first to insiders. Would you expect a physician working as a clerk in the Post Office? Of course not. Then, if there is no qualified person in the service, the position will be offered to an outsider through an ad in a newspaper.

My son Lester, a computer science graduate from Michigan State University, wrote a letter to the Postal Service headquarters in Washington DC to inquire about postal employment. He received the following letter, which is self-explanatory:

UNITED STATES POSTAL SERVICE
475 L'Enfant Plaza, SW
Washington, DC 20260

February 23, 1987

Mr. Lester A. Bartista
Post Office Box 299
East Detroit, Michigan   48021

Dear Mr. Bartista:

Thank you for your February 16 letter seeking information concerning Postal Service employment.

The majority of professional staff positions advertised are filled by qualified applicants from within the Postal Service. However, occasionally we will be unable to fill a position from within and will subsequently advertise outside the Service, usually through advertisements in the local newspapers. Headquarters ads usually appear in the Washington Post, New York Times and Wall Street Journal.

Usually, the positions which are advertised outside the Service fall in the technical fields (computer analyst, programmer, engineer, architect, etc.). I would urge you, if you are interested in Postal Service employment in the computer field, to watch for Postal Service ads in your local paper for local positions, or the Washington Post for Headquarters positions. Your public library probably has a subscription and should have the paper available on a regular basis. In addition, I would urge you to check with the personnel office at your local post office on a periodic basis.

I hope this information is of help to you. Best wishes as you graduate and begin your career.

Sincerely,

Roberta S. Kroggel
Administrative Coordinator
Marketing Department

As indicated in the letter, if you are interested in a technical position, such as computer analyst, programmer, or engineer, watch for postal ads in the local newspapers for local positions or in the *Washington Post* for headquarters positions. If you have a friend or a relative in the local management sectional center, let him or her advise you of any vacancies for those positions. Vacancy announcements are posted on the bulletin board. In that way you'll know where the vacancies are; you may contact the local office or the headquarters, when the Postal Service advertises in the local paper for local positions or in the *Washington Post* for headquarters positions.

It's a Good Idea, But Not in the Bag

If you're a computer programmer or an analyst and if you want to get a job in a large postal installation or at headquarters in Washington, you may take a clerk-carrier exam. Make a high mark; when you're called for employment, accept a clerk position. (That's $21,230 to $28,630 a year, plus overtime.) When you have seniority, bid for a position as computer programmer or computer analyst. Because these jobs are offered first to insiders (like you), you have the edge in competing with outside programmers and analysts. Still, there's no guarantee that you'll get the job. Before you follow this strategy, it's best to talk with the personnel department of your local post office or the sectional center. Ask if it's really a good idea and what your chances are.

How to Select the Job You Want

Match your education, training, experience, interests, and abilities with the job classifications in this book. Part II lists positions open to the general public that require passing entrance exams or having job interviews. Part III lists positions that are offered to current Postal career employees. Many of the positions listed in Part III require passing in-service exams; others do not. Part III also describes positions that are available to current employees, such as medical officers, engineers, and computer personnel, but which mostly cannot be filled because few technical people are currently employed in the Postal Service. This is the time that the Postal Service invites outsiders, who are not given written exams but are employed on the basis of education, training, experience, and other qualifications.

Canvassing of Eligibles

If you are a civil service eligible, whether for the position of mark-up clerk, automated, clerk-typist or whatever, you can request the transfer of your eligibility to any city of your choice. (See **Eligibility is Transferable,** page 10.) Below is a letter from the Detroit, MI Post Office, which is self-explanatory.

UNITED STATE POST OFFICE
DETROIT MICHIGAN 48233-9998   7850:op9:851024:EB

October 25, 1985

Lester A. Bautista
23323 Teppert
East Detroit, MI 48021

Dear Mr. Bautista:

The Detroit, Michigan Post Office is establishing a register of eligibles from which future Distribution Clerk-Machine, MPLSM Operators, PS Level 5, beginning salary $9.48 per hour clerk vacancies may be filled.

The duties and responsibilities of the Distribution Clerk-Machine, MPLSM Operator are: Operates an electro mechanical machine in the distribution of letter sized mail requiring the knowledge and application of (1) two approved schemes, or (2) city primary or secondary schemes, or (3) memory items used for holdouts or non ZIP Coded mail, or (4) machine schemes consisting of the distribution by any direct and alphabetical or geographical grouping or read the ZIP Code in each letter as it is positioned. Must be able to demonstrate in examination, operation of the machine requiring an accuracy rate of 98%.

Based on your eligibility on the Royal Oak, MI Distribution Clerk-Machine, MPLSM Register, you are being canvassed by the Detroit, MI Post Office to transfer your eligibility to the Detroit, MI register for Distribution Clerk-Machine, MPLSM Operator register, for Keyboard Dexterity Training and possible employment.

You will have one hundred and eighty (180) days from the date the transfer of your active rating from Royal Oak, MI register to transfer your active rating back to Royal Oak, MI if you should decide you do not wish to remain on the Detroit, MI register. However, your eligibility must be active in order for you to transfer it back to Royal Oak, MI during the one hundred and eighty (180) day period. Your eligibility becomes inactive if you are (1) appointed to a career position or (2) if you fail to meet the training requirements of the position.

If you do not transfer your eligibility to the Detroit, MI register, it will remain active on the Royal Oak, MI Distribution Clerk-Machine, MPLSM register.

Where the Jobs Are   5

Before we discuss where the jobs are, it would be best to take a look at the organization of the U.S. Postal Service. Headed by the Postmaster General, the USPS has its general headquarters at 475 L'Enfant Plaza SW, Washington, DC 20260. The USPS is divided into four regions: Western, Southern, Northeastern, and Central. The regions are divided into divisions and the divisions are divided into Management Sectional Centers (MSC's) and General Mail Facilities (GMF's) that manage associate offices. The Detroit division, for instance, includes the Detroit General Mail Facilities (GMF) and the Royal Oak Post Office whose management sectional center (MSC) is situated in Troy, Michigan. In the Royal Oak sectional center, mail from all cities whose zip codes begin with 480 or 483 is brought for processing and forwarding. In the sectional centers such as this, mail is processed through letter sorting machines (LSM's) and optical character reader machines (OCR's). Here, the mail is postmarked, sorted and sent back to different local post offices for distribution. (Mail for out-of-state post offices is forwarded from sectional centers directly to its destination.)

Openings for most Postal Service jobs are not restricted to particular states or divisional or regional areas; rather, they are distributed in direct proportion to the volume of mail processed, or the size of a particular area or city. You can expect to find more letter carriers in thickly populated states like California, New York, Texas, or Florida. You can also expect large numbers of distribution clerks (machine), mail handlers, mark-up clerks (automated), and mail processors to be concentrated in GMF's and MSC's.

Technical Positions

For technical positions such as computer programmer, computer analyst, engineer, or architect, you'll have a better chance of being employed in the Postal Service Headquarters in Washington. These technical jobs are offered first to current career employees through vacancy announcements sheets, which are distributed throughout the post offices, particularly GMF's and MSC's. If the positions can't be filled up by qualified "insiders," they are advertised in newspapers, particularly in the *Washington Post*, which may be available in your local library. Technical jobs in your area are advertised in the local newspapers.

If you want to live and work in any of these states but can't get a postal job there, take postal exams and get a job in the state where you live. Then, after one or two years, request a transfer to the city where you want to live. To increase your chances of getting a postal job anywhere, you must take as many exams as possible. But before you do so, you must be prepared to score high on these exams and beat the competition. You must remember that thousands of people take a single exam but only a small number will be called for immediate employment. The rest will be placed on the waiting list.

Beat the Competition!

To know about scheduled postal exams, call several or many MSCs and GMFs (see Supplement B: **National Directory of U.S. Postal Service Examination Centers**). You can also subscribe to a biweekly newspaper that publishes postal exam announcements. Write: **Federal Jobs Digest,** 325 Pennsylvania Avenue, SE, Washington DC 20003.

You can also get a technical job, not only in the headquarters in Washington but also in field regions and divisions. For instance, computer programmers are hired at the Software Branch Systems, Data Operations Divisions, in San Mateo, California, and in St. Louis. Computer system analysts are hired in the Rates and Classification Center in the Eastern Region in Philadelphia. Telecommunications hardware technicians are hired at network operations branches such as that in Network Communications Division, National Information Systems Development Center in Raleigh, North Carolina.

Mail processing maintenance mechanics, letter box mechanics, electronic technicians, blacksmith/welders, and other skilled or semi-skilled workers can be hired in sectional centers.

The best plan is to be hired by the Postal Service, as a clerk, a carrier, or whatever. Remember that the present salary for a carrier is $21,230 to $28,630 per year. Once you're in, you'll get a better view of the service, and through vacancy announcements you'll know where the jobs are. As I said before, other jobs in the postal service are offered first to "insiders" before they're offered to "outsiders." So whether you're a mechanic, a plumber, or a computer expert, get a postal job first. As the saying goes, "If you can't beat them, join them!"

Know Where the Jobs Are

Veterans in the Postal Service

6

Veterans are given preference for employment in Federal jobs. If you are a veteran, a certain number of points will be added to your basic rating on the exam, so long as you make at least 70% on the exam. This is what the law dictates: if you have served in the Armed Forces of the United States, you deserve some kind of priority in government employment.

Whether you are a veteran who participated in World II, Vietnam war, or Grenada war, you will receive this preference so long as you were honorably discharged or separated from the Armed Forces of the United States.

In the competitive tests for appointment to the positions in the Postal Service, these preference benefits are given to veterans under certain conditions.

If you are claiming the ten-point veteran disability preference, you are more fortunate than someone who is eligible for the ordinary five-point preference. Why? Because veteran eligibles who have service-connected disabilities and have extra ten points are placed first at the top of the register in the order of their scores.

(See, **Civil Service Eligibility,** page 19.)

That simply means that you're followed by all other eligibles, including the five-point preference veterans, who are listed according to their ratings. So if you're a ten-point preference veteran, you'll be on top of the list, even if your basic score is lower than the top scorers. You'll bump the other eligibles as if to say, *"Move down, move down, move down!"* The so-called *preference eligibles* who receive five points additional are listed with the other eligibles (civilians) according to scores. On the other hand, if you are a five-point preference veteran, it does not mean you will be ahead of those who make higher scores than yours. If you score 75, including your five points, you won't be listed above a nonpreference eligible who scores 76. However, if you are a preference eligible, you'll be listed ahead of the nonpreference eligibles who make the same scores as you.

Standard Form 15

If you're claiming veteran preference, you'll have to fill out and submit Standard Form 15 to prove that you really served in the Armed Forces.

Questions and complaints have come up because of the veteran preference. One woman who bought this book from me and scored 100% score on a Postal exam complained to her congressman that she was discriminated against because people with lower scores than hers were appointed to positions while she was still on the waiting list. The postmaster had to explain that those who were appointed were veterans.

Because of the veteran preference, many who have retired from the Army, Navy, and Air Force have been appointed to postal positions after making the required scores on civil service exams.

In the competitive tests for appointment to the positions in the Postal Service, these preference benefits are given to veterans under certain conditions:

1. Five points are added to the basic rating of an examinee who scores at least 70 percent (the passing grade). If you make a score of 70, your final score will be 75; if you score 98 on the exam, your final score will be 103.

2. Ten points are added to the basic rating of an examinee who scores 70 percent or above and who is:
   a. a disabled veteran or a veteran who has received a Purple Heart award. Physical requirements are waived for persons who receive this preference, so long as they can do efficiently the duties of a postal worker.
   b. the wife of a disabled veteran if the veteran is physically disqualified by his service-connected disability for civil service appointment to positions along the line of his prewar or usual occupation.

c. the widow of a serviceman who died on active duty while serving in the Armed Forces, but only if she has not married again. (The law does not say whether she'll be disqualified if she fails in love again.)

d. The mother of a deceased or disabled veteran son or daughter, if she is either widowed, divorced, or separated, or if her present husband is permanently and totally disabled.

Veteran Preference Explained

With regard to the veterans preference, the **Postal Bulletin,** in its issue of May 30, 1985 stated:

> "The following revises Handbook P-11, Personnel Operations, Section 241.31. The principal change is to incorporate the minimum service requirements for veterans preference as provided in Section 408 of *Public Law 87-306*, enacted October 14, 1982, which amended Title 38 *U.S. Code of Federal Regulations* Section 3103A. To obtain veterans preference in Federal employment, a person who enlists after September 7, 1980 (or begins active duty on or after October 14, 1982, and has not previously completed 24 months of continuous active duty), must perform active duty in the Armed Forces during a war or in a campaign or expedition for which a campaign badge has been authorized, and serve for 2 years or the full period called or ordered to active duty. The time limit does not affect eligibility for veterans preference based on peacetime service exceeding 180 days from 1955 to 1976. This change is effective immediately and will be included in a future transmittal letter.

> **"241.3 Kinds of Veteran Preference**

> **.31 5-Point Preference.** Five point preference is given to honorably separated veterans (see 241.5) who served on active duty in the armed forces of the United States:

>> "*a.* During a war; or

>> "*b.* During the period April 28, 1952 to July 1, 1955; or

>> "*c.* In any campaign or expedition for which a campaign badge has been authorized (exception: a person who enlisted after September 7, 1980; or begins active duty on or after October 14, 1982, and has not previously completed 24 months of continuous active duty must perform active duty in the armed forces, during a war or in a campaign or expedition for which a campaign badge has been authorized, and serve for 2 years or the full period called or ordered for active duty . The law excepts a person who is discharged or released from active duty (a) for a disability incurred or aggravated in the line of duty, or (b) under 10 U.S.C. 1171 or 1173 for hardship or other reasons or"

"*d.* For more than 180 consecutive days any part of which occurred after January 31, 1955, and before October 15, 1976. (An initial period of active duty for training under the 6-month Reserve or National Guard Program does not count.)"

How to Mark Circles on the Answer Sheet

7

Your answer sheet is separate from the question sheet. This answer sheet is corrected by computer in California. The USPS furnishes lead pencils to be used during the examination; you may not use your own. You must make the pencil point *broad enough* to mark or darken the circle in one or *two* strokes.

Don't Sharpen the Point of Your Pencil.

The USPS Way

The sample below is included in a booklet published by the USPS, but it is not sent out. It is used only by organized groups that are participating in the Postal Service's affirmative action program by preparing applicants for the tests. This sample shows how an answer sheet is to be marked.

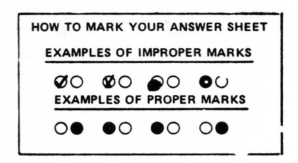

Some reviewers advise that you make this kind of mark. Others do not even discuss how a circle is to be marked.

A book on postal tests says that the instructions you receive at the time of the official test will include instructions on how to blacken the answer sheet. It reminds you to follow the instructions strictly and not to misinterpret the directions.

According to that book you are to darken completely the circle you have selected as the correct answer, like this:

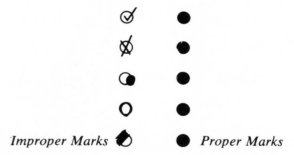

The Bautista Version

When I took an exam for the Warren (Michigan) Post Office, I tried to blacken the circles almost completely. I tried to be a Picasso; my final score was 78.5%. Then I decided to change my stroke in marking the circles after I had devised some other test systems. I made the mark smaller; the smaller it became, the higher score I made.

Pablo R. Abesamis of Glendale, California marked the circles better than I did (much smaller marks), and this is what he wrote to me:

"It's unbelievable! Just imagine, using your method I got five

scores of 100% on postal entrance examinations. I also acquired 98.80% and 97.00% on two other exams. Your systems really work..."

I received a flood of letters from readers, congratulating me for my efforts for showing them my own way of marking the circles. I included illustrations of how Abesamis and scores of many others marked the circles and made high scores.

In **Booklist,** a publication of the American Library Association, a reviewer writes:

"Bautista provides valuable advice for passing the civil service exams necessary to obtain several U.S. Postal jobs....the text supplies practical background on eligibility for post office jobs, on the veteran preference system, on the actual contents of the exams, and on techniques for studying and memorization."

Here's how I made the markings:

Your exam score may be higher when you don't complete mark the whole circles on the answer sheet. It's simply common sense that when you compare addresses and mark the circles on a six-minute, 95-question test, you have to work fast. To compare 95 sets of addressees in six minutes, you must take less than four seconds to answer each question, including marking the circles on the answer sheet. If you blacken the circles completely, (as advised by other postal books), you won't be able to answer all the 95 questions, but only about one-half of the questions. The smaller you mark the circle, the more questions you'll answer because of the time limit.

On the basis of my experience in taking exams, the marking depends on what type of test you're taking. If you're taking the 470 Battery Test and the 460 Rural Carrier Associate Exam (address-checking and memory-for-address tests), you can make a smaller mark; if you're taking the arithmetic and reading comprehension portions of the exam, you can make the mark bigger simply because you've the time to do it.

You can chat with your local carrier or any other current postal employee and ask him or her how he made the markings on the answer sheet when he took the exam. Maybe he did the right thing; if not, he could not have been employed in the Postal Service.

Many other people who bought my manual and did what I did also made high scores on tests. When Bautista talks, people listen.

From all over the United States, readers have written to tell me that they made high marks after they had followed my step-by-step instructions.

If You Follow My Instructions,
This Won't Happen to You.

Brains of Humans and Machines

8

Maybe you're wondering why I am writing about the brains of humans and machines. This is very important, for you must use your brain like a computer when you do memory work during your test.

Similarity Between Brains and Computers

In these days of computerization, comparisons are always being made between the human brain and the computer. They are alike — in fact, it's said that the computer is patterned after the human brain. Your brain senses what you see, hear, or touch, thinks about it, and stores it. When you put information into your biocomputer, it is called *input;* when you retrieve information, it is called *output.* It's like depositing and withdrawing money at the bank, but without a deposit you cannot make any withdrawal. The same is true with the computer.

The human brain, however, has feelings. The computer doesn't; it cannot fall in and out of love.

Short-Term and Long-Term Memory

The human brain has two kinds of memory: *short-term* and *long-term.* Short-term memory keeps track of immediate concerns; for instance, remembering your date at seven that evening or where you put your eye glasses. Long-term memory stores information such as memories of playing hide-and-seek with the girl or boy who also became your playmate in adulthood.

The computer has also the short-term and long-term memory, called the *RAM* and *ROM.* RAM stands for *random access memory;* the CPU (central processing unit), the brains of the computer, can add to or take from this memory at any time. When a CPU adds information to the memory, it is called *writing;* when information is taken out, it is called *reading.*

ROM stands for *read only memory.* Although the CPU has access to ROM, ROM cannot be changed; it was "born" with the computer because the manufacturer placed it there. According to an author on computers, a ROM is like a phonograph record, because the information is stored permanently, as a long-term memory, while RAM is like a cassette tape on which you can add, delete, or retrieve information, like short-term memory.

Your Own Computer

Your brain will work like a computer when you do memory work for your exams and when you work as a mark-up clerk, automated. When you store names and numbers in your brain, you'll be using keywords or codes, just as when you do a computer input and output.

For instance, when you do the memory work for the memory-for-address test, (See **Strategies for Memory-for-Address Test,** pages 107-112), you'll use your memory by creating keywords or codes, such as certain letters of the name and two numbers of the address. You do the input. Then you retrieve the information by recalling these codes. The computer does the same. (See **Mark-Up Clerk, Automated).** The operator enters a certain individual's change of address (COA) by having an extract code: the first three letters of the last name and the last two numbers of the address. When the operator wants to generate a label for this COA, he or she has only to type the first three letters of the last name and the last

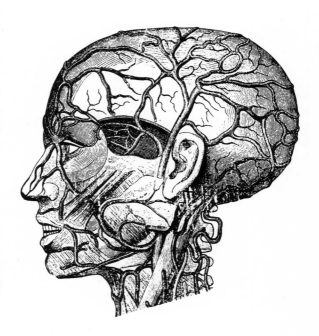

The Human Computer

two numbers of the address and the label with the new address comes out.

Information Storage and Retrieval

As you can see, the brain and the computer work the same way to store and retrieve information, so the system used in this book has a scientific basis. In short, it *works.*

Let's take this example below:

Box A

```
┌─────────────────────┐
│ 1700-2599 Wood      │
│ Dushore             │
│ 8500-8699 Lang      │
│ Lott                │
│ 6200-6399 James     │
└─────────────────────┘
```

If you're a mark-up clerk, automated, you'll enter the change of address with an *extract code,* keying the first three letters of the person's last name and the last two numbers of the address. But in preparing for the memory-for-address test, you should remember the first three letters of the addressee's name and the first two numbers (instead of the last two numbers) of the address. For your own purpose, the extract codes are Dus17, Dus85, and Lot62.

To memorize Dus17 and Dus85, think of a boy named Duso, who is 17 years old and who will die at 85. Think of Lot62 as Lolita, who is already 62 years old, or that you met your own Lolita in 1962. Now you have memorized Box A. Then using the same procedure, memorize boxes B, C, D, and E. In other words, associate the names with the numbers. (See **Strategies for Memory-for-Address Test,** pages 107-112). This system is based on what the computer does to enter information into the system and to retrieve it. You can use your brain the same way as you use the computer.

Other Storage Systems

There are other systems for storing information, (See **Strategies for Memory-for-Address Test,** pages 107-112) but the principle is the same: the use of extract codes. For instance, if you bought this book directly from me, your name has probably been entered into the system on a disk. If your name is John Houston, I'll type your first initial and the first three letters of your last name, (Jhou) and my computer will retrieve the information about your name, address, date of purchase, and date of delivery.

Yes, your name and address will be in the *system,* unless, of course, the disk drive eats the disk.

Program Your Brain

Different kinds of extract codes can be used, depending on the various programs being used. The programs depend on the computer programmer. You, too, can be a programmer of your very own computer!

Just concentrate well when you are "programming" and creating your extract codes. Don't worry. Your head won't explode—it's like a computer. A computer seldom explodes; it just loses its memory.

I HAVE A DREAM

• • • • •

*...that one day
you will rise up,
top the postal exams
and live out
the true meaning of our creed:
"We hold these truths
to be self-evident,
that all men
are not created equal.*

Carrier: The Man or the Woman on the Road 9

Carrier (City Carrier, Rural Carrier, Rural Carrier Associate)

Grade: Level 5

Salary Range: $26,063 - $36,835

Persons Eligible to Apply: Open to the general public

Examination Requirement: Must pass the 470 Battery Test and the driving test

As a carrier (whether city or rural) you'll be required to sort, rack, and tie mail at the post office before you start making deliveries within your route or area of delivery. In sorting letters, you must arrange them in the same order as the streets occur on the route. Letters and magazines for occupants of an apartment complex must be tied together with a rubber band or a belt. If you make a mistake in reading an addresses, the letter may go into the wrong home mailbox, causing a delay in delivery. The next day, you may find a note that says, *"This is not ours. Opened by mistake."* The letter might be a a "deadline" letter, an order from the court, or a warning from a creditor.

As a carrier, you'll also maintain required information, record changes of addresses, maintain other reports, and forward undeliverable-as-addressed mail.

In some ways, a rural carrier's duty is different from that of a city carrier. If you are hired as a rural carrier or a rural carrier associate, you'll be a jack of all trades; you'll also be a "walking post office." You may carry stamps, scales, and other equipment and supplies to serve the people of the rural area you cover. For this reason, you must know how to compute the cost of a piece of mail or a package whether it's going to a neighboring city, Somalia, or the North Pole.

Regular Route

Once you're a carrier, you'll have a regular route. Day in and day out, you'll walk on the same streets and open the same mailboxes. You won't get lost and you'll probably have time for a cup of coffee at McDonald's or Burger King after you've finished covering your route.

As a letter carrier you can become "the great observer." As you pound on the streets on your route, you'll notice unusual lawn ornaments, flagpoles, signs, and other out-of-the-ordinary things.

Once a letter carrier saw this sign nailed to a wooden fence: *"Dogs: Beware of Letter Carriers."*

**This is Not How
the Mail Room Looks Today**

If you're still a flexible carrier, that's a different story. Sometimes, as a *flex*, you'll cover different routes everyday. Before you go out, you'll have to look at the city map to see where you are going so that you'll finish delivering all your mail. You'll cover the routes of carriers who are off on a particular day or who have called in sick. Don't worry — once they were flexibles, and your time will come. Seniority is the rule in the post office.

Love Notes

If you are carrier, you must remember names as well as you can. If you don't, you'll receive many notes, on envelopes: *"How many times have we told you that this man moved five years ago!"* or *"I've told you a dozen times that this man has long been dead!"*

Once a friend of mine who is a letter carrier found some notes on an envelope returned to him: *"Gone! Not back! Not coming back anymore!"*

Road Adventures

I asked my friend whether he had ever been accosted by anyone on the streets while he was covering his route.

"Yes, many times," he said.

"By thieves?" I asked.

"No .....by retirees," he responded.

Sometimes in the spring or the fall, you'll have to bring an umbrella or a raincoat. When it rains, it pours. You may also wish to put a sticker on the back bumper of your car or jeep that says: *"Warning—I Give a 'Break' to Animals."*

When It Rains, It Pours.

Undeliverable-As-Addressed (UAA) Mail

Undeliverable-as-addressed mail is sent to the Computerized Forwarding System (CFS) unit in every sectional center, where the mail is processed. Previously processed by the mark-up clerks in every post office, undeliverable-as-addressed mail goes to the CFS for forwarding. Changes of addresses are computerized, and every change of address (COA) is entered into the system, where it is stored on disks. When the letter, magazine, or package is keyed—that is, when the operator types in the first three letters of the last name and the last two numbers of the street address—the computer generates a corresponding label.

No Record ("N") Mail

As a carrier, you will also send mail that has no change of address to the CFS. This mail (called "N" mail) will be returned to you for proper disposition. N mail has a "returned to sender, undeliverable as addressed" label with the letter N, meaning that there's no record of the address in the CFS or that a change of address has not been submitted to the CFS. Maybe you didn't send in the Form 3575 (change-of-address card), filled in properly by the one whose family moved. At times like this you will exchange some kind of note with the people in the CFS.

Once when a carrier received an N mail letter, he was angry because he had already written the word "deceased" on the envelope, but it was returned to him anyway as N mail. He wrote a note on the envelope and sent it back to the CFS. The note said: *"This man is already dead. Where shall I deliver the mail—to hell?"*

Form 3575

He might have been right. But he should have filled out Form 3575, the change-of-address card, with the name and address of the dead person and the "deceased" under "new address." This information is entered into the computer, and the mail is returned to the sender. When a CFS mark-up clerk keys this address, the label that is produced will say, *"Return to Sender, Moved, Left No Address."*

Examination Requirements

As an applicant, you have to pass an entrance examination. The clerk-carrier exam is the most commonly given exam in the Postal Service. It consists of Part A I: address-checking test and Part B or II: memory-for-address test. You have to score 95-100% so that you will beat the competition.

To be a carrier, you must have an operator's permit for driving and you must undergo a road test.

New York City Letter Carriers, Circa 1868. A group of the city's mail carriers in new uniforms, off to deliver their letters. (*Harper's Weekly*, December 26, 1868; Paul Frenzeny.)

Clerk Position: Key to Other Postal Jobs

10

Distribution Clerk (Manual)

Grade: L-5

Salary Range: $26,063 - $36,835

Persons Eligible to Apply: Open to the general public

Examination Requirement: Must pass the 470 Battery Test.

Clerk may be the jack-of-all-trades position in the U.S. Postal Service. If you score high on the 470 Battery Test and land a job in the Postal Service, you can be a a manual distribution clerk.

As a distribution clerk, you'll work indoors and will handle sacks of mail weighing as heavy as 70 pounds. You'll sort mail and distribute it by using a complicated scheme, which must be memorized. (See *How to Score 95-100% on Scheme Tests.*) You'll place letters or flats (magazines and pieces of mail in big envelopes into the correct boxes or pigeonholes. If you make a mistake in reading addresses or numbers, the letter will go to the wrong box, thus causing a delay in delivery. Letters from different boxes in a "case" go to different carriers, who will distribute the mail door to door.

As a distribution clerk, you'll also dump sacks of mail onto conveyors for culling and sorting; you'll load and unload sacks and trays of mail on and off mail transporters, such as APCs (All-Purpose Containers) and BMCs (Bulk Mail Containers). As a clerk, you may also be assigned to a public counter or window, doing such jobs as selling stamps and weighing parcels, and you'll be personally responsible for all money and stamps.

How Not to Unload Parcels

A friend of mine who works in a post office has told me this story.

While he was still a flexible employee at the post office in Mt. Clemens, Michigan Post Office, he was assigned to unload parcels from a BMC. He had to work fast because there were several BMCs to be unloaded. While he was unloading a big parcel, the bottom of it suddenly gave way, and hundreds of nuts poured onto the floor! He was embarrassed and had a hard time picking up the nuts, and some of the other employees helped him. Then, on one side of the carton that had contained the nuts, my red-faced friend read a note: *Glass—please handle with care.*

As a distribution clerk, you will be responsible for sorting letters. You put letters or flats (magazines and pieces of mail in big envelopes) into the correct boxes or pigeonholes. If you make a mistake in reading addresses or numbers, the letter will go to the wrong box, thus causing a delay in delivery. Letters from different boxes in a case go to different routes or carriers.

Clerk-Typist

Grade: L-4 to L-6

Salary Range: $24.500 - $37,827

Persons Eligible to Apply: Open to the general public

Examination Requirements: Must pass Examination 710 (See page 145) and a typing test.

Duties: Originates and maintains routine records; composes memoranda and letters; acts as receptionist, answering telephone calls, talking and relaying messages and furnishing information requested; relieves office clerks; does all other related clerical jobs.

Qualifications: Ability to read and understand instructions, to perform basic arithmetic computations, to maintain accurate records, to prepare reports and correspondence, and to operate office machines, such as calculator, adding machine, and duplicator.

Experience Requirements:
A. For PS-Level 4 or PMS-Level, 1 year
B. For PS-Level 5 or PMS-Level, 2 years
C. PS-Level 6 or PMS-level, 3 years

Substitution of Education for Experience: Successful completion of a full 4-year high school course, including credits in commercial or business subjects, such as general business education, business arithmetic, or office practice, may be substituted for 1 year of the required experience

Study completed in a business or secretarial school or an academic institution above high school level may be substituted for a maximum of 1 year of experience on the basis of 36 weeks of study for 1 year of experience. Credit will be allowed for full-time or part-time study at the rate of 20 class hours of instruction for one week of study in such subjects as business English, office machines, filing and indexing, office practice, business mathematics, accounting or bookkeeping.

Typing Requirement: Ability to type 40 words per minute for 5 minutes with no more than two errors. This ability will be tested in the performance section of the examination.

Clerk-Stenographer

Grades: L-4 to L-6

Salary Range: $24,599 - #37,827 (COLA included)

Persons Eligible to Apply: Open to the general public

Examination Requirements: Applicants must pass Examination 710. They must also pass the dictation test.

Duties: Same as the duties performed by a clerk-typist, except that he or she must also take dictation.

Dictation Requirement: Ability to take dictation in shorthand or on a shorthand machine at 80 words per minute. This ability will be tested in the performance section of the examination.

Typing Requirement: Ability to type 40 words per minute for 5 minutes with no more than two errors. This ability will be tested in the performance section of the examination.

If There's No Opening Yet

If you're planning to take Examination 710, which is the exam for clerk-typist and clerk-stenographer, but there are no openings yet, there's an easier way to get one of these positions. Take the 470 Battery Test (for me, it's the easiest) and obtain a clerk position.

After you have gained enough seniority, submit your bid for a clerk-typist or clerk-stenographer position, if there are any vacancies. You won't take a written examination, but you'll have to take a typing test for a clerk-typist position, and a typing test and shorthand dictation for a clerk-stenographer position.

After you pass the test, you'll obtain the position if you win in the bidding on the basis of seniority, experience, and qualifications. Before such a position is offered to an eligible (who made a high score on an entrance exam), it is offered to an insider (like you).

Other Positions

From your clerk position, you can also transfer to an accounting technician position, if you love working with figures, or to any other available position in the Postal Service. Some positions may require you to pass "in-service" examinations or training; others do not. For instance, if you're an letter sorting machine (LSM) operator and are already tired of hitting machine keys, you can move to a manual distribution clerk position. As a distribution clerk or any other kind of clerk, you can move from one job to another (moving forward, not backward, of course) by submitting a bid and winning the job on the basis of your seniority, education, and other qualifications.

Mark-Up Clerk: The Mail Forwarder   11

Grade: L-4

Salary Range: $24,599 - $35,949

Persons Eligible to Apply: Open to the general public

Examination Requirement: Applicants must pass the 470 Battery Test and the typing test.

Mark-up clerks process mail that is undeliverable as addressed. Previously they were just known as mark-up clerks, but now they are known as mark-up clerks, automated. Your duty as a mark-up clerk, automated consists of keying on the machine, labeling, and other related jobs.

Mark-up clerks used to mark undeliverable-as-addressed mail with rubber stamps that said "Return to Sender, Address Unknown," etc. (but not with the words "Return to Sender, Went to Heaven or Hell!"). They used to stick, pre-printed labels with new addresses on envelopes. These labels were inserted between change-of-address cards, arranged alphabetically in an index card tray.

Computerized Forwarding System Units

Today, CFS units are installed in USPS sectional centers throughout the country. If a CFS unit is to be established by a post office, or if a CFS unit needs additional employees, postal officials will have to give a 470 Battery Test. Those already in the service may get these jobs if they wish, by bidding for positions. But they must pass a special written exam and a typing test. Civilian employees in military headquarters or offices may also request transfer to mark-up clerks, as in other positions. But they must pass the written and typing tests.

The first priority of the CFS in establishing a data bank for all changes of address in a sectional center is the conversion program (CP). All the changes of addresses in post offices under the jurisdiction of a certain sectional center is entered into the system. The change-of-address notice is contained on a card known as Form 3575.

Change-of-Address Input

On the basis of the information on the change-of-address card, the mark-up clerk enters the change of address (COA) into the system.

The operator goes to the data management (DM) program. The first words to appear on the computer screen are *Zone* and *Function*. Zone means the ZIP code and the function asks if you're entering a COA for the first time or if you are modifying the file that is already in the system.

For instance:

Zone: 48336

Extract Code: Smit431 (In entering the extract code you type the first four letters of the family name and the last three numbers of the address. If it's a business address change, then you have to type the first four numbers of the business name and the last three numbers of the address.)

Function: ( )

A - Add
M - Modify
E - EC

Usually you'll type the A or M.

When you select the A, this will appear:

Zone:
Extraction Code:
Address Selection:
1. Street Address
2. P.O. Box
3. Rural Route
4. Hwy Contract
5. General Delivery
6. Foreign

For instance, if the original (or old) address is a street, then select 1, and this information will appear:

COA Information: FP4

The FP4 indicates that this is a permanent (P) address for a family (F). If it's for an individual, it should be IP4. If the change is temporary, then it should be FT4 or IT4. The 4 indicates that the addressee is willing to pay for 4th class mail forwarded to the new address.

Start Date:
Last Name:
First Name:
Number:
Pre-Directional:
Apt/Suite No:
DNF Code:
Additional Extraction Code:

(Note: the Last Name and the First Name will be changed to Business, if it's a business moving.)

If you are to enter the new address, this information will appear on the screen:

Number:
Pre Directional:
Street Name:
Post Directional:
Apt/Suite No.
City:
State:
ZIP:

If the person is moving from a P.O. Box and you check the selection P.O. Box, this will appear on the screen:

COA Info:
Start Date:
Last Name:
First Name:
P.O. Box:
DNF Code:
Additional Extract Code:

After this, as in the street address, you must select whether the person or the business is moving to a street, a P.O. Box, a rural route, etc.

In generating labels, the mark-up clerk then goes to the Label Generation (LG) Program and the zone and extraction code questions appear. (The machinable letters pass in front of the operator through a revolving mini-conveyor, as if asking "Where am I going?") The operator then keys the extra code (as if answering, "I don't know!") for each piece of mail passing by, typing the first four letters of the last name or first four letters of the business name and the last three numbers of the address. Then bingo! The computer automatically generates the yellow label (installed in a built-in case on the machine). This machine is different from the computer wherein COAs (changes of addresses) are entered. The letters are directed to different bins: some to the "local bin," others to the "out-of-town bin," some others to the "return-to-sender" bin, etc.

Why Do People Move?

Why do many people move so often? Because they want a change of environment or atmosphere: they seek new jobs, find new friends, and, if they are already in good financial shape, they want to live where the rich or the retirees live. Sometimes people can no longer bear the bitter cold and blizzards in northern states, so they move temporarily to places like Florida, California, or Arizona. People are like birds: they fly to certain places, depending on the season. Some of the changes are not for families, but for individuals when members of a family move to different places. For instance, two people find they no longer care for each other, so they move to different places to try to forget each other and to find new playmates.

Extraction Codes

Why does a mark-up clerk enter additional extraction codes? The reason for this is that we think differently. An operator must type the first four letters of the family name and last three numbers of the old address to produce the label for a new address. But sometimes he or she doesn't know which is which. Here are some examples:

Bock Lim Ping
King Lok Bong

Which are the family names? (Sometimes those sending out letters put the last name last and sometimes first in addresses.) You don't know? I don't know, either. In other words, the last name on an address is not necessarily the family name, so you must include all the possible extraction codes: Bock, Lim-, Ping, and Kim-, Lok-, and Bong, plus the last three numbers of the old address. (A hyphen is added to the extract code if it consists only of three letters.) In this way, no matter which code the mark-up clerks keys in, a label with the new address is generated.

Last names that begin with MC or MAC or with O should have two extract codes. Such family names are McDonald, MacFadden, O'Neal, DeLeon, etc. The first extraction codes of the family names are McDo, Macf, Onea, and Dele. The second extraction codes of the same family names are Dona, Fadd, Neal, and Leon, which like the other codes, are combined with the last three numbers of the old addresses.

In a nutshell, a mark-up clerk, automated operates a computer with a printer that produces labels with new addresses, from 450 to more than a 1,000 labels per hour, depending on the speed of the operator. The operator reads the addresses of machinable mail passing in front of him or her (from left to right) through a revolving belt, and hits the proper keys. This is called *keying.* The operator controls the machine. The speed of the machine depends on how fast the operator keys the mail. For every machinable mail, seven keys are hit: the first four letters of the last name or the business name. The label may contain words such as *"NO FORWARDING ORDER ON FILE, UNABLE TO FORWARD, RETURN TO SENDER," "MOVED, LEFT NO ADDRESS, UNABLE TO FORWARD RETURN TO SENDER," "DO NOT FORWARD, DO NOT RETURN,"* and *"RETURN TO SENDER, POSTAGE DUE $.29."* All letters with correct forwarding address, except those with temporary changes, contain the words "NOTIFY SENDER OF NEW ADDRESS."

Different Shifts

Mark-up clerks work in shifts: one may come at 6 a.m., another at 8:00 a.m., and another at 3:30 p.m.

LSM Operator: The Worker With a Walkman   12

Distribution Clerk, Machine (Letter Sorting Machine) Operator

Grade: L-5

Salary Range: $26,063 - $36,835

Persons Eligible to Apply: Open to the general public

Examination Requirements: Must pass the 470 Battery Test.and the LSM training

A Letter Sorting Machine (LSM) operator is a clerk who operates a machine (called a console) that is attached to a giant letter-sorting machine. The console has a keyboard similar to that of a piano. Some people say that if you're a pianist or know how to play the piano (even if the music is not in rhythm), you'll be a good LSM operator.

There are two kinds of LSM operators. One is assigned to learn one or more distribution schemes; the other is assigned to key ZIP codes.

Every post office has its *schemes,* based on its ZIP codes. For example, Warren, Michigan has four ZIP codes: 48089, 48091, 48092, and 48093. The scheme involves the routes to which letter carriers are assigned. For instance, a carrier may be assigned to Route 38, which covers certain streets. Sometimes a street is divided into several routes. Also, letters must be diverted to their proper routes. This is the job of an LSM operator (distribution clerk, machine). A manual distribution clerk sorts letters according to their routes by putting letters into pigeonholes on a *case.*

Scheme Operator

If you're assigned to key schemes, you must hit the right keys (two) on the machine (all numbers) as you read the addresses on envelopes that are moving from right to left at the speed of about 50 letters per minute. Your vision must not move back and forth as if you're watching a smiling John McEnroe and a frowning basketball star Magic Johnson in a tennis exhibition game. Your sight must be focused in front of you. Your eyes must be on *red alert* for the letters passing by, and you must hit the proper keys as soon as each letter passes. Sometimes, while you're deciding what route a letter is destined for, it is already going going—gone! If that happens, go on to the next letter. All letters keyed wrong or unkeyed go to the *nixies*. You must not make many mistakes because you are allowed only a certain percentage of errors.

ZIP Code Operator

If you're assigned to key ZIP codes, you have to key only the first *three numbers* in the ZIP code. Your speed must be 60 letters per minute. The letters you're keying may go to different ZIP codes (for instance, Mt. Clemens: 48043, 48044, 48045, and 48046). While the ZIP code operator keys three numbers, the scheme operator keys two numbers. What makes the difference? The scheme operator hits only two keys because he or she has to think of the route (where it's going) before he or she hits the keys. Sometimes the letter is already gone by the time the right number pops out of his mind. The ZIP code operator hits three keys because he or she has to read only the first three numbers of the zip code written on the mail. He must consult his biocomputer only when the sender didn't know the zip code or forgot to put it on the letter.

In other words, the ZIP code operator drives at 60 miles an hour while the scheme operator drives at 50.

Do you think you can handle the job? Why not? They're doing it. As the saying goes, if they can do it, you can do it, too. (You must undergo training, of course, and must pass that training.)

If you don't believe me, just imagine that you're observing LSM operators doing their job. Some of them are seated with crossed legs; some have tiny radios strapped around their waists and plugged into their ears; some are singing their favorite songs to themselves; others are shaking their bodies as if they were running a marathon. The way they work, they seem to be enjoying it!

Other Major Jobs in the Postal Service

## 13

Mail Handler

Grade: L-4

Salary Range: $24,599 - $35,949

Persons Eligible to Apply: Open to the general public

Examination Requirement: Must pass the 470 Battery Test.

If you get a job as a mail handler, you'll work mostly in the dock area, the canceling section, and the operation area. As the title indicates, you'll load and unload mail onto and off trucks and perform duties incidental to the movement and processing of mail.

As a mail handler, your duties include separating mail sacks to go to different routes or cities; canceling parcel post stamps; rewrapping parcels; and operating canceling machines, addressographs, mimeographs, and fork-lifts.

Mail Processor

Grade: L-4

Salary Range: $24,599 - $35,949

Persons Eligible to Apply: Open to the general public. Occasionally, positions are open only to current employees.

Examination Requirement: Must pass the 470 Battery Test

If you're appointed as a mail processor, you'll process mail using a variety of automated mail processing equipment. You'll work at the optical character reader (OCR) mail processing equipment.

Among your duties are starting and stopping equipment, culling and loading mail, clearing jams, sweeping mail from bins, and performing other related tasks.

As an applicant, you must have the ability to cull non-processable letters and to load mail on the transport unit for introduction into the distribution unit. You must also have the ability to sweep mail from bins and to place it into trays, carts, racks, and pouches.

Flat Sorting Machine Operator

Grade: L. 5

Salary Range: $26,063 - $36,835

Persons Eligible to Apply: Open to the general public

Examination Requirement: Must pass the 470 Battery Test

As a flat sorting machine operator, your major duty is to operate a single- or multi-position operator-paced electromechanical machine in the distribution of flats. (Flats are mailed material mostly contained in manila envelopes and other self-sealed mail, and are fed to the machine by an operator to go to different cities or routes.) You may also be assigned to work in other areas as needed.

As an applicant, you must have skills in operating an electromechanical machine and in the application of approved machine distribution. Heavy lifting is also required.

Data Conversion Operator

Grade: L-4

Salary Range: $9.74 per hour
Persons Eligible to Apply: Open to the general public

Examination Requirements: Must pass Examination 710, and the Computer-Based Test 714, and a keyboard qualification test. (See pages 145-168.)

If you get high score on Examination 710 and pass the computer test and a keyboard qualification test, you may be hired as a data conversion operator in a Remote Encoding Center.

As a data conversion operator, you'll use a computer terminal to prepare mail for automated sorting equipment.

You'll key the essential information needed so that an address bar code can be applied to each letter.

460 RCA Examination (Same as 470 Battery Test)

The U.S. Postal Service has replaced the **470 Battery Test** with the new **Test 473-473-C**, a new exam for major entry-level jobs: **City Carriers, Mail Processing Clerks, Mail Handlers,** and **Sales, Services,** and **Distribution Associates.** (See Chapter 35, page 327).

It is interesting to note that the **470 Battery Test** and the **460 Exam** for Rural Carrier Associates **are the same**. The 470 Test used to be the exam for seven Post Office jobs: Clerk, Carrier (City and Rural Carrier), Mail Handler, Mark-Up Clerk, (Automated), Mail Processor, Flat-Sorting Machine Operator, and Distribution Clerk, Machine. To repeat it, Test 473/473-C has replaced the Test 470. However, since this chapter, used to be titled **470 Battery Test)**, may be used for reviewing for the **460 Exam**, since they are the same. (See Part 2 of 460 Exam starts on Page 261-326)

Exam 460 exam covers the following parts:

Part A: Address Checking
Part B: Memory for Address
Part C: Number series
Part D: Following Oral Instructions.

Part II of 460 RCA exam starts on page 261.

There are 10 practice tests (Chapter 34, see pages 276-326.

(See: **Techniques for Address-Checking Test** on pages 77-81.)
(See **Memory-for-Address Test: Tips & Strategies** on pages 106-112.)

(**Note:** The old 470 Battery Test: Pages 61-146, can be used for review of the 460 RCA exam because they are the same.)

TEST 470 APPLICANT INSTRUCTIONS

YOU MUST BRING THE FOLLOWING TO BE ADMITTED:

Completed Sample Answer Sheet,
Admission Card/Notice,
Photo ID and
2 Sharpened No. 2 Pencils

LATECOMERS WILL NOT BE ADMITTED.

No. 2 pencil,

Social Security card,

ZIP Code for current address and

ZIP+4 Code for current address.

These instructions will prepare you for the exam. Please take time to **carefully read ALL of the instructions. THIS IS YOUR RESPONSIBILITY.** You should read all of the instructions and complete the required items even if you have taken a Postal exam before. **We are providing you with:**

1. *A SAMPLE ANSWER SHEET TO FILL OUT AT HOME.* This will enable you to complete the Answer Sheet in the exam room.

2. *WHAT YOU CAN EXPECT DURING THE ACTUAL TEST PART OF THE EXAM SESSION.*

3. *SAMPLE QUESTIONS FOR PRACTICE.* So that you will be familiar with the type of questions on the test, sample questions are included for practice.

4. *HOW THE FOUR PARTS OF THE TEST WILL BE SCORED.*

To fill out the Sample Answer Sheet, you will need:

This booklet,

Sample Answer Sheet,

Your Admission Card/Notice,

In the exam room, you will be given 15 minutes to copy your work from the Sample Answer Sheet to the Answer Sheet. The test will begin soon thereafter. **You will not have time in the exam room to become familiar with these instructions.**

The Answer Sheet will be given to you in the exam room. It is processed by a high-speed scanner. It is important that you precisely complete the grids on the Sample Answer Sheet. This is so you will know exactly how to fill out the Answer Sheet in the exam room.

You are responsible for correctly completing the Sample Answer Sheet. When you report to take the test, you must bring it with you.

Your Sample Answer Sheet will be checked for accurate and total completion. You may not have time to fix any errors or complete items not filled out before the session starts. Only those who have a properly completed Sample Answer Sheet will be admitted. Those who still have an incomplete Sample Answer Sheet by the time the exam starts will NOT be admitted.

THE FOLLOWING INSTRUCTIONS EXPLAIN HOW TO FILL OUT EACH GRID ON THE SAMPLE ANSWER SHEET.

EFFECTIVE SEPTEMBER 1993

Examples of correct and incorrect marks are:

CORRECT MARKS	INCORRECT MARKS
● ● ● ●	⊘ ⊗ ◉ ⊖

1 NAME. Use your full, legal name when completing this grid. Use the same name every time you take a postal exam. Use of a nickname could result in a delay in processing the result.

GRID 1 is divided into three parts: **Last Name, First Name and MI (Middle Initial).** Each part is surrounded by a border. **Each part of your name must be entered ONLY in the place for that part.**

Last Name. Enter your last name one letter to a box. **You must start with the first square box to the left.**

If you are a JR, SR, III or IV, this should be included as a part of your last name. After entering your last name, skip a box and enter the correct letters.

To help you complete the grids correctly, you will use the **EDGE** of the Admission Card/Notice or the envelope as a guide. Place the Admission Card/Notice or envelope on top of GRID 1 so that the edge is to the LEFT of the first column. For **example,** when the last name is "HALL III":

Last Name

EDGE

Grid showing boxes: H A L L (blank) I I I with bubble columns A–L below each.

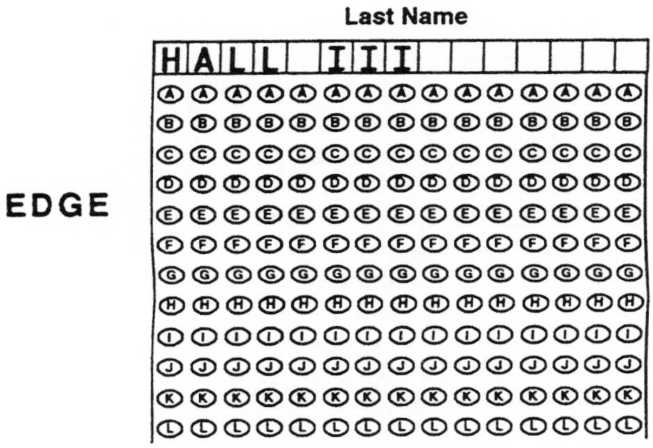

(If you are left handed, place the edge to the RIGHT of the first column.)

For the letter in the box, find the matching circle in the column below and darken that circle.

Next, move the edge **with one hand** so that it is against the **next** column. Darken the circle **with the other hand** for that letter.

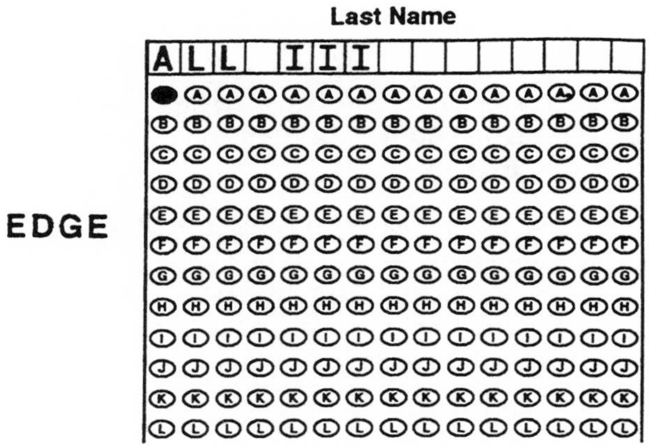

Last Name

EDGE

Grid showing boxes: A L L (blank) I I I with bubble columns A–L below each.

Then proceed until you have darkened the circle for each letter you have entered in a box.

If your name has the letter "O" in it, make sure to darken the circle that comes after "N". Do not mistake the letter "Q" for the letter "O".

When you come to a blank box, do nothing.

The following is an **example of a completed grid** when the last name is "HALL III":

Last Name

Grid showing boxes: H A L L (blank) I I I with darkened bubbles for H, A, L, L, I, I, I.

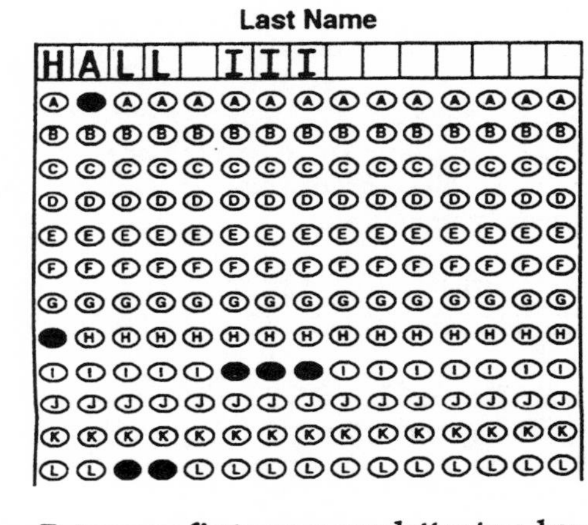

First Name. Enter your first name one letter to a box. **You must start with the first box after the border line.**

As you did for **Last Name,** take the edge and place it on top of this grid against the first column.

Find the matching circle below and darken that circle. Next, move the edge so it is against the next column. Darken the circle for that letter. Then proceed until you have darkened the circle for each letter you have entered in a box.

Do not mistake the letter "Q" for the letter "O".

When you come to a blank box, do nothing.

MI (Middle Initial). Enter your middle initial and darken the circle for the letter. **If you do not have a middle initial,** do not enter anything in the box or darken a circle.

2 SOCIAL SECURITY NUMBER. Look at your Social Security Number card. Compare the number with the one on the Admission Card/Notice. If the number on the Admission Card/Notice is not correct, draw a line through it and make the correction.

Enter your correct Social Security Number in GRID 2 on the Sample Answer Sheet.

Using the edge, darken the matching numerical circles.

3 BIRTH DATE. For GRID 3, in the box labeled "MM", enter the two numbers for your birth month, **one number to a box.** If you were born in January through September, you would enter a "0" in the first box and the number for the month in the second box. Using the edge, darken the matching circles.

In the box labeled "DD", enter the two numbers for your day of birth, **one number to a box. If your day of birth is from one to nine,** enter a "0" in the first box and the number for the day in the second box. Using the edge, darken the matching circles.

In the box labeled "YY", enter the last two numbers of the year in which you were born, **one number to a box. Do not use the current year.** Using the edge, darken the matching circles.

WHEN YOU FINISH GRID 3, YOU SHOULD HAVE ENTERED AND GRIDDED SIX NUMBERS.

4 LEAD OFFICE/INSTALLATION FINANCE NUMBER. Look at the Admission Card/Notice. On it there is a six digit number and the name of the office for which you have applied. With your pencil, enter this number in GRID 4, one number to a box. Using the edge, darken the matching numerical circles.

5 JOB CHOICE. This test is being given for seven jobs which are very different. Read the descriptions below and then make a choice by darkening the corresponding circle for the job. You may choose from one to seven jobs.

City Carriers deliver and collect mail. They walk and/or drive trucks. Carriers must be outdoors in all kinds of weather. Almost all carriers have to carry mail bags on their shoulders, and **a mail bag full of mail can weigh up to 35 pounds.** Carriers have to load and unload sacks of **mail weighing as much as 70 pounds.**

City Carriers applicants must have **a current valid state drivers license** and are required to have a **safe driving record.** In some offices, City Carriers are required to work on weekends.

Clerks work indoors. Clerks have to handle parcels, bundles and sacks of mail weighing as much as **70 pounds.** They sort mail by ZIP Code or by a memorized plan. Some clerks work at public windows doing such jobs as selling stamps and weighing parcels, and are **personally responsible for all money and stamps.** Clerks may have to be **on their feet all day.** They also have to stretch, reach, and bend frequently when distributing mail. In some offices, clerks are required to work at night and on weekends.

Distribution Clerks, Machine operate a letter sorting machine to distribute letters by a memorized plan or by reading the ZIP Code. They enter codes using a special purpose keyboard to **distribute letters at the rate of up to 60 per minute.**

Applicants must be able to demonstrate the **operation of the machine at an accuracy rate of 98 percent.** They must have the ability to maintain close visual attention for long periods of time. Operators must also load or unload machines. Distribution Clerks, Machine are usually required to work at night and on weekends.

Flat Sorting Machine Operators operate a machine to distribute large flat pieces of mail by a memorized plan or by reading the ZIP Code. They enter codes using a special purpose keyboard to **distribute flats at the rate of up to 45 per minute.**

Applicants must be able to demonstrate the **operation of the machine at an accuracy rate of 98 percent.** They must have an ability to maintain close visual attention for long periods of time. Operators must also load or unload machines. Flat Sorting Machine Operators are usually required to work at night and on weekends.

Mail Handlers load, unload and move bulk mail and sacks. They may have to be **on their feet all day** in an industrial environment. They also have to **repeatedly lift up to 70 pounds.**

Applicants must be able to demonstrate their ability

to lift by passing a test of strength and stamina. In some offices Mail Handlers are required to work at night and on weekends.

Mail Processors are required to stand for long periods of time loading and unloading mail from a variety of automated mail processing equipment. Their work is performed in large mail-processing facilities in an industrial environment. Mail Processors are normally required to work nights and weekends.

Mark Up Clerks enter change of address data into a computer base, process mail and perform other clerical functions. Mark Up Clerks operate a keyboard in order to process changes.

Applicants for Mark Up Clerks must have good data entry skills and are required to pass a typing test. They may be required to work at night and on weekends.

6 TEST SERIES. Do nothing with GRID 6.

7 EXAM DATE. Look at the Admission Card/Notice for the date you are scheduled to take this exam. For GRID 7, in the box labeled "MM", enter the two numbers for the exam month, one number to a box. If the exam is in January through September, you would enter a "0" in the first box and the number for the month in the second box. Using the edge, darken the matching circles.

In the box labeled "DD", enter the two numbers for your day of exam, one number to a box. If your day of exam is from one to nine, enter a "0" in the first box and the number for the day in the second box. Using the edge, darken the matching circles.

In the box labeled "YY", enter the last two numbers of the year of the exam, one number to a box. Using the edge, darken the matching circles.

WHEN YOU FINISH GRID 7, YOU SHOULD HAVE ENTERED AND GRIDDED SIX NUMBERS.

IMPORTANT NOTE. If you are a current career Postal employee OR your Admission Card/Notice is stamped "INSERVICE", DO NOT COMPLETE GRIDS 8, 9, 17, 18 AND 19.

8 YOUR CHOICE OF INSTALLATIONS.   Do nothing with GRID 8.

9 VETERAN PREFERENCE. If you are not eligible to claim Veteran Preference, do nothing with GRID 9. The following is an explanation of the different types of Veteran Preference:

5 Points (tentative). This preference is usually given to honorably separated veterans who served on active duty in the Armed Forces of the United States under one of the following conditions:

a. During a declared war (the last one was World War II); or

b. During the period April 28, 1952 to July 1, 1955; or

c. During the period February 1, 1955 through October 14, 1976 for which any part of more than 180 consecutive days was served. (An initial period of active duty for training under the 6-month Reserve or National Guard Program does not count.)

d. In any campaign or expedition for which a campaign badge was authorized.

Veterans who served in Southwest Asia or in the surrounding contiguous waters or air space on or after August 2, 1990 AND who were awarded the Southwest Asia Service Medal can claim five points.

10 Points - Compensable (Less than 30%). This preference is given to honorably separated veterans who served on active duty in the Armed Forces at any time and have a service-connected disability for which compensation is provided at 10% or more, but less than 30%.

10 Points - Compensable (30% or more). This preference is given to honorably separated veterans who served on active duty in the Armed Forces at any time and have a service-connected disability for which compensation is provided at 30% or more.

10 Points (other). This preference is claimed by a variety of people:

a. Veterans who were awarded the Purple Heart; or

b. Veterans who have a recognized service-connected disability for which no compensation is received or a recognized nonservice-connected disability; or

c. Until remarried, the widow or widower of an honorably separated veteran, provided the deceased veteran served in active duty during a war, or the veteran died while in the Armed Forces; or

d. Spouses of certain veterans with a service-connected disability; or

e. Mothers of certain deceased or disabled veterans.

Darken only one circle in GRID 9 if you wish to claim Veteran Preference. Do not darken more than one circle.   Points claimed will be added to your score ONLY if you pass the exam with a score of 70 or better.

10   EXAM TYPE. In GRID 10, for:

Entrance, darken this circle if you applied for this exam in response to a public announcement or are taking the test for other reasons (see 11 below). **Current career Postal Employees do NOT darken this circle.**

Inservice, darken this circle if you are a **current career Postal employee.** Also, darken this circle if you are taking this exam on a noncompetitive basis — your **Admission Card/Notice will be stamped "INSERVICE."**

11   SPECIAL INSTRUCTIONS. If you do not have "DELAYED" or "REOPENED" stamped on your Admission Card/Notice, do nothing with GRID 11. This grid is only for people who are taking this exam because they either:

a. missed an opportunity to take the exam when last opened to the public because they were on active military duty, **"DELAYED"** status OR

b. entitled to 10 point Veteran Preference, **"REOPENED"** status.

Grid the circle labeled **"3"** for **"DELAYED",** or the circle labeled **"4"** for **"REOPENED."**

12   LEAD OFFICE (Name). **Look at the right side of the Admission Card/Notice for the name of the installation for which you are applying. Print the name in the block labeled: "Lead Office/Installation (Please Print)".** Print the two letter abbreviation for the state in the block labeled **"State."**

Sign your name in the block labeled **"Signature."**

13 PRINT YOUR CITY AND STATE. Turn to Page 2 of the Sample Answer Sheet. **Print the city and state of your current mailing address.**

14 STREET ADDRESS. This is for the one line address that will be used to deliver your test result. If you pass **and** later your score is reached for consideration, the address you grid will be used to notify you. The address you grid **must** meet Postal standards. Study the following examples:

1234 MAIN ST APT 999

45678 MADISON BLVD S

33 1/2 IVY DR SW

4329-02 MONTGOMERY PL

2342 NW SMITH RD

RR 2 BOX 50

PO BOX 4502

You must use the correct shortened format for your one line address. Also, such an address will be easier and quicker to grid.

This grid is different from the other ones because it contains numbers, special symbols and letters. Enter your one line address in the boxes. **You must start with the first box to the left.** Skip a **blank box** where there needs to be a space. By using the edge and starting with the first column to the left, darken the circles.

Do not mistake the letter "Q" for the letter "O".

When you come to a blank box, do nothing.

15 ZIP (Code). **You must have your correct ZIP Code to complete this grid. An incorrect ZIP Code will result in a delay in sending your rating to you.** Your ZIP Code is found on magazines, utility bills and other business mail you receive at home. **Enter your correct five digit ZIP Code in the boxes. Then use the edge to darken the matching numerical circles.**

16 +4 (Code). **You must have your correct ZIP+4 Code to complete this grid.** Your ZIP+4 is usually found on mail you receive at home. This four digit number appears **after** the five digit ZIP Code. Enter this number in GRID 16. Use the edge and darken the numerical circles.

FOR GRIDS 17, 18 AND 19, read the General Instructions for the RESEARCH QUESTIONNAIRE on Page 2 of the Sample Answer Sheet.

17   SEX. Darken the appropriate circle in GRID 17.

18 DISABILITY CODE.   If you do **not** have a disability, enter 0 in the first box and 5 in the second box in GRID 18. Code **"05"** indicates **"No Disability."** Using the edge, darken the numerical circles.

A disability refers to a physical or mental disability or history of such disability which is likely to cause difficulty in obtaining, maintaining, or advancing in employment. On Page 4, you will find a list of various disabilities. Each of the disabilities has a number. If you have a disability, read the list carefully and select the code that best describes your disability. If you have multiple disabilities, choose the code for the one that is most disabling. Enter the two numbers of the disability code in the boxes at the top of GRID 18. If your disability is not listed, enter zero in the first column and six in the second column. Using the edge, darken the numerical circles.

19 RACIAL AND NATIONAL ORIGIN. This grid is for the collection of your racial and national origin. Darken the circle for the category that applies to you. If you are of mixed racial and/or national origin, you should identify yourself by the one category for which you most closely associate yourself by darkening the appropriate circle in GRID 19.

Checking your work. After you have finished, go back and check your work. For a letter or number in a box, you should have only one circle darkened in the column found directly below. Make sure that you have completed all items as requested.

After checking your work, go back to Page 1 of the Sample Answer Sheet. In the upper left corner is the United States Postal Service eagle. Draw a circle around the eagle.

Get someone else to check your work. Since the scanner that reads the Answer Sheet only picks up what is gridded, you should have someone else check your work. Let them tell you if you made a mistake so that you can correct it. This will help make sure that you do the best job you possibly can on the Answer Sheet in the exam room.

1  **SAMPLE ANSWER SHEET**
for
TEST 470

USE NO. 2 PENCIL ONLY

---

1 In the boxes below, print your last name, first name and middle initial in the proper sections as indicated, one letter per box. Below each box, blacken the oval which is lettered the same as the letter in the box. For each blank letter box, do not blacken any of the ovals.

Last Name   **First Name**   **MI**

(ovals A through Z for each letter column in Last Name, First Name, and MI)

2 Social Security Number

(ovals 0 through 9)

3 Birth Date

MM	DD	YY

(ovals 0 through 9)

A false or dishonest answer in blocks 1, 2 or 3 may be grounds for not employing you or for dismissing you after you begin work.

4 Lead Office/ Installation Finance Number

(ovals 0 through 9)

5 Job Choice

- ◯ City Carrier
- ◯ Clerk
- ◯ Dist. Clerk, Machine
- ◯ Flat Sorter Machine
- ◯ Mail Handler
- ◯ Mail Processor
- ◯ Mark Up Clerk
- ◯ Other

6 Test Series

(ovals 0 through 9)
DO NOT COMPLETE

7 Exam Date

MM	DD	YY

(ovals 0 through 9)

8 Your choice of installations where you want to be considered (not more than 3)

1 2 3 4 5 6 7 8 9 10
11 12 13 14 15 16 17 18 19 20
21 22 23 24 25 26 27 28 29 30
31 32 33 34 35 36 37 38 39 40
41 42 43 44 45 46 47 48 49 50

9 Veteran Preference

- ◯ 5 points (tentative)
- ◯ 10 points-Compensable (Less than 30%)
- ◯ 10 points-Compensable (30% or more)
- ◯ 10 points (other)

10 Exam Type

- ◯ Entrance
- ◯ In Service

11 Special Instructions

1 2 3 4 5 6 7 8 9 10 11 12 13 14 15 16 17 18 19 20 21 22 23 24

12 Lead Office/Installation (Please Print) | State | Signature

PS Form **8155-S**, July 1993

13 Print your city and state ⟶

14 In the boxes below, print your street address or post office box (one letter, number, or symbol per box).

15 ZIP

16 +4

(grids of ovals with digits 0–9 for boxes 14, 15, 16, and letter/number grids A–Z below)

17 Indicate Sex

○ Male

○ Female

18 Disability Code
see page 4

(grid of ovals 0–9)

19 The categories below are designed to identify your basic racial and national origin category. If you are of mixed racial and/or national origin, indicate the category with which you most closely identify yourself.

Name of Category	Definition of Category
○ American Indian or Alaskan Native	A person having origins in any of the original peoples of North America, and who maintains cultural identification through community recognition or tribal affiliation.
○ Asian or Pacific Islander	A person having origins in any of the original peoples of the Far East, Southeast Asia, the Indian subcontinent, or the Pacific Islands. This area includes, for example China, India, Japan, Korea, the Philippine Islands, Samoa, and Vietnam.
○ Black, not of Hispanic Origin	A person having origins in any of the black racial groups of Africa. Does not include persons of Mexican, Puerto Rican, Cuban, Central or South American, or other Spanish cultures or origins (see Hispanic).
○ Hispanic	A person of Mexican, Puerto Rican, Cuban, Central or South American, or other Spanish cultures or origins. Does not include persons of Portuguese culture or origin.
○ White, not of Hispanic Origin	A person having origins in any of the original peoples of Europe, North Africa, or the Middle East. Does not include persons of Mexican, Puerto Rican, Cuban, Central or South American, or other Spanish cultures or origins (see Hispanic). Also includes persons not included in other categories.

DID YOU READ **ALL** OF THE
INSTRUCTIONS?

THANK YOU FOR FOLLOWING THE
DIRECTIONS AND COMPLETING
THE SAMPLE ANSWER SHEET.

THE UNITED STATES POSTAL SERVICE IS
AN EQUAL OPPORTUNITY EMPLOYER.

Disability Code Listing

CODE	GENERAL	CODE	PARTIAL PARALYSIS *(continued)*
01	Disability Not Reported	66	Both arms, any part
05	No Disability	67	One side of body, including one arm and one leg
06	Disability Not Listed on This Form	68	Three or more major parts of the body *(arms and legs)*

CODE	SPEECH IMPAIRMENTS	CODE	COMPLETE PARALYSIS
13	Severe speech malfunction or inability to speak, hearing is normal. Example: defects of articulation *(unclear language sounds)*; stuttering; aphasia; laryngectomy *(removal of the voice box)*.		*(Because of a brain, nerve, or muscle problem, including palsy and cerebral palsy, there is complete loss of ability to move or use a part of the body, including legs, arms and/or trunk.)*
		70	One hand

CODE	HEARING IMPAIRMENTS	CODE	
15	Hard of hearing; correctable by hearing aid	71	Both hands
16	Total deafness with understandable speech	72	One arm
17	Total deafness with inability to speak clearly	73	Both arms
	VISION IMPAIRMENTS	74	One leg
22	Can read ordinary size print with glasses, but with loss of peripheral *(side)* vision	75	Both legs
		76	Lower half of body, including legs
23	Cannot read ordinary size print; not correctable by glasses	77	One side of body, including one arm and one leg
24	Blind in one eye	78	Three or more major parts of the body *(arms and legs)*
25	Blind in both eyes		OTHER IMPAIRMENTS

CODE	MISSING EXTREMITIES	CODE	OTHER IMPAIRMENTS
27	One hand	80	Heart disease with no restriction or limitation of activity *(history of heart problem with complete recovery)*
28	One arm		
29	One foot	81	Heart disease with restriction or limitation of activity
32	One leg		
33	Both hands or arms	82	Convulsive disorder *(e.g., epilepsy)*
34	Both feet or legs		
35	One hand or arm and one foot or leg	83	Blood disease *(e.g., sickle cell disease, leukemia, hemophilia)*
36	One hand or arm and both feet or legs		
37	Both hands or arms and one foot or leg	84	Diabetes
38	Both hands or arms and both feet or legs		

CODE	NONPARALYTIC ORTHOPEDIC IMPAIRMENTS *(Because of chronic pain, stiffness, or weakness in bones or joints, there is some loss of ability to move or use a part of the body.)*	CODE	
		86	Pulmonary or respiratory *(e.g., tuberculosis, emphysema, asthma)*
44	One or both hands	87	Kidney dysfunctioning *(e.g., use of an artificial kidney machine)*
45	One or both feet		
46	One or both arms	88	Cancer *(history of cancer with complete recovery)*
47	One or both legs		
48	Hip or pelvis	89	Cancer *(undergoing surgical and/or medical treatment)*
49	Back		
57	Any combination of two or more parts of the body	92	Severe distortion of limbs and/or spine *(e.g., dwarfism, kyphosis — severe distortion of back, etc.)*

CODE	PARTIAL PARALYSIS *(Because of a brain, nerve, or muscle problem, including palsy and cerebral palsy, there is some loss of ability to move or use a part of the body, including legs, arms, and/or trunk.)*	CODE	
		93	Disfigurement of face, hands, or feet *(e.g., distortion of features on skin, such as those caused by burns, gunshot injuries, and birth defects, gross facial birth marks, club feet, etc.)*
61	One hand		MENTAL RETARDATION/EMOTIONAL PROBLEMS
62	One arm, any part	90	A chronic and lifelong condition involving a limited ability to learn, to be educated and to be trained for useful productive employment as certified by a State Vocational Rehabilitation Agency.
63	One leg, any part	91	Mental or emotional illness *(history of treatment for mental or emotional problems)*
64	Both hands		
65	Both legs, any part	94	Learning Disability

Sample Questions
470 Battery Test
(U.S. Postal Service)

TEST INSTRUCTIONS

During the test session, it will be your responsibility to pay close attention to what the examiner has to say and to follow all instructions. One of the purposes of the test is to see how quickly and accurately you can work. Therefore, each part of the test will be carefully timed. You will not START until being told to do so. Also, when you are told to STOP, you must immediately STOP answering the questions. When you are told to work on a particular part of the examination, regardless of which part, you are to work on that part ONLY. If you finish a part before time is called, you may review your answers for that part, but you will not go on or back to any other part. Failure to follow ANY directions given to you by the examiner may be grounds for disqualification. Instructions read by the examiner are intended to ensure that each applicant has the same fair and objective opportunity to compete in the examination.

SAMPLE QUESTIONS

Study carefully before the examination.

The following questions are like the ones that will be on the test. Study these carefully. This will give you practice with the different kinds of questions and show you how to mark your answers.

Part A: Address Checking

In this part of the test, you will have to decide whether two addresses are alike or different. If the two addresses are exactly *Alike* in every way, darken circle A for the question. If the two addresses are *Different* in any way, darken circle D for the question.

Mark your answers to these sample questions on the Sample Answer Grid at the right.

1...2134 S 20th St   2134 S 20th St

Since the two addresses are exactly alike, mark A for question 1 on the Sample Answer Grid.

2...4608 N Warnock St   4806 N Warnock St

3...1202 W Girard Dr   1202 W Girard Rd

4...Chappaqua NY 10514   Chappaqua NY 10514

5...2207 Markland Ave   2207 Markham Ave

Sample Answer Grid		
1	(A)	(D)
2	(A)	(D)
3	(A)	(D)
4	(A)	(D)
5	(A)	(D)

The correct answers to questions 2 to 5 are: 2D, 3D, 4A, and 5D.

Your score on Part A of the actual test will be based on the number of wrong answers as well as on the number of right answers. Part A is scored right answers minus wrong answers. Random guessing should not help your score. For the Part A test, you will have six minutes to answer as many of the 95 questions as you can. It will be to your advantage to work as quickly and as accurately as possible. You will not be expected to be able to answer all the questions in the time allowed.

Part B: Memory for Addresses

In this part of the test, you will have to memorize the locations (A, B, C, D, or E) of 25 addresses shown in five boxes, like those below. For example, "Sardis" is in Box C, "6800-6999 Table" is in Box B, etc. (The addresses in the actual test will be different.)

A	B	C	D	E
4700-5599 Table	6800-6999 Table	5600-6499 Table	6500-6799 Table	4400-4699 Table
Lismore	Kelford	Joel	Tatum	Ruskin
5600-6499 West	6500-6799 West	6800-6999 West	4400-4699 West	4700-5599 West
Hesper	Musella	Sardis	Porter	Nathan
4400-4699 Blake	5600-6499 Blake	6500-6799 Blake	4700-5599 Blake	6800-6999 Blake

Study the locations of the addresses for five minutes. As you study, silently repeat these to yourself. Then cover the boxes and try to answer the questions below. Mark your answers for each question by darkening the circle as was done for questions 1 and 2.

1. Musella
2. 4700-5599 Blake
3. 4700-5599 Table
4. Tatum
5. 4400-4699 Blake
6. Hesper
7. Kelford
8. Nathan
9. 6500-6799 Blake
10. Joel
11. 4400-4699 Blake
12. 6500-6799 West
13. Porter
14. 6800-6999 Blake

Sample Answer Grid

1	Ⓐ ● Ⓒ Ⓓ Ⓔ	5	Ⓐ Ⓑ Ⓒ Ⓓ Ⓔ	9	Ⓐ Ⓑ Ⓒ Ⓓ Ⓔ	13	Ⓐ Ⓑ Ⓒ Ⓓ Ⓔ
2	Ⓐ Ⓑ Ⓒ ● Ⓔ	6	Ⓐ Ⓑ Ⓒ Ⓓ Ⓔ	10	Ⓐ Ⓑ Ⓒ Ⓓ Ⓔ	14	Ⓐ Ⓑ Ⓒ Ⓓ Ⓔ
3	Ⓐ Ⓑ Ⓒ Ⓓ Ⓔ	7	Ⓐ Ⓑ Ⓒ Ⓓ Ⓔ	11	Ⓐ Ⓑ Ⓒ Ⓓ Ⓔ		
4	Ⓐ Ⓑ Ⓒ Ⓓ Ⓔ	8	Ⓐ Ⓑ Ⓒ Ⓓ Ⓔ	12	Ⓐ Ⓑ Ⓒ Ⓓ Ⓔ		

The correct answers for questions 3 to 14 are: 3A, 4D, 5A, 6A, 7B, 8E, 9C, 10C, 11A, 12B, 13D, and 14E.

During the examination, you will have three practice exercises to help you memorize the location of addresses shown in five boxes. After the practice exercises, the actual test will be given. Part B is scored right answers minus one-fourth of the wrong answers. Random guessing should not help your score. But, if you can eliminate one or more alternatives, it is to your advantage to guess. For the Part B test, you will have five minutes to answer as many of the 88 questions as you can. It will be to your advantage to work as quickly and as accurately as you can. You will not be expected to be able to answer all the questions in the time allowed.

Part C: Number Series

For each *Number Series* question there is at the left a series of numbers which follow some definite order and at the right five sets of two numbers each. You are to look at the numbers in the series at the left and find out what order they follow. Then decide what the next two numbers in that series would be if the same order were continued. Mark your answers on the Sample Answer Grid.

1. 1 2 3 4 5 6 7 .... A) 1 2   B) 5 6   C) 8 9   D) 4 5   E) 7 8

The numbers in this series are increasing by 1. If the series were continued for two more numbers, it would read: 1 2 3 4 5 6 7 8 9. Therefore the correct answer is 8 and 9 and you should have darkened C for question 1.

2. 15 14 13 12 11 10 9 . . . .   A) 2 1   B) 17 16   C) 8 9   D) 8 7   E) 9 8

The numbers in this series are decreasing by 1. If the series were continued for two more numbers, it would read: 15 14 13 12 11 10 9 8 7. Therefore the correct answer is 8 and 7 and you should have darkened D for question 2.

3. 20 20 21 21 22 22 23 . . . .   A) 23 23   B) 23 24   C) 19 19   D) 22 23   E) 21 22

Each number in this series is repeated and then increased by 1. If the series were continued for two more numbers, it would read: 20 20 21 21 22 22 23 23 24. Therefore the correct answer is 23 and 24 and you should have darkened B for question 3.

4. 17 3 17 4 17 5 17 . . . .   A) 6 17   B) 6 7   C) 17 6   D) 5 6   E) 17 7

This series is the number 17 separated by numbers increasing by 1, beginning with the number 3. If the series were continued for two more numbers, it would read: 17 3 17 4 17 5 17 6 17. Therefore the correct answer is 6 and 17 and you should have darkened A for question 4.

5. 1 2 4 5 7 8 10 . . . .   A) 11 12   B) 12 14   C) 10 13   D) 12 13   E) 11 13

The numbers in this series are increasing first by 1 (plus 1) and then by 2 (plus 2). If the series were continued for two more numbers, it would read: 1 2 4 5 7 8 10 (plus 1) 11 and (plus 2) 13. Therefore the correct answer is 11 and 13 and you should have darkened E for question 5.

Now read and work sample questions 6 through 10 and mark your answers on the Sample Answer Grid.

6. 21 21 20 20 19 19 18 . . . .   A) 18 18   B) 18 17   C) 17 18   D) 17 17   E) 18 19

7. 1 22 1 23 1 24 1 . . . .   A) 26 1   B) 25 26   C) 25 1   D) 1 26   E) 1 25

8. 1 20 3 19 5 18 7 . . . .   A) 8 9   B) 8 17   C) 17 10   D) 17 9   E) 9 18

9. 4 7 10 13 16 19 22 . . . .   A) 23 26   B) 25 27   C) 25 26   D) 25 28   E) 24 27

10. 30 2 28 4 26 6 24 . . . .   A) 23 9   B) 26 8   C) 8 9   D) 26 22   E) 8 22

Sample Answer Grid			
6 (A) (B) (C) (D) (E)	8 (A) (B) (C) (D) (E)	9 (A) (B) (C) (D) (E)	10 (A) (B) (C) (D) (E)
7 (A) (B) (C) (D) (E)			

The correct answers to sample questions 6 to 10 are: 6B, 7C, 8D, 9D and 10E. Explanations follow.

6. Each number in the series repeats itself and then decreases by 1 or minus 1; *21* (repeat) *21* (minus 1) *20* (repeat) *20* (minus 1) *19* (repeat) *19* (minus 1) *18* (repeat) *?* (minus 1) *?*

7. The number 1 is separated by numbers which begin with 22 and increased by 1; *1 22 1* (increase 22 by 1) *23 1* (increase 23 by 1) *24 1* (increase 24 by 1) *?*

8. This is best explained by two alternating series — one series starts with 1 and increases by 2 or plus 2; the other series starts with 20 and decreases by 1 or minus 1.

1	^	3	^	5	^	7	^	?
	20		19		18		?	

9. This series of numbers increases by 3 (plus 3) beginning with the first number — *4 7 10 13 16 19 22 ? ?*

10. Look for two alternating series — one series starts with 30 and decreases by 2 (minus 2); the other series starts with 2 and increases by 2 (plus 2).

Now try questions 11 to 15.

11. 5 6 20 7 8 19 9 .... A) 10 18   B) 18 17   C) 10 17   D) 18 19   E) 10 11

12. 4 6 9 11 14 16 19 .... A) 21 24   B) 22 25   C) 20 22   D) 21 23   E) 22 24

13. 8 8 1 10 10 3 12 .... A) 13 13   B) 12 5   C) 12 4   D) 13 5   E) 4 12

14. 10 12 50 15 17 50 20 .... A) 50 21   B) 21 50   C) 50 22   D) 22 50   E) 22 24

15. 20 21 23 24 27 28 32 33 38 39 . A) 45 46   B) 45 52   C) 44 45   D) 44 49   E) 40 46

Sample Answer Grid
11 ⒶⒷⒸⒹⒺ   13 ⒶⒷⒸⒹⒺ   14 ⒶⒷⒸⒹⒺ   15 ⒶⒷⒸⒹⒺ
12 ⒶⒷⒸⒹⒺ

The correct answers to the sample questions above are: 11A, 12A, 13B, 14D and 15A.

It will be to your advantage to answer every question in Part C that you can, since your score on this part of the test will be based on the number of questions that you answer correctly. Answer first those questions which are easiest for you. For the Part C test, you will have 20 minutes to answer as many of the 24 questions as you can.

Part D: Following Oral Instructions

In this part of the test, you will be told to follow directions by writing in a test booklet and then on an answer sheet. The test booklet will have lines of material like the following five samples:

SAMPLE 1.   5 __

SAMPLE 2.   1   6   4   3   7

SAMPLE 3.   D   B   A   E   C

SAMPLE 4. (8 __) (5 __) (2 __) (9 __) (10 __)

SAMPLE 5. (7 __) [6 __] (1 __) [12 __]

To practice this part of the test, tear off page 11. Then have somebody read the instructions to you and you follow the instructions. When he or she tells you to darken the space on the Sample Answer Grid, use the one on this page.

	Sample Answer Grid			
1 (A)(B)(C)(D)(E)	4 (A)(B)(C)(D)(E)	7 (A)(B)(C)(D)(E)	10 (A)(B)(C)(D)(E)
2 (A)(B)(C)(D)(E)	5 (A)(B)(C)(D)(E)	8 (A)(B)(C)(D)(E)	11 (A)(B)(C)(D)(E)
3 (A)(B)(C)(D)(E)	6 (A)(B)(C)(D)(E)	9 (A)(B)(C)(D)(E)	12 (A)(B)(C)(D)(E)

Your score for part D will be based on the number of questions that you answer correctly. Therefore, if you are not sure of an answer, it will be to your advantage to guess. Part D will take about 25 minutes.

KEEP THESE INSTRUCTIONS FOR FUTURE REFERENCE. YOUR PARTICIPATION AND COOPERATION IN THIS POSTAL EXAM IS APPRECIATED.

Instructions to be read **(the words in parentheses should NOT be read aloud)**

You are to follow the instructions that I shall read to you. I cannot repeat them.

Look at the samples. Sample 1 has a number and a line beside it. On the line write A as in ace. **(Pause 2 seconds.)** Now on the Sample Answer Grid, find the number 5 **(pause 2 seconds)** and darken the letter you just wrote on the line. **(Pause 2 seconds.)**

Look at Sample 2. **(Pause slightly.)** Draw a line under the third number. **(Pause 2 seconds.)** Now look on the Sample Answer Grid, find the number under which you just drew a line and darken B as in boy. **(Pause 5 seconds.)**

Look at the letters in Sample 3. **(Pause slightly.)** Draw a line under the third letter in the line. **(Pause 2 seconds.)** Now on your Sample Answer Grid, find number 9 **(pause 2 seconds)** and darken the letter under which you drew a line. **(Pause 5 seconds.)**

Look at the five circles in Sample 4. **(Pause slightly.)** Each circle has a number and a line in it. Write D as in dog on the line in the last circle. **(Pause 2 seconds.)** Now on the Sample Answer Grid, darken the number-letter combination that is in the circle you just wrote in. **(Pause 5 seconds.)**

Look at Sample 5. **(Pause slightly.)** There are two circles and two boxes of different sizes with numbers in them. **(Pause slightly.)** If 4 is more than 2 and if 5 is less than 3, write A as in ace in the smaller circle. **(Pause slightly.)** Otherwise write C as in car in the larger box. **(Pause 2 seconds.)** Now on the Sample Grid, darken the number-letter combination in the box or circle in which you just wrote. **(Pause 5 seconds.)**

Now look at the Sample Answer Grid. **(Pause slightly.)** You should have darkened 4B, 5A, 9A, 10D, and 12C on the Sample Answer Grid. **(If the person preparing to take the examination made any mistakes, try to help him or her see why he or she made the wrong marks.)**

Techniques for Address-Checking Test   15

The **Address Checking Test** forms Part B of the **460 RCA Exam** and the old **470 Battery Test** (replaced by the new **Test 473/473-C**) which are the same. On this test, you must determine whether two addresses are *alike* or *different*. It's like comparing sexy Sharon Stone with sassy Drew Barrymore; the size of their bodies, the shape of their legs or noses, and so on. In comparing addresses, too, you are to see how they are *alike* or *different*. If they are *alike* in numbers, roads, streets, or spellings, you answer *A* (for *alike*); if they are *different* in numbers, roads, streets, or spelling, you answer *D* (for *different*).

You're Not a Walkathon Participant

(460 Exam, pages 61-146. See more practice tests on pages 276-326.)

If you had plenty of time to take this test, as if participating in a walkathon, you might score 100%. But you are racing against time; there is a time limit. You must compare 95 sets of addresses in only 6 minutes. In other words, you are like in a participant in a Grand Prix race. Your eyes must zoom from left to right in seconds! To finish comparing the 95 sets of addresses, you must take less than 4 seconds to answer each question, including the marking of circles on your answer sheet. (See **How to Mark Circles on the Answer Sheets,** page 33.) The examiner may tell you, however, that you don't have to answer all the questions (few do) to make a high score.

Let Your Fingers Do the Walking

In comparing addresses (in two columns), you can point at the streets and the numbers with your fingers. Place the little finger of your nonwriting hand on one column of address and the index finger of the same hand on the other column. Move your hand downward as you make comparisons, while your right hand marks the answers.

Widen the Focus of Your Eyes!

Pretend that you're driving a car. Your sight is focused to the front as far as you can see, but you can still see to your left and to your right. You don't need the eyes of an E.T. to do this, but do remember that comparing addresses is faster than the so-called speed reading. If possible, just make one or two "eye sweeps" of the addresses.

Things to Do, In a Nutshell

■ Compare the two addresses (left and right) by one or two eye sweeps of the line. It's also a good idea to fold the paper so that the number, for instance, "2134" of the second address will be near the "St." or "Rd." of the first address (on the same line, of course). It's like taking a photo of an excited Bill Clinton and Hillary Rodman at their anniversary ball— you want them to be close together so that you can get a good close-up shot. The question sheet and the answer sheet should be lying side by side; the question sheet on your non-writing side, the answer sheet on your writing side. In this way, your sight doesn't travel too far. Don't jerk your neck from left to right as you read; just let your eyes do the sweeping. While you do this, hold your pencil in your writing hand and don't move your nonwriting hand from the answer sheet. Then move it downward as you mark a circle with two or three strikes by your writing hand. Be sure that the line you are marking corresponds to the question you are answering.

■ **Spellings:** Note the spellings of street, city, state, and numbers in the ZIP code. Sometimes the first address has a ZIP code of 48012 and the second address has a ZIP code of 48021.

■ **Differences:** Most of the time there are differences in abbreviations, such as St., Rd., or Ave. Sometimes the first address (left) is abbreviated as St. and the second address (right) is abbreviated as Rd., or vice versa.

■ **Guide:** It's best to use a bookmark or some other kind of guide with your nonwriting hand: place it just below the line you are comparing and slide it straight down to the next line as you continue with the test. This prevents you from comparing the first address or number with an address or number in the wrong line. You can also place the little finger of your nonwriting hand on the left column and the index finger of the same hand on the right column of addresses. Move your nonwriting hand downward as you make the comparisons, while you mark the answers with your writing hand.

How to Compare the Addresses

There are four ways to compare the addresses. Use whichever is most comfortable for you:

First Way: Compare the two addresses by moving your eyes from left to right; that is, compare the address on the left to the one on the right. Make *one* or *two* "eye sweeps" of the addresses. It's like sweeping snow from your car, but you do it in a snap. If possible, the "eye sweep" should be faster than the speed of sound.

Example:

2134 S 20th St	2134 S 20th St

Since the addresses are alike, the answer is *A*.

Second Way: Focus your sight on the space between the two addresses. You can look at the addresses simultaneously from the center. With this method you can get a complete view of both addresses, like looking at Bo Derek and Raquel Welch at the same time while they are smiling at you.

Example:

7507 Wyngate Dr   ●   7505 Wyngate Dr

Since the street numbers are different, the answer is *D*.

Third Way: First, compare only the street name and the abbreviations: *St, Rd,* or *Ave.* If they are alike, then compare the street numbers on the left to the numbers on the right. If they are alike, answer *A*.

Example:

2207 Markland Ave   2207 Markham

When you use the third way in this example, first compare the street name and the abbreviation *Rd* or *Ave.* Since there's a difference in street names (one is Mark*land* and the other is Mark*ham),* you immediately mark circle *D,* meaning that they are different. Do not continue comparing anymore, but proceed at once to the next line or number. If the street names are alike, then compare the left-hand numbers to the numbers on the right. If they are still alike, answer *A;* if the figures are different, answer *D.*

Fourth Way: This can be discussed by analyzing the example below.

Example:

  5428 N Shelbourne Rd   5482   N   Shelbourne   Rd

You compare the numbers at the left to the numbers at right, ignoring the initial, street name, and abbreviation (Rd. etc.). Once you see a difference (*28* and *82)* darken circle *D* right away. Do not go on to compare the street names because you've already found a difference between the *two* addresses. In a nutshell, differences may occur in numbers, abbreviations, or names.

UNITED STATES POSTAL SERVICE

SAMPLE QUESTIONS—STUDY CAREFULLY BEFORE YOU GO TO THE EXAMINATION ROOM

The questions on this sheet are like the ones you will take in the test. Study them carefully. This sheet will give you practice with the different kinds of questions and show you how to mark your answers.

Address Checking Test

In this test you will have to decide whether two addresses are alike or different. If the two addresses are exactly *Alike* in every way, darken space A for the question. If the two addresses are *Different* in any way, darken space D for the question.

Mark your answers to these sample questions on the Sample Answer Sheet at the right.

1.. 2134 S 20th St   2134 S 20th St
Since the two addresses are exactly alike, mark A for question 1 on the Sample Answer Sheet.
2.. 4608 N Warnock St   4806 N Warnock St
3.. 1202 W Girard Dr   1202 W Girard Rd
4.. Chappaqua N Y 10514   Chappaqua N Y 10514
5.. 2207 Markland Ave   2207 Markham Ave

The answers to samples 2 to 5 are: 2D, 3D, 4A, and 5D.

```
Sample Answer Sheet

   1 Ⓐ Ⓓ

   2 Ⓐ Ⓓ

   3 Ⓐ Ⓓ

   4 Ⓐ Ⓓ

   5 Ⓐ Ⓓ
```

Address-Checking Practice Test
Work—3 Minutes

Decide whether the two addresses are *Alike* or *Different*. If they are *Alike*, darken or mark space A; if they are *Different*, darken space D. Mark the answers on the answer sheet to the right. Work exactly 3 minutes.

			Test A	Test B
1.	2134 S 20th St	2134 S 20th St	1 Ⓐ Ⓓ	1 Ⓐ Ⓓ
2.	4608 N Warnock St	2806 N Warnock St	2 Ⓐ Ⓓ	2 Ⓐ Ⓓ
3.	1202 W Girard Dr	1202 W Girard Rd	3 Ⓐ Ⓓ	3 Ⓐ Ⓓ
4.	3120 S Harcourt St	3120 S Harcourt St	4 Ⓐ Ⓓ	4 Ⓐ Ⓓ
5.	4618 W Addison St	4618 E Addison St	5 Ⓐ Ⓓ	5 Ⓐ Ⓓ
6.	Sessums Miss	Sessoms Miss	6 Ⓐ Ⓓ	6 Ⓐ Ⓓ
7.	6425 N Delancey	6425 N Delencey	7 Ⓐ Ⓓ	7 Ⓐ Ⓓ
8.	5407 Columbia Rd	5407 Columbia Rd	8 Ⓐ Ⓓ	8 Ⓐ Ⓓ
9.	2106 Southern Ave	2106 Southern Ave	9 Ⓐ Ⓓ	9 Ⓐ Ⓓ
10.	Highfalls NC 27259	Highlands NC 27259	10 Ⓐ Ⓓ	10 Ⓐ Ⓓ
11.	2873 Pershing Dr	2873 Pershing Dr	11 Ⓐ Ⓓ	11 Ⓐ Ⓓ
12.	1329 N H Ave NW	1329 N J Ave NW	12 Ⓐ Ⓓ	12 Ⓐ Ⓓ
13.	1316 N Quinn St	1316 N Quinn St	13 Ⓐ Ⓓ	13 Ⓐ Ⓓ
14.	7507 Wyngate Dr	7505 Wyngate Dr	14 Ⓐ Ⓓ	14 Ⓐ Ⓓ
15.	2918 Colesville Rd	2918 Colesvale Rd.	15 Ⓐ Ⓓ	15 Ⓐ Ⓓ
16.	2071 E Belvedere Dr	2071 E Belvedere Dr	16 Ⓐ Ⓓ	16 Ⓐ Ⓓ
17.	Palmer Wash	Palmer Mich	17 Ⓐ Ⓓ	17 Ⓐ Ⓓ
18.	2106 16th SW	2106 16th St SW	18 Ⓐ Ⓓ	18 Ⓐ Ⓓ
19.	2207 Markland Ave	2207 Markham Ave	19 Ⓐ Ⓓ	19 Ⓐ Ⓓ
20.	5345 16th St SW	5345 16th St SE	20 Ⓐ Ⓓ	20 Ⓐ Ⓓ
21.	239 Summit Pl NE	239 Summit Pl NE	21 Ⓐ Ⓓ	21 Ⓐ Ⓓ
22.	152 Continental Pkwy	152 Continental Blvd	22 Ⓐ Ⓓ	22 Ⓐ Ⓓ
23.	8092 13th Rd S	8029 13th Rd S	23 Ⓐ Ⓓ	23 Ⓐ Ⓓ
24.	3906 Queensbury Rd	3906 Queensbury Rd	24 Ⓐ Ⓓ	24 Ⓐ Ⓓ
25.	4719 Linnean Ave NW	4719 Linnean Ave NE	25 Ⓐ Ⓓ	25 Ⓐ Ⓓ
26.	Bradford Me	Bradley Me	26 Ⓐ Ⓓ	26 Ⓐ Ⓓ
27.	Parrott Ga 31777	Parrott Ga 31177	27 Ⓐ Ⓓ	27 Ⓐ Ⓓ
28.	4312 Lowell Lane	4312 Lowell Lane	28 Ⓐ Ⓓ	28 Ⓐ Ⓓ
29.	6929 W 135th Place	6929 W 135th Plaza	29 Ⓐ Ⓓ	29 Ⓐ Ⓓ
30.	5143 Somerset Cir	5143 Somerset Cir	30 Ⓐ Ⓓ	30 Ⓐ Ⓓ
31.	8501 Kennedy St	8501 Kennedy St	31 Ⓐ Ⓓ	31 Ⓐ Ⓓ
32.	2164 E McLean Ave	2164 E McLean Ave	32 Ⓐ Ⓓ	32 Ⓐ Ⓓ
33.	7186 E St NW	7186 F St NW	33 Ⓐ Ⓓ	33 Ⓐ Ⓓ
34.	2121 Beechcrest Rd	2121 Beechcroft Rd	34 Ⓐ Ⓓ	34 Ⓐ Ⓓ
35.	3609 E Montrose St	3609 E Montrose St	35 Ⓐ Ⓓ	35 Ⓐ Ⓓ
36.	324 S Alvadero St	324 S Alverado St	36 Ⓐ Ⓓ	36 Ⓐ Ⓓ
37.	2908 Plaza Estrellas	2908 Plaza Estrellas	37 Ⓐ Ⓓ	37 Ⓐ Ⓓ
38.	223 Great Falls Rd	223 Great Falls Dr	38 Ⓐ Ⓓ	38 Ⓐ Ⓓ
39.	Kelton SC 29354	Kelton SC 29354	39 Ⓐ Ⓓ	39 Ⓐ Ⓓ
40.	3201 Landover Rd	3201 Landover Rd	40 Ⓐ Ⓓ	40 Ⓐ Ⓓ

Correct Answers

Address-Checking Test

Part A

1.	A	21.	A
2.	D	22.	D
3.	D	23.	D
4.	A	24.	A
5.	D	25.	D
6.	D	26.	D
7.	D	27.	D
8.	A	28.	A
9.	A	29.	D
10.	D	30.	A
11.	A	31.	A
12.	D	32.	A
13.	A	33.	D
14.	D	34.	D
15.	D	35.	A
16.	A	36.	D
17.	D	37.	A
18.	D	38.	D
19.	D	39.	A
20.	D	40.	A

Address-Checking Practice Test
Work—6 Minutes

These addresses are like the ones in the address-checking test.

Decide whether the two addresses are Alike, or Different. Mark the answers on the answer sheet to the right. Work as fast as you can without making too many errors. Work exactly 6 minutes.

ANSWER SHEET

			Test A	Test B

1. 3157 W Vincent Dr — 3157 E Vincent Dr — 1. Ⓐ Ⓓ — 1. Ⓐ Ⓓ
2. 721 Foreman Ctr E — 721 Foreman Ctr E — 2. Ⓐ Ⓓ — 2. Ⓐ Ⓓ
3. 9530 Campbell Ct NW — 9530 Campbell Ct NW — 3. Ⓐ Ⓓ — 3. Ⓐ Ⓓ
4. 3129 E Popcorn Lake St — 3129 N Popcon Lake — 4. Ⓐ Ⓓ — 4. Ⓐ Ⓓ
5. 9292 Burns Rd W — 9229 Burris Rd W — 5. Ⓐ Ⓓ — 5. Ⓐ Ⓓ
6. 3197 Lovers Lane — 3197 Lovers Lane — 6. Ⓐ Ⓓ — 6. Ⓐ Ⓓ
7. 812 Albuquerque St SW — 812 Albuquerque St SW — 7. Ⓐ Ⓓ — 7. Ⓐ Ⓓ
8. 7315 Norway Blvd S — 7315 Norway Blvd S — 8. Ⓐ Ⓓ — 8. Ⓐ Ⓓ
9. 5930 N Prospect Way — 5930 N Prospect Way — 9. Ⓐ Ⓓ — 9. Ⓐ Ⓓ
10. 7296 Holbroke Trl — 7298 Holbroke Trl — 10. Ⓐ Ⓓ — 10. Ⓐ Ⓓ
11. 18185 Southfield Rd — 18185 Southland Rd — 11. Ⓐ Ⓓ — 11. Ⓐ Ⓓ
12. 2178 Gibson Ave NW — 2178 Gibson St NW — 12. Ⓐ Ⓓ — 12. Ⓐ Ⓓ
13. 28091 Hickory Sq E — 28091 Hickory Sq E — 13. Ⓐ Ⓓ — 13. Ⓐ Ⓓ
14. 2156 Crawford Lake Rd — 431 S Little Town Trl — 14. Ⓐ Ⓓ — 14. Ⓐ Ⓓ
15. 6593 5th Ave SW — 6593 5th Ave SW — 15. Ⓐ Ⓓ — 15. Ⓐ Ⓓ
16. 9051 Pleasant Rd E — 9057 Pleasant Rd E — 16. Ⓐ Ⓓ — 16. Ⓐ Ⓓ
17. 8105 Pumpkin Trl S — 8105 Pumpkin Ctr S — 17. Ⓐ Ⓓ — 17. Ⓐ Ⓓ
18. 9232 E Thomas Pkwy — 9232 E Thomas Pky — 18. Ⓐ Ⓓ — 18. Ⓐ Ⓓ
19. 3741 Edmenton Ct N — 3741 Edmenton Ct N — 19. Ⓐ Ⓓ — 19. Ⓐ Ⓓ
20. 3961 Butterfield Ave — 3961 Butternut Ave — 20. Ⓐ Ⓓ — 20. Ⓐ Ⓓ
21. 93441 Royal Oak 48068 — 93441 Royal Oak 48066 — 21. Ⓐ Ⓓ — 21. Ⓐ Ⓓ
22. 3492 Hudson Dr SW — 3492 Hudson Dr SE — 22. Ⓐ Ⓓ — 22. Ⓐ Ⓓ
23. 10313 Kennedy Sq — 10313 Kennedy Sq — 23. Ⓐ Ⓓ — 23. Ⓐ Ⓓ
24. 4491 Kingman Blvd — 4491 Kingman Blvd — 24. Ⓐ Ⓓ — 24. Ⓐ Ⓓ
25. 5270 Gratiot Ave NW — 5279 Gratiot Ave NW — 25. Ⓐ Ⓓ — 25. Ⓐ Ⓓ
26. 8121 St Agustine Pl — 8121 St Agustine Pl — 26. Ⓐ Ⓓ — 26. Ⓐ Ⓓ
27. 7677 NW Evanston Crescent — 7677 NW Evanston Cres — 27 Ⓐ Ⓓ — 27. Ⓐ Ⓓ
28. 9570 Newman Rd — 5790 Newman Rd — 28. Ⓐ Ⓓ — 28. Ⓐ Ⓓ
29. 23323 Madison Trl — 23323 Madison Sq — 29. Ⓐ Ⓓ — 29. Ⓐ Ⓓ
30. 1015 Marathon Way — 1015 Mareathon Way — 30. Ⓐ Ⓓ — 30. Ⓐ Ⓓ
31. 7350 Evans Rd — 7550 Evans Rd — 31. Ⓐ Ⓓ — 31. Ⓐ Ⓓ
32. 4651 Orchard Lake Rd — 4651 Orchard Lake Rd — 32. Ⓐ Ⓓ — 32. Ⓐ Ⓓ
33. 8569 Crying Pig St — 8560 Crying Pig St — 33. Ⓐ Ⓓ — 33. Ⓐ Ⓓ
34. 5118 Winchester Ave — 5118 Minchester Ave — 34. Ⓐ Ⓓ — 34. Ⓐ Ⓓ
35. 931 France Rd — 9317 France Rd — 35. Ⓐ Ⓓ — 35. Ⓐ Ⓓ
36. 8965 Manila Pl — 8965 Manila Pl — 36. Ⓐ Ⓓ — 36. Ⓐ Ⓓ
37. 9731 Vancouver Ct — 9731 Vancouver Ave — 37. Ⓐ Ⓓ — 37. Ⓐ Ⓓ
38. 2561 Oakwood Rdg — 2562 Oaklane Rdg — 38. Ⓐ Ⓓ — 38. Ⓐ Ⓓ

Go on to the next number on the next page.

39. 6750 Michigan Ave	6750 Michigan Ave	39. Ⓐ Ⓓ	39. Ⓐ Ⓓ
40. 1584 Milford Rd	1684 Milford Rd	40. Ⓐ Ⓓ	40. Ⓐ Ⓓ
41. 931 Pontiac Trl	931 Pontiac Trl	41 Ⓐ Ⓓ	41. Ⓐ Ⓓ
42. 7145 S Green Tree Rd	7135 S Green Tree Rd	42. Ⓐ Ⓓ	42. Ⓐ Ⓓ
43. 8503 Cambridge Blvd	8503 Cambridge Blvd	43. Ⓐ Ⓓ	43. Ⓐ Ⓓ
44. 1856 E Bradford Rd	1859 E Bradford Rd	44. Ⓐ Ⓓ	44. Ⓐ Ⓓ
45. 567 Sloan Dr	567 Sloan Dr	45. Ⓐ Ⓓ	45. Ⓐ Ⓓ
46. 3056 Weeping Tree Hts	3156 Weeping Tree Hts	46. Ⓐ Ⓓ	46. Ⓐ Ⓓ
47. 1069 Lindenmere Rd	1069 Lindenmere St	47. Ⓐ Ⓓ	47. Ⓐ Ⓓ
48. 27351 Woodward Ave	27351 Woodward Ave	48. Ⓐ Ⓓ	48. Ⓐ Ⓓ
49. 10527 Geraldine Ln	10627 Geraldine Ln	49. Ⓐ Ⓓ	49. Ⓐ Ⓓ
50. 7857 Main St SW	8757 Main St SE	50. Ⓐ Ⓓ	50. Ⓐ Ⓓ
51. 81351 Ypsilanti Cir	81351 Upsilanti Cir	51. Ⓐ Ⓓ	51. Ⓐ Ⓓ
52. 5296 Meadowbrook Ave	5296 Meadowbrooke Ave	52. Ⓐ Ⓓ	52. Ⓐ Ⓓ
53. 27 6th St SW	27 6th St SE	53. Ⓐ Ⓓ	53. Ⓐ Ⓓ
54. 393 Crossroad Pl	398 Crossrad Pl	54. Ⓐ Ⓓ	54. Ⓐ Ⓓ
55. 47651 Burntree St	47651 Burntree Rd	55. Ⓐ Ⓓ	55. Ⓐ Ⓓ
56. 927 Clinton Blvd	927 Clinton Blvd	56. Ⓐ Ⓓ	56. Ⓐ Ⓓ
57. 8531 Capitol Ave	8531 Capitol Ave	57. Ⓐ Ⓓ	57. Ⓐ Ⓓ
58. 4683 Falcon Cress Way	4688 Falcon Cress Way	58. Ⓐ Ⓓ	58. Ⓐ Ⓓ
59. 7536 Atlans Spring	7536 Atlas Spring	59. Ⓐ Ⓓ	59. Ⓐ Ⓓ
60. 9736 Sleepy Holllow Rdg	9736 Sleeping Hollow Rdg	60. Ⓐ Ⓓ	60. Ⓐ Ⓓ
61. 1530 Laughing Twins Pl	1539 Laughing Twins Pl	61. Ⓐ Ⓓ	61. Ⓐ Ⓓ
62. 8819 Los Amigos St	8819 Los Amigos St	62. Ⓐ Ⓓ	62. Ⓐ Ⓓ
63. 7081 Renegade Pl	7081 Renegate Pl	63. Ⓐ Ⓓ	63. Ⓐ Ⓓ
64. 4047 Bates Ave	4047 Bates Ave	64. Ⓐ Ⓓ	64. Ⓐ Ⓓ
65. 3250 Hidden Valley Trl	3259 Hidden Valley Trl	65. Ⓐ Ⓓ	65. Ⓐ Ⓓ
66. 1212 Blake St	1212 Blake Trl	66. Ⓐ Ⓓ	66. Ⓐ Ⓓ
67. 590 James Pl	590 Jamison Pl	67. Ⓐ Ⓓ	67. Ⓐ Ⓓ
68. 6060 Porter Rd	6060 Port Rd	68. Ⓐ Ⓓ	68. Ⓐ Ⓓ
69. 1345 Johnson Dr	145 Johnson Dr	69. Ⓐ Ⓓ	69. Ⓐ Ⓓ
70. 67616 Walking Skeleton St	67616 Walking Sleleton St	70. Ⓐ Ⓓ	70. Ⓐ Ⓓ
71. 3052 145th St NW	3052 148th St NW	71. Ⓐ Ⓓ	71. Ⓐ Ⓓ
72. 61990 Barkley Lane	61990 Barkley Lane	72. Ⓐ Ⓓ	72. Ⓐ Ⓓ
73. 90771 Fox Parkway	90771 Fox Parklawn	73. Ⓐ Ⓓ	73. Ⓐ Ⓓ
74. 2010 Lester Bay	2010 Lester Bay	74. Ⓐ Ⓓ	74. Ⓐ Ⓓ
75. 2070 Kimberly St	2079 Kimberly St	75. Ⓐ Ⓓ	75. Ⓐ Ⓓ
76. 44336 Hubert Way	44336 Hubert Way	76. Ⓐ Ⓓ	76. Ⓐ Ⓓ
77. 4606 Henry Rdg	4660 Henry Rdg	77. Ⓐ Ⓓ	77. Ⓐ Ⓓ
78. 83197 Mocking Bird Pl	83107 Mocking Bird Pl	78. Ⓐ Ⓓ	78. Ⓐ Ⓓ
79. 381 Xanado St	381 Xanadoe St	79. Ⓐ Ⓓ	79. Ⓐ Ⓓ
80. 30089 Hermoso Park Blvd	30080 Hermoso park Blvd	80. Ⓐ Ⓓ	80. Ⓐ Ⓓ
81. 4663 Winter Ln	463 Winter Rd	81. Ⓐ Ⓓ	81. Ⓐ Ⓓ
82. 16111 Plymuth St	16111 Plymoth St	82. Ⓐ Ⓓ	82 Ⓐ Ⓓ
83. 1409 Jordan Trl	1409 Jordan Pl	83. Ⓐ Ⓓ	83. Ⓐ Ⓓ
84. 26711 Liberty Ave	26711 Liberty Ave	84. Ⓐ Ⓓ	84. Ⓐ Ⓓ
85. 4012 Jackson Blvd	4012 Jackson Blvd	85. Ⓐ Ⓓ	85. Ⓐ Ⓓ
86. 2630 Ann Arbor St	2830 Ann Arbor St	86. Ⓐ Ⓓ	86. Ⓐ Ⓓ
87. 2905 Quial St N	2905 Queal St N	87. Ⓐ Ⓓ	87. Ⓐ Ⓓ
88. 4572 Northville Park	4573 Northville Park	88. Ⓐ Ⓓ	88. Ⓐ Ⓓ

Go on to the next number on the next page.

89. 50883 Hagertown Blvd S	50383 Hagertown Blvd S	89. Ⓐ Ⓓ	89. Ⓐ Ⓓ
90. 7728 Carson Trl	7723 Carson Trl	90. Ⓐ Ⓓ	90. Ⓐ Ⓓ
91. 5735 Brooksfield Crescent	5735 Brookshield Crescent	91. Ⓐ Ⓓ	91. Ⓐ Ⓓ
92. 1495 Smoky Mountain Rd	1495 Smoky Mountain Rd	92. Ⓐ Ⓓ	92. Ⓐ Ⓓ
93. 1165 Hermansville Rdg	1165 Hermansvil Rdg	93. Ⓐ Ⓓ	93. Ⓐ Ⓓ
94. 3689 Cuyahoga Pl	3689 Cuyahoga Pl	94. Ⓐ Ⓓ	94. Ⓐ Ⓓ
95. 1531 Winchester Hwy	1531 Winchester Hwy	95. Ⓐ Ⓓ	95. Ⓐ Ⓓ

STOP

**If you finish before the time is up, check your answers for Part A.
Do not go to any other part.**

(See the correct answers on the next page.)

Correct Answers

Address-Checking Test

1. D	25. D	49. D	73. D
2. A	26. A	50. D	74. A
3. A	27. D	51. D	75. D
4. D	28. D	52. D	76. A
5. D	29. D	53. D	77. D
6. A	30. D	54. D	38. D
7. A	31. D	55. D	79. D
8. A	32. A	56. A	80. D
9. A	33. D	57. A	81. D
10. D	34. D	58. D	82. D
11. D	35. D	59. D	83. D
12. D	36. A	60. D	84. A
13. A	37. D	61. D	85. A
14. D	38. D	62. A	86. D
15. A	39. A	63. D	87. D
16. D	40. D	64. A	88. D
17. D	41. A	65. D	89. D
!8. D	42. D	66. D	90. D
19. A	43. A	67. D	91. D
20. D	44. D	68. D	92. A
21. D	45. A	69. D	93. D
22. D	46. D	70 D	94. A
23. A	47. D	71. D	95. A
24. A	48. A	72. A	

Address-Checking Practice Test
Work—6 Minutes

These addresses are like the ones in the address-checking test.

Decide whether the two addresses are Alike, or Different. Mark the answers on the answer sheet to the right. Work as fast as you can without making too many errors. Work exactly 6 minutes.

ANSWER SHEET

		Test A	Test B
1. 429 Judson Ct	37. 429 Judson Ct	1. Ⓐ Ⓓ	1. Ⓐ Ⓓ
2. 2500 University St	38. 2509 University St	2. Ⓐ Ⓓ	2. Ⓐ Ⓓ
3. 85651 Walton Way	85651 Walton Way	3. Ⓐ Ⓓ	3. Ⓐ Ⓓ
4. 4395 Leane St	4305 Leane St	4. Ⓐ Ⓓ	4. Ⓐ Ⓓ
5. 4275 Circle Dr	4375 Circle Dr	5. Ⓐ Ⓓ	5. Ⓐ Ⓓ
6. 1219 E Mansfield	1219 W Mansfield	6. Ⓐ Ⓓ	6. Ⓐ Ⓓ
7. 23210 Fourth St	23110 Fourth Rd	7. Ⓐ Ⓓ	7. Ⓐ Ⓓ
8. 10101 Price St	10101 Price Rd	8. Ⓐ Ⓓ	8. Ⓐ Ⓓ
9. 4441 Emerson Trl	4441 Emersion Trl	9. Ⓐ Ⓓ	9. Ⓐ Ⓓ
10. 1231 N Johnson Blvd	1231 E Johnson Blvd	10. Ⓐ Ⓓ	10. Ⓐ Ⓓ
11. 89265 Woodland Ln E	89263 Woodland Ln E	11. Ⓐ Ⓓ	11. Ⓐ Ⓓ
12. 1397 Cherryhill Rd	1397 Cherrylane Rd	12. Ⓐ Ⓓ	12. Ⓐ Ⓓ
13. 5256 Apple Lane St	5256 Apple Lane St	13. Ⓐ Ⓓ	13. Ⓐ Ⓓ
14. 44571 E Walton Way	44571 E Walton Way	14. Ⓐ Ⓓ	14. Ⓐ Ⓓ
15. 3800 Grandville Rd	3800 Grandmall Rd	15. Ⓐ Ⓓ	15. Ⓐ Ⓓ
16. 40105 W Huron Dr	41005 W Huron Dr	16. Ⓐ Ⓓ	16. Ⓐ Ⓓ
17. 52990 Blaine St	52999 Blaine St	17. Ⓐ Ⓓ	17. Ⓐ Ⓓ
18. 8265 State Rd W	8265 State Rd W	18. Ⓐ Ⓓ	18. Ⓐ Ⓓ
19. 15025 S Highwood St	15025 S Highwood St	19. Ⓐ Ⓓ	19. Ⓐ Ⓓ
20. 6814 Forgrove Cir	6914 Forgrove Cir	20. Ⓐ Ⓓ	20. Ⓐ Ⓓ
21. 11224 N Moore St	11234 N Moore St.	21. Ⓐ Ⓓ	21. Ⓐ Ⓓ
22. 3957 Lynch Crescent	3957 Lynch Crescent	22. Ⓐ Ⓓ	22. Ⓐ Ⓓ
23. 264 N Hillside Way	264 E Hillside Way	23. Ⓐ Ⓓ	23. Ⓐ Ⓓ
24. 10558 W Chicago Rd	19558 W Chicago Rd	24. Ⓐ Ⓓ	24. Ⓐ Ⓓ
25. 9948 Dixie Highway Rd	9948 Dixie Highway Rd	25. Ⓐ Ⓓ	25. Ⓐ Ⓓ
26. 2641 Fairchild St SW	2641 Fairchild St SW	26. Ⓐ Ⓓ	26. Ⓐ Ⓓ
27. 64521 E Campbell St	64521 N Campbell St	27 Ⓐ Ⓓ	27. Ⓐ Ⓓ
28. 4925 Auburn Dr SW	4925 Auburn Cir SW	28. Ⓐ Ⓓ	28. Ⓐ Ⓓ
29. 36101 Joslyn Rd	36191 Joslyn Rd	29. Ⓐ Ⓓ	29. Ⓐ Ⓓ
30. 41417 Maine St	41417 Maine St	30. Ⓐ Ⓓ	30. Ⓐ Ⓓ
31. 3416 S Shirley Rd	3416 S Shirly Rd	31. Ⓐ Ⓓ	31. Ⓐ Ⓓ
32. 9713 N Paddock St	9713 N Paddock St	32. Ⓐ Ⓓ	32. Ⓐ Ⓓ
33. 20501 Miller Hwy NW	20501 Miller Way NW	33. Ⓐ Ⓓ	33. Ⓐ Ⓓ
34. 69102 Mork St	69102 Mork St	34. Ⓐ Ⓓ	34. Ⓐ Ⓓ
35. 2539 E Bloomfield	2530 E Bloomfield	35. Ⓐ Ⓓ	35. Ⓐ Ⓓ
36. 18681 Riker Rd	18681 Riker Rd	36. Ⓐ Ⓓ	36. Ⓐ Ⓓ
37. 45001 S Saginaw St	37. 45001 S Saginaw St	37. Ⓐ Ⓓ	37. Ⓐ Ⓓ
38. 5483 Warren Rd W	38. 5483 Warren Rd W	38. Ⓐ Ⓓ	38. Ⓐ Ⓓ

Go on to the next number on the next page.

39. 46431 Brush Ln	46437 Brush Ln	39. Ⓐ Ⓓ	39. Ⓐ Ⓓ
40. 79019 W New York	79010 W New York	40. Ⓐ Ⓓ	40. Ⓐ Ⓓ
41. 14009 E Colgate	14009 E Colgate	41 Ⓐ Ⓓ	41. Ⓐ Ⓓ
42. 50517 Cherrylawn Rd	50517 Cherrylane Rd	42. Ⓐ Ⓓ	42. Ⓐ Ⓓ
43. 2300 Pine St	2300 Pine St	43. Ⓐ Ⓓ	43. Ⓐ Ⓓ
44. 28910 Southfield Trl E	28910 Southfield Trl E	44. Ⓐ Ⓓ	44. Ⓐ Ⓓ
45. 10129 Sanford St	10129 Sanford Rd	45. Ⓐ Ⓓ	45. Ⓐ Ⓓ
46. 1604 Dearborn SW	1804 Dearborn SW	46. Ⓐ Ⓓ	46. Ⓐ Ⓓ
47. 8679 Westway Ave	8670 Westway Ave	47. Ⓐ Ⓓ	47. Ⓐ Ⓓ
48. 14919 Broadway Rd	14019 Broadway Rd	48. Ⓐ Ⓓ	48. Ⓐ Ⓓ
49. 10456 Hickory Cr	10456 Hickory Cr	49. Ⓐ Ⓓ	49. Ⓐ Ⓓ
50. 2169 Wayne St	2169 Wayne St	50. Ⓐ Ⓓ	50. Ⓐ Ⓓ
51. 60517 Wedgewood NW	60817 Wedgewood NW	51. Ⓐ Ⓓ	51. Ⓐ Ⓓ
52. 10821 E Birwood St	18421 E Birwood St	52. Ⓐ Ⓓ	52. Ⓐ Ⓓ
53. 41642 Parkway W	41642 Parkway W	53. Ⓐ Ⓓ	53. Ⓐ Ⓓ
54. 32101 E Lakeside Rd	32101 E Lakeside Rd	54. Ⓐ Ⓓ	54. Ⓐ Ⓓ
55. 27509 Hillsdale Ave	27509 Hillsdale Ave	55. Ⓐ Ⓓ	55. Ⓐ Ⓓ
56. 20614 W Ann Arbor	20614 W Ann Arbor	56. Ⓐ Ⓓ	56. Ⓐ Ⓓ
57. 89607 Benson Dr	89607 Benson St	57. Ⓐ Ⓓ	57. Ⓐ Ⓓ
58. 48336 Lanson Pky	48836 Lanson Pakway	58. Ⓐ Ⓓ	58. Ⓐ Ⓓ
59. 6511 Colony Rd SW	6511 Colony Rd NW	59. Ⓐ Ⓓ	59. Ⓐ Ⓓ
60. 73011 Allen Park Way	73011 Allen Park Way	60. Ⓐ Ⓓ	60. Ⓐ Ⓓ
61. 1800 Ronald Lane	1800 Ronald Lane	61. Ⓐ Ⓓ	61. Ⓐ Ⓓ
62. 7457 Cass Ave	7458 Cass Ave	62. Ⓐ Ⓓ	62. Ⓐ Ⓓ
63. 2715 Northway Rd	2775 Northway Rd	63. Ⓐ Ⓓ	63. Ⓐ Ⓓ
64. 42061 Bennet Way	42061 Bennet Way	64. Ⓐ Ⓓ	64. Ⓐ Ⓓ
65. 48260 W Amy Ln	48260 W Amy Ln	65. Ⓐ Ⓓ	65. Ⓐ Ⓓ
66. 36412 Ward St	36413 Ward St	66. Ⓐ Ⓓ	66. Ⓐ Ⓓ
67. 29840 Clark Ct NW	29840 Clark Ct NW	67. Ⓐ Ⓓ	67. Ⓐ Ⓓ
68. 3561 Middlebelt SW	3861 Middlebelt SW	68. Ⓐ Ⓓ	68. Ⓐ Ⓓ
69. 4912 S Lakeshore Cr	4012 S Lakeshore Cr	69. Ⓐ Ⓓ	69. Ⓐ Ⓓ
70. 6721 Cresent Ave	6721 Cresent Rd	70. Ⓐ Ⓓ	70. Ⓐ Ⓓ
71. 8921 Waldo Ave E	8921 Waldo Ave W	71. Ⓐ Ⓓ	71. Ⓐ Ⓓ
72. 22518 Grandtour E	22518 Grandtour S	72. Ⓐ Ⓓ	72. Ⓐ Ⓓ
73. 41658 Southwest Way	41659 Southwest Way	73. Ⓐ Ⓓ	73. Ⓐ Ⓓ
74. 1416 Meadowlawn Pl	1418 Meadowlawn Pl	74. Ⓐ Ⓓ	74. Ⓐ Ⓓ
75. 6210 Oakland Ave	6210 Oakland Rd	75. Ⓐ Ⓓ	75. Ⓐ Ⓓ
76. 15012 Manhattan Way	15012 Manhattan Way	76. Ⓐ Ⓓ	76. Ⓐ Ⓓ
77. 9051 W Lexington R	9951 W Lexington Rd	77. Ⓐ Ⓓ	77. Ⓐ Ⓓ
78. 24615 N Gidding Rd	24815 N Gidding Rd	78. Ⓐ Ⓓ	78. Ⓐ Ⓓ
79. 84115 Vernon Rd	84115 Vernon Rd	79. Ⓐ Ⓓ	79. Ⓐ Ⓓ
80. 5846 Martin Luther King St	5346 Martin Luther King St	80. Ⓐ Ⓓ	80. Ⓐ Ⓓ
81. 8987 Northview Pl	8087 Northview Pl	81. Ⓐ Ⓓ	81. Ⓐ Ⓓ
82. 3516 Bay Rd	3517 Bay St	82. Ⓐ Ⓓ	82 Ⓐ Ⓓ
83. 8264 S Eastway Cir	8264 S Eastway Cir	83. Ⓐ Ⓓ	83. Ⓐ Ⓓ
84. 32890 Lauren Ave	32890 Lauren Ave	84. Ⓐ Ⓓ	84. Ⓐ Ⓓ
85. 72110 Ball St S	72110 Ball St S	85. Ⓐ Ⓓ	85. Ⓐ Ⓓ
86. 938 Osmun NW	938 Osmun NW	86. Ⓐ Ⓓ	86. Ⓐ Ⓓ
87. 1265 Franklane W	1265 Franklane W	87. Ⓐ Ⓓ	87. Ⓐ Ⓓ
88. 44251 W Fairmont Way	44251 W Fairmont Way	88. Ⓐ Ⓓ	88. Ⓐ Ⓓ

Go on to the next number on the next page.

89. 9308 Fairground Blvd	9303 Fairground Blvd	89. Ⓐ Ⓓ	89. Ⓐ Ⓓ
90. 2847 Robinwood St N	2847 Robinwood St W	90. Ⓐ Ⓓ	90. Ⓐ Ⓓ
91. 4750 E Salley Ln	4750 E Salley Ln	91. Ⓐ Ⓓ	91. Ⓐ Ⓓ
92. 59465 Michigan Ave SW	59465 Michigan Rd SW	92. Ⓐ Ⓓ	92. Ⓐ Ⓓ
93. 3138 N Morgan St	3138 N Morgan St	93. Ⓐ Ⓓ	93. Ⓐ Ⓓ
94. 11517 Oxford Rd	11517 Oxford Rd	94. Ⓐ Ⓓ	94. Ⓐ Ⓓ
95. 47518 Clawsan Parkway	47518 Clawson Parkway	95. Ⓐ Ⓓ	95. Ⓐ Ⓓ

STOP

**If you finish before the time is up, check your answers for Part A.
Do not go to any other part.**

(See the correct answers on the next page.)

Correct Answers

Address-Checking Test

1. A	25. A	49. A	73. D
2. D	26. A	50. A	74. D
3. A	27. D	51. D	75. D
4. D	28. D	52. D	76. A
5. D	29. D	53. A	77. D
6. D	30. A	54. A	78. D
7. D	31. D	55. A	79. A
8. D	32. A	56. A	80. D
9. D	33. D	57. D	81. D
10. D	34. A	58. D	82. D
11. D	35. D	59. D	83. A
12. D	36. A	60. A	84. A
13. A	37. A	61. A	85. A
14. A	38. A	62. D	86. A
15. D	39. D	63. D	87. A
16. D	40. D	64. A	88. A
17. D	41. A	65. A	89. D
18. A	42. D	66. D	90. D
19. A	43. A	67. A	91. A
20. D	44. A	68. D	92. D
21. D	45. D	69. D	93. A
22. A	46. D	70. D	94. A
23. D	47. D	71. D	95. D
24. D	48. D	72. D	

Address-Checking Practice Test
Work—6 Minutes

These addresses are like the ones in the address-checking test.

Decide whether the two addresses are *Alike* or *Different*. If they are *Alike*, darken or mark space A; if they are *Different*, darken space D. Mark the answers on the answer sheet to the right. Work as fast as you can without making too many errors. Work exactly 6 minutes.

ANSWER SHEET

#	Address 1	Address 2	Test A	Test B
1.	38201 River Ave E	38201 River Ave E	1 Ⓐⓓ	1 Ⓐⓓ
2.	6061 Trumbull Ave S	6061 Trumbull Ave N	2 Ⓐⓓ	2 Ⓐⓓ
3.	15058 Campbell St	15058 Campbell St	3 Ⓐⓓ	3 Ⓐⓓ
4.	7538 Emerson Rd	7583 Emerson Rd	4 Ⓐⓓ	4 Ⓐⓓ
5.	1189 Grand Blvd E	1189 Grand Blvd E	5 Ⓐⓓ	5 Ⓐⓓ
6.	824 Smith St	824 Smyth St	6 Ⓐⓓ	6 Ⓐⓓ
7.	1810 Northridge Rd	1810 Northridge Rd	7 Ⓐⓓ	7 Ⓐⓓ
8.	4809 Winchester St	4809 Winchester St	8 Ⓐⓓ	8 Ⓐⓓ
9.	3138 Ongkama Ter	3183 Ongkama Ter	9 Ⓐⓓ	9 Ⓐⓓ
10.	2633 Meridian Sq	2633 Meridian Sq	10 Ⓐⓓ	10 Ⓐⓓ
11.	42473 Teppert St	42473 Teppert St	11 Ⓐⓓ	11 Ⓐⓓ
12.	50506 Shaftsbury Pl	50056 Shaftsbury Pl	12 Ⓐⓓ	12 Ⓐⓓ
13.	6562 Marigold Rd E	6526 Marigold Rd E	13 Ⓐⓓ	13 Ⓐⓓ
14.	35405 Courtland Cir	35405 Cortland Cir	14 Ⓐⓓ	14 Ⓐⓓ
15.	9544 Wesley Ln NE	9544 Wesley Ln SW	15 Ⓐⓓ	15 Ⓐⓓ
16.	4265 Bauerle Rd E	4265 Bauerle Rd E	16 Ⓐⓓ	16 Ⓐⓓ
17.	15993 Ann Ln	15993 Annie Ln	17 Ⓐⓓ	17 Ⓐⓓ
18.	1744 Burris Dr SW	1744 Burris Dr SE	18 Ⓐⓓ	18 Ⓐⓓ
19.	6303 Ryan Rd	6308 Ryan Rd	19 Ⓐⓓ	19 Ⓐⓓ
20.	3796 Albuquerque Cir	3769 Albuquerque Cir	20 Ⓐⓓ	20 Ⓐⓓ
21.	62778 Townely Sq	62778 Townley Sq	21 Ⓐⓓ	21 Ⓐⓓ
22.	3240 Kelly Rd E	3240 Kelly Rd W	22 Ⓐⓓ	22 Ⓐⓓ
23.	7970 Milford St	7970 Milford St	23 Ⓐⓓ	23 Ⓐⓓ
24.	1219 Sullivan Ln	1219 Sullivan Ln	24 Ⓐⓓ	24 Ⓐⓓ
25.	9113 Bradley Ct SE	9113 Bradley CT SW	25 Ⓐⓓ	25 Ⓐⓓ
26.	52305 Northwind Cir	52305 Northwind Cir	26 Ⓐⓓ	26 Ⓐⓓ
27.	5665 Gratiot Ave	5995 Gratiot Ave	27 Ⓐⓓ	27 Ⓐⓓ
28.	18143 Shaw Ave E	18143 Shaw Ave E	28 Ⓐⓓ	28 Ⓐⓓ
29.	1297 St Andrews Dr	1297 St Andrews Ave	29 Ⓐⓓ	29 Ⓐⓓ
30.	1435 Greenbrush Cir	1435 Greenbush Cir	30 Ⓐⓓ	30 Ⓐⓓ
31.	1569 Moore St	1596 Moore St	31 Ⓐⓓ	31 Ⓐⓓ
32.	170 Prospect Ave	170 Prospect Ave	32 Ⓐⓓ	32 Ⓐⓓ
33.	7621 Tonawanda Dr	7621 Tonakawa Dr	33 Ⓐⓓ	33 Ⓐⓓ
34.	92512 Plateau Rd	92512 Plateau Cir	34 Ⓐⓓ	34 Ⓐⓓ
35.	3764 Kennedy Sq	3764 Kennedy Sq	35 Ⓐⓓ	35 Ⓐⓓ
36.	8388 Anthony Ln	8838 Kennedy Sq	36 Ⓐⓓ	36 Ⓐⓓ
37.	8161 Laurel Way	8161 Laurel Way	37 Ⓐⓓ	37 Ⓐⓓ
38.	3653 Caverhill Dr	3654 Caverhill Dr	38 Ⓐⓓ	38 Ⓐⓓ
39.	46961 Maverick St	49691 Maverick St	39 Ⓐⓓ	39 Ⓐⓓ
40.	6211 Vernor Ave W	6211 Vernor Ave W	40 Ⓐⓓ	40 Ⓐⓓ

Go on to the next number on the next page.

41.	2002 Clarkston Cir	2020 Clarkston Cir	41 Ⓐ Ⓓ	41 Ⓐ Ⓓ
42.	15913 Winfield Pkwy	15913 Winfield Pkwy	42 Ⓐ Ⓓ	42 Ⓐ Ⓓ
43.	5688 Oakwood Rd	5868 Oakwood Rd	43 Ⓐ Ⓓ	43 Ⓐ Ⓓ
44.	9273 Butterfield Dr	9273 Butterfield Dr	44 Ⓐ Ⓓ	44 Ⓐ Ⓓ
45.	4203 Moody St	4203 Moody St	45 Ⓐ Ⓓ	45 Ⓐ Ⓓ
46.	3561 Kraft Cir	3561 Craft Cir	46 Ⓐ Ⓓ	46 Ⓐ Ⓓ
47.	1688 Bradford St	1866 Bradford St	47 Ⓐ Ⓓ	47 Ⓐ Ⓓ
48.	9725 Frandor Dr	9725 Frandor Dr	48 Ⓐ Ⓓ	48 Ⓐ Ⓓ
49.	89678 Pleasant St	89678 Pleasant St	49 Ⓐ Ⓓ	49 Ⓐ Ⓓ
50.	1531 Rather Way	1513 Rather Way	50 Ⓐ Ⓓ	50 Ⓐ Ⓓ
51.	3720 Cavanaugh W	3720 Cavanaugh E	51 Ⓐ Ⓓ	51 Ⓐ Ⓓ
52.	4172 Main St	4172 Main St	52 Ⓐ Ⓓ	52 Ⓐ Ⓓ
53.	31069 Bailey Dr	31069 Bailey Dr	53 Ⓐ Ⓓ	53 Ⓐ Ⓓ
54.	4171 Waterford NW	4171 Waterford NE	54 Ⓐ Ⓓ	54 Ⓐ Ⓓ
55.	1876 Bessley Sq	1876 Bessley Sq	55 Ⓐ Ⓓ	55 Ⓐ Ⓓ
56.	2151 Stadium Dr	2151 Stadium Dr	56 Ⓐ Ⓓ	56 Ⓐ Ⓓ
57.	9792 Browne St	9729 Browne St	57 Ⓐ Ⓓ	57 Ⓐ Ⓓ
58.	5498 Lenon Ave	5498 Lenon Ave	58 Ⓐ Ⓓ	58 Ⓐ Ⓓ
59.	7533 Armstrong	7533 Armstrong	59 Ⓐ Ⓓ	59 Ⓐ Ⓓ
60.	3421 Spencer St	3421 Spencer St	60 Ⓐ Ⓓ	60 Ⓐ Ⓓ
61.	21384 Chestnut Rd	21384 Chestnut Rd	61 Ⓐ Ⓓ	61 Ⓐ Ⓓ
62.	7317 Foxbury Ln	7317 Foxbury Ln	62 Ⓐ Ⓓ	62 Ⓐ Ⓓ
63.	6367 Whitehouse Rd	6376 Whitehouse Rd	63 Ⓐ Ⓓ	63 Ⓐ Ⓓ
64.	7397 Belwood Pkwy	7397 Bellewood Pkwy	64 Ⓐ Ⓓ	64 Ⓐ Ⓓ
65.	59513 Burntree St	5951 Burntree St	65 Ⓐ Ⓓ	65 Ⓐ Ⓓ
66.	3964 Yakely Rd	3964 Yakely Rd	66 Ⓐ Ⓓ	66 Ⓐ Ⓓ
67.	2044 Elkhart St	2044 Elkhart St	67 Ⓐ Ⓓ	67 Ⓐ Ⓓ
68.	5954 Cavalry Ln NE	5954 Cavalry Ln NW	68 Ⓐ Ⓓ	68 Ⓐ Ⓓ
69.	37371 Sominole Rd	37371 Seminole Rd	69 Ⓐ Ⓓ	69 Ⓐ Ⓓ
70.	263 Emmons Ave	2363 Emmons Ave	70 Ⓐ Ⓓ	70 Ⓐ Ⓓ
71.	8502 Larson Sq	8502 Larson Sq	71 Ⓐ Ⓓ	71 Ⓐ Ⓓ
72.	1396 Capitol St	1396 Capitol St	72 Ⓐ Ⓓ	72 Ⓐ Ⓓ
73.	5584 Dragon Dr	5854 Dragon Dr	73 Ⓐ Ⓓ	73 Ⓐ Ⓓ
74.	6109 Cornelia Rd	6109 Cornelia Rd	74 Ⓐ Ⓓ	74 Ⓐ Ⓓ
75.	1606 Patricia Ln	1606 Patricia Ln	75 Ⓐ Ⓓ	75 Ⓐ Ⓓ
76.	1887 Winfield Ave	1878 Winfield Ave	76 Ⓐ Ⓓ	76 Ⓐ Ⓓ
77.	2104 Waverly Cir	2104 Waverly Cir	77 Ⓐ Ⓓ	77 Ⓐ Ⓓ
78.	35017 Fairfax St SW	35017 Fairfax St SE	78 Ⓐ Ⓓ	78 Ⓐ Ⓓ
79.	4433 Oaklawn Sq	4343 Oaklawn	79 Ⓐ Ⓓ	79 Ⓐ Ⓓ
80.	1402 Cedar Rd S	1402 Cedar Rd S	80 Ⓐ Ⓓ	80 Ⓐ Ⓓ
81.	9562 Williamston Rd	9652 Williamston Rd	81 Ⓐ Ⓓ	81 Ⓐ Ⓓ
82.	3555 Huebner Dr	3555 Hubbard Dr	82 Ⓐ Ⓓ	82 Ⓐ Ⓓ
83.	17573 Burlington St	1775 Burlington St	83 Ⓐ Ⓓ	83 Ⓐ Ⓓ
84.	8421 Springfield Way	8421 Springfield Way	84 Ⓐ Ⓓ	84 Ⓐ Ⓓ
85.	5340 Abbot Ln	5340 Abbot Ln	85 Ⓐ Ⓓ	85 Ⓐ Ⓓ
86.	2505 Reuther Rd	2505 Reuther Rd	86 Ⓐ Ⓓ	86 Ⓐ Ⓓ
87.	3135 Glaser St	3135 Glaser St	87 Ⓐ Ⓓ	87 Ⓐ Ⓓ
88.	151 Hudson Sq	151 Hudson Sq	88 Ⓐ Ⓓ	88 Ⓐ Ⓓ
89.	8612 Newman Ave	8612 Neuman Ave	89 Ⓐ Ⓓ	89 Ⓐ Ⓓ

Go on to the next number on the next page.

90.	59183 Edmenton St NE	59183 Edmenton St NW	90 Ⓐ Ⓓ	90 Ⓐ Ⓓ
91.	2587 Gold St	2587 Gold St	91 Ⓐ Ⓓ	91 Ⓐ Ⓓ
92.	1731 Falcon Crest	1731 Falcon Crest	92 Ⓐ Ⓓ	92 Ⓐ Ⓓ
93.	4986 Tumolo Ave	4968 Tumolo Ave	93 Ⓐ Ⓓ	93 Ⓐ Ⓓ
94.	90859 Newton St	90859 Newton St	94 Ⓐ Ⓓ	94 Ⓐ Ⓓ
95.	23323 Teppert St	22323 Teppert St	95 Ⓐ Ⓓ	95 Ⓐ Ⓓ

STOP.

**If you finish before the time is up, check your answers for Part A.
Do not go to any other part.**

(See the correct answers on the next page.)

Correct Answers

Address-Checking Test

1. A	25. D	49. A	73. D
2. D	26. A	50. D	74. A
3. A	27. D	51. D	75. A
4. D	28. A	52. A	76. D
5. A	29. D	53. A	77. A
6. D	30. D	54. D	78. D
7. A	31. D	55. A	79. D
8. A	32. A	56. A	80. A
9. D	33. D	57. D	81. D
10. A	34. D	58. A	82. D
11. A	35. A	59. A	83. D
12. D	36. D	60. A	84. A
13. D	37. A	61. A	85. A
14. D	38. D	62. A	86. A
15. D	39. D	63. D	87. A
16. A	40. A	64. D	88. A
17. D	41. D	65. D	89. D
18. D	42. A	66. A	90. D
19. D	43. D	67. A	91. A
20. D	44. A	68. D	92. A
21. D	45. A	69. D	93. D
22. D	46. D	70. D	94. A
23. A	47. D	71. A	95. D
24. A	48. A	72. A	

Address-Checking Practice Test
Work—6 Minutes

These addresses are like the ones in the address-checking test.

Decide whether the two addresses are *Alike* or *Different*. If they are *Alike*, darken or mark space A; if they are *Different*, darken space D. Mark the answers on the answer sheet to the right. Work as fast as you can without making too many errors. Work exactly 6 minutes.

ANSWER SHEET

			Test A	Test B
1.	405 Winter Rd NW	405 Winter Rd NW	1 ⒶⒹ	1 ⒶⒹ
2.	607 S Calaveras Rd	607 S Calaveras Rd	2 ⒶⒹ	2 ⒶⒹ
3.	8406 La Casa St	8406 La Cosa St	3 ⒶⒹ	3 ⒶⒹ
4.	121 N Rippon St	121 N Rippon St	4 ⒶⒹ	4 ⒶⒹ
5.	Wideman Ark	Wiseman Ark	5 ⒶⒹ	5 ⒶⒹ
6.	Sodus NY 14551	Sodus NY 14551	6 ⒶⒹ	6 ⒶⒹ
7.	3429 Hermosa Dr	3429 Hermoso Dr	7 ⒶⒹ	7 ⒶⒹ
8.	3628 S Zeeland St	3268 S Zealand St	8 ⒶⒹ	8 ⒶⒹ
9.	1330 Cheverly Ave NE	1330 Cheverly Ave NE	9 ⒶⒹ	9 ⒶⒹ
10.	1689 N Derwood Dr	1689 N Derwood Dr	10 ⒶⒹ	10 ⒶⒹ
11.	3886 Sunrise Ct	3886 Sunrise Ct	11 ⒶⒹ	11 ⒶⒹ
12.	635 La Calle Mayor	653 La Calle Mayor	12 ⒶⒹ	12 ⒶⒹ
13.	2560 Lansford Pl	2560 Lansford St	13 ⒶⒹ	13 ⒶⒹ
14.	4631 Central Ave	4631 Central Ave	14 ⒶⒹ	14 ⒶⒹ
15.	Mason City Iowa 50401	Mason City Iowa 50401	15 ⒶⒹ	15 ⒶⒹ
16.	758 Los Arboles Ave SE	758 Los Arboles Ave SW	16 ⒶⒹ	16 ⒶⒹ
17.	3282 E Downington St	3282 E Dunnington St	17 ⒶⒹ	17 ⒶⒹ
18.	7117 N Burlingham Ave	7117 N Burlingham Ave	18 ⒶⒹ	18 ⒶⒹ
19.	32 Oaklawn Blvd	32 Oakland Blvd	19 ⒶⒹ	19 ⒶⒹ
20.	1274 Manzana Rd	1274 Manzana Rd	20 ⒶⒹ	20 ⒶⒹ
21.	4598 E Kenilworth Dr	4598 E Kenilworth Dr	21 ⒶⒹ	21 ⒶⒹ
22.	Dayton Okla 73449	Dagton Okla 73449	22 ⒶⒹ	22 ⒶⒹ
23.	1172 W 83rd Ave	1127 W 83rd Ave	23 ⒶⒹ	23 ⒶⒹ
24.	6434 E Pulaski St	6434 E Pulaski Ct	24 ⒶⒹ	24 ⒶⒹ
25.	2764 N Rutherford Pl	2764 N Rutherford Pl	25 ⒶⒹ	25 ⒶⒹ
26.	565 Greenville Blvd SE	565 Greenview Blvd SE	26 ⒶⒹ	26 ⒶⒹ
27.	Washington DC 20013	Washington DC 20018	27 ⒶⒹ	27 ⒶⒹ
28.	3824 Massasoit St	3824 Massasoit St	28 ⒶⒹ	28 ⒶⒹ
29.	22 Sagnaw Pkwy	22 Saganaw Pkwy	29 ⒶⒹ	29 ⒶⒹ
30.	Byram Conn 10573	Byram Conn 10573	30 ⒶⒹ	30 ⒶⒹ
31.	1928 S Fairfield Ave	1928 S Fairfield St	31 ⒶⒹ	31 ⒶⒹ
32.	36218 Overhills Dr	36218 Overhills Dr	32 ⒶⒹ	32 ⒶⒹ
33.	516 Avenida de Las Am	516 Avenida de Las Am	33 ⒶⒹ	33 ⒶⒹ
34.	7526 Naraganset Pl SW	7526 Naraganset Pl SW	34 ⒶⒹ	34 ⒶⒹ
35.	52626 W Ogelsby Dr	52626 W Ogelsby Dr	35 ⒶⒹ	35 ⒶⒹ
36.	1003 Winchester Rd	1003 Westchester RD	36 ⒶⒹ	36 ⒶⒹ
37.	3478 W Cavanaugh Ct	3478 W Cavenaugh Ct	37 ⒶⒹ	37 ⒶⒹ
38.	Kendall Calif 90551	Kendell Calif 90551	38 ⒶⒹ	38 ⒶⒹ
39.	225 El Camino Blvd	225 El Camino Ave	39 ⒶⒹ	39 ⒶⒹ
40.	7310 Via delos Pisos	7310 Via de los Pinos	40 ⒶⒹ	40 ⒶⒹ

Go on to the next number on the next page.

41.	1987 Wellington Ave SW	1987 Wellington Ave SW	41 Ⓐ Ⓓ	41 Ⓐ Ⓓ
42.	3124 S 71st St	3142 S 71st St	42 Ⓐ Ⓓ	42 Ⓐ Ⓓ
43.	729 Lincolnwood Blvd	729 Lincolnwood Blvd	43 Ⓐ Ⓓ	43 Ⓐ Ⓓ
44.	1166 N Beaumont Dr	1166 S Beaumont Dr	44 Ⓐ Ⓓ	44 Ⓐ Ⓓ
45.	3224 W Winecona Pl	3224 W Winecona Pl	45 Ⓐ Ⓓ	45 Ⓐ Ⓓ
46.	608 Calle Bienvenida	607 Calle Bienvenida	46 Ⓐ Ⓓ	46 Ⓐ Ⓓ
47.	La Molte Iowa 52045	La Molte Iowa 52045	47 Ⓐ Ⓓ	47 Ⓐ Ⓓ
48.	8625 Armitage Ave NW	8625 Armitage Ave NW	48 Ⓐ Ⓓ	48 Ⓐ Ⓓ
49.	2343 Broadview Ave	2334 Broadview Ave	49 Ⓐ Ⓓ	49 Ⓐ Ⓓ
50.	4279 Sierra Grande Ave	4279 Sierra Grande Dr	50 Ⓐ Ⓓ	50 Ⓐ Ⓓ
51.	165 32nd Ave	165 32nd Ave	51 Ⓐ Ⓓ	51 Ⓐ Ⓓ
52.	12742 N Deerborn St	12724 N Deerborn St	52 Ⓐ Ⓓ	52 Ⓐ Ⓓ
53.	114 Estancia Ave	141 Estancia Ave	53 Ⓐ Ⓓ	53 Ⓐ Ⓓ
54.	351 S Berwyn Rd	351 S Berwyn Pl	54 Ⓐ Ⓓ	54 Ⓐ Ⓓ
55.	7732 Avenida Manana SW	7732 Avenida Manana SW	55 Ⓐ Ⓓ	55 Ⓐ Ⓓ
56.	6337 C St SW	6337 G St SW	56 Ⓐ Ⓓ	56 Ⓐ Ⓓ
57.	57895 E Drexyl Ave	58795 E Drexyl Ave	57 Ⓐ Ⓓ	57 Ⓐ Ⓓ
58.	Altro Tex 75923	Altra Tex 75923	58 Ⓐ Ⓓ	58 Ⓐ Ⓓ
59.	3465 S Nashville St	3465 N Nashville St	59 Ⓐ Ⓓ	59 Ⓐ Ⓓ
60.	1226 Odell Blvd NW	1226 Oddell Blvd NW	60 Ⓐ Ⓓ	60 Ⓐ Ⓓ
61.	94002 Chappel Ct	94002 Chappel Ct	61 Ⓐ Ⓓ	61 Ⓐ Ⓓ
62.	512 La Vega Dr	512 La Veta Dr	62 Ⓐ Ⓓ	62 Ⓐ Ⓓ
63.	8774 W Winona Pl	8774 R Winona	63 Ⓐ Ⓓ	63 Ⓐ Ⓓ
64.	6431 Ingleside St SE	6431 Ingleside St SE	64 Ⓐ Ⓓ	64 Ⓐ Ⓓ
65.	2270 N Leanington St	2270 N Leanington St	65 Ⓐ Ⓓ	65 Ⓐ Ⓓ
66.	235 Calle de Vecinos	235 Calle de Vecinos	66 Ⓐ Ⓓ	66 Ⓐ Ⓓ
67.	3987 E Westwood Ave	3987 W Westwood Ave	67 Ⓐ Ⓓ	67 Ⓐ Ⓓ
68.	Skamokawa Wash	Skamohawa Wash	68 Ⓐ Ⓓ	68 Ⓐ Ⓓ
69.	2674 E Champlain Cir	2764 E Champlain Cir	69 Ⓐ Ⓓ	69 Ⓐ Ⓓ
70.	8751 Elmhurst Blvd	8751 Elmwood Blvd	70 Ⓐ Ⓓ	70 Ⓐ Ⓓ
71.	6649 Solano Dr	6649 Solana Dr	71 Ⓐ Ⓓ	71 Ⓐ Ⓓ
72.	4423 S Escenaba St	4423 S Escenaba St	72 Ⓐ Ⓓ	72 Ⓐ Ⓓ
73.	1198 N St NW	1198 M St NW	73 Ⓐ Ⓓ	73 Ⓐ Ⓓ
74.	Sparta GA	Sparta Va	74 Ⓐ Ⓓ	74 Ⓐ Ⓓ
75.	96753 Wrightwood Ave	96753 Wrightwood Ave	75 Ⓐ Ⓓ	75 Ⓐ Ⓓ
76.	2445 Sangamow Ave SE	2445 Sangamow Ave SE	76 Ⓐ Ⓓ	76 Ⓐ Ⓓ
77.	5117 E 67 Pl	5171 E 67 Pl	77 Ⓐ Ⓓ	77 Ⓐ Ⓓ
78.	847 Mesa Grande Pl	847 Mesa Grande Ct	78 Ⓐ Ⓓ	78 Ⓐ Ⓓ
79.	1100 Cermaken St	1100 Cermaker St	79 Ⓐ Ⓓ	79 Ⓐ Ⓓ
80.	321 Tijeras Ave NW	321 Tijeras Ave NW	80 Ⓐ Ⓓ	80 Ⓐ Ⓓ
81.	3405 Prospect St	3405 Prospect St	81 Ⓐ Ⓓ	81 Ⓐ Ⓓ
82.	6643 Burlington Pl	6643 Burlingtown Pl	82 Ⓐ Ⓓ	82 Ⓐ Ⓓ
83.	851 Esperanza Blvd	851 Esperanza Blvd	83 Ⓐ Ⓓ	83 Ⓐ Ⓓ
84.	Jenkinjones W Va	Jenkinjones W Va	84 Ⓐ Ⓓ	84 Ⓐ Ⓓ
85.	1006 Pennsylvania Ave	1008 Pennsylvania Ave	85 Ⓐ Ⓓ	85 Ⓐ Ⓓ
86.	2924 26th St N	2929 26th St N	86 Ⓐ Ⓓ	86 Ⓐ Ⓓ
87.	7115 Highland Dr	7115 Highland Dr	87 Ⓐ Ⓓ	87 Ⓐ Ⓓ
88.	Chaptico MD	Chaptica MD	88 Ⓐ Ⓓ	88 Ⓐ Ⓓ
89.	3508 Camron Mills Rd	3508 Camron Mills Rd	89 Ⓐ Ⓓ	89 Ⓐ Ⓓ

Go on to the next number on the next page.

90. 67158 Capston Dr	67158 Capston Dr	90 Ⓐ Ⓓ	90 Ⓐ Ⓓ
91. 3613 S Taylor Ave	3631 S Taylor Ave	91 Ⓐ Ⓓ	91 Ⓐ Ⓓ
92. 2421 Menokin Dr	2421 Menokin Dr	92 Ⓐ Ⓓ	92 Ⓐ Ⓓ
93. 3226 M St NW	3226 N St NW	93 Ⓐ Ⓓ	93 Ⓐ Ⓓ
94. 1201 S Court House Rd	1201 S Court House Rd	94 Ⓐ Ⓓ	94 Ⓐ Ⓓ
95. Findlay Ohio 45840	Findley Ohio 45840	95 Ⓐ Ⓓ	95 Ⓐ Ⓓ

STOP
If you finish before the time is up, check your answers for Part A.
Do not go to any other part.

(See the correct answers on the next page.)

Correct Answers

Address-Checking Test

1. A	25. A	49. D	73. D
2. A	26. D	50. D	74. D
3. D	27. D	51. A	75. A
4. A	28. A	52. D	76. A
5. D	29. D	53. D	77. D
6. A	30. A	54. D	78. D
7. D	31. D	55. A	79. D
8. D	32. A	56. D	80. A
9. A	33. A	57. D	81. A
10. A	34. A	58. D	82. D
11. A	35. A	59. D	83. A
12. D	36. D	60. D	84. A
13. D	37. D	61. A	85. D
14. A	38. D	62. D	86. D
15. A	39. D	63. D	87. A
16. D	40. D	64. A	88. D
17. D	41. A	65. A	89. A
18. A	42. D	66. A	90. A
19. D	43. A	67. D	91. D
20. A	44. D	68. D	92. A
21. A	45. A	69. D	93. D
22. D	46. D	70. D	94. A
23. D	47. A	71. D	95. D
24. D	48. A	72. A	

United States Postal Service

Interpretation of Test Scores
on Sample Address-Checking Test

For the Address Checking (Part A), count the number that you got right and the number that you got wrong. (If you didn't mark anything for a question, it doesn't get counted.)

From the number right _____
Subtract the number wrong _____
This number (the difference) is your score ▶ _____

The meaning of the score is as follows:

52 or higher -- Good.

Between 32 and 51-- Fair.
Below 32 ---------------------------------- You need more practice.

Go back and see where you made your mistakes. Were you careless? Did you work too slowly?

Author's Note: According to my own estimate, when you get more than half of the answers correct (address checking, part A, 95 numbers), you'll pass the exam. I based this estimate on scores acquired by several examinees. However, you need to make high scores to beat the competition and be called immediately.

Address-Checking Practice Test
Work—6 Minutes

These addresses are like the ones in the address-checking test.

Decide whether the two addresses are *Alike*, or *Different*. If they are *Alike*, darken or mark space A; if they are *Different*, darken space D. Mark the answers on the answer sheet to the right. Work as fast as you can without making too many errors. Work exactly 6 minutes.

ANSWER SHEET

#	Address 1	Address 2	Test A	Test B
1.	15647 Dequindre Rd	15647 Dequindre Rd	1 Ⓐ Ⓓ	1 Ⓐ Ⓓ
2.	48075 Solis St	48057 Solis St	2 Ⓐ Ⓓ	2 Ⓐ Ⓓ
3.	31822 Dowland Ln	31822 Dowland Ln	3 Ⓐ Ⓓ	3 Ⓐ Ⓓ
4.	2319 Sherman Ct	2319 Sherman Ct	4 Ⓐ Ⓓ	4 Ⓐ Ⓓ
5.	5157 Orchard Lake	5157 Orchard Lake	5 Ⓐ Ⓓ	5 Ⓐ Ⓓ
6.	8366 Belvidere Rd	8366 Belvidere Rd	6 Ⓐ Ⓓ	6 Ⓐ Ⓓ
7.	32184 Dickinson St	32148 Dickinson St	7 Ⓐ Ⓓ	7 Ⓐ Ⓓ
8.	7505 Chalmers Ave	7505 Chalmers Ave	8 Ⓐ Ⓓ	8 Ⓐ Ⓓ
9.	28377 Hoover Rd	28777 Hoover St	9 Ⓐ Ⓓ	9 Ⓐ Ⓓ
10.	4204 Gilford Sq	4204 Gilford Sq	10 Ⓐ Ⓓ	10 Ⓐ Ⓓ
11.	8309 Thorneycroft Dr	8309 Thorneycroft Dr	11 Ⓐ Ⓓ	11 Ⓐ Ⓓ
12.	62114 Hennings Ln	62114 Jennings Ln	12 Ⓐ Ⓓ	12 Ⓐ Ⓓ
13.	1445 Cologne St	1445 Cologne St	13 Ⓐ Ⓓ	13 Ⓐ Ⓓ
14.	23209 Gratiot Ave	23290 Gratiot Ave	14 Ⓐ Ⓓ	14 Ⓐ Ⓓ
15.	6243 Briarcliff Rd	6243 Briarcliff Rd	15 Ⓐ Ⓓ	15 Ⓐ Ⓓ
16.	1730 Little Mack Rd	1730 Little Mack Rd	16 Ⓐ Ⓓ	16 Ⓐ Ⓓ
17.	461 Woodall St	461 Woodall St	17 Ⓐ Ⓓ	17 Ⓐ Ⓓ
18.	61992 Normandy Rd	619912 Normandy Rd	18 Ⓐ Ⓓ	18 Ⓐ Ⓓ
19.	15986 Toepfer St	15968 Toepfer St	19 Ⓐ Ⓓ	19 Ⓐ Ⓓ
20.	4353 Harper	4353 Harper	20 Ⓐ Ⓓ	20 Ⓐ Ⓓ
21.	22479 Ironwood Ln	22479 Ironwood Rd	21 Ⓐ Ⓓ	21 Ⓐ Ⓓ
22.	8200 Schoenherr Rd	8200 Schoenherr Rd	22 Ⓐ Ⓓ	22 Ⓐ Ⓓ
23.	79394 Brookwood St	79349 Bropokwood St	23 Ⓐ Ⓓ	23 Ⓐ Ⓓ
24.	5211 Melbourne Ave	5211 Melbourne Ave	24 Ⓐ Ⓓ	24 Ⓐ Ⓓ
25.	91864 Weller Sq	91864 Weller Sq	25 Ⓐ Ⓓ	25 Ⓐ Ⓓ
26.	9317 Shader Ln	9317 Shader Ln	26 Ⓐ Ⓓ	26 Ⓐ Ⓓ
27.	3225 Mulberry Way	2114 Mulberry Way	27 Ⓐ Ⓓ	27 Ⓐ Ⓓ
28.	33353 Chateau St	33335 Chateau St	28 Ⓐ Ⓓ	28 Ⓐ Ⓓ
29.	4902 Wagner Rd	4902 Wagner Rd	29 Ⓐ Ⓓ	29 Ⓐ Ⓓ
30.	23129 Kellog Ln	23219 Kellog Ln	30 Ⓐ Ⓓ	30 Ⓐ Ⓓ
31.	43208 Colman Rd	43208 Coleman	31 Ⓐ Ⓒ	31 Ⓐ Ⓓ
32.	16190 Westminster Ave	16190 Westminster Ave	32 Ⓐ Ⓓ	32 Ⓐ Ⓓ
33.	9493 Colony Sq	9439 Colony Sq	33 Ⓐ Ⓓ	33 Ⓐ Ⓓ
34.	1683 Glouchester	1638 Glouchester	34 Ⓐ Ⓓ	34 Ⓐ Ⓓ
35.	3905 Breckenridge St	3905 Breckenridge St	35 Ⓐ Ⓓ	35 Ⓐ Ⓓ
36.	2123 Beechwood Rd	2123 Beechhaven Rd	36 Ⓐ Ⓓ	36 Ⓐ Ⓓ
37.	30629 Beacon St	30629 Deacon St	37 Ⓐ Ⓓ	37 Ⓐ Ⓓ
38.	1523 Jefferson Ave	1523 Jefferson Ave	38 Ⓐ Ⓓ	38 Ⓐ Ⓓ
39.	8545 Vaughn Pkwy	8545 Vaughn Pkwy	39 Ⓐ Ⓓ	39 Ⓐ Ⓓ
40.	46354 Huntington Rd	46534 Huntington Dr	40 Ⓐ Ⓓ	40 Ⓐ Ⓓ

Go on to the next number on the next page.

41.	1681 Gaukler Way	1681 Gaukler Way	41 Ⓐ Ⓓ	41 Ⓐ Ⓓ
42.	9515 Audrey Rd	9515 Audrey Rd	42 Ⓐ Ⓓ	42 Ⓐ Ⓓ
43.	38111 Sprenger St	38111 Sprenger St	43 Ⓐ Ⓓ	43 Ⓐ Ⓓ
44.	18541 Lapeer Rd NE	18541 Lapeer Rd SE	44 Ⓐ Ⓓ	44 Ⓐ Ⓓ
45.	31816 Wildray Circle	31816 Wildray Circle	45 Ⓐ Ⓓ	45 Ⓐ Ⓓ
46.	8352 Kennedy Square	8532 Kennedy Square	46 Ⓐ Ⓓ	46 Ⓐ Ⓓ
47.	44199 Normandale St	41199 Normandale St	47 Ⓐ Ⓓ	47 Ⓐ Ⓓ
48.	13434 Sutherland Rd	13434 Sutherland Rd	48 Ⓐ Ⓓ	48 Ⓐ Ⓓ
49.	5521 Peachwood Way	5521 Beachwood Way	49 Ⓐ Ⓓ	49 Ⓐ Ⓓ
50.	37716 Riviera Lane	37761 Riviera Lane	50 Ⓐ Ⓓ	50 Ⓐ Ⓓ
51.	46858 Lakeville View	46858 Lakeville View	51 Ⓐ Ⓓ	51 Ⓐ Ⓓ
52.	8135 Robertson St	8135 Robertson Rd	52 Ⓐ Ⓓ	52 Ⓐ Ⓓ
53.	22315 Peck Sq SE	22315 Peck Sq SW	53 Ⓐ Ⓓ	53 Ⓐ Ⓓ
54.	49225 Hayes Rd	49225 Hayes Rd	54 Ⓐ Ⓓ	54 Ⓐ Ⓓ
55.	1964 Martin Pkwy	1964 Martin Pkwy	55 Ⓐ Ⓓ	55 Ⓐ Ⓓ
56.	25556 Barton St	25556 Barton St	56 Ⓐ Ⓓ	56 Ⓐ Ⓓ
57.	1821 Pearson Cir	1812 Pearson Cir	57 Ⓐ Ⓓ	57 Ⓐ Ⓓ
58.	29436 Hazelwood Way	29436 Hazelwood Way	58 Ⓐ Ⓓ	58 Ⓐ Ⓓ
59.	21458 Merryweather St	21458 Merryweather St	59 Ⓐ Ⓓ	59 Ⓐ Ⓓ
60.	37740 Collingwood SW	37740 Collingwood SE	60 Ⓐ Ⓓ	60 Ⓐ Ⓓ
61.	9109 Aurora Ave	9198 Aurora Ave	61 Ⓐ Ⓓ	61 Ⓐ Ⓓ
62.	2832 Tuscany Ln	2823 Tuscany Ln	62 Ⓐ Ⓓ	62 Ⓐ Ⓓ
63.	3023 Canterbury Rd	3023 Canterbury Rd	63 Ⓐ Ⓓ	63 Ⓐ Ⓓ
64.	151031 Eaglehart Way	151031 Englehart Way	64 Ⓐ Ⓓ	64 Ⓐ Ⓓ
65.	2094 Milton Cir	2094 Milton Ln	65 Ⓐ Ⓓ	65 Ⓐ Ⓓ
66.	39426 Camelot Pl	30472 Camelot Pl	66 Ⓐ Ⓓ	66 Ⓐ Ⓓ
67.	2260 Kramer Rd	2260 Kramer St	67 Ⓐ Ⓓ	67 Ⓐ Ⓓ
68.	4228 Deepwood St	4228 Deepwood	68 Ⓐ Ⓓ	68 Ⓐ Ⓓ
69.	2094 Alden Dr	2093 Alden Dr	69 Ⓐ Ⓓ	69 Ⓐ Ⓓ
70.	42835 Parkridge St	42835 Parkridge St	70 Ⓐ Ⓓ	70 Ⓐ Ⓓ
71.	203 Woodbridge Ln	203 Woodbridge Ln	71 Ⓐ Ⓓ	71 Ⓐ Ⓓ
72.	45866 Patterson St	48566 Patterson St	72 Ⓐ Ⓓ	72 Ⓐ Ⓓ
73.	3604 Semprau Way	3604 Semprau	73 Ⓐ Ⓓ	73 Ⓐ Ⓓ
74.	29150 Erben Rd	29150 Erben Ave	74 Ⓐ Ⓓ	74 Ⓐ Ⓓ
75.	24564 Coolidge Ave	24654 Coolidge Ave	75 Ⓐ Ⓓ	75 Ⓐ Ⓓ
76.	12907 Frazho View	12907 Frazho View	76 Ⓐ Ⓓ	76 Ⓐ Ⓓ
77.	259 Mulberry Pl	259 Mulberry Pl	77 Ⓐ Ⓓ	77 Ⓐ Ⓓ
78.	28249 Gilbert Rd	28249 Gilbert Rd	78 Ⓐ Ⓓ	78 Ⓐ Ⓓ
79.	37235 Bender Cir	37325 Bender Cir	79 Ⓐ Ⓓ	79 Ⓐ Ⓓ
80.	29055 Bohn Pkwy S	29055 Bohn Pkwy E	80 Ⓐ Ⓓ	80 Ⓐ Ⓓ
81.	1985 Ohmer Ter	1985 Ohmer Ter	81 Ⓐ Ⓓ	81 Ⓐ Ⓓ
82.	2654 Rosedale Cres	2645 Rosedale Crest	82 Ⓐ Ⓓ	82 Ⓐ Ⓓ
83.	25192 Bryan St	25192 Bryan St	83 Ⓐ Ⓓ	83 Ⓐ Ⓓ
84.	24204 Dowland Ln	24240 Dowland Ln	84 Ⓐ Ⓓ	84 Ⓐ Ⓓ
85.	358 Brooks Cir	358 Brooke Cir	85 Ⓐ Ⓓ	85 Ⓐ Ⓓ
86.	37927 Masch Rd	36862 Mash Rd	86 Ⓐ Ⓓ	86 Ⓐ Ⓓ
87.	4533 Williamston St	4533 Williamson St	87 Ⓐ Ⓓ	87 Ⓐ Ⓓ
88.	36518 Almont Sq	36158 Almont Sq	88 Ⓐ Ⓓ	88 Ⓐ Ⓓ
89.	2614 Westbury View	2614 Westbury View	89 Ⓐ Ⓓ	89 Ⓐ Ⓓ

Go on to the next number on the next page.

90. 75445 Driftwood St W	75445 Driftwood Sq	90 Ⓐ Ⓓ	90 Ⓐ Ⓓ
91. 6409 Rosalino Ln	6409 Rosalino Ln	91 Ⓐ Ⓓ	91 Ⓐ Ⓓ
92. 22466 Sycamore Ter	22466 Sycamore Ln	92 Ⓐ Ⓓ	92 Ⓐ Ⓓ
93. 181 Spitz Rd NE	181 Spitz Rd NW	93 Ⓐ Ⓓ	93 Ⓐ Ⓓ
94. 22405 Walker Dr E	22045 Waler Dr E	94 Ⓐ Ⓓ	94 Ⓐ Ⓓ
95. 4221 Visnaw Rdg	4221 Visnaw Rdg	95 Ⓐ Ⓓ	95 Ⓐ Ⓓ

STOP
If you finish before the time is up, check your answers for Part A.
Do not go to any other part.

(See the correct answers on the next page.)

(For more **Address-Checking Practice Tests**, see pages 276-296.)

Correct Answers

Address-Checking Test

1. A	25. A	49. D	73. D
2. D	26. A	50. D	74. D
3. A	27. D	51. A	75. D
4. A	28. D	52. D	76. A
5. A	29. A	53. D	77. A
6. A	30. D	54. A	78. A
7. D	31. D	55. A	79. D
8. A	32. A	56. A	80. D
9. D	33. D	57. D	81. A
10. A	34. D	58. A	82. D
11. A	35. A	59. A	83. A
12. D	36. D	60. D	84. D
13. A	37. D	61. D	85. D
14. D	38. A	62. D	86. D
15. A	39. A	63. A	87. D
16. A	40. D	64. D	88. D
17. A	41. A	65. D	89. A
18. D	42. A	66. D	90. D
19. D	43. A	67. D	91. A
20. A	44. D	68. D	92. D
21. D	45. A	69. D	93. D
22. A	46. D	70. A	94. D
23. D	47. D	71. A	95. A
24. A	48. A	72. D	

Memory-for-Address Test: Tips & Strategies 16

The *Memory-for-Address Test* forms Part B of the **460 Battery Test.** In this part of the test, you must memorize the locations (A, B, C, D, or E) of 25 addresses shown in 5 boxes. You'll be sent a sample test when you file an application for examinations. But the addresses in the actual test will be different from your sample test.

In determining in which box each address is located, you must memorize every address in the 5 boxes. The location of the addresses is easy to memorize if you use some strategies. Based on my experience in postal test taking, I have developed the following strategies for memory-for-address test:

■ **Shortcut:** Just remember the *first two numbers* in each address in a box and the *first syllable* of each name in the same box. For examples, Hubert and Lester are *Hu-Les* when combined. In answering, read only the first two numbers of each address and the first syllable of the name of street, and answer the question by marking the correct circle. Proceed immediately to the next number: You don't have to use a bookmark or any guide in your nonwriting hand. Just point the index finger of that hand to the name or address you are working on. Immediately place the tip of your pencil in your writing hand on the next line on the answer sheet, as you move your nonwriting hand's index finger downward.

■ **Caution:** Once in every five or six numbers, before you mark the circle, be sure that the *circle* corresponds to the proper *line.* That is, the circle belonging to item number 9, for instance, should answer question number 9. Sometimes when you're in a hurry, you may mark circles that do not correspond to the questions you're answering. That happened to me once.

(460 Exam, pages 61-146. See more practice tests on pages 276-326.)

■ **Be in a hurry:** Skip the questions you don't know. Go back to them, however, if you finish working on the test early.

■ **Memorization:** Don't try to write down addresses or notes on your palm. You'll have no time to do that. You can try to remember only the *first digit* of each address, but the trouble is that sometimes the first digits are the same. It's better to remember *two* numbers.

■ **Side by side:** Don't place the question sheet and the answer sheet far from each other or far from your body. Your eyes must not travel long distances. If you don't follow this advice, it's like traveling to Africa instead of to California!

Memory for Addresses Test

In this test you will have to memorize the locations (A, B, C, D, or E) of twenty-five addresses shown in five boxes, like those below. For example, "Sardis" is in Box C, 5200–5799 West is in Box B, etc. (The addresses in the actual test are, of course, different.)

A	B	C	D	E
4700–5599 Table	6800–6999 Table	5600–6499 Table	6500–6799 Table	4400–4699 Table
Lismore	Kelford	Joel	Tatum	Ruskin
4800–5199 West	5200–5799 West	3200–3499 West	3500–4299 West	4300–4799 West
Hesper	Musella	Sardis	Porter	Somers
5500–6399 Blake	4800–5499 Blake	6400–7299 Blake	4300–4799 Blake	7300–7499 Blake

Study the locations of the addresses for 5 minutes. As you study, sound them to yourself. Then cover the boxes and try to answer the questions below. Mark your answers for each question by darkening the space as was done for questions 1 and 2.

1. Musella
2. 4300–4799 Blake
3. 4700–5599 Table
4. Tatum
5. 5500–6399 Blak
6. Hesper
7. Kelford
8. Somers
9. 6400–7299 Blake
10. Joel
11. 5500–6399 Blake
12. 5200–5799 West
13. Porter
14. 7300–7499 Blake

Sample Answer Sheet

| 1 Ⓐ ● Ⓒ Ⓓ Ⓔ | 3 Ⓐ Ⓑ Ⓒ Ⓓ Ⓔ | 5 Ⓐ Ⓑ Ⓒ Ⓓ Ⓔ | 7 Ⓐ Ⓑ Ⓒ Ⓓ Ⓔ | 9 Ⓐ Ⓑ Ⓒ Ⓓ Ⓔ | 11 Ⓐ Ⓑ Ⓒ Ⓓ Ⓔ | 13 Ⓐ Ⓑ Ⓒ Ⓓ Ⓔ |
| 2 Ⓐ Ⓑ Ⓒ ● Ⓔ | 4 Ⓐ Ⓑ Ⓒ Ⓓ Ⓔ | 6 Ⓐ Ⓑ Ⓒ Ⓓ Ⓔ | 8 Ⓐ Ⓑ Ⓒ Ⓓ Ⓔ | 10 Ⓐ Ⓑ Ⓒ Ⓓ Ⓔ | 12 Ⓐ Ⓑ Ⓒ Ⓓ Ⓔ | 14 Ⓐ Ⓑ Ⓒ Ⓓ Ⓔ |

The correct answers for questions 3 to 14 are: 3A, 4D, 5A, 6A, 7B, 8E, 9C, 10C, 11A, 12B, 13D, and 14E.

Memory-for-Address Test

In the example below, there are various techniques for memorizing the names and addresses in five minutes.

A	B	C	D	E
1700-2599 Wood Dushore 8500-8699 Lang Lott 6200-6399 James	2700-3299 Wood Jeriel 8700-9399 Lang Vanna 5700-6199 James	1300-1699 Wood Levering 9400-9499 Lang Ekron 6400-6499 James	3300-3599 Wood Bair 8000-8499 Lang Viborg 5000-5699 James	2600-2699 Wood Danby 9500-9999 Lang Lycan 4700-4999 James

The best thing to do is to remember only *two* numbers, the *first two* digits of the addresses. Combine the *first* syllables of the two names in each box, to make it only one name; example, *DusLot (Dus*hore and *Lot*t.)

For Box A	Box B	Box C	Box D	Box E
17	27	13	33	26
85	87	94	80	95
62	57	64	50	47

To remember the names:

Box A	Box B	Box C	Box D	Box E
DusLot	JeVa	LeEk	BaVi	DanLy

Decide which is the best way for you to memorize the numbers above: from **top** to **bottom** or from **left to right.**

One way is from **top** to **botttom,** by boxes.

A	B	C	D	E
17 ⬇	27 ⬇	13 ⬇	33 ⬇	26 ⬇
85 ⬇	87 ⬇	94 ⬇	80 ⬇	95 ⬇
62 ⬇	57 ⬇	64 ⬇	50 ⬇	47 ⬇
DusLot ⬇	JeVa ⬇	LeEk ⬇	BaVi ⬇	DanLy ⬇

Memorize the combined names from **left to right.**

Another way is to memorize *A* and *B* **vertically** and *C, D,* and *E* **horizontally.**

A	B	C	D	E
17 ⬇	27 ⬇	13 ➡	33 ➡	26
85 ⬇	87 ⬇	94 ➡	80 ➡	95
62 ⬇	57 ⬇	64 ➡	50 ➡	47
DusLot ⬇	JeVa ⬇	LeEk ➡	BaVi ➡	DanLy

Important! Important! Important!

Lately, the U.S. Postal Service has been including two or three "same numbers" in the addresses in the five boxes (Memory-for-Address test).

This creates confusion. (You cannot just remember the *first two numbers*. You must remember the *first two numbers*, along with the name of the *street*.

Part B: Memory for Addresses

In this part of the test, you will have to memorize the locations (A, B, C, D, or E) of 25 addresses shown in five boxes, like those below. For example, "Sardis" is in Box C, "6800-6999 Table" is in Box B, etc. (The addresses in the actual test will be different.)

A	B	C	D	E
4700-5599 Table	6800-6999 Table	5600-6499 Table	6500-6799 Table	4400-4699 Table
Lismore	Kelford	Joel	Tatum	Ruskin
5600-6499 West	6500-6799 West	6800-6999 West	4400-4699 West	4700-5599 West
Hesper	Musella	Sardis	Porter	Nathan
4400-4699 Blake	5600-6499 Blake	6500-6799 Blake	4700-5599 Blake	6800-6999 Blake

If you examine the boxes above, you'll see the identical numbers:

1. Three 4700-5599s:

4700-5599 Table (Box A), 4700-5599 Blake (Box D), and 4700-5599 Table (Box E);

2. Three 5600-6499s:

5600-6499 West (A), 5600-6499 Blake (B), and 5600-6499 Table (C);

3. Three 4400-4699s:

4400-4699 Blake (A), 4400-4699 West (D), 4400-4699 Table (E);

4. Three 6800-6999s:

6800-6999 Table (B), 6800-6999 West (C), and 6800-6999 Blake (E).

5. And *three* 6500-6799s:

6500-6799 West (B), 6500-6799 Blake (C) and 6500-6799 Table (D).

Instruction: To avoid confusion and to remember to which box the numbers belong, remember the *first two numbers* along with the name of the *streets*:

Example: 47 Table (Box A); 47 Blake (Box D) and 47 West (Box E).

For Box A, for instance, you may remember the numbers and names of streets as follows (Box A):

A	B	C	D	E
47 Table	68 Table	56 Table	65 Table	44 Table
56 West	65 West	68 West	44 West	47 West
44 Blake	56 Blake	65 Blake	47 Blake	68 Blake
LisHe	KelMu	JoSar	TaPor	RusNa

LisHe (Combination of the first syllables of Lismore and Hesper.)

You may memorize the *first two numbers* vertically; for example, 47, 56, 44. Then remember that in every box the *first street* is **Table**; the *second*, **West**, and the *third*, **Blake.** Or you may find your own way of memorizing them.

How to Remember
Names and Numbers

In memorizing numbers or names, associate them with numbers or names familiar to you, so that you can retrieve them instantly from your mind. Visualize! A thing visualized is not usually forgotten. That is, create key words or extraction codes. In entering information into a computer, you need to have a *code* so that you can retrieve the information. Without it, you cannot retrieve the facts and figures you stored on the disk. Your brain, which is your own computer, operates in the same way.

Use Your Imagination

To memorize Box A, for example, I'll remember *17* as the age of a beautiful teenaged girl living in the neighborhood; I'll remember *85* (1985) as the year I invaded Grenada; and *62* (1962) as the year my wife and I promised to each other "*to love and cherish, for better or worse, till death do us part.*" I'll remember *Dus-Lot* by visualizing that I'll go to the *lot* which is full of *dust* to play games.

Since you have to memorize the names and addresses in five boxes in five minutes, you'll have to memorize each box in sixty seconds. Actually, you'll do the memorization in eight minutes, including the three minutes for the practice test. But don't rely on that. Count on only five minutes. I have done it and many of my students have done it. If the computer can do it, your brain can do it, too!

In your case, think of years or numbers that you can associate with the numbers in Box A. For example, your youngest brother or sister may be *17* years old (or make him or her 17), you visited Beirut in year *85 (1985),* and for *62,* you may remember that the Texas Rangers won the World Series in 1962. You may remember *Dus-Lot* by recalling the name *Dusty* Baker, who has a *lot* of chewing gum in his mouth. Or you may recall names of your friends which sound like *Dus* or *Lot.*

Associate Numbers
with Things or Events

You can think of many things. Associate numbers with age, weight, height, numbers of floors in buildings, dates, or events. Associate names with well-known personalities: actors, actresses, politicians, athletes, and others.

When you see the number, you can associate it easily with things familiar to you. Associate it with the first thing that comes into your mind. Different people will usually have different key numbers or key words.

In a nutshell, you'll have to remember only the first two numbers of addresses and the first syllables of two names. Forget about the street names, such as Wood or Lang. *Combine two names* into *one* and kill two birds with one stone. Imagine too that you're writing numbers and names on an invisible computer screen!

Combine Two Names Into One.

Sample Questions for Memory for Addresses

In this test you will have five boxes labeled A, B, C, D, and E. Each box contains five addresses. Three of the five are groups of street addresses like 1700-2599 Wood, 8500-8699 Lang, and 6200-6399 James, and two are names of places. They are different in each box.

You will also be given two lists of names. You will have to decide which box each name belongs in. When you are working on the first list, you will have the boxes with the names in front of you. When you are working on the second list, you will not be able to look at the boxes.

The addresses you will use for the Practice Test are given in the boxes below.

A	B	C	D	E
1700-2599 Wood Dushore 8500-8699 Lang Lott 6200-6399 James	2700-3299 Wood Jeriel 8700-9399 Lang Vanna 5700-6199 James	1300-1699 Wood Levering 9400-9499 Lang Ekron 6400-6499 James	3300-3599 Wood Bair 8000-8499 Lang Viborg 5000-5699 James	2600-2699 Wood Danby 9500-9999 Lang Lycan 4700-4999 James

Questions 1 through 5 show the way the questions look. You have to decide in which lettered box (A, B, C, D, or E) the address belongs and then mark that answer on the Sample Answer Sheet on this page.

1. Levering
   This address is in box C. So darken circle C on the Sample Answer Sheet.
2. 2700-3299 Wood
   This address is in box B. So darken circle B on the Sample Answer Sheet.
3. Vanna
   This address is in box B. So darken circle B on the Sample Answer Sheet.
4. 6200-6399 James
5. Bair

The answers for samples 4 and 5 are 4A and 5D.

(Author's Note: Memorize the above addresses and names in five boxes, according to my instructions, in five to eight minutes (three minutes additional in practice test before the actual exam.)

Before the actual test, you'll be allowed three minutes to do the practice test. During this practice test, work on two or three questions only and continue memorizing the numbers and names. You must not waste a second and you must really concentrate on memorizing them.

Now that you have memorized the addresses and names in five to eight minutes, turn to the next page for your test.

Go For It!

Sample Questions for Memory-for-Address Test

In this test you will have five boxes labeled A, B, C, D, and E. Each box contains five addresses. Three of the five are groups of street addresses like 4000-4599 Henry, 8600-9899 Fox, and 2100-2699 Johnson, and two are names of places. They are different in each box.

You will also be given two lists of names. You will have to decide in which box each name belongs. When you are working on the first list, you will have the boxes with the names in front of you. When you are working on the second list, you will not be able to look at the boxes.

The addresses you will use for the practice test are given in the boxes below.

A	B	C	D	E
4000-4599 Henry	6400-8999 Henry	1700-3299	4600-6399 Henry	3300-3999 Henry
Herbert	Ingleside	Capitol	Memphis	Lincoln
8600-9899 Fox	2300-6499 Fox	8800-9999 Fox	6500-7699 Fox	7700-8799 Fox
Lester	Lewis	Drexel	Lansford	Saginaw
2100-2699 Johnson	1500-1899 Johnson	3700-4299 Johnson	2700-3699 Johnson	1900-2099 Johnson

Questions 1 through 5 show the way the questions look. You have to decide in which lettered box (A, B, C, D, or E) the address belongs and then mark that answer on the sample answer sheet on this page.

1. Saginaw
   This address is in box E, so darken circle E on the sample answer sheet.

2. 8600-9899 Fox
   This address is in box A, so darken circle A on the sample answer sheet.

3. Drexel
   This address is in box C, so darken circle C on the sample answer sheet.

4. 2300-6499 Fox

5. Lansford

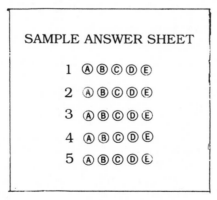

SAMPLE ANSWER SHEET

1 Ⓐ Ⓑ Ⓒ Ⓓ Ⓔ

2 Ⓐ Ⓑ Ⓒ Ⓓ Ⓔ

3 Ⓐ Ⓑ Ⓒ Ⓓ Ⓔ

4 Ⓐ Ⓑ Ⓒ Ⓓ Ⓔ

5 Ⓐ Ⓑ Ⓒ Ⓓ Ⓔ

The answers for samples 4 and five are 4B and 5D.

Author's Note: Memorize the above addresses and names in five boxes, according to my instructions, in five to eight minutes (three minutes additional in practice test before the actual exam.)

Memory-for-Address Test

Work—3 Minutes

Answer each question on a piece of paper to show the letter of the box in which the address belongs. Try to remember the location of as many addresses as you can. If you are not sure of an address, guess. Work only three minutes.

A	B	C	D	E
1700-2599 Wood Dushore 8500-8699 Lang Lott 6200-6399 James	2700-3299 Wood Jeriel 8700-9399 Lang Vanna 5700-6199 James	1300-1699 Wood Levering 19400-9499 Lang Ekron 6400-6499 James	3300-3599 Wood Bair 8000-8499 Lang Viborg 5000-5699 James	2600-2699 Wood Danby 9500-9999 Lang Lycan 4700-4999 James

1. 1700-2599 Wood
2. Ekron
3. Vanna
4. 2700-3299 Wood
5. Jeriel
6. Lycan
7. 5000-5699 James
8. Viborg
9. 9400-9499 Lang
10. Vanna
11. 6400-6499 James
12. Ekron
13. 5000-5699 James
14. 4700-4999 James
15. Jeriel
16. Viborg
17. 6400-6499 James
18. 2600-2699 Wood
19. 1300-1699 Wood
20. 9500-9999 Lang
21. Vanna
22. Dushore
23. Levering
24. 5000-5699 James

25. 3300-3599 Wood
26. Danby
27. Viborg
28. Dushore
29. 8000-8499 Lang
30. Lott
31. 8500-8699 Lang
32. 3300-3599 Wood
33. 6200-6399 James
34. Danby
35. 2700-3299 Wood
36. Bair
37. 8700-9399 Lang
38. 3300-3599 Wood
39. Lott
40. 2600-2699 Wood
41. Vanna
42. Bair
43. 6200-6399 James
44. Lycan
45. Lott
46. Bair
47. Jeriel
48. 6200-6399 James

49. Bair
50. Viborg
51. Danby
52. 5700-6199 James
53. 3300-3599 Wood
54. 8700-9399 Lang
55. Ekron
56. Vanna
57. 3300-3599 Wood
58. 1300-1699 Wood
59. Danby
60. 1700-2599 Wood
61. 5700-6199 James
62. 9500-9999 Lang
63. 2700-3299 Wood
64. Lott
65. Levering
66. Dushore
67. 3300-3599 Wood
68. Jeriel
69. 6400-6499 James
70. 6200-6399 James
71. 2600-2699 Wood
72. Viborg

73. Jeriel
74. Dushore
75. 2700-3299 Wood
76. Lott
77. 1700-2599 Wood
78. Lycan
79. Jeriel
80. 6200-6399 James
81. Dushore
82. Viborg
83. Lycan
84. Bair
85. 4700-4999 James
86. Jeriel
87. 8500-8699 Lang
88. Ekron

STOP

When the time is up, go on to the next page for the correct answers.

(**Author's Note:** The sample test above is known as the memory-for-address test in the 470 Battery Test. This Part B is considered as a practice test. You'll be allowed to look at the names and addresses in the boxes, as you are instructed to answer as many questions as possible in three minutes. In the next part, however, you will be asked to answer the 88 questions in five minutes and you won't be allowed to look at the names and addresses. During the three-minute practice test, answer only a few questions. Spend most of the three minutes in memorizing the placement of numbers and names (just the first two numbers of each address and the first syllables of names, combining two syllables into one. Now, answer a few questions and memorize the names and addresses in preparation for the next part.)

Correct Answers

Memory-for-Address Test

1.	A	31.	A	61.	B
2.	C	32.	D	62.	E
3.	B	33.	A	63.	B
4.	B	34.	E	64.	A
5.	B	35.	B	65.	C
6.	E	36.	D	66.	A
7.	D	37.	B	67.	D
8.	D	38.	D	68.	B
9.	C	39.	A	69.	C
10.	B	40.	E	70.	A
11.	C	41.	B	71.	E
12.	C	42.	D	72.	D
13.	D	43.	A	73.	B
14.	E	44.	E	74.	A
15.	B	45.	A	75.	B
16.	D	46.	D	76.	A
17.	C	47.	B	77.	A
18.	E	48.	A	78.	E
19.	C	49.	D	79.	B
20.	E	50.	D	80.	A
21.	B	51.	E	81.	A
22.	A	52.	B	82.	D
23.	C	53.	D	83.	E
24.	D	54.	B	84.	D
25.	D	55.	C	85.	E
26.	E	56.	B	86.	B
27.	D	57.	D	87.	A
28.	A	58.	C	88.	C
29.	D	59.	E		
30.	A	60.	A		

Memory-for-Address Test

(USPS)

Work—5 Minutes

This is the section that counts.

Decide in which box each name or address belongs. Don't look back at the boxes with the addresses in them. Work for 5 minutes. For each question, mark the answers on the answer sheet to the right.

ANSWER SHEET

	Test A	Test B
1. Jeriel	1 Ⓐ Ⓑ Ⓒ Ⓓ Ⓔ	1 Ⓐ Ⓑ Ⓒ Ⓓ Ⓔ
2. Dushore	2 Ⓐ Ⓑ Ⓒ Ⓓ Ⓔ	2 Ⓐ Ⓑ Ⓒ Ⓓ Ⓔ
3. 5000-5699 James	3 Ⓐ Ⓑ Ⓒ Ⓓ Ⓔ	3 Ⓐ Ⓑ Ⓒ Ⓓ Ⓔ
4. 1300-1699 Wood	4 Ⓐ Ⓑ Ⓒ Ⓓ Ⓔ	4 Ⓐ Ⓑ Ⓒ Ⓓ Ⓔ
5. 8500-8699 Lang	5 Ⓐ Ⓑ Ⓒ Ⓓ Ⓔ	5 Ⓐ Ⓑ Ⓒ Ⓓ Ⓔ
6. Bair	6 Ⓐ Ⓑ Ⓒ Ⓓ Ⓔ	6 Ⓐ Ⓑ Ⓒ Ⓓ Ⓔ
7. 5700-6199 James	7 Ⓐ Ⓑ Ⓒ Ⓓ Ⓔ	7 Ⓐ Ⓑ Ⓒ Ⓓ Ⓔ
8. Levering	8 Ⓐ Ⓑ Ⓒ Ⓓ Ⓔ	8 Ⓐ Ⓑ Ⓒ Ⓓ Ⓔ
9. Danby	9 Ⓐ Ⓑ Ⓒ Ⓓ Ⓔ	9 Ⓐ Ⓑ Ⓒ Ⓓ Ⓔ
10. Viborg	10 Ⓐ Ⓑ Ⓒ Ⓓ Ⓔ	10 Ⓐ Ⓑ Ⓒ Ⓓ Ⓔ
11. 8000-8499 Lang	11 Ⓐ Ⓑ Ⓒ Ⓓ Ⓔ	11 Ⓐ Ⓑ Ⓒ Ⓓ Ⓔ
12. 2700-3299 Wood	12 Ⓐ Ⓑ Ⓒ Ⓓ Ⓔ	12 Ⓐ Ⓑ Ⓒ Ⓓ Ⓔ
13. 9400-9499 Lang	13 Ⓐ Ⓑ Ⓒ Ⓓ Ⓔ	13 Ⓐ Ⓑ Ⓒ Ⓓ Ⓔ
14. 3300-3599 Wood	14 Ⓐ Ⓑ Ⓒ Ⓓ Ⓔ	14 Ⓐ Ⓑ Ⓒ Ⓓ Ⓔ
15. 4700-4999 James	15 Ⓐ Ⓑ Ⓒ Ⓓ Ⓔ	15 Ⓐ Ⓑ Ⓒ Ⓓ Ⓔ
16. 9500-9999 Lang	16 Ⓐ Ⓑ Ⓒ Ⓓ Ⓔ	16 Ⓐ Ⓑ Ⓒ Ⓓ Ⓔ
17. Ekron	17 Ⓐ Ⓑ Ⓒ Ⓓ Ⓔ	17 Ⓐ Ⓑ Ⓒ Ⓓ Ⓔ
18. 1300-1699 Wood	18 Ⓐ Ⓑ Ⓒ Ⓓ Ⓔ	18 Ⓐ Ⓑ Ⓒ Ⓓ Ⓔ
19. Vanna	19 Ⓐ Ⓑ Ⓒ Ⓓ Ⓔ	19 Ⓐ Ⓑ Ⓒ Ⓓ Ⓔ
20. Lycan	20 Ⓐ Ⓑ Ⓒ Ⓓ Ⓔ	20 Ⓐ Ⓑ Ⓒ Ⓓ Ⓔ
21. 8700-9399 Lang	21 Ⓐ Ⓑ Ⓒ Ⓓ Ⓔ	21 Ⓐ Ⓑ Ⓒ Ⓓ Ⓔ
22. Dushore	22 Ⓐ Ⓑ Ⓒ Ⓓ Ⓔ	22 Ⓐ Ⓑ Ⓒ Ⓓ Ⓔ
23. 6200-6399 James	23 Ⓐ Ⓑ Ⓒ Ⓓ Ⓔ	23 Ⓐ Ⓑ Ⓒ Ⓓ Ⓔ
24. Lott	24 Ⓐ Ⓑ Ⓒ Ⓓ Ⓔ	24 Ⓐ Ⓑ Ⓒ Ⓓ Ⓔ
25. 2700-3299 Wood	25 Ⓐ Ⓑ Ⓒ Ⓓ Ⓔ	25 Ⓐ Ⓑ Ⓒ Ⓓ Ⓔ
26. 5700-6199 James	26 Ⓐ Ⓑ Ⓒ Ⓓ Ⓔ	26 Ⓐ Ⓑ Ⓒ Ⓓ Ⓔ
27. Levering	27 Ⓐ Ⓑ Ⓒ Ⓓ Ⓔ	27 Ⓐ Ⓑ Ⓒ Ⓓ Ⓔ
28. 9500-9999 Lang	28 Ⓐ Ⓑ Ⓒ Ⓓ Ⓔ	28 Ⓐ Ⓑ Ⓒ Ⓓ Ⓔ
29. 2600-2699 Wood	29 Ⓐ Ⓑ Ⓒ Ⓓ Ⓔ	29 Ⓐ Ⓑ Ⓒ Ⓓ Ⓔ
30. 3300-3599 Wood	30 Ⓐ Ⓑ Ⓒ Ⓓ Ⓔ	30 Ⓐ Ⓑ Ⓒ Ⓓ Ⓔ
31. Viborg	31 Ⓐ Ⓑ Ⓒ Ⓓ Ⓔ	31 Ⓐ Ⓑ Ⓒ Ⓓ Ⓔ
32. 9400-9499 Lang	32 Ⓐ Ⓑ Ⓒ Ⓓ Ⓔ	32 Ⓐ Ⓑ Ⓒ Ⓓ Ⓔ
33. Jeriel	33 Ⓐ Ⓑ Ⓒ Ⓓ Ⓔ	33 Ⓐ Ⓑ Ⓒ Ⓓ Ⓔ
34. Bair	34 Ⓐ Ⓑ Ⓒ Ⓓ Ⓔ	34 Ⓐ Ⓑ Ⓒ Ⓓ Ⓔ
35. 8500-8699 Lang	35 Ⓐ Ⓑ Ⓒ Ⓓ Ⓔ	35 Ⓐ Ⓑ Ⓒ Ⓓ Ⓔ

Go on to the next number on the next page.

36.	1700-2599 Wood		36 Ⓐ Ⓑ Ⓒ Ⓓ Ⓔ	36 Ⓐ Ⓑ Ⓒ Ⓓ Ⓔ
37.	8000-8499 Lang		37 Ⓐ Ⓑ Ⓒ Ⓓ Ⓔ	37 Ⓐ Ⓑ Ⓒ Ⓓ Ⓔ
38.	Danby		38 Ⓐ Ⓑ Ⓒ Ⓓ Ⓔ	38 Ⓐ Ⓑ Ⓒ Ⓓ Ⓔ
39.	Ekron		39 Ⓐ Ⓑ Ⓒ Ⓓ Ⓔ	39 Ⓐ Ⓑ Ⓒ Ⓓ Ⓔ
40.	4700-4999 James		40 Ⓐ Ⓑ Ⓒ Ⓓ Ⓔ	40 Ⓐ Ⓑ Ⓒ Ⓓ Ⓔ
41.	Dushore		41 Ⓐ Ⓑ Ⓒ Ⓓ Ⓔ	41 Ⓐ Ⓑ Ⓒ Ⓓ Ⓔ
42.	Vanna		42 Ⓐ Ⓑ Ⓒ Ⓓ Ⓔ	42 Ⓐ Ⓑ Ⓒ Ⓓ Ⓔ
43.	5000-5699 James		43 Ⓐ Ⓑ Ⓒ Ⓓ Ⓔ	43 Ⓐ Ⓑ Ⓒ Ⓓ Ⓔ
44.	Lott		44 Ⓐ Ⓑ Ⓒ Ⓓ Ⓔ	44 Ⓐ Ⓑ Ⓒ Ⓓ Ⓔ
45.	1300-1699 Wood		45 Ⓐ Ⓑ Ⓒ Ⓓ Ⓔ	45 Ⓐ Ⓑ Ⓒ Ⓓ Ⓔ
46.	Levering		46 Ⓐ Ⓑ Ⓒ Ⓓ Ⓔ	46 Ⓐ Ⓑ Ⓒ Ⓓ Ⓔ
47.	5700-6199 James		47 Ⓐ Ⓑ Ⓒ Ⓓ Ⓔ	47 Ⓐ Ⓑ Ⓒ Ⓓ Ⓔ
48.	9500-9999 Lang		48 Ⓐ Ⓑ Ⓒ Ⓓ Ⓔ	48 Ⓐ Ⓑ Ⓒ Ⓓ Ⓔ
49.	Bair		49 Ⓐ Ⓑ Ⓒ Ⓓ Ⓔ	49 Ⓐ Ⓑ Ⓒ Ⓓ Ⓔ
50.	8700-9399 Lang		50 Ⓐ Ⓑ Ⓒ Ⓓ Ⓔ	50 Ⓐ Ⓑ Ⓒ Ⓓ Ⓔ
51.	6200-6399 James		51 Ⓐ Ⓑ Ⓒ Ⓓ Ⓔ	51 Ⓐ Ⓑ Ⓒ Ⓓ Ⓔ
52.	9400-9499 Lang		52 Ⓐ Ⓑ Ⓒ Ⓓ Ⓔ	52 Ⓐ Ⓑ Ⓒ Ⓓ Ⓔ
53.	Viborg		53 Ⓐ Ⓑ Ⓒ Ⓓ Ⓔ	53 Ⓐ Ⓑ Ⓒ Ⓓ Ⓔ
54.	8000-8499 Lang		54 Ⓐ Ⓑ Ⓒ Ⓓ Ⓔ	54 Ⓐ Ⓑ Ⓒ Ⓓ Ⓔ
55.	4700-4999 James		55 Ⓐ Ⓑ Ⓒ Ⓓ Ⓔ	55 Ⓐ Ⓑ Ⓒ Ⓓ Ⓔ
56.	Lycan		56 Ⓐ Ⓑ Ⓒ Ⓓ Ⓔ	56 Ⓐ Ⓑ Ⓒ Ⓓ Ⓔ
57.	Vanna		57 Ⓐ Ⓑ Ⓒ Ⓓ Ⓔ	57 Ⓐ Ⓑ Ⓒ Ⓓ Ⓔ
58.	Danby		58 Ⓐ Ⓑ Ⓒ Ⓓ Ⓔ	58 Ⓐ Ⓑ Ⓒ Ⓓ Ⓔ
59.	5700-6199 James		59 Ⓐ Ⓑ Ⓒ Ⓓ Ⓔ	59 Ⓐ Ⓑ Ⓒ Ⓓ Ⓔ
60.	Lott		60 Ⓐ Ⓑ Ⓒ Ⓓ Ⓔ	60 Ⓐ Ⓑ Ⓒ Ⓓ Ⓔ
61.	2700-3299 Wood		61 Ⓐ Ⓑ Ⓒ Ⓓ Ⓔ	61 Ⓐ Ⓑ Ⓒ Ⓓ Ⓔ
62.	5000-5699 James		62 Ⓐ Ⓑ Ⓒ Ⓓ Ⓔ	62 Ⓐ Ⓑ Ⓒ Ⓓ Ⓔ
63.	1700-2599 Wood		63 Ⓐ Ⓑ Ⓒ Ⓓ Ⓔ	63 Ⓐ Ⓑ Ⓒ Ⓓ Ⓔ
64.	8000-8499 Lang		64 Ⓐ Ⓑ Ⓒ Ⓓ Ⓔ	64 Ⓐ Ⓑ Ⓒ Ⓓ Ⓔ
65.	9400-9499 Lang		65 Ⓐ Ⓑ Ⓒ Ⓓ Ⓔ	65 Ⓐ Ⓑ Ⓒ Ⓓ Ⓔ
66.	Jeriel		66 Ⓐ Ⓑ Ⓒ Ⓓ Ⓔ	66 Ⓐ Ⓑ Ⓒ Ⓓ Ⓔ
67.	9500-9999 Lang		67 Ⓐ Ⓑ Ⓒ Ⓓ Ⓔ	67 Ⓐ Ⓑ Ⓒ Ⓓ Ⓔ
68.	Dushore		68 Ⓐ Ⓑ Ⓒ Ⓓ Ⓔ	68 Ⓐ Ⓑ Ⓒ Ⓓ Ⓔ
69.	2600-2699 Wood		69 Ⓐ Ⓑ Ⓒ Ⓓ Ⓔ	69 Ⓐ Ⓑ Ⓒ Ⓓ Ⓔ
70.	8500-8699 Lang		70 Ⓐ Ⓑ Ⓒ Ⓓ Ⓔ	70 Ⓐ Ⓑ Ⓒ Ⓓ Ⓔ
71.	Levering		71 Ⓐ Ⓑ Ⓒ Ⓓ Ⓔ	71 Ⓐ Ⓑ Ⓒ Ⓓ Ⓔ
72.	5000-5699 James		72 Ⓐ Ⓑ Ⓒ Ⓓ Ⓔ	72 Ⓐ Ⓑ Ⓒ Ⓓ Ⓔ
73.	Dushore		73 Ⓐ Ⓑ Ⓒ Ⓓ Ⓔ	73 Ⓐ Ⓑ Ⓒ Ⓓ Ⓔ
74.	8000-8499 Lang		74 Ⓐ Ⓑ Ⓒ Ⓓ Ⓔ	74 Ⓐ Ⓑ Ⓒ Ⓓ Ⓔ
75.	Bair		75 Ⓐ Ⓑ Ⓒ Ⓓ Ⓔ	75 Ⓐ Ⓑ Ⓒ Ⓓ Ⓔ
76.	Ekron		76 Ⓐ Ⓑ Ⓒ Ⓓ Ⓔ	76 Ⓐ Ⓑ Ⓒ Ⓓ Ⓔ
77.	6200-6399 James		77 Ⓐ Ⓑ Ⓒ Ⓓ Ⓔ	77 Ⓐ Ⓑ Ⓒ Ⓓ Ⓔ
78.	3300-3599 Wood		78 Ⓐ Ⓑ Ⓒ Ⓓ Ⓔ	78 Ⓐ Ⓑ Ⓒ Ⓓ Ⓔ
79.	8700-9399 Lang		79 Ⓐ Ⓑ Ⓒ Ⓓ Ⓔ	79 Ⓐ Ⓑ Ⓒ Ⓓ Ⓔ
80.	Viborg		80 Ⓐ Ⓑ Ⓒ Ⓓ Ⓔ	80 Ⓐ Ⓑ Ⓒ Ⓓ Ⓔ
81.	4700-4999 James		81 Ⓐ Ⓑ Ⓒ Ⓓ Ⓔ	81 Ⓐ Ⓑ Ⓒ Ⓓ Ⓔ
82.	Lycan		82 Ⓐ Ⓑ Ⓒ Ⓓ Ⓔ	82 Ⓐ Ⓑ Ⓒ Ⓓ Ⓔ
83.	1700-2599 Wood		83 Ⓐ Ⓑ Ⓒ Ⓓ Ⓔ	83 Ⓐ Ⓑ Ⓒ Ⓓ Ⓔ
84.	8500-8699 Lang		84 Ⓐ Ⓑ Ⓒ Ⓓ Ⓔ	84 Ⓐ Ⓑ Ⓒ Ⓓ Ⓔ

Go on to the next number on the next page.

85. 1300-1699 Wood   85 Ⓐ Ⓑ Ⓒ Ⓓ Ⓔ   85 Ⓐ Ⓑ Ⓒ Ⓓ Ⓔ
86. Jeriel   86 Ⓐ Ⓑ Ⓒ Ⓓ Ⓔ   86 Ⓐ Ⓑ Ⓒ Ⓓ Ⓔ
87. Danby   87 Ⓐ Ⓑ Ⓒ Ⓓ Ⓔ   87 Ⓐ Ⓑ Ⓒ Ⓓ Ⓔ
88. 6400-6499 James   88 Ⓐ Ⓑ Ⓒ Ⓓ Ⓔ   88 Ⓐ Ⓑ Ⓒ Ⓓ Ⓔ

**If you finish before the time is up,
go back and check your answers.**

(See the correct answers on the next page.)

Correct Answers

Memory-for-Address Test

1. B	31. D	61. B
2. A	32. C	62. D
3. D	33. B	63. A
4. C	34. D	64. D
5. A	35. A	65. C
6. D	36. A	66. B
7. B	37. D	67. E
8. C	38. E	68. A
9. E	39. C	69. E
10. D	40. E	70. A
11. D	41. A	71. C
12. B	42. B	72. D
13. C	43. D	73. A
14. D	44. A	74. D
15. E	45. C	75. D
16. E	46. C	76. C
17. C	47. B	77. A
18. C	48. E	78. D
19. B	49. D	79. B
20. E	50. B	80. D
21. B	51. A	81. E
22. A	52. C	82. E
23. A	53. D	83. A
24. A	54. D	84. A
25. B	55. E	85. C
26. B	56. E	86. B
27. C	57. B	87. E
28. E	58. E	88. C
29. E	59. B	
30. D	60. A	

Sample Questions for Address-Code Memory Test

In this test you will have five boxes labeled A, B, C, D, and E. Each box contains five addresses. Three of the five are groups of street addresses like 1900-2299 Reagan, 2000-2999 Kelly and 2200-2899 King, and two are names of places. They are different in each box.

You will also be given two lists of names. You will have to decide in which box each name belongs. When you are working on the first list, you will have the boxes with the names in front of you. When you are working on the second list, you will not be able to look at the boxes.

The addresses you will use for the practice test are given in the boxes below.

A	B	C	D	E
2200-2899 King	1200-1499 King	3200-3900 King	1500-2199 King	2900-3199 King
Pamela	Haven	Abbot	Janet	Namath
1600-1899 Reagan	2500-4199 Reagan	2300-2499 Reagan	1900-2299 Reagan	1300-1599 Reagan
Lancaster	Scott	Dennis	Davis	Sheila
4400-4899 Kelly	1400-1999 Kelly	3000-4399 Kelly	4900-5900 Kelly	2000-2999 Kelly

Questions 1 through 5 show the way the questions look. You have to decide in which lettered box (A, B, C, D, or E) the address belongs and then mark that answer on the sample answer sheet on this page.

1. Janet
   This address is in box D. So darken circle D on the sample answer sheet.

2. 2500-4199 Reagan
   This address is in box B. So darken circle B on the sample answer sheet.

3. Sheila
   This address is in box E. So darken circle E on the sample answer sheet.

4. 3000-4399 Kelly

5. Davis

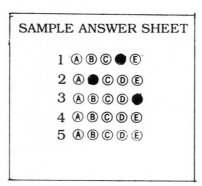

```
SAMPLE ANSWER SHEET

1  Ⓐ Ⓑ Ⓒ ● Ⓔ
2  Ⓐ ● Ⓒ Ⓓ Ⓔ
3  Ⓐ Ⓑ Ⓒ Ⓓ ●
4  Ⓐ Ⓑ Ⓒ Ⓓ Ⓔ
5  Ⓐ Ⓑ Ⓒ Ⓓ Ⓔ
```

The answers for samples 4 and five are 4C and 5D.

Author's Note: Memorize the above names and addresses in five boxes, according to my instructions, in five to eight minutes with three additional minutes in practice test before the actual exam.

Memory-for-Address Test

Work—3 Minutes

Answer each question on a piece of paper to show the letter of the box in which the address belongs. Try to remember the location of as many addresses as you can. If you are not sure of an address, guess. Work only three minutes.

A	B	C	D	E
2200-2899 King Pamela 1600-1899 Reagan Lancaster 4400-4899 Kelly	1200-1499 King Haven 2500-4199 Reagan Scott 1400-1999 Kelly	3200-3900 King Abbot 2300-2499 Reagan Dennis 3000-4399 Kelly	1500-2199 King Janet 1900-2299 Reagan Davis 4900-5900 Kelly	2900-3199 King Namath 1300-1599 Reagan Sheila 2000-2999 Kelly

1. 1200-1499 King
2. Scott
3. 1900-2299 Reagan
4. 1400-1999 Kelly
5. 3200-3900 King
6. 2200-2899 King
7. 1400-1999 Kelly
8. Namath
9. Haven
10. Abbot
11. 2300-2499 Reagan
12. Davis
13. Lancaster
14. 4900-5900 Kelly
15. Janet
16. 1500-2199 King
17. Lancaster
18. Scott
19. 4900-5900 Kelly
20. 2000-2999 Kelly
21. 2900-3199 King
22. Abbot
23. Sheila
24. 4400-4899 Kelly
25. 1300-1599 Reagan
26. 26. 2300-2499 Reagan
27. 1400-1999 Kelly
28. Davis
29. Sheila
30. 1900-2299 Reagan
31. Pamela
32. 3000-4399 Kelly
33. 2200-2899 King
34. 1900-2299 Reagan
35. Davis
36. 2000-2999 Kelly
37. 2500-4199 Reagan
38. 4400-4899 Kelly
39. 1300-1599 Reagan
40. Abbot
41. Pamela
42. Namath
43. Janet
44. Davis
45. Pamela
46. Lancaster
47. 1600-1899 Reagan
48. Dennis
49. 1900-2299 Reagan
50. 4900-5900 Kelly
51. Davis
52. Sheila
53. Haven
54. Pamela
55. 1600-1899 Reagan
56. 4900-5900 Kelly
57. Janet
58. 4400-4899 Kelly
59. 1300-1599 Reagan
60. Lancaster
61. 1600-1899 Reagan
62. 4900-5900 Kelly
63. 3000-4399 Kelly
64. 1900-2299 Reagan
65. Davis
66. 4900-5900 Kelly
67. Sheila
68. 2900-3199 King
69. Pamela
70. 4900-5900 Kelly
71. Namath
72. 1600-1899 Reagan
73. Janet
74. 2000-2999 Kelly
75. 1500-2199 King
76. 1400-1999 Kelly
77. 3200-3900 King
78. Lancaster
79. Sheila
80. Scott
81. Namath
82. Davis
83. 1400-1899 Kelly
84. Haven
85. Dennis
86. Sheila
87. 1500-2199 King
88. Lancaster

STOP

When the time is up, go on to the next page for the correct answers.

Author's Note: The sample test above is known as the memory-for-address test in the **470 Battery Test.** See **Strategies for Memory-for-Address Test,** pages 107-112 and **How to Mark Circles on the Answer Sheet,** pages 33-36. This part B is considered as a practice test. You'll be allowed to look at the names and addresses in the boxes, as you are instructed to answer as many questions as possible in three minutes. In the next part, however, you will be asked to answer the 88 questions in five minutes and you won't be allowed to look at the names and addresses. During the three-minute practice, answer only a few questions. Spend most of the three minutes in memorizing the placement of numbers and names: the first two numbers of each address and the first syllables of the names, combining two syllables into one. Now, answer a few questions and memorize the names and addresses in preparation for the next part.

Correct Answers

Memory-for-Address Test

1.	B	31.	A	61.	A
2.	B	32.	C	62.	D
3.	D	33.	A	63.	C
4.	B	34.	D	64.	D
5.	C	35.	D	65.	D
6.	A	36.	E	66.	D
7.	B	37.	B	67.	E
8.	E	38.	A	68.	E
9.	B	39.	E	69.	A
10.	C	40.	C	70.	D
11.	C	41.	A	71.	E
12.	D	42.	E	72.	A
13.	A	43.	D	73.	D
14.	D	44.	D	74.	E
15.	D	45.	A	75.	D
16.	D	46.	A	76.	B
17.	A	47.	A	77.	C
18.	B	48.	C	78.	A
19.	D	49.	D	79.	E
20.	E	50.	D	80.	B
21.	E	51.	D	81.	E
22.	C	52.	E	82.	D
23.	E	53.	B	83.	B
24.	A	54.	A	84.	B
25.	E	55.	A	85.	C
26.	C	56.	D	86.	E
27.	B	57.	D	87.	D
28.	D	58.	A	88.	A
29.	E	59.	E		
30.	D	60.	A		

Memory-for-Address Test

Work—3 Minutes

Answer each question on a piece of paper to show the letter of the box in which the address belongs. Try to remember the location of as many addresses as you can. If you are not sure of an address, guess. Work only three minutes.

A	B	C	D	E
4000-4599 Henry Herbert 8600-9899 Fox Lester 2100-2699 Johnson	6400-8999 Henry Ingleside 2300-6499 Fox Lewis 1500-1899 Johnson	1700-3299 Henry Capitol 8800-9999 Fox Drexel 3700-4299 Johnson	4600-6399 Henry Memphis 6500-7699 Fox Lansford 2700-3699 Johnson	3300-3999 Henry Lincoln 7700-8799 Fox Saginaw 1900-2099 Johnson

1. Ingleside
2. 6500-7699 Fox
3. 8600-9899 Fox
4. Lewis
5. Drexel
6. 7700-8799 Fox
7. 4000-4599 Henry
8. 1900-2099 Johnson
9. Lewis
10. 4600-6399 Henry
11. 3300-3999 Henry
12. 1900-2099 Johnson
13. Ingleside
14. Drexel
15. Saginaw
16. 2100-2699 Johnson
17. 3700-4299 Johnson
18. Lester
19. 2300-6499 Fox
20. 6500-7699 Fox
21. Lansford
22. 4600-6399 Henry
23. 2700-3699 Johnson
24. Lewis

25. 3300-3999 Henry
26. 8800-9999 Fox
27. 1900-2099 Johnson
28. 2100-2699 Johnson
29. 1700-3299 Henry
30. Capitol
31. Lansford
32. 2100-2699 Johnson
33. Drexel
34. 8800-9999 Fox
35. Herbert
36. Memphis
37. Lansford
38. 8600-9899 Fox
39. Lewis
40. Capitol
41. Herbert
42. Saginaw
43. Drexel
44. 3700-4299 Johnson
45. Capitol
46. Lincoln
47. Lewis
48. Drexel

49. Lincoln
50. Herbert
51. Lansford
52. Capitol
53. 8600-9899 Fox
54. Lincoln
55. 2700-3699 Johnson
56. Saginaw
57. 2700-3699 Johnson
58. Herbert
59. Memphis
60. 8800-9999 Fox
61. 6400-8999 Henry
62. 7700-8799 Fox
63. 2300-6499 Fox
64. Lester
65. Lewis
66. Herbert
67. Lansford
68. 6500-7699 Fox
69. 4000-4599 Henry
70. 1700-3299 Henry
71. Memphis
72. Saginaw

73. 8800-9999 Fox
74. 1900-2099 Johnson
75. Lester
76. 6500-7699 Fox
77. Lewis
78. 4600-6399 Henry
79. 2300-6499 Fox
80. Lincoln
81. 3300-3999 Henry
82. Drexel
83. 1500-1899 Johnson
84. Capitol
85. 2100-2699 Johnson
86. 4600-6399 Henry
87. 3300-3999 Henry
88. Herbert

STOP

When the time is up, go on to the next page for the correct answers.

(**Note:** See the author's note on page 123.)

Correct Answers

Memory-for-Address Test

1. B	31. D	61. B
2. D	32. A	62. E
3. A	33. C	63. B
4. B	34. C	64. A
5. C	35. A	65. B
6. E	36. D	66. A
7. A	37. D	67. D
8. E	38. A	68. D
9. B	39. B	69. A
10. D	40. C	70. C
11. E	41. A	71. D
12. E	42. E	72. E
13. B	43. C	73. C
14. C	44. C	74. E
15. E	45. C	75. A
16. A	46. E	76. D
17. C	47. B	77. B
18. A	48. C	78. D
19. B	49. E	79. B
20. D	50. A	80. E
21. D	51. D	81. E
22. D	52. C	82. C
23. D	53. A	83. B
24. B	54. E	84. C
25. E	55. D	85. A
26. C	56. E	86. D
27. E	57. D	87. E
28. A	58. A	88. A
29. C	59. D	
30. C	60. C	

Address-Code Memory Test

Work—5 Minutes

This is the section that counts.

Decide in which box each name or address belongs. Don't look back at the boxes with the addresses in them. Work for 5 minutes. For each question, mark the answers on the answer sheet to the right.

ANSWER SHEET

		Test A	Test B
1.	1500-2199 King	1 Ⓐ Ⓑ Ⓒ Ⓓ Ⓔ	1 Ⓐ Ⓑ Ⓒ Ⓓ Ⓔ
2.	2500-4199 Reagan	2 Ⓐ Ⓑ Ⓒ Ⓓ Ⓔ	2 Ⓐ Ⓑ Ⓒ Ⓓ Ⓔ
3.	2300-2499 Reagan	3 Ⓐ Ⓑ Ⓒ Ⓓ Ⓔ	3 Ⓐ Ⓑ Ⓒ Ⓓ Ⓔ
4.	Scott	4 Ⓐ Ⓑ Ⓒ Ⓓ Ⓔ	4 Ⓐ Ⓑ Ⓒ Ⓓ Ⓔ
5.	1900-2299 Reagan	5 Ⓐ Ⓑ Ⓒ Ⓓ Ⓔ	5 Ⓐ Ⓑ Ⓒ Ⓓ Ⓔ
6.	1400-1999 Kelly	6 Ⓐ Ⓑ Ⓒ Ⓓ Ⓔ	6 Ⓐ Ⓑ Ⓒ Ⓓ Ⓔ
7.	2300-2499 Reagan	7 Ⓐ Ⓑ Ⓒ Ⓓ Ⓔ	7 Ⓐ Ⓑ Ⓒ Ⓓ Ⓔ
8.	Sheila	8 Ⓐ Ⓑ Ⓒ Ⓓ Ⓔ	8 Ⓐ Ⓑ Ⓒ Ⓓ Ⓔ
9.	3000-4399 Kelly	9 Ⓐ Ⓑ Ⓒ Ⓓ Ⓔ	9 Ⓐ Ⓑ Ⓒ Ⓓ Ⓔ
10.	Lancaster	10 Ⓐ Ⓑ Ⓒ Ⓓ Ⓔ	10 Ⓐ Ⓑ Ⓒ Ⓓ Ⓔ
11.	4400-4899 Kelly	11 Ⓐ Ⓑ Ⓒ Ⓓ Ⓔ	11 Ⓐ Ⓑ Ⓒ Ⓓ Ⓔ
12.	Pamela	12 Ⓐ Ⓑ Ⓒ Ⓓ Ⓔ	12 Ⓐ Ⓑ Ⓒ Ⓓ Ⓔ
13.	2500-4199 Reagan	13 Ⓐ Ⓑ Ⓒ Ⓓ Ⓔ	13 Ⓐ Ⓑ Ⓒ Ⓓ Ⓔ
14.	Dennis	14 Ⓐ Ⓑ Ⓒ Ⓓ Ⓔ	14 Ⓐ Ⓑ Ⓒ Ⓓ Ⓔ
15.	2900-3199 King	15 Ⓐ Ⓑ Ⓒ Ⓓ Ⓔ	15 Ⓐ Ⓑ Ⓒ Ⓓ Ⓔ
16.	3000-4399 Kelly	16 Ⓐ Ⓑ Ⓒ Ⓓ Ⓔ	16 Ⓐ Ⓑ Ⓒ Ⓓ Ⓔ
17.	1600-1899 Reagan	17 Ⓐ Ⓑ Ⓒ Ⓓ Ⓔ	17 Ⓐ Ⓑ Ⓒ Ⓓ Ⓔ
18.	Abbot	18 Ⓐ Ⓑ Ⓒ Ⓓ Ⓔ	18 Ⓐ Ⓑ Ⓒ Ⓓ Ⓔ
19.	Haven	19 Ⓐ Ⓑ Ⓒ Ⓓ Ⓔ	19 Ⓐ Ⓑ Ⓒ Ⓓ Ⓔ
20.	Sheila	20 Ⓐ Ⓑ Ⓒ Ⓓ Ⓔ	20 Ⓐ Ⓑ Ⓒ Ⓓ Ⓔ
21.	Lancaster	21 Ⓐ Ⓑ Ⓒ Ⓓ Ⓔ	21 Ⓐ Ⓑ Ⓒ Ⓓ Ⓔ
22.	Janet	22 Ⓐ Ⓑ Ⓒ Ⓓ Ⓔ	22 Ⓐ Ⓑ Ⓒ Ⓓ Ⓔ
23.	Scott	23 Ⓐ Ⓑ Ⓒ Ⓓ Ⓔ	23 Ⓐ Ⓑ Ⓒ Ⓓ Ⓔ
24.	Namath	24 Ⓐ Ⓑ Ⓒ Ⓓ Ⓔ	24 Ⓐ Ⓑ Ⓒ Ⓓ Ⓔ
25.	Davis	25 Ⓐ Ⓑ Ⓒ Ⓓ Ⓔ	25 Ⓐ Ⓑ Ⓒ Ⓓ Ⓔ
26.	Pamela	26 Ⓐ Ⓑ Ⓒ Ⓓ Ⓔ	26 Ⓐ Ⓑ Ⓒ Ⓓ Ⓔ
27.	3000-4399 Kelly	27 Ⓐ Ⓑ Ⓒ Ⓓ Ⓔ	27 Ⓐ Ⓑ Ⓒ Ⓓ Ⓔ
28.	1200-1499 King	28 Ⓐ Ⓑ Ⓒ Ⓓ Ⓔ	28 Ⓐ Ⓑ Ⓒ Ⓓ Ⓔ
29.	Sheila	29 Ⓐ Ⓑ Ⓒ Ⓓ Ⓔ	29 Ⓐ Ⓑ Ⓒ Ⓓ Ⓔ
30.	2300-2499 Reagan	30 Ⓐ Ⓑ Ⓒ Ⓓ Ⓔ	30 Ⓐ Ⓑ Ⓒ Ⓓ Ⓔ
31.	4900-5900 Kelly	31 Ⓐ Ⓑ Ⓒ Ⓓ Ⓔ	31 Ⓐ Ⓑ Ⓒ Ⓓ Ⓔ
32.	Scott	32 Ⓐ Ⓑ Ⓒ Ⓓ Ⓔ	32 Ⓐ Ⓑ Ⓒ Ⓓ Ⓔ
33.	Haven	33 Ⓐ Ⓑ Ⓒ Ⓓ Ⓔ	33 Ⓐ Ⓑ Ⓒ Ⓓ Ⓔ
34.	1500-2199 King	34 Ⓐ Ⓑ Ⓒ Ⓓ Ⓔ	34 Ⓐ Ⓑ Ⓒ Ⓓ Ⓔ
35.	Pamela	35 Ⓐ Ⓑ Ⓒ Ⓓ Ⓔ	35 Ⓐ Ⓑ Ⓒ Ⓓ Ⓔ
36.	3000-4399 Kelly	36 Ⓐ Ⓑ Ⓒ Ⓓ Ⓔ	36 Ⓐ Ⓑ Ⓒ Ⓓ Ⓔ
37.	Lancaster	37 Ⓐ Ⓑ Ⓒ Ⓓ Ⓔ	37 Ⓐ Ⓑ Ⓒ Ⓓ Ⓔ
38.	4900-5900 Kelly	38 Ⓐ Ⓑ Ⓒ Ⓓ Ⓔ	38 Ⓐ Ⓑ Ⓒ Ⓓ Ⓔ
39.	Namath	39 Ⓐ Ⓑ Ⓒ Ⓓ Ⓔ	39 Ⓐ Ⓑ Ⓒ Ⓓ Ⓔ
40.	Scott	40 Ⓐ Ⓑ Ⓒ Ⓓ Ⓔ	40· Ⓐ Ⓑ Ⓒ Ⓓ Ⓔ

Go on to the next number on the next page.

41. 3200-3900 King	41 Ⓐ Ⓑ Ⓒ Ⓓ Ⓔ	41 Ⓐ Ⓑ Ⓒ Ⓓ Ⓔ
42. Dennis	42 Ⓐ Ⓑ Ⓒ Ⓓ Ⓔ	42 Ⓐ Ⓑ Ⓒ Ⓓ Ⓔ
43. Janet	43 Ⓐ Ⓑ Ⓒ Ⓓ Ⓔ	43 Ⓐ Ⓑ Ⓒ Ⓓ Ⓔ
44. 4400-4899 Kelly	44 Ⓐ Ⓑ Ⓒ Ⓓ Ⓔ	44 Ⓐ Ⓑ Ⓒ Ⓓ Ⓔ
45. Sheila	45 Ⓐ Ⓑ Ⓒ Ⓓ Ⓔ	45 Ⓐ Ⓑ Ⓒ Ⓓ Ⓔ
46. Haven	46 Ⓐ Ⓑ Ⓒ Ⓓ Ⓔ	46 Ⓐ Ⓑ Ⓒ Ⓓ Ⓔ
47. Abbot	47 Ⓐ Ⓑ Ⓒ Ⓓ Ⓔ	47 Ⓐ Ⓑ Ⓒ Ⓓ Ⓔ
48. Lancaster	48 Ⓐ Ⓑ Ⓒ Ⓓ Ⓔ	48 Ⓐ Ⓑ Ⓒ Ⓓ Ⓔ
49. 4900-5900 Kelly	49 Ⓐ Ⓑ Ⓒ Ⓓ Ⓔ	49 Ⓐ Ⓑ Ⓒ Ⓓ Ⓔ
50. 3200-3900 King	50 Ⓐ Ⓑ Ⓒ Ⓓ Ⓔ	50 Ⓐ Ⓑ Ⓒ Ⓓ Ⓔ
51. Pamela	51 Ⓐ Ⓑ Ⓒ Ⓓ Ⓔ	51 Ⓐ Ⓑ Ⓒ Ⓓ Ⓔ
52. Namath	52 Ⓐ Ⓑ Ⓒ Ⓓ Ⓔ	52 Ⓐ Ⓑ Ⓒ Ⓓ Ⓔ
53. Davis	53 Ⓐ Ⓑ Ⓒ Ⓓ Ⓔ	53 Ⓐ Ⓑ Ⓒ Ⓓ Ⓔ
54. 2000-2999 Kelly	54 Ⓐ Ⓑ Ⓒ Ⓓ Ⓔ	54 Ⓐ Ⓑ Ⓒ Ⓓ Ⓔ
55. 1500-2199 King	55 Ⓐ Ⓑ Ⓒ Ⓓ Ⓔ	55 Ⓐ Ⓑ Ⓒ Ⓓ Ⓔ
56. 1200-1499 King	56 Ⓐ Ⓑ Ⓒ Ⓓ Ⓔ	56 Ⓐ Ⓑ Ⓒ Ⓓ Ⓔ
57. 1900-2299 Reagan	57 Ⓐ Ⓑ Ⓒ Ⓓ Ⓔ	57 Ⓐ Ⓑ Ⓒ Ⓓ Ⓔ
58. Lancaster	58 Ⓐ Ⓑ Ⓒ Ⓓ Ⓔ	58 Ⓐ Ⓑ Ⓒ Ⓓ Ⓔ
59. 3200-3900 King	59 Ⓐ Ⓑ Ⓒ Ⓓ Ⓔ	59 Ⓐ Ⓑ Ⓒ Ⓓ Ⓔ
60. Namath	60 Ⓐ Ⓑ Ⓒ Ⓓ Ⓔ	60 Ⓐ Ⓑ Ⓒ Ⓓ Ⓔ
61. Scott	61 Ⓐ Ⓑ Ⓒ Ⓓ Ⓔ	61 Ⓐ Ⓑ Ⓒ Ⓓ Ⓔ
62. Abbot	62 Ⓐ Ⓑ Ⓒ Ⓓ Ⓔ	62 Ⓐ Ⓑ Ⓒ Ⓓ Ⓔ
63. 2000-2999 Kelly	63 Ⓐ Ⓑ Ⓒ Ⓓ Ⓔ	63 Ⓐ Ⓑ Ⓒ Ⓓ Ⓔ
64. 1200-1499 King	64 Ⓐ Ⓑ Ⓒ Ⓓ Ⓔ	64 Ⓐ Ⓑ Ⓒ Ⓓ Ⓔ
65. Dennis	65 Ⓐ Ⓑ Ⓒ Ⓓ Ⓔ	65 Ⓐ Ⓑ Ⓒ Ⓓ Ⓔ
66. Pamela	66 Ⓐ Ⓑ Ⓒ Ⓓ Ⓔ	66 Ⓐ Ⓑ Ⓒ Ⓓ Ⓔ
67. Sheila	67 Ⓐ Ⓑ Ⓒ Ⓓ Ⓔ	67 Ⓐ Ⓑ Ⓒ Ⓓ Ⓔ
68. Davis	68 Ⓐ Ⓑ Ⓒ Ⓓ Ⓔ	68 Ⓐ Ⓑ Ⓒ Ⓓ Ⓔ
69. Scott	69 Ⓐ Ⓑ Ⓒ Ⓓ Ⓔ	69 Ⓐ Ⓑ Ⓒ Ⓓ Ⓔ
70. 1600-1899 Reagan	70 Ⓐ Ⓑ Ⓒ Ⓓ Ⓔ	70 Ⓐ Ⓑ Ⓒ Ⓓ Ⓔ
71. Namath	71 Ⓐ Ⓑ Ⓒ Ⓓ Ⓔ	71 Ⓐ Ⓑ Ⓒ Ⓓ Ⓔ
72. 2300-2499 Reagan	72 Ⓐ Ⓑ Ⓒ Ⓓ Ⓔ	72 Ⓐ Ⓑ Ⓒ Ⓓ Ⓔ
73. 2900-3199 King	73 Ⓐ Ⓑ Ⓒ Ⓓ Ⓔ	73 Ⓐ Ⓑ Ⓒ Ⓓ Ⓔ
74. 1400-1999 Kelly	74 Ⓐ Ⓑ Ⓒ Ⓓ Ⓔ	74 Ⓐ Ⓑ Ⓒ Ⓓ Ⓔ
75. Abbot	75 Ⓐ Ⓑ Ⓒ Ⓓ Ⓔ	75 Ⓐ Ⓑ Ⓒ Ⓓ Ⓔ
76. 2200-2899 King	76 Ⓐ Ⓑ Ⓒ Ⓓ Ⓔ	76 Ⓐ Ⓑ Ⓒ Ⓓ Ⓔ
77. Davis	77 Ⓐ Ⓑ Ⓒ Ⓓ Ⓔ	77 Ⓐ Ⓑ Ⓒ Ⓓ Ⓔ
78. 1300-1599 Reagan	78 Ⓐ Ⓑ Ⓒ Ⓓ Ⓔ	78 Ⓐ Ⓑ Ⓒ Ⓓ Ⓔ
79. 4900-5900 Kelly	79 Ⓐ Ⓑ Ⓒ Ⓓ Ⓔ	79 Ⓐ Ⓑ Ⓒ Ⓓ Ⓔ
80. Abbot	80 Ⓐ Ⓑ Ⓒ Ⓓ Ⓔ	80 Ⓐ Ⓑ Ⓒ Ⓓ Ⓔ
81. Lancaster	81 Ⓐ Ⓑ Ⓒ Ⓓ Ⓔ	81 Ⓐ Ⓑ Ⓒ Ⓓ Ⓔ
82. Dennis	82 Ⓐ Ⓑ Ⓒ Ⓓ Ⓔ	82 Ⓐ Ⓑ Ⓒ Ⓓ Ⓔ
83. Janet	83 Ⓐ Ⓑ Ⓒ Ⓓ Ⓔ	83 Ⓐ Ⓑ Ⓒ Ⓓ Ⓔ
84. Sheila	84 Ⓐ Ⓑ Ⓒ Ⓓ Ⓔ	84 Ⓐ Ⓑ Ⓒ Ⓓ Ⓔ
85. Haven	85 Ⓐ Ⓑ Ⓒ Ⓓ Ⓔ	85 Ⓐ Ⓑ Ⓒ Ⓓ Ⓔ
86. 3000-4399 Kelly	86 Ⓐ Ⓑ Ⓒ Ⓓ Ⓔ	86 Ⓐ Ⓑ Ⓒ Ⓓ Ⓔ
87. 2200-2899 King	87 Ⓐ Ⓑ Ⓒ Ⓓ Ⓔ	87 Ⓐ Ⓑ Ⓒ Ⓓ Ⓔ
88. Namath	88 Ⓐ Ⓑ Ⓒ Ⓓ Ⓔ	88 Ⓐ Ⓑ Ⓒ Ⓓ Ⓔ

(See the correct answers on the next page.)

Correct Answers

Address-Code Memory Test

1. D	31. D	61. B
2. B	32. B	62. C
3. C	33. B	63. E
4. B	34. D	64. B
5. D	35. A	65. C
6. B	36. C	66. A
7. C	37. A	67. E
8. E	38. D	68. D
9. C	39. E	69. B
10. A	40. B	70. A
11. A	41. C	71. E
12. A	42. C	72. C
13. B	43. D	73. E
14. C	44. A	74. B
15. E	45. E	75. C
16. C	46. B	76. A
17. A	47. C	77. D
18. C	48. A	78. E
19. B	49. D	79. D
20. E	50. C	80. C
21. A	51. A	81. A
22. D	52. E	82. C
23. B	53. D	83. D
24. E	54. E	84. E
25. D	55. D	85. B
26. A	56. B	86. C
27. C	57. D	87. A
28. B	58. A	88. E
29. E	59. C	
30. C	60. E	

Memory-for-Address Test
Work—5 Minutes
This is the section that counts.

Decide in which box each name or address belongs. Don't look back at the boxes with the addresses in them. Work for 5 minutes. For each question, mark the answers on the answer sheet to the right.

ANSWER SHEET

		Test A	Test B
1.	4600-6399 Henry	1 Ⓐ Ⓑ Ⓒ Ⓓ Ⓔ	1 Ⓐ Ⓑ Ⓒ Ⓓ Ⓔ
2.	Saginaw	2 Ⓐ Ⓑ Ⓒ Ⓓ Ⓔ	2 Ⓐ Ⓑ Ⓒ Ⓓ Ⓔ
3.	8800-9999 Fox	3 Ⓐ Ⓑ Ⓒ Ⓓ Ⓔ	3 Ⓐ Ⓑ Ⓒ Ⓓ Ⓔ
4.	1500-1899 Johnson	4 Ⓐ Ⓑ Ⓒ Ⓓ Ⓔ	4 Ⓐ Ⓑ Ⓒ Ⓓ Ⓔ
5.	4000-4599 Henry	5 Ⓐ Ⓑ Ⓒ Ⓓ Ⓔ	5 Ⓐ Ⓑ Ⓒ Ⓓ Ⓔ
6.	1900-2099 Johnson	6 Ⓐ Ⓑ Ⓒ Ⓓ Ⓔ	6 Ⓐ Ⓑ Ⓒ Ⓓ Ⓔ
7.	Drexel	7 Ⓐ Ⓑ Ⓒ Ⓓ Ⓔ	7 Ⓐ Ⓑ Ⓒ Ⓓ Ⓔ
8.	4600-6399 Henry	8 Ⓐ Ⓑ Ⓒ Ⓓ Ⓔ	8 Ⓐ Ⓑ Ⓒ Ⓓ Ⓔ
9.	2300-6499 Fox	9 Ⓐ Ⓑ Ⓒ Ⓓ Ⓔ	9 Ⓐ Ⓑ Ⓒ Ⓓ Ⓔ
10.	8800-9999 Fox	10 Ⓐ Ⓑ Ⓒ Ⓓ Ⓔ	10 Ⓐ Ⓑ Ⓒ Ⓓ Ⓔ
11.	1500-1899 Johnson	11 Ⓐ Ⓑ Ⓒ Ⓓ Ⓔ	11 Ⓐ Ⓑ Ⓒ Ⓓ Ⓔ
12.	8600-9899 Fox	12 Ⓐ Ⓑ Ⓒ Ⓓ Ⓔ	12 Ⓐ Ⓑ Ⓒ Ⓓ Ⓔ
13.	Herbert	13 Ⓐ Ⓑ Ⓒ Ⓓ Ⓔ	13 Ⓐ Ⓑ Ⓒ Ⓓ Ⓔ
14.	Lansford	14 Ⓐ Ⓑ Ⓒ Ⓓ Ⓔ	14 Ⓐ Ⓑ Ⓒ Ⓓ Ⓔ
15.	6500-7699 Fox	15 Ⓐ Ⓑ Ⓒ Ⓓ Ⓔ	15 Ⓐ Ⓑ Ⓒ Ⓓ Ⓔ
16.	1900-2099 Johnson	16 Ⓐ Ⓑ Ⓒ Ⓓ Ⓔ	16 Ⓐ Ⓑ Ⓒ Ⓓ Ⓔ
17.	4000-4599 Henry	17 Ⓐ Ⓑ Ⓒ Ⓓ Ⓔ	17 Ⓐ Ⓑ Ⓒ Ⓓ Ⓔ
18.	Drexel	18 Ⓐ Ⓑ Ⓒ Ⓓ Ⓔ	18 Ⓐ Ⓑ Ⓒ Ⓓ Ⓔ
19.	Memphis	19 Ⓐ Ⓑ Ⓒ Ⓓ Ⓔ	19 Ⓐ Ⓑ Ⓒ Ⓓ Ⓔ
20.	Saginaw	20 Ⓐ Ⓑ Ⓒ Ⓓ Ⓔ	20 Ⓐ Ⓑ Ⓒ Ⓓ Ⓔ
21.	3700-4299 Johnson	21 Ⓐ Ⓑ Ⓒ Ⓓ Ⓔ	21 Ⓐ Ⓑ Ⓒ Ⓓ Ⓔ
22.	Lincoln	22 Ⓐ Ⓑ Ⓒ Ⓓ Ⓔ	22 Ⓐ Ⓑ Ⓒ Ⓓ Ⓔ
23.	Lester	23 Ⓐ Ⓑ Ⓒ Ⓓ Ⓔ	23 Ⓐ Ⓑ Ⓒ Ⓓ Ⓔ
24.	3300-3999 Henry	24 Ⓐ Ⓑ Ⓒ Ⓓ Ⓔ	24 Ⓐ Ⓑ Ⓒ Ⓓ Ⓔ
25.	7700-8799 Fox	25 Ⓐ Ⓑ Ⓒ Ⓓ Ⓔ	25 Ⓐ Ⓑ Ⓒ Ⓓ Ⓔ
26.	Ingleside	26 Ⓐ Ⓑ Ⓒ Ⓓ Ⓔ	26 Ⓐ Ⓑ Ⓒ Ⓓ Ⓔ
27.	8800-9999 Fox	27 Ⓐ Ⓑ Ⓒ Ⓓ Ⓔ	27 Ⓐ Ⓑ Ⓒ Ⓓ Ⓔ
28.	4000-4599 Henry	28 Ⓐ Ⓑ Ⓒ Ⓓ Ⓔ	28 Ⓐ Ⓑ Ⓒ Ⓓ Ⓔ
29.	Lewis	29 Ⓐ Ⓑ Ⓒ Ⓓ Ⓔ	29 Ⓐ Ⓑ Ⓒ Ⓓ Ⓔ
30.	Capitol	30 Ⓐ Ⓑ Ⓒ Ⓓ Ⓔ	30 Ⓐ Ⓑ Ⓒ Ⓓ Ⓔ
31.	3300-3999 Henry	31 Ⓐ Ⓑ Ⓒ Ⓓ Ⓔ	31 Ⓐ Ⓑ Ⓒ Ⓓ Ⓔ
32.	Herbert	32 Ⓐ Ⓑ Ⓒ Ⓓ Ⓔ	32 Ⓐ Ⓑ Ⓒ Ⓓ Ⓔ
33.	2300-6499 Fox	33 Ⓐ Ⓑ Ⓒ Ⓓ Ⓔ	33 Ⓐ Ⓑ Ⓒ Ⓓ Ⓔ
34.	Lansford	34 Ⓐ Ⓑ Ⓒ Ⓓ Ⓔ	34 Ⓐ Ⓑ Ⓒ Ⓓ Ⓔ
35.	Saginaw	35 Ⓐ Ⓑ Ⓒ Ⓓ Ⓔ	35 Ⓐ Ⓑ Ⓒ Ⓓ Ⓔ
36.	2100-2699 Johnson	36 Ⓐ Ⓑ Ⓒ Ⓓ Ⓔ	36 Ⓐ Ⓑ Ⓒ Ⓓ Ⓔ
37.	4600-6399 Henry	37 Ⓐ Ⓑ Ⓒ Ⓓ Ⓔ	37 Ⓐ Ⓑ Ⓒ Ⓓ Ⓔ
38.	Capitol	38 Ⓐ Ⓑ Ⓒ Ⓓ Ⓔ	38 Ⓐ Ⓑ Ⓒ Ⓓ Ⓔ
39.	Ingleside	39 Ⓐ Ⓑ Ⓒ Ⓓ Ⓔ	39 Ⓐ Ⓑ Ⓒ Ⓓ Ⓔ
40.	2700-3699 Johnson	40 Ⓐ Ⓑ Ⓒ Ⓓ Ⓔ	40 Ⓐ Ⓑ Ⓒ Ⓓ Ⓔ

Go on to the next number on the next page.

41. Lincoln	41 Ⓐ Ⓑ Ⓒ Ⓓ Ⓔ	41 Ⓐ Ⓑ Ⓒ Ⓓ Ⓔ
42. Drexel	42 Ⓐ Ⓑ Ⓒ Ⓓ Ⓔ	42 Ⓐ Ⓑ Ⓒ Ⓓ Ⓔ
43. Lansford	43 Ⓐ Ⓑ Ⓒ Ⓓ Ⓔ	43 Ⓐ Ⓑ Ⓒ Ⓓ Ⓔ
44. 6400-8999 Henry	44 Ⓐ Ⓑ Ⓒ Ⓓ Ⓔ	44 Ⓐ Ⓑ Ⓒ Ⓓ Ⓔ
45. 1500-1899 Johnson	45 Ⓐ Ⓑ Ⓒ Ⓓ Ⓔ	45 Ⓐ Ⓑ Ⓒ Ⓓ Ⓔ
46. Memphis	46 Ⓐ Ⓑ Ⓒ Ⓓ Ⓔ	46 Ⓐ Ⓑ Ⓒ Ⓓ Ⓔ
47. Herbert	47 Ⓐ Ⓑ Ⓒ Ⓓ Ⓔ	47 Ⓐ Ⓑ Ⓒ Ⓓ Ⓔ
48. Saginaw	48 Ⓐ Ⓑ Ⓒ Ⓓ Ⓔ	48 Ⓐ Ⓑ Ⓒ Ⓓ Ⓔ
49. 3300-3999 Henry	49 Ⓐ Ⓑ Ⓒ Ⓓ Ⓔ	49 Ⓐ Ⓑ Ⓒ Ⓓ Ⓔ
50. Capitol	50 Ⓐ Ⓑ Ⓒ Ⓓ Ⓔ	50 Ⓐ Ⓑ Ⓒ Ⓓ Ⓔ
51. 2700-3699 Johnson	51 Ⓐ Ⓑ Ⓒ Ⓓ Ⓔ	51 Ⓐ Ⓑ Ⓒ Ⓓ Ⓔ
52. 2300-6499 Fox	52 Ⓐ Ⓑ Ⓒ Ⓓ Ⓔ	52 Ⓐ Ⓑ Ⓒ Ⓓ Ⓔ
53. 8600-9899 Fox	53 Ⓐ Ⓑ Ⓒ Ⓓ Ⓔ	53 Ⓐ Ⓑ Ⓒ Ⓓ Ⓔ
54. 1900-2099 Johnson	54 Ⓐ Ⓑ Ⓒ Ⓓ Ⓔ	54 Ⓐ Ⓑ Ⓒ Ⓓ Ⓔ
55. 1700-3299 Henry	55 Ⓐ Ⓑ Ⓒ Ⓓ Ⓔ	55 Ⓐ Ⓑ Ⓒ Ⓓ Ⓔ
56. Herbert	56 Ⓐ Ⓑ Ⓒ Ⓓ Ⓔ	56 Ⓐ Ⓑ Ⓒ Ⓓ Ⓔ
57. Lansford	57 Ⓐ Ⓑ Ⓒ Ⓓ Ⓔ	57 Ⓐ Ⓑ Ⓒ Ⓓ Ⓔ
58. Drexel	58 Ⓐ Ⓑ Ⓒ Ⓓ Ⓔ	58 Ⓐ Ⓑ Ⓒ Ⓓ Ⓔ
59. Lester	59 Ⓐ Ⓑ Ⓒ Ⓓ Ⓔ	59 Ⓐ Ⓑ Ⓒ Ⓓ Ⓔ
60. Capitol	60 Ⓐ Ⓑ Ⓒ Ⓓ Ⓔ	60 Ⓐ Ⓑ Ⓒ Ⓓ Ⓔ
61. 4000-4599 Henry	61 Ⓐ Ⓑ Ⓒ Ⓓ Ⓔ	61 Ⓐ Ⓑ Ⓒ Ⓓ Ⓔ
62. 3700-4299 Johnson	62 Ⓐ Ⓑ Ⓒ Ⓓ Ⓔ	62 Ⓐ Ⓑ Ⓒ Ⓓ Ⓔ
63. 2300-6499 Fox	63 Ⓐ Ⓑ Ⓒ Ⓓ Ⓔ	63 Ⓐ Ⓑ Ⓒ Ⓓ Ⓔ
64. Lincoln	64 Ⓐ Ⓑ Ⓒ Ⓓ Ⓔ	64 Ⓐ Ⓑ Ⓒ Ⓓ Ⓔ
65. 6500-7699 Fox	65 Ⓐ Ⓑ Ⓒ Ⓓ Ⓔ	65 Ⓐ Ⓑ Ⓒ Ⓓ Ⓔ
66. 1900-2099 Johnson	66 Ⓐ Ⓑ Ⓒ Ⓓ Ⓔ	66 Ⓐ Ⓑ Ⓒ Ⓓ Ⓔ
67. Ingleside	67 Ⓐ Ⓑ Ⓒ Ⓓ Ⓔ	67 Ⓐ Ⓑ Ⓒ Ⓓ Ⓔ
68. Herbert	68 Ⓐ Ⓑ Ⓒ Ⓓ Ⓔ	68 Ⓐ Ⓑ Ⓒ Ⓓ Ⓔ
69. 7700-8799 Fox	69 Ⓐ Ⓑ Ⓒ Ⓓ Ⓔ	69 Ⓐ Ⓑ Ⓒ Ⓓ Ⓔ
70. Drexel	70 Ⓐ Ⓑ Ⓒ Ⓓ Ⓔ	70 Ⓐ Ⓑ Ⓒ Ⓓ Ⓔ
71. Lewis	71 Ⓐ Ⓑ Ⓒ Ⓓ Ⓔ	71 Ⓐ Ⓑ Ⓒ Ⓓ Ⓔ
72. Memphis	72 Ⓐ Ⓑ Ⓒ Ⓓ Ⓔ	72 Ⓐ Ⓑ Ⓒ Ⓓ Ⓔ
73. Lincoln	73 Ⓐ Ⓑ Ⓒ Ⓓ Ⓔ	73 Ⓐ Ⓑ Ⓒ Ⓓ Ⓔ
74. 3300-3999 Henry	74 Ⓐ Ⓑ Ⓒ Ⓓ Ⓔ	74 Ⓐ Ⓑ Ⓒ Ⓓ Ⓔ
75. Lester	75 Ⓐ Ⓑ Ⓒ Ⓓ Ⓔ	75 Ⓐ Ⓑ Ⓒ Ⓓ Ⓔ
76. Capitol	76 Ⓐ Ⓑ Ⓒ Ⓓ Ⓔ	76 Ⓐ Ⓑ Ⓒ Ⓓ Ⓔ
77. 7700-8799 Fox	77 Ⓐ Ⓑ Ⓒ Ⓓ Ⓔ	77 Ⓐ Ⓑ Ⓒ Ⓓ Ⓔ
78. Herbert	78 Ⓐ Ⓑ Ⓒ Ⓓ Ⓔ	78 Ⓐ Ⓑ Ⓒ Ⓓ Ⓔ
79. 1700-3299 Henry	79 Ⓐ Ⓑ Ⓒ Ⓓ Ⓔ	79 Ⓐ Ⓑ Ⓒ Ⓓ Ⓔ
80. 2100-2699 Johnson	80 Ⓐ Ⓑ Ⓒ Ⓓ Ⓔ	80 Ⓐ Ⓑ Ⓒ Ⓓ Ⓔ
81. Saginaw	81 Ⓐ Ⓑ Ⓒ Ⓓ Ⓔ	81 Ⓐ Ⓑ Ⓒ Ⓓ Ⓔ
82. 8600-9899 Fox	82 Ⓐ Ⓑ Ⓒ Ⓓ Ⓔ	82 Ⓐ Ⓑ Ⓒ Ⓓ Ⓔ
83. 7700-8799 Fox	83 Ⓐ Ⓑ Ⓒ Ⓓ Ⓔ	83 Ⓐ Ⓑ Ⓒ Ⓓ Ⓔ
84. Ingleside	84 Ⓐ Ⓑ Ⓒ Ⓓ Ⓔ	84 Ⓐ Ⓑ Ⓒ Ⓓ Ⓔ
85. Capitol	85 Ⓐ Ⓑ Ⓒ Ⓓ Ⓔ	85 Ⓐ Ⓑ Ⓒ Ⓓ Ⓔ
86. Lansford	86 Ⓐ Ⓑ Ⓒ Ⓓ Ⓔ	86 Ⓐ Ⓑ Ⓒ Ⓓ Ⓔ
87. 8600-9899 Fox	87 Ⓐ Ⓑ Ⓒ Ⓓ Ⓔ	87 Ⓐ Ⓑ Ⓒ Ⓓ Ⓔ
88. Lincoln	88 Ⓐ Ⓑ Ⓒ Ⓓ Ⓔ	88 Ⓐ Ⓑ Ⓒ Ⓓ Ⓔ

**If you finish before the time is up,
go back and check your answers.
(See the correct answers on the next page.)**

Correct Answers

Memory-for-Address Test

1. D	31. E	61. A
2. E	32. A	62. C
3. C	33. B	63. B
4. B	34. D	64. E
5. A	35. E	65. D
6. E	36. A	66. E
7. C	37. D	67. B
8. D	38. C	68. A
9. B	39. B	69. E
10. C	40. D	70. C
11. B	41. E	71. B
12. A	42. C	72. D
13. A	43. D	73. E
14. D	44. B	74. E
15. D	45. B	75. A
16. E	46. D	76. C
17. A	47. A	77. E
18. C	48. E	78. A
19. D	49. E	79. C
20. E	50. C	80. A
21. C	51. D	81. E
22. E	52. B	82. A
23. A	53. A	83. E
24. E	54. E	84. B
25. E	55. C	85. C
26. B	56. A	86. D
27. C	57. D	87. A
28. A	58. C	88. E
29. B	59. A	
30. C	60. C	

(For more **Memory-for-Address Practice Tests**, see pages 297-326.)

(United States Postal Service)

Interpretation of Test Scores on Sample Address-Checking and Memory-for-Address Tests

For the Address Checking (Part A), count the number that you got right and the number that you got wrong. (If you didn't mark anything for a question, it doesn't get counted.)

From the number right _____
Subtract the number wrong _____
This number (the difference) is your score ▸ _____

The meaning of the score is as follows:

52 or higher --- Good.

Between 32 and 51--- Fair.

Below 32 ----------------------------------- You need more practice.

Go back and see where you made your mistakes. Were you careless? Did you work too slowly?

For the Memory for Address (Part B), count the number that you got right and the number that you got wrong. (If you didn't mark anything for a question, it doesn't get counted.)

Divide the number wrong by 4. _____

From the number right _____
Subtract $\frac{1}{4}$ the number wrong_____
This number (the difference) is your score ▸_____

The meaning of the score is as follows.

44 or higher --- Good.

Between 26 and 43 --- Fair.

Below 26 ----------------------------------- You need more practice.

Go back and see where you made your mistakes. Were you careless? Did you work too slowly?

(Author's Note: According to my own estimate, when you get more than half of the answers correct (address checking, part A, 95 numbers); you'll pass the exam. I based this estimate on scores acquired by several examinees. This also applies to memory-for-address test (part B, 88 numbers); when you get more than half the answers correct, you pass. However, you need to make high scores to beat the competition and be called immediately.)

Number Series Test   17

The *Number Series Test* involves a series of numbers that follows some definite pattern. For each number series question, there is a series of numbers that progresses from left to right and follows some definite order. All you must do is to determine what the next two last numbers or the last two pairs of numbers will be if the same order is continued. The test, which is considered nonverbal, measures your ability to find the "missing link."

Here are some strategies:

Strategy 1: Find the rule that creates the series of numbers.

Strategy 2: Found out which number comes next or is missing.

Strategy 3: Find the patterns used.

In this test, you'll discover that the pattern or the relationship may involve the use of the following:

- addition
- subtraction
- multiplication
- division
- squaring
- cubing
- square root
- cube root

At first, the sequence of numbers is easier to determine. For instance, the number may increase by 2, 4, 5, etc.; sometimes, the number may decrease by 1, 3, 5, etc. But sometimes, the series involves the alternating uses of addition and subtraction, which may appear a little more complex.

Simple Number Series. Each of the three sample questions below gives a series of seven numbers. Each number follows a certain pattern or order. Choose what will be the next one or two numbers in that series if the pattern is continued.

    1.   6   8   10   12   14   16   18   ....

460 RCA Examination (470 Battery Test): Pages 61-146.

A) 22
B) 20
C) 24
D) 21
E) 23

In this question, the pattern is to add 2 to each number: 6 + 2 = 8; 8 + 2 = 10; 10 + 2 = 12; 12 + 2 14; 14 + 2 = 16; 16 + 2 = 18. The next number in the series is 18 + 2 which equals 20. B is the correct answer. Here's how it's done:

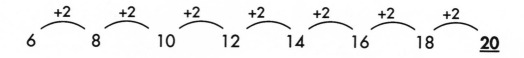

2.   7   9   12   15   17   20   23   ...

A) 29
B) 27
C) 26
D) 25
E) 39

In this question, the pattern is to add 2 to the first number (7 + 2 = 9); add 3 to the second number (9 + 3 = 12; add 3 to the third number (12 + 3 = 15); add 2 to the fourth number (15 + 2 = 17); add 3 to the fifth number (17 + 3 = 20); add 3 to the sixth number (20 + 3) = 23). To continue the series, add 2 to the next number (23 + 2) = 25). D is the correct answer. Here's how it's done:

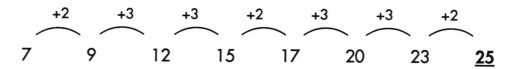

As you can see, the order or pattern is to add 2 once, then add 3 twice. Get it?

3.   9   10   8   9   7   8   6   ...   ...

A) 7
B) 5
C) 9

D) 8
E) 6

In this question, the pattern is to add 1 to the first number, subtract 2 from the next, add 1, subtract 2, and so on. (9 + 1 = 10; 10 - 2 = 8; 8 + 1 = 9; 9 - 2 = 7; 7 + 1 = 8; 8 - 2 = 6; 6 + 1 = 7). Thus A is the correct answer. Here's how it's done:

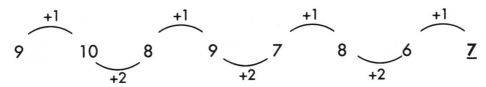

Complex Number Series. These questions are more difficult and the correct answer must be chosen from sets of two numbers. Your job is to select the correct set of two numbers.

The technique used in this type of question is to compare the first number to the third number, the second to the fourth, the third to the fifth, and so on. To make it easier, draw lines to join the numbers as you analyze the pattern. So that you won't be confused, draw the lines both above and below the numbers. (When you finish answering the questions, you may erase these lines on the question or answer sheet. It's as simple as connecting Monday to Wednesday, Wednesday to Friday, Tuesday to Thursday, and Thursday to Saturday. Then all you have to do is find the pattern within each group of numbers.

1.   7   13   8   15   10   17   13   19   17   ...   ...

A) 23 24
B) 21 22
C) 25 26
D) 27 28
E) 28 30

There two patterns in this series. Add 2 to the second, fourth, sixth, and the eight numbers and add to the first, third, fifth, seventh, and ninth numbers as follows: + 1, + 2, +3, +4, +5. B is the correct answer. Here's how it's done:

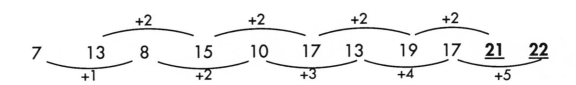

2.   1   7   2   6   4   5   7   4   ...   ...

A) 13 3
B) 15 2
C) 11 3
D) 17 2
E) 12 2

For the first, third, fifth, and seventh numbers, you must to add 1, add 2, add 3, and add 4. For the second, fourth, sixth, and eight numbers, subtract 1 each time. C is the correct answer. Here's how it's done:

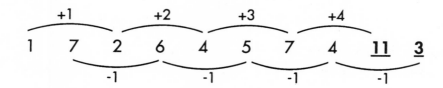

In this test, you are allotted 20 minutes to complete 24 number series questions. In other words, if you have a hard time on a particular question, skip it and go to the next number, etc. Then if you have enough time left, go back to any of the unanswered questions.

Number Series
Practice Test

1. 8 14 9 16 11 18 14 20 18 ... ...   1. ....

    A) 24 22   C) 22 30   E) 20 23
    B) 22 23   D) 16 22

2. 12 17 12 16 12 15 12   ... ...   2. ....

    A) 12 13   C) 14 12   E) 14 13
    B) 12 14   D) 13 14

3. 12 3 4 12 5 6 12 ... ...   3. ....

    A) 6 7   C) 7 8   E) 7 12
    B) 7 7   D) 12 7

4. 1 5 3 7 5 9 7 ... ...   4. ....

    A) 5 3   C) 11 15   E) 5 9
    B) 11 9   D) 9 11

5. 5 8 10 13 15 18 ... ...   5. ....

    A) 21 24   C) 20 22   E) 19 21
    B) 20 23   D) 21 23

6. 20 7 17 19 6 16 18 ... ...   6. ....

    A) 5 17   C) 17 5   E) 5 15
    B) 4 14   D) 15 17

7. 8 9 10 6 7 8 4 ... ...   7. ....

    A) 5 6   C) 6 7   E) 5 3
    B) 6 4   D) 4 5

8. 17 4 5 17 6 7 17 ... ...   8. ....

    A) 8 9   C) 17 6   E) 17 8
    B) 8 8   D) 7 8

9. 19 8 7 18 9 8 17 10 9 ... ...   9. ....

    A) 16 9   C) 18 11   E) 16 11
    B) 18 10   D) 18 9

10. 11 18 12 19 13 20 14 ... ...   10. ....

    A) 21 15   C) 14 21   E) 15 16
    B) 14 15   D) 15 21

11. 18 17 11 16 15 12 14 ... ...   11. ....

    A) 11 13   C) 13 13   E) 13 11
    B) 15 11   D) 11 15

12. 15 7 14 8 13 9 12 ... ...   12. ....

    A) 10 13   C) 12 11   E) 11 10
    B) 10 12   D) 10 11

13. 15 26 24 23 21 20 18 ... ...   13. ....

    A) 17 15   C) 16 15   E) 13 14
    B) 16 14   D) 19 17

14. 23 29 28 21 27 26 18 25 24 14 23 ... ... 14. ....

    A) 18 17   C) 13 12   E) 22 9
    B) 24 10   D) 23 21

15. 10 8 13 11 16 14 19 17 22 ... ... 15. ....

    A) 25 20   C) 20 25   E) 23 26
    B) 20 23   D) 25 28

(See the correct answers on page 142.)

Number Series Practice Test

Here's how it's done.

1. 8   14   9   16   11   18   14   20   18   **22**   **23**
    (+2 between 14, 16, 18, 20, 22; +1, +2, +3, +4, +5 between 8, 9, 11, 14, 18)

2. 12   17   12   16   12   15   12   **14**   **12**
    (−1 between 17, 16, 15, 14)

3. 12   3   4   12   5   6   12   **7**   **8**
    (+2 between 4, 6, 8; +2 between 3, 5, 7)

4. 1   5   3   7   5   9   7   **11**   **9**
    (+2 between 5, 7, 9, 11; +2 between 1, 3, 5, 7)

5. 5   8   10   13   15   18   **20**   **23**
    (+5 between 8, 13, 18, 23; +5 between 5, 10, 15, 20)

6. 20   7   17   19   6   16   18   **5**   **15**
    (−1 between 7, 6, 5; −1 between 19, 18, ...)

7. 8   9   10   6   7   8   4   **5**   **6**
    (−2 between 10, 8, 6; −2 between ...)

8. 17   4   5   17   6   7   17   **8**   **9**
    (+2 between 4, 6, 8; +2 between 5, 7, 9)

9.   19   8   7   18   9   8   17   10   9   **16**   **11**

Top arcs: +1 (8→9), +1 (9→10), +1 (10→11)
Bottom arcs: −1 (19→18), −1 (18→17), −1 (17→16)

10.   11   18   12   19   13   20   14   **21**   **15**

Top arcs: +1 (11→12), +1 (12→13), +1 (13→14), +1 (14→15)
Bottom arcs: +1 (18→19), +1 (19→20), +1 (20→21)

11.   18   17   11   16   15   12   14   **13**   **13**

Top arcs: +1 (11→12), +1 (12→13)
Bottom arcs: −1 (18→17), −1 (16→15), −1 (14→13)

12.   15   7   14   8   13   9   12   **10**   **11**

Top arcs: +1 (7→8), +1 (8→9), +1 (9→10)
Bottom arcs: −1 (15→14), −1 (14→13), −1 (13→12), −1 (12→11)

13.   15   26   24   23   21   20   18   **17**   **15**

Top arcs: −3 (24→21), −3 (21→18), −3 (18→15)
Bottom arcs: −3 (26→23), −3 (23→20), −3 (20→17)

14.   23   29   28   21   27   26   18   25   24   14   23   **22**   **9**

Top arcs: −2 (23→21), −3 (21→18), −4 (18→14), −5 (14→9)
Bottom arcs: −1 (29→28), −1 (27→26), −1 (25→24), −1 (23→22)

15.   10   8   13   11   16   14   19   17   22   **20**   **25**

Top arcs: +3 (10→13), +3 (13→16), +3 (16→19), +3 (19→22)
Bottom arcs: +3 (8→11), +3 (11→14), +3 (14→17), +3 (17→20), +3 (20→25)

Correct Answers

Number Series Test

1. 22 23		8. 8 9	
2. 14 12		9. 16 11	
3. 7 8		10. 21 15	
4. 11 9		11. 13 13	
5. 20 23		12. 10 11	
6. 5 15		13. 17 15	
7. 5 6		14. 22 9	
		15. 20 25	

Following Oral Instructions Test 18

Part D of the **470 Battery Test** consists of the *Following Oral Instructions Test* that involves directions to be given by the examiner to job applicants. When the examiner talks, you listen. If you don't, that's the end of the story; you'll fail on this exam. It's because during the test, direction for answering questions will be given orally, and if you miss those questions, the examiner will not repeat them. You better listen carefully to the instructions, and follow them.

The suggested answers to each questions are lettered. You choose the *best* answer, whichever it is.

To practice for the test, you might have a friend read the directions to you, while you mark your answers on the sample answer sheet on page 2.

You will be told to follow directions by writing in a test booklet and then on an answer sheet. The test booklet will have lines of material like the following four samples:

SAMPLE 8. 5 _____

SAMPLE 9. 1 6 4 3 7

SAMPLE 10. D B A E C

SAMPLE 11. (8__) (5__) (2__) (9__) (10__)

SAMPLE 12. (7__) [6__] (1__) [12__]

460 RCA Examination (470 Battery Test): Pages 61-146.

To practice this test, tear off page 3. Then have somebody read the instructions to you. When you are told to darken a space on the sample answer sheet, use the one on this page.

Sample Answer Sheet

1 Ⓐ Ⓑ Ⓒ Ⓓ Ⓔ	7 Ⓐ Ⓑ Ⓒ Ⓓ Ⓔ
2 Ⓐ Ⓑ Ⓒ Ⓓ Ⓔ	8 Ⓐ Ⓑ Ⓒ Ⓓ Ⓔ
3 Ⓐ Ⓑ Ⓒ Ⓓ Ⓔ	9 Ⓐ Ⓑ Ⓒ Ⓓ Ⓔ
4 Ⓐ Ⓑ Ⓒ Ⓓ Ⓔ	10 Ⓐ Ⓑ Ⓒ Ⓓ Ⓔ
5 Ⓐ Ⓑ Ⓒ Ⓓ Ⓔ	11 Ⓐ Ⓑ Ⓒ Ⓓ Ⓔ
6 Ⓐ Ⓑ Ⓒ Ⓓ Ⓔ	12 Ⓐ Ⓑ Ⓒ Ⓓ Ⓔ

Instructions to be read (the words in parentheses should not be read aloud):
You are to follow the instructions that I shall read to you. I cannot repeat them.

Look at the samples. Sample 1 has a number and a line beside it. On the line write an A. (Pause 2 seconds.) Now on the sample answer sheet, find number 5 (pause 2 seconds) and darken the space for the letter you just wrote on the line. (Pause 2 seconds.)

Look at Sample 2. (Pause slightly.) Draw a line under the third number. (Pause 2 seconds.) Now look on the sample answer sheet, find the number under which you just drew a line, and darken space B as in "baker" for that number. (Pause 5 seconds.)

Look at Sample 3. (Pause slightly.) Draw a line under the third letter in the line. (Pause 2 seconds.) Now on your answer sheet, find number 9 (pause 2 seconds) and darken the space for the letter under which you drew a line. (Pause 5 seconds.)

Look at the five circles in Sample 4. (Pause slightly.) Each circle has a number and a line in it. Write D as in "dog" on the blank in the last circle. (Pause 2 seconds.) Now on the sample answer sheet, darken the space for the number-letter combination that is in the circle you just wrote in (pause 5 seconds.)

Now look at the sample answer sheet. (Pause slightly.) You should have darkened spaces 4B, 5A, 9A, and 10D on the sample answer sheet. (If the person preparing to take the examination made any mistakes, try to help him see why he made wrong marks.)

(Data Conversion Operator, Clerk-Typist, Clerk Stenographer)

The following questions are samples of the types of questions that will be used on Examination 710. Study these questions carefully. Each question has several suggested answers. You are to decide which one is the **best answer**. Next, on the Sample Answer Sheet below, find the answer space that is numbered the same number as the question, then darken the space that is lettered the same as the answer you have selected. After you have answered all the questions, compare your answers with the ones given in the Correct Answers to Sample Questions below the Sample Answer Sheets.

Sample Questions 1 through 14 - **Clerical Aptitude**

In Sample Questions 1 through 3 below, there is a name or code in a box at the left, and four other names or codes in alphabetical or numerical order at the right. Find the correct space for the boxed name or number so that it will be in alphabetical and/or numerical order with the others and mark the letter of that space as your answer on your Sample Answer Sheet below.

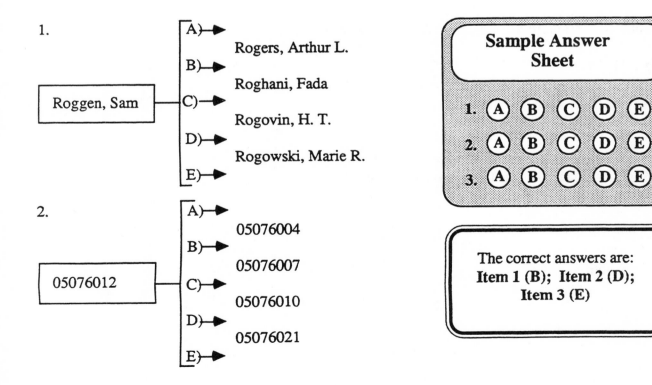

1.

A) ➤
　　　Rogers, Arthur L.
B) ➤
　　　Roghani, Fada

Roggen, Sam   C) ➤
　　　Rogovin, H. T.
D) ➤
　　　Rogowski, Marie R.
E) ➤

Sample Answer Sheet

1. Ⓐ Ⓑ Ⓒ Ⓓ Ⓔ
2. Ⓐ Ⓑ Ⓒ Ⓓ Ⓔ
3. Ⓐ Ⓑ Ⓒ Ⓓ Ⓔ

2.

A) ➤
　　　05076004
B) ➤
　　　05076007

05076012   C) ➤
　　　05076010
D) ➤
　　　05076021
E) ➤

The correct answers are:
**Item 1 (B); Item 2 (D);
Item 3 (E)**

3.

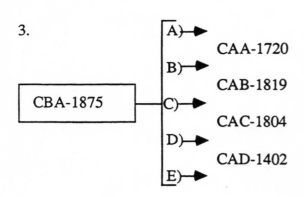

CBA-1875

A)→ CAA-1720

B)→ CAB-1819

C)→ CAC-1804

D)→ CAD-1402

E)→

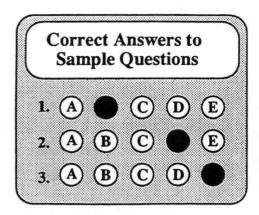

Correct Answers to Sample Questions

1. (A) ● (C) (D) (E)
2. (A) (B) (C) ● (E)
3. (A) (B) (C) (D) ●

Sample Questions 4 through 8 require you to compare names, addresses, or codes. In each line across the page, there are three names, addresses or codes that are much alike. Compare the three and decide which ones are exactly alike. On the Sample Answer Sheet at the bottom, mark the answers:

A   if **ALL THREE** names, addresses, or codes are exactly **ALIKE**
B   if only the **FIRST** and **SECOND** names, addresses, or codes are exactly **ALIKE**
C   if only the **FIRST** and **THIRD** names, addresses, or codes are exactly **ALIKE**
D   if only the **SECOND** and **THIRD** names, addresses, or codes are exactly **ALIKE**
E   if **ALL THREE** names, addresses, or codes are **DIFFERENT**

4.	Helene Bedell	Helene Beddell	Helene Beddell
5.	F. T. Wedemeyer	F. T. Wedemeyer	F. T. Wedmeyer
6.	3214 W. Beaumont St.	3214 Beaumount St.	3214 Beaumont St.
7.	BC 3105T-5	BC 3015T-5	BC 3105T-5
8.	4460327	4460327	4460327

For the next two questions, find the correct spelling of the word and darken the appropriate answer space on your Sample Answer Sheet. If none of the alternatives are correct, darken Space D.

9.   A) accomodate
     B) acommodate
     C) accommadate
     D) none of the above

10. A) manageble
     B) manageable
     C) manegeable
     D) none of the above

Sample Answer Sheet

4. (A) (B) (C) (D) (E)
5. (A) (B) (C) (D) (E)
6. (A) (B) (C) (D) (E)
7. (A) (B) (C) (D) (E)
8. (A) (B) (C) (D) (E)
9. (A) (B) (C) (D)
10. (A) (B) (C) (D)

The correct answers are:
Item 4 (D);
Item 5 (B);
Item 6 (E);
Item 7 (C);
Item 8 (A);
Item 9 (D);
Item 10 (B)

Correct Answers to Sample Questions

4. (A) (B) (C) ● (E)
5. (A) ● (C) (D) (E)
6. (A) (B) (C) (D) ●
7. (A) (B) ● (D) (E)
8. ● (B) (C) (D) (E)
9. (A) (B) (C) ●
10. (A) ● (C) (D)

For Questions 11 through 14, perform the computation as indicated in the question and find the answer among the list of alternative responses. Mark your Sample Answer Sheet A, B, C, or D for the correct answer; or, if your answer is not among these, mark E for that question.

Sample Answer Sheet

11. (A) (B) (C) (D) (E)
12. (A) (B) (C) (D) (E)
13. (A) (B) (C) (D) (E)
14. (A) (B) (C) (D) (E)

11.   32 + 26 =

   A)   69
   B)   59
   C)   58
   D)   54
   E)   none of the above

12.   57 - 15 =

   A)   72
   B)   62
   C)   54
   D)   44
   E)   none of the above

The correct answers are:
Item 11 (C); Item 12 (E);
Item 13 (B); Item 14 (A)

13.   23 x 7 =

   A)   164
   B)   161
   C)   154
   D)   141
   E)   none of the above

14.   160 / 5 =

   A)   32
   B)   30
   C)   25
   D)   21
   E)   none of the above

Correct Answers to Sample Questions

11. (A) (B) ● (D) (E)
12. (A) (B) (C) (D) ●
13. (A) ● (C) (D) (E)
14. ● (B) (C) (D) (E)

Sample Questions 15 through 22 - **Verbal Abilities**

Sample items 15 through 17 below test the ability to follow instructions. They direct you to mark a specific number and letter combination on your Sample Answer Sheet. The answers that you are instructed to mark are, for the most part, NOT in numerical sequence (·i.e., you would not use Number 1 on your answer sheet to answer Question 1; Number 2 for Question 2, etc.). Instead, you must mark the number and space specifically designated in each test question.

> **Sample Answer Sheet**
>
> 15. (A) (B) (C) (D) (E)
> 16. (A) (B) (C) (D) (E)
> 17. (A) (B) (C) (D) (E)

15. Look at the letters below. Draw a circle around the middle letter. Now, on your Sample Answer Sheet, find Number 16 and darken the space for the letter you just circled.

     R   C   H

> The correct answers are:
> **Item 15 (B); Item 16 (C);
> Item 17 (A)**

16. Draw a line under the number shown below that is more than 10 but less than 20. Find that number on your Sample Answer Sheet, and darken Space A.

     5   9   17   22

17. Add the numbers 11 and 4 and write your answer on the blank line below. Now find this number on your Sample Answer Sheet and darken the space for the second letter in the alphabet.

     _____

> **Correct Answers to
> Sample Questions**
>
> 15. (A) ● (C) (D) (E)
> 16. (A) (B) ● (D) (E)
> 17. ● (B) (C) (D) (E)

Answer the remaining Sample Test Questions on the Sample Answer Sheet in numerical sequence (i.e., Number 18 on the Sample Answer Sheet for Question 18; Number 19 for Question 19, etc.).

Sample Answer Sheet

18. Ⓐ Ⓑ Ⓒ Ⓓ
19. Ⓐ Ⓑ Ⓒ Ⓓ
20. Ⓐ Ⓑ Ⓒ Ⓓ

Select the sentence below which is most appropriate with respect to grammar, usage, and punctuation suitable for a formal letter or report.

18.   A) He should of responded to the letter by now.
      B) A response to the letter by the end of the week.
      C) The letter required his immediate response.
      D) A response by him to the letter is necessary.

In questions 19 and 20 below, you will be asked to decide what the highlighted word means.

The correct answers are:
**Item 18 (C); Item 19 (B);
Item 20 (D)**

19.   The payment was **authorized** yesterday. **Authorized** most nearly means

      A) expected
      B) approved
      C) refunded
      D) received

20.   Please **delete** the second paragraph. **Delete** most nearly means

      A) type
      B) read
      C) edit
      D) omit

Corrected Answers to Sample Questions

18. Ⓐ Ⓑ ● Ⓓ
19. Ⓐ ● Ⓒ Ⓓ
20. Ⓐ Ⓑ Ⓒ ●

In questions 21 and 22 below, you are asked to read a paragraph, then answer the question that follows it.

21. "Window Clerks working for the Postal Service have direct financial responsibility for the selling of postage. In addition, they are expected to have a thorough knowledge concerning the acceptability of all material offered by customers for mailing. Any information provided to the public by these employees must be completely accurate."

The paragraph best supports the statement that Window Clerks

A) must account for the stamps issued to them for sale

B) have had long training in other Postal Service jobs

C) must help sort mail to be delivered by carriers

D) inspect the contents of all packages offered for mailing

22. "The most efficient method for performing a task is not always easily determined. That which is economical in terms of time must be carefully distinguished from that which is economical in terms of expended energy. In short, the quickest method may require a degree of physical effort that may be neither essential nor desirable."

The paragraph best supports the statement that

A) it is more efficient to perform a task slowly than rapidly

B) skill in performing a task should not be acquired at the expense of time

C) the most efficient execution of a task is not always the one done in the shortest time

D) energy and time cannot both be considered in the performance of a single task

Sample Answer Sheet

21. Ⓐ Ⓑ Ⓒ Ⓓ
22. Ⓐ Ⓑ Ⓒ Ⓓ

The correct answers are:
Item 21 (A); Item 22 (C)

Corrected Answers to Sample Questions

21. Ⓑ Ⓒ Ⓓ
22. Ⓐ Ⓑ Ⓓ

UNITED STATES
POSTAL SERVICE

Sample Questions for Stenography
Examination 711

The sample below shows the length of material dictated. Have someone dictate the passage to you so that you can see how well prepared you are to take dictation at 80 words a minute. Each pair of lines is dictated in 10 seconds. Dictate periods, but not commas. Read the exercise with the expression the punctuation indicates.

I realize that this practice dictation is not a part of the examination	10 sec.
proper and is not to be scored.(Period) When making a study of the private	20 sec.
pension structure and its influence on turnover. the most striking feature is its	30 sec.
youth.(Period) As has been shown, the time of greatest growth began just a few years	40 sec.
ago.(Period) The influence that this growth has had on the labor market and	50 sec.
worker attitudes is hard to assess, partly because the effects have not yet fully	1 min.
evolved and many are still in the growing stage.(Period) Even so, most pension	10 sec.
plans began with much more limited gains than they give now.(Period) For example,	20 sec.
as private plans mature they grant a larger profit and a greater range of gains to	30 sec.
more workers and thereby become more important.(Period) Plans which protect accrued pension	40 sec.
credits are rather new and are being revised in the light of past trends.(Period)	50 sec.
As informal and formal information on pension plans spreads, the workers become more	2 min.
aware of the plans and their provisions increase, their impact on employee attitudes	10 sec.
and decisions will no doubt become stronger.(Period) Each year, more and more workers	20 sec.
will be retiring with a private pension, their firsthand knowledge of the benefits to	30 sec.
be gained from private pensions will spread to still active workers.(Period) Thus, workers	40 sec.
may less often view pensions as just another part of the security package	50 sec.
based on service and more often see them as unique benefits.(Period)	3 min.

On the back page, the TRANSCRIPT and WORD LIST for part of the above dictation are similar to those each competitor will receive for the dictation test. Many words have been omitted from the TRANSCRIPT. Compare your notes with it. When you come to a blank space in the TRANSCRIPT, decide which word (or words) belongs in the space. Look for the missing word in the WORD LIST. Notice what letter is printed beside the word. Write that letter in the blank. B is written in blank 1 to show how you are to record your choice. Write E if the exact answer is NOT in the WORD LIST. You may also write the word (or words) or the shorthand for it, if you wish. The same choice may belong in more than one blank.

EFFECTIVE APRIL 1993

ALPHABETIC WORD LIST

Write E if the answer is NOT listed.

at - D	make - A
attitudes - C	making - B
be - B	market - B
been - C	markets - D
began - D	marking - D
being - A	never - B
completely - A	not - D
examination - A	over - C
examine - B	part - C
examining - D	partly - D
feat - A	pension - C
feature - C	practical - C
full - B	practice - B
fully - D	private - D
greater - D	proper - C
grow - B	section - D
growing - C	so - B
had - D	still - A
has - C	structure - D
has been - B	structured - B
has had - A	to - D
has made - A	to be - C
in - C	trial - A
in part - B	turn - D
influence - A	turnover - B
labor - C	values - A
main - B	yet - C

TRANSCRIPT

I realize that this ----- dictation is ----- a ----- of the
                  B
                  1   2   3

----- ----- and is ----- ----- scored.
4   5   6   7

When ----- a ----- of the ----- ----- ----- and its
       8   9   10   11   12

----- on -----, the most striking ----- is its youth. As
13   14   15

----- shown, the time of ----- growth began just a few
16   17

years ago. The ----- that this growth ----- on the labor
                 18   19

----- and worker ----- is hard to assess, ----- because
20   21   22

the effects have not yet ----- evolved and many are ----
                          23   24

in the ----- stage....
        25

(For the next sentences there would be another WORD LIST, if the entire sample dictation were transcribed.)

You will be given an answer sheet like the sample at the left, below, on which your answers can be scored by machine. Each number on the answer sheet stands for the blank with the same number in the transcript. Darken the space below the letter that is the same as the letter you wrote in the transcript. If you have not finished writing letters in the blanks in the transcript, or if you wish to make sure that you have lettered them correctly, <u>you may continue to use your notes after you begin marking the answer sheet</u>.

Answer Sheet for Sample Transcript

Correct Answers for Sample Transcript

Analyzing Examination 710   20

I. Clerical Aptitude

Sample Questions 1 through 14

In sample questions 1 through 3, there is a name or a code in a box at the left. There are also four other names or codes in alphabetical or numeral order at the right. All you have to do is find out the appropriate place (A to D) at right, so that it will be in alphabetical and/or numerical order with the others. Mark the letter of that space as your answer on the sample answer sheet. In other words, know how to alphabetize or do numerical arrangement.

You are required by sample questions 4 through 8 to compare names, addresses, and codes. In each line across the page, there are three names, addresses, or codes that are much alike. You must compare the three and decide which ones are exactly alike or the same. You must answer A, B, C, D, or E.

On the same sample answer sheet at the right, mark the answer as follows:

A If **ALL THREE** names, addresses, or codes are exactly **ALIKE**
B If only the **FIRST** and **SECOND** names, addresses, or codes are exactly **ALIKE**
C If only the **FIRST** and **THIRD** names, addresses, or codes are exactly **ALIKE**
D If only the **SECOND** and **THIRD** names, addresses, or codes are exactly **ALIKE**
E If **ALL THREE** names, addresses, or codes are **DIFERENT**

To make it easier for me to answer the questions, I developed my own system of memorization and comparison. Here is my code, which is easy to remember.

A = 123 (first, second, and third alike)
B = 12 (first and second alike)
C = 13 (first and third alike)
D = 23 (second and third alike)
E = 0 (all different)

(Note: This examination is for Data Conversion Operator, Clerk-Typist, and Clerk-Stenographer)

It is to be emphasized that you'll look for names, addresses, and codes that are ALIKE, except answer E. In other words, in answering E, you look for those names, and addresses, and codes that are all different. Memorize and use my code for this kind of test.

Examples:

4. Helene Bedell	Helene Beddell	Helene Beddell
5. F. T. Wedemeyer	F. T. Wedemeyer	F. T. Wedmeyer
6. 3214 W. Beaumont St.	3214 Beaumount St.	3214 Beaumont St.
7. BC 3105T-5	BC 3015T-5	BC 3105T-5
8. 4460327	4460327	4460327

General Rule: In comparing names or numbers, compare the first column with the second column, then the second with the third. So that you won't get confused, place a minus sign (- for different) or a plus sign (+ for alike) between the first column and the second column and between the second column and the third column. These plus and minus signs are my own codes, not the Postal Service's.

Example 1: (No. 4)

Helen Bedell   -   Helene Beddell   +   Helene Beddell

The code is 23 (second and third alike), so the answer is D.

In the above example, the first and second columns are different (the first column has one *d*, while the second column has a double *d*) and the second and third columns are alike (both have a double *d*). You must not compare the third and first columns to see whether they are different or alike. In short, the third and first columns are different. Hence, the answer is D (code 23).

Example 2: (No. 5)

F. T. Wedemeyer   +   F. T. Wedemeyer   -   F. T. Wedmeyer

In the above example, the first and second columns are alike (with a plus sign) and the second and third columns are different, the third column having only three *e*'s (with a minus sign). You don't need to compare the third column with the first. It is understood that they are different.

The code is 12 (first and second columns are alike). The correct answer is B.

Example 3: (No.6)

3214 W. Beaumont St.   -   3214 Beaumount St.   -   3214 Beaumont St.

If the first and the second columns are different (with a minus sign), and the third and second columns, are different, the code is 0 (all are different). As you can see, the first column has a direction, which is W (West), while the second and third columns have different spellings of streets. The second street is spelled "Beau*mount*) while the third is spelled "Beau*mont*." The correct answer is E, the code being 0.

Example 4: (No. 7)

BC 3105T-5   -   BC 3015T-5   -   BC 3105T-5

In the above example, the first and second columns are different (with a minus sign) and the second and third are different (with a minus sign). You still need to compare the third column with the first, to see if there is any similarity or difference. The first and third columns have the same letters and figures. So the code is 13 (first and third are alike). Therefore, the correct answer is C.

Example 5: (No.) 8

4460327   +   4460327   +   4460327

As you can see, the first and second columns (with a plus sign) are alike and the second and third columns are alike (with a plus sign). Since they are alike, the code is 123 (first, second, and third columns are alike). So the correct answer is A.

As explained in the above examples, you have to know which columns are alike.

After writing the answers, you should erase the plus and minus signs you made on the question sheet. However, if you have no more time to do it, then leave them alone.

Spelling

(See **Spelling Techniques**.)

For the next two questions, find the correct spelling of the word and darken the appropriate answer space on your sample answer sheet. If none of the alternatives are correct, darken Space D.

9.
A) accomodate
B) acommodate
C) accommadate
D) none of the above

10.
A) manageble
B) manageable
C) manegeable
D) none of the above

If you are practicing speed reading, you can glance at the words from A to D in a snap in the above example (question 9). You can immediately disregard A, B, and C because merely by looking at them you'll know they are awkwardly spelled. Pronounce the words to yourself and you'll know what I mean. D is the correct answer. As to question 10, B is the correct answer. The words *manage* and *able* are combined.

Arithmetic

For questions 11 through 14, perform the computation as indicated in the question and find the answer among the list of alternative responses. Mark your sample answer sheet A, B, C, or D for the correct answer; or if your answer is not among these, mark E for that question.

11.

32 + 26 =

A) 69
B) 59
C) 58
D) 54
E) none of the above

12.

57 - 15 =

A) 72
B) 62
C) 54
D) 44
E) none of the above

13.

23 x 7 =

A) 164
B) 161
C) 154
D) 141
E) none of the above

14.

160/5 =

A) 32
B) 30
C) 25
D) 21
E) none of the above

Now, for the analyses of questions 11 to 14.

You don't need to be an Einstein to score high on arithmetic tests. What you need to do is use some techniques and try them out with your own biocomputer. The Postal Service gives only simple mathematical problems, and you can surely make a perfect score if you have enough time to answer the questions. The problem is that time is limited, so you have to use some techniques to beat the system.

11. Addition problem (32 + 26):

$$\begin{array}{r} 32 \\ + 26 \\ \hline 58 \end{array}$$

The numbers 32 and 26 are to be added together. The solution to the addition, 58 in this case, is called the "sum."

If the problem is as simple as this, without any carrying, you can simply add the numbers mentally from left to right—not

---

Sample Answer Sheet

11. (A) (B) (C) (D) (E)
12. (A) (B) (C) (D) (E)
13. (A) (B) (C) (D) (E)
14. (A) (B) (C) (D) (E)

The correct answers are:
Item 11 (C); Item 12 (E);
Item 13 (B); Item 14 (A)

Correct Answers to Sample Questions

11. (A) (B) ● (D) (E)
12. (A) (B) (C) (D) ●
13. (A) ● (C) (D) (E)
14. ● (B) (C) (D) (E)

from right to left, which is taught in school. It's much simpler and faster from left to right.

12. Subtraction problem (57 - 15):

```
  57
- 15
  42
```

The number 15 is to be subtracted from 57. Simply deduct 1 from 5 and 5 from 7 (starting from the left, because you don't need borrowing. If you need to borrow, then start from right to left).

13. In the multiplication problem (23 x 7):

```
   23
  x 7
  161
```

In a simple multiplication problem like this, try to work mentally to save time. (When you write it down, you spend several seconds. Think to yourself, 7 x 3 = 21 (just remember 1 and carry 2): 7 x 2 = 14 + 2 = 16. Put the 1 after 16 and the answer is 161 or B.

14. Division problem (160/5):

5/160 = 32

The division given in the sample test is as simple as this, but remember, there's a time limit. You can do the division mentally, too by dividing 16 by 5 = 3 (with the extra 1). Place the extra 1 before 0 and the answer is 10. Dividing 10 by 5 = 2. Put 2 after 3 and the answer is 32 or A.

*(Also see **Numbers and Mathematics,** and **Strategies for Standardized Tests,** Solving Mathematics Problems.)*

II. Verbal Abilities

Sample questions 15 through 22

Sample questions 15 through 17 below tests the ability to follow instructions. They direct you to mark a specific number and letter combination on your sample answer sheet. The answers that you are instructed to mark are, for the most part, NOT in numerical sequence (i.e., you would not use number 1 on your answer sheet to answer question 1; number 2 for question 2, etc.). Instead, you must mark the number and space specifically designated in each test question, as specified in the following sample questions:

15. Look at the letters below. Draw a circle around the middle letter. Now, on your sample answer sheet, find Number 16 and darken the space for the letter you just circled.

R   C   H

So you darken the circle with letter C on number 16. In other words, you are not told to darken the letter C on number 15. The answer to question 15 is to be marked on number 16. So number 16 has C as the answer. How about the answer to number 15? Just continue.

16. Draw a line under the number shown below that is more than 10 but less than 20. Find that number on your sample sheet, and darken space A.

5   9   17   22

So the answer to question number 16 is to be marked on question number 17, which is A. So darken space A on Number 17. In other words, the answer to question number 16 is A, which happened to be on number 17.

17. Add the numbers 11 and 4 and write your answer on the blank line below. Now find this number on your sample answer sheet and darken the space for the second letter in the alphabet.

_____

Add 11 and 4 and the answer is 15. So find number 15 on the sample answer sheet. Darken the second letter in the alphabet, which happens to be B. So darken space B on number 15.

Sample Answer Sheet

15. (A) (B) (C) (D) (E)
16. (A) (B) (C) (D) (E)
17. (A) (B) (C) (D) (E)

The correct answers are:
**Item 15 (B);   Item 16 (C);
Item 17 (A)**

Correct Answers to Sample Questions

15. (A) ● (C) (D) (E)
16. (A) (B) ● (D) (E)
17. ● (B) (C) (D) (E)

In other words, the darkening of spaces started from number 16, then to number 17 and back to number 15. As you can see, the questions are easy to answer but the Postal Service is trying to confuse you and me!

Answer the remaining sample test questions on the sample answer sheet in numerical sequence (i.e., number 18 on the sample answer sheet for question 18; number 19 for question 19, etc.).

Select the sentence below that is the most appropriate with respect to grammar, usage, and punctuation for a formal letter or report.

18.

A) He should be of responded to the letter by now.
B) A response to the letter by the end of the week.
C) The letter required his immediate response.
D) A response by him to the letter is necessary.

If you analyze the sentences, you'll see the question A is awkward and question B is incomplete. So neither of them is the answer. C is grammatically correct. D, although a complete sentence, seems to be awkward, too. So C is the answer. Darken space C.

In questions 19 and 20 below, you'll be asked to decide what the highlighted word means:

19. The payment was **authorized** yesterday. **Authorized** means

---

Sample Answer Sheet

18. Ⓐ Ⓑ Ⓒ Ⓓ
19. Ⓐ Ⓑ Ⓒ Ⓓ
20. Ⓐ Ⓑ Ⓒ Ⓓ

The correct answers are:
Item 18 (C); Item 19 (B); Item 20 (D)

Corrected Answers to Sample Questions

18. Ⓐ Ⓑ ● Ⓓ
19. Ⓐ ● Ⓒ Ⓓ
20. Ⓐ Ⓑ Ⓒ ●

A) expected
B) approved
C) refunded
D) received

In an instance, you'll know that *approved* (B) is the answer. Why? Because *expected, refunded,* and *received,* mean something else.

20. Please *delete* the second paragraph. *Delete* most nearly means

A) type
B) read
C) edit
D) omit

The letters *de* before *lete* indicate a negative action. That is, *de* means *from* which may mean take it out or away from something. So naturally, omit or D is the correct answer.

In questions 21 and 22 below, you are asked to read a paragraph, then answer the question that follows it:

21. "Window clerks working for the Postal Service have direct financial responsibility for the selling of postage. In addition, they are expected to have a thorough knowledge concerning the acceptability of all material offered by customers for mailing. Any information provided to the public by these employees must be completely accurate."

The paragraph best supports the statement that window clerks

A) must account for stamps issued to them for sale
B) have had long training in other Postal Service jobs
C) must help sort mail to be delivered by carriers
D) inspect the contents of all packages offered for mailing

(Reading Comprehension)

(See **Reading Comprehension**, page 177.)

In choosing answers to reading comprehension questions, look for the main idea in the statement. In question 20, look for the main idea in the statement "Window clerks...." If you read it carefully, you'll see that the main point in the paragraph is the financial responsibility for the selling of postage. Hence, "A) must account for the stamps issued to them for sale" best supports the statement about Window Clerks.

22. "The most efficient method for performing a task is not always easily determined. That which is economical in terms of time must be carefully distinguished from that which is economical in terms of expended energy. In short, the quickest method may require a degree of physical effort that may be neither essential nor desirable."

The paragraph best supports the statement that

A) it is more efficient to perform a task slowly than rapidly

B) skill in performing a task should not be acquired at the expense of time

C) the most efficient execution of a task is not always the one done in the shortest time

D) energy and time cannot both be considered in the performance of a single task

If you analyze the statement in question 22, the sentence "the most efficient method for performing a task is not always easily determined" clearly indicates that it is the main idea in the statement. As you'll note, there's the word *efficient* in the first sentence of the statement and there's also the word *efficient* in two answer choices: "A) it is more efficient to perform a task slowly than rapidly" and "C) the most efficient execution of a task is not always the one done in the shortest time." So the correct answer is from either these two choices. And it is. C is the correct answer.

Sample Answer Sheet

21. Ⓐ Ⓑ Ⓒ Ⓓ
22. Ⓐ Ⓑ Ⓒ Ⓓ

The correct answers are:
Item 21 (A); Item 22 (C)

Corrected Answers to Sample Questions

21. ● Ⓑ Ⓒ Ⓓ
22. Ⓐ Ⓑ ● Ⓓ

Typing Test

As an applicant, you must show that you can type forty words per minute for five minutes with no more than two errors. Space, paragraph, spell, punctuate, capitalize, and begin and end each line precisely as shown in the exercise.

In the examination, you will have five minutes in which to copy the test exercise. When you complete the exercise, simply double space and begin again. In the test you must type at least sixteen lines to be eligible in speed. At that minimum speed, your paper should not have more than two errors. The number of errors permitted increases with the number of words typed.

Below is an example of the type of material that appears on the typing test:

> This is an example of the type of material which will be presented to you as the actual typewriting examination. Each competitor will be required to typewrite the practice material exactly as it appears on the copy. You are to space, capitalize, punctuate, spell, and begin and end each line exactly as it is presented in the copy. Each time you reach the end of the paragraph you should begin again and continue to practice typing the practice paragraph on scratch paper until the examiner tells you to stop. You are advised that it is more important to type accurately than to type rapidly.

I must repeat that to be a clerk-typist or mark-up clerk, automated, you should type at least forty words per minute and pass the last part of the exam: the typing test. I usually type fifty to sixty words per minute accurately, so whenever I take this typing test, and I have already made one mistake, I try to increase my speed to type more words. For example, when I took an automated mark-up clerk exam in Michigan (including the typing test), I increased my speed as soon as I knew I had made one error. I typed about sixty words per minute with only two errors. You are allowed more errors if you type more than forty words per minute.

Techniques

Try to be at the examination room at least thirty minutes before the test time. Select a typewriter that you like; remember, it will be your word processor, which will produce at least forty words per minute.

From the looks of the machine, you'll know whether you like it and it likes you. Check out the size and shape. Place your fingers in the proper places; see if they fit the keys. See if all the parts work: release the margins and make new ones, especially for the paragraph. How about the spaces? Is the typewriter set for the single space? How about the ribbon? Is it new? If the typewriter is an electric one, it might have a film ribbon, which is no problem.

Gentle Touch

Now feel the keys; be gentle with them. Feel how they react to your touch; touch every part, including the carriage return. Do you like the way it responds to your touch?

Probably, you are now breathing fast. Try typing some words, slowly. Then make a few strong strokes; see if the keys respond quickly to your strokes, or if they like your touch. Now you know your partner; you know which parts are sensitive and which aren't. You know where to touch it and when to touch it.

Now you are ready for your test. Concentrate hard and don't look at any other typewriter. Stare at your typewriter as if it's staring at you too. Say to your partner, "We'll make it."

Take Your Time

When the examiner says "Start!" don't rush and type at full speed. Although your fingers may be trembling and you may be breathing fast, make your every move correct and don't let your fingers slip from the keys. Be gentle with them, and as you become familiar with your typewriter's sensitiveness, you'll know when and how fast to make your move. Little by little, as you make your strokes, you'll notice that you are moving *with* your typewriter.

Little by little, you can increase your speed, but try to be accurate. You have now regained your composure and confidence.

Type in small groups of letters: example: ma-te-ri-al, ex-am-in-a-tion, par-a-graph, im-por-tune. (Forget the hyphen; it's invisible.) Now you are on the way to your destiny!

Answer Want Ads

To become an expert in taking typing tests, answer want ads for typists in the newspapers and tell the advertiser you want to take a typing test. Take the tests for practice only. Make it a routine until you don't get nervous anymore.

When the time comes for your postal typing test, tell yourself, "This is *not* a test. This is the real thing. This is it!"

CB Test 714

## 21

(Data Conversion Operator)

SAMPLE ITEMS FOR COMPUTER BASED TEST 714

The CB 714 is a computer administered and scored exam. Applicants are assisted with the start-up of the exam and with the exam instructions. **You do <u>not</u> need prior experience on a computer terminal to take this test.**

The exam contains a list of alphanumeric postal data entry items just as you see in the sample items below. Applicants must demonstrate that they can type these items on the computer terminal at the following rate(s) based on the requirements of the position. The lower level passing rate is 5 correct lines per minute. The higher level passing rate is 7 correct lines per minute. Credit is given only for correctly typed lines. Practice for the exam by typing the sample provided below.

<u>Type each line as shown in the exercise</u>, beginning with the first column. You may use lower-case or capital letters when typing the sample exercise. When you reach the end of a line, single space and begin typing the next line. If you reach the end of the sample items in the first column, continue with the items in the second column. If you finish both columns, simply begin again with the first column and continue to type until the five minutes have elapsed.

See whether you can copy the entire Sample Test once in a five minute timing. Now count the number of lines you typed correctly and divide this number by five to determine your per minute score. Correctly typing only the items in column 1 is approximately equal to typing 5 correct lines per minute. Correctly typing all of the items in both columns is approximately equal to typing 7 correct lines per minute.

In the exam you will have five minutes in which to type the test material. Keep in mind that in order to pass the test you must type both rapidly and accurately.

(See Data Conversion Operator, page 60.)

SAMPLE TEST COPY

```
  4.90 STEERING DAMPER          18.25 DOWN SPRING
16.55 REAR DOOR LATCH           3.10 UC GASKET
23.80 TIMING CHAIN            35.45 ROCKER ARM
8721 8906                      4973 5261
2013 2547                      6057 7382
5972 6841                      2783 4195
HANOVER RD. 600 - 699          GREENBRIAR DR. 1100 - 1399
ARKANSAS AVE. 4000 - 4199      MADISON ST. 3700 - 3799
SO. MAIN ST. 1200 - 1299       BRUNSWICK AVE. 8100 - 8199
CAPITOL DR. 500 - 599          INDUSTRIAL RD. 2300 - 2499
L ON MAPLEWOOD PL.
RETRACE TO 421
R ON MOHICAN TO TOWER
4478267 LSM/LSM
4478271 MPLSM
4478289 EGR SECONDARY
KNIGHT, J.R. 04/17/67
CHARLES, S.M. 11/19/68
JEFFERSON, W.A. 08/20/69
SPRINGFIELD 07215
GREENSBORO 07098
LEXINGTON 07540
FOURTH CLASS 363
INTN. SECTION 27
200 BOX 10
```

EFFECTIVE DATE FEBRUARY 1992

Vocabulary, Spelling & Reading Comprehension

22

In several post office examinations, you'll answer questions pertaining to vocabulary, spelling, and reading comprehension. For instance, in the meaning of words test, you'll be asked what a word or a phrase means. In each question, a word or a phrase is printed in italics. Five other words or phrases (lettered A, B, C, D, and E) are given as possible meanings. You must pick only one correct answer.

Example:

The letter was *short. Short* means most nearly

A) tall
B) wide
C) brief

D) heavy
E) dark

A: Vocabulary Systems

You can use various techniques or systems for answering questions on the meaning of words. Let me discuss them with you one by one.

1. The Dissecting Words System

We can dissect words as medical students dissect frogs or human bodies by studying their prefixes, suffixes, and roots.

Here are some examples: (Taken from my book *How to Teach Your Child.*)

Native English Prefixes and Roots

Prefix	Meaning	Root	Example
fore	ahead, before	cast	**fore**cast
mis	not correct	lead	**mis**lead
under	below	estimate	**under**estimate
a	in, on, at	wake	**a**wake
in	in, into	doors	**in**doors
out	outside, beyond	distance	**out**distance
un	not	sure	**un**sure

Native English Suffixes and Roots

Suffix	Meaning	Root	Example
ly	like when, how	kind	kind**ly**
		week	week**ly**
er	one who, that which	box	box**er**
hood	state of	nation	nation**hood**
less	without, lacking	shoe	shoe**less**
some	inclined to	hand	hand**some**

Latin Prefixes

Prefix	Meaning	Example
ab	away from	**ab**sent
ad	to, forward	**ad**vance
de	away from	**de**part
dis	apart, opposite of	**dis**assemble
in, im,	not	**in**appropriate
		improper
ir, il)		**ir**regular
		illegitimate
pre	before	**pre**cede
re	again, back	**re**turn
sub	under, below	**sub**marine

Latin Suffixes

Suffix	Meaning	Example
an, ian	one who	Iran**ian**
ment	act of	entertain**ment**

ive	of, relating to	objec**tive**
ic	like,	ton**ic**
	having to do with	
ary, ory	relating to	diction**ary**
		cremat**ory**

Latin Roots

Root	*Meaning*	*Example*
dict	tell	pre**dict**
mit	send	trans**mit**
script	write	tran**script**
vers, vert	turn	re**verse**, di**vert**
voke	call	pro**voke**

Greek Stems or Word Parts

Word Part	*Meaning*	*Example*
auto	self	**auto**matic
bio	life	**bio**graphy
micro	small	**micro**scope
phone	sound	micro**phone**
tele	far off	**tele**phone
thermo	heat	**thermo**stat
meter	measurement	speedo**meter**

In studying the roots of words, we must know that thousands of English words have Greek or Latin stems or origins. Not only that. We also import words just as we import cars from Japan or from European Europe. The word *pizza* is Italian, and the word *vodka* is Russian.

We use these foreign stems and other prefixes and suffixes in analyzing words. We can divide words into different parts to learn their meaning. The secret is knowing *word keys.*

Here's an example of word keys: *-ar, -er, -r.* Any one of these suffixes means *one who* or *that which.*

Examples:

compute*r* — a machine that computes
barbe*r* — one who cuts hair.
Kille*r* — one who kills.

2. The "It Makes the Difference" System

With what I call the *it makes the difference system,* you select the answer that looks different from the other four answers. Let me give you an example: *red, white, blue,* and *green.* The possible answer is *green,* because it's the different one, not being in the American flag. In the case of the sample question above, the words *tall* and *wide* seem to be similar and the words *heavy* and *dark* seem to be alike too. The word *brief* looks different from them: it stands alone. So the correct answer is *brief.*

3. The Elimination System

In selecting the answer, especially when you don't know the *correct* one, you must use the so-called *elimination* system. That is, eliminate the wrong choices one by one, starting with the word that is the least likely answer, until only one word or phrase is left. It's like Bob Barker announcing five finalists in the **Miss Planet Earth** contest. He starts with the fourth runner-up. When the second runner-up is named, only two contestants remain. When the first runner-up is announced, there's no more choice; the remaining finalist is automatically proclaimed the most beautiful girl in the universe!

Miss Planet Earth Contest

B: Spelling Techniques

Find the correct spelling of the word and darken the proper answer space. If no suggested spelling is correct, darken *D*.

A) careacteristic   C) cheracteristic

B) characteristic   D) none of these

If you are practicing speed reading, you can glance at the words from *A* to *D* in a snap. You can immediately disregard *A* and *C* because merely by looking at them you'll know they are awkwardly spelled. Pronounce the words to yourself and you'll know what I mean. *B* is the correct answer. Since *B* is the correct answer, just disregard *D*.

How to Be a Super Speller

You can be a super speller when you have a good vocabulary, so you must also study *prefixes*, *suffixes*, and *roots*. You can also memorize words which are difficult to spell. However, the best way to be good in spelling is to study some rules of spelling. There are some rules, but there are also exceptions to these rules.

Verbs That End in *-ize* or *-ise*

Thousands of words end in *-ize*. They are very common words such as antagon*ize*, colon*ize*, mechan*ize*, American*ize*, victim*ize*, util*ize*, and individual*ize*.

As you study verbs that end in *-ize* or *-ise*, you can make your own rules. For instance, you can say that after the letter *m* and *n*, use only *-ize*, never *ise*. (See above samples.)

There are only a few verbs that end in *-ise*, so it's better to spend your time on them. Some of the most confusing words are ad*vise*, super*vise*, advert*ise*, desp*ise*, rev*ise*, dev*ise*, surpr*ise*, chast*ise*, improv*ise*, and exerc*ise*.

You can make a list of verbs that end in either *-ize* or *-ise*. If you are in doubt about the correct spelling, consult the dictionary. If you have a computer, run the disk containing your letter or report or manuscript with **Word Plus** or **Perfect Speller,** the computer's spelling bee champions.

To Double or Not to Double

Often you may be confused about words that should (or should not) have double *s*, *r*, *p*, *l*, or *n*. Again, here are some rules to follow:

Double *s* (ss): Examples: *mis*spell, *mis*spend, *mis*state, *dis*similar, *dis*satisfy.

As you can see, all the examples contain double *s*. *Mis-* is attached to the front of a word to make it *negative*. So when you attach *mis-* to the word *spell*, it will contain a double *s*. However, some words that start with *mis-* have no double *s*. The reason is simple: the words that *mis-* is attached to *do not* start with an *s*. Examples: *mis*guide, *mis*judge, *mis*interpret, *mis*inform.

The prefix *dis-* attached to the front of a word makes it *negative*, too. Examples: *dis*comfort, *dis*connect, *dis*continue, *dis*honor, *dis*-simulate, *dis*satisfy. When we connect *dis-* to the beginning of a word that starts with letter *s* to make it negative, the new word contains double *s (ss)*. Example: *dis*satisfy.

Double *n (nn)*: To make a *noun* out of an *adjective*, we just add the suffix *-ness* to the adjective. Examples: malicious*ness*, mad*ness*, ugli*ness*, short*ness*.

Remember that when you attach the suffix *-ness* to an adjective that -ends with an *n*, the newly formed noun contains double *n*. Examples: drunken*ness*, thin*ness*.

Double *l (ll)*: To make an *adverb* out of an *adjective* we just add *-ly*. Examples: adverse becomes adverse*ly*; hot becomes hot*ly*; *dynastic* (from dynasty) becomes dynastical*ly*.   When we connect *-ly* to an *adjective* that already ends in *l*, the word then has a double *l (ll)*. Examples: beautiful — beautiful*ly*; *masterful — masterfully*; sexual — sexual*ly*.

Double *p (pp)* or *r (rr)*. In the case of words that should have double *p*, *r*, or *s*, it's better just to memorize them. Remember: emba*rr*ass-ment, ha*r*assment, Mississi*pp*i.

Combinations *ie* or *ei*: These pairs of vowels are really confusing. Sometimes, you can't figure out which comes first. Of these two combinations, *ie* is the more common. Examples: bel*ie*f, rel*ie*f, sh*ie*k. Samples of words with *ei*: rec*ei*pt, rec*ei*ve, dec*ei*ve, perc*ei*ve.

Generally, the letter *c* is followed by *-ei* instead of *-ie*. Here are rules to remember:

1. If the letter *c* is pronounced as an *s*, as in receive, it is followed by *-ei*, not *-ie*.

2. In certain words, *-ei* is used for the long *e* sound, even if the preceding letter is not *c*. Examples: s*ei*ze, l*ei*sure, sh*ei*k, prot*ei*n, caff*ei*ne.

3. Otherwise, *-ie* is often used in long *e* syllables. Examples: bel*ie*ve, rel*ie*ve, ach*ie*ve.

Double *r (rr)*, *t (tt)* or other *double consonants*: Sometimes we don't know whether or not to *double* the consonant. (As you probably know, the vowels are the letters *a, e, i, o,* and *u*. *Y* is sometimes used as a vowel. All the other letters of the alphabet are consonants.)

Rules to remember in doubling a letter:

The word must end in a *single* consonant, Examples: refer — referred; compel — compelled. In the case of the word desist, *t* is not doubled because the word ends in two consonants *(st)*.

2. The word must be accented on the last syllable. Example: commit — committed, committing, etc.

3. You must double the *consonant* when adding a suffix that starts with a *vowel,* so long as the accent on the *last* syllable of the original word remains. Example: occur — occurrence. However, *pre*fer becomes preference because the accent goes back to the *first* syllable; hence, the *r* is not doubled.

One-Syllable Words

What do we do with single-syllable words? Do we double the consonant at the end of the word when we add a suffix? Certainly, yes. The reason is simple. The rules state that when a word ends in a *single* consonant preceded by a *single* vowel (not two or more) and the *accent* is on the *final* syllable, the consonant must be *doubled.* Hence the consonant is always *doubled* in a *one-syllable* word. Why? Because there's no choice! The *first* and *last* (only) syllable receives the accent. However, fix — fixed and play — played are exceptions.

Examples: drag — dragged; drug — drugged; drop-dropped; beg — begged; run — runner.

Addition of Suffixes

Are you sometimes confused when you add suffixes such as *-ly,* *-ness,* and *-ment* to words that end in *e?*

When we add suffixes *-ly,* *-ness,* and *-ment* to words that end in *e,* we retain the *e.* Examples: sincere — sincerely; immediate — immediately; measure — measurement.

However, when we add *-ment* to words that end in *-dge,* the final *e* is dropped. Example: judge — judgment.

The Addition of *-able*

What do we do when we add *-able* to words that end in *e?* Do we drop the *e* or not?

Rules to remember:

1. The final *e* should be retained when words end in *-ce* or *-ge.* The purpose is to keep the *c* and *g* "soft" before the *a* in *-able.* Examples: notice — noticeable; manage — manageable.

2. The final *e* should be dropped when words end in *e* preceded by any other consonant. Examples: machine — machin*able*; like — lik*able*.

3. If a word ends in an *e* preceded by a consonant, the final *e* is dropped before any suffix that starts with a vowel. Examples: drive — driv*ing*; like — lik*ing*; arrive — arriv*ing*; *live* — *living*.

4. *Y* is considered a vowel when it is used as a suffix. Therefore, the final *e*, when preceded by a consonant, is dropped before suffix *-y* is added. Example: stone — ston*y*.

The -Able or *-Ible* Suffixes

Probably these two suffixes are the most confusing in the English language.

Things to remember:

1. There are more *-able* than *-ible* words. So when in doubt, use *able*. It's that simple.

2. *-Able* is added to a complete word. On the other hand, *-ible* is added to a root that is *not* a complete word. Examples: admit — admit*table*; regret — regret*table*; but divis- — divis*ible*.

3. Drop *e* and add *-ible* if a word ends in *-nce*, *-rce* or *uce*. Examples: convince — convin*cible*; produce — produ*cible*; force — for*cible*.

4. *-Ible* is used when a root word ends in *-ns*. Examples: offense — offen*sible*; defense — defen*sible*.

5. Roots that end in *-miss* take *-ible*. Examples: dismiss — dis*missible*.

No Rules; Just Memorize

We cannot apply rules in the spelling of many words. Some words are just hard to spell. First, you must know the root and its meaning; then you *may* know the correct spelling. If you cannot do this, then just memorize the word and associate it with things you know, and it will be easier to store in and retrieve from your own biocomputer. When you are at a loss for spelling certain words, look them up in the dictionary.

Some English experts say the best spellers seem to be those who "take pictures" of words. A good speller, they say, has seen a word correctly and remembers how it's supposed to look. That's one good reason why you should do a lot of reading!

C: Reading Comprehension

In order to make a high score on reading comprehension, you must improve in reading. You should be able to read fast, but you must also comprehend or understand what you have read.

When you read a certain paragraph, just pick out the main ideas; formulate questions; relate the material to whatever is already known; and locate and understand key words or key phrases.

You don't have to read word by word but phrase by phrase. For instance, a word-by-word beginning reader may read the following sentence as follows:

1. Iran's *Khomeini* **declares** *war* **with** *U.S.*

To avoid the word-by-word method, group the words in pair as follows:

2. Iran's Khomeini *declares war* **with U.S.**

This grouping of words into twos can remind you of **Laverne and Shirley.**

To improve your reading, however, divide the sentence into the following groups of three words:

3. Iran's Khomeini declares *war with U.S.*

In order not to forget this example, just think of **Three's Company.**

However, we don't use only the two-word or three-word technique. Sometimes we have to make a larger group into a phrase. So in reading, we have the so-called duplex speed, triplex speed, and multiplex speed for two-word, three-word, and many-word phrases.

In reading, speed and concentration are essential. You have to ignore your surroundings. During a test, don't listen to what your neighbor is asking you, even if you imagine that he is John Travolta or she is Victoria Principal. Not this time! You have an appointment with destiny!

We have two kinds of vision: *macular* and *peripheral vision.* In reading a phrase such as this:

We live to●die someday

the eyes focus on an invisible black spot in the middle of the phrase; *macular vision* enables you to see clearly the word or words in the center of the phrase. On the other hand, *peripheral vision* lets you see, though less clearly, the words at ends of the phrase.

To help give you an idea of the sharpness of your peripheral vision, a group of words is arranged below in the form of a pyramid. Fix your eyes at the top of an imaginary line that goes down the middle of the pyramid. Move your eyes *vertically*, not *horizontally*.

A
•
woman
•
believed
•
to be the oldest
•
resident of Pennsyl-
•
vania died at Somerset
•
State Hospital at age 111.
•
Fairy Florence Pile, a native
•
of Jefferson Township, Somerset
•
County, had been a resident of the
•
state mental hospital institution for
•
ninety-nine years before her death.

Pittsburgh Post Gazette

If you were able to read more than half of the above sentence without any *horizontal* eye movements, you should practice reading newspaper stories, for they have narrower columns. It is a good exercise for your eyes. If possible, read the columns by making only two fixations on each line. Make two thin imaginary lines vertically down the column; in this way you can keep the two fixations. The column will look something like this:

The Hertfordshire County
• •
(England) Civil Defense Com-
• •
mittee has appointed Joseph
• •
Brady of Shenley village to the
• •
post of Local Contingency Warn-
• •
ing Supervisor.

"In the event of a nuclear war,
Mr. Brady's job is to run down
the main street of the village
banging a trash can lid," said a
Defense Committee spokesman.
"We realize that a whistle is the
ideal instrument for this purpose; however, you can make a
lot of noise with a trash can lid in
four minutes."

Kansas City Times

Reading

"The secretarial profession is a very old one and has increased in importance with the passage of time. In modern times, the vast expansion of business and industry has greatly increased the need and opportunities for secretaries, and for the first time in history their number has become large."

The quotation best supports the statement that the secretarial profession

A) is older than business and industry
B) demands higher training than it did formerly
C) did not exist in ancient times
D) has greatly increased in size

The Main Idea

Get the main idea of the quotation. Look for key words. The quotation says that the secretarial profession is a very old one, but it does not say it is older than business and industry, so the correct answer is not A. It does not say that it now demands higher training, so B is not the answer. It does not say that it did not exist in ancient times, so C is not the correct answer. As you can see, the word *increased* (the key word) is mentioned twice, and the phrase *has become large* (which means *increased)* is mentioned once. So D, *has greatly increased in size,* is the correct choice.

In choosing the correct answer, look for the main idea or the key words. However, sometimes the person who prepares the questions will use words in a statement that are also in the quotation. This is to confuse you so that you may choose it as the possible answer, even if it is not correct. So in looking for the *key words,* use your own interpretation. Sometimes the answer or the words used in a statement *(A or* whatever) are not mentioned directly in the quotation. You have to interpret what the quotation means or expresses.

Cleaner, Custodian & Custodial Laborer Test   23

The positions of cleaner, custodian, and custodial laborer are exclusively for veterans and present employees. Only individuals entitled to veteran preference are eligible to take this entrance exam.

Cleaner

Grade: L-2

Salary Range: $21,923 - $34,348 (COLA included)

Persons Eligible to Apply: Open to veterans only

Examination Requirements: All applicants will be required to take Examination M/N 911 to test their ability to interpret and follow instructions. The test and completion of the forms will require approximately 1 1/2 hours. Competitors will be rated on a scale of 100 and must score 70 to be eligible.

Duties: Performs light and heavy manual cleaning and housekeeping at a postal facility.

Custodian

Grade: L-2

Salary Range $21,923 - $34,348 (COLA included)

Persons Eligible to Apply: Open to veterans only

Examination Requirements: Applicants will be required to take Examination M/N 911 to test their ability to interpret and follow instructions.

Duties: Performs heavier manual cleaning, housekeeping, and buildings and grounds maintenance tasks at a postal facility.

Custodial Laborer

Grade: L-3

Salary Range: $22,253 - $35,113 (COLA included)

Persons Eligible to Apply: Open to veterans only

Examination Requirements: Must pass Examination M/N 911 to determine the ability to interpret and follow instructions.

Duties: Performs manual labor in maintaining and cleaning buildings and grounds of a postal facility.

Examination 911

United States Postal Service

Sample Questions

STUDY CAREFULLY BEFORE YOU GO TO THE EXAMINATION ROOM

The purpose of this booklet is to illustrate the types of questions you will use in Examination M/N 911. It also shows you how the questions are to be answered.

The suggested answers to each question are lettered. Select the *best* answer, and make a heavy pencil mark in the space on the sample answer sheet by darkening the space for the best answer to that question. Each mark must be dense black. Each mark must cover more than half of the area of the space, and must not extend into neighboring spaces. If the answer to sample 1 is B, you would mark the sample answer sheet like this:

Record your answers to each sample question. Then compare your answers with those given in the sample question instructions.

During the test, directions for answering questions will be given orally. You are to listen closely to the directions and follow them. To practice for the test, you might have a friend read the directions to you while you mark your answers on the sample answer sheet on the next page.

You will be told to follow directions by writing in a test booklet and then on an answer sheet. The test booklet will have lines of material like the following four samples:

SAMPLE 1   5 _____

SAMPLE 2   1   6   4   3   7

SAMPLE 3   D   B   A   E   C

SAMPLE 4   (8__)   (5__)   (2__)   (9__)   (10__)

SAMPLE 5   (7__)   [6__]   (1__)   [12__]

To practice this test, tear off page 3. Then have somebody read the instructions to you. When you are told to darken a space on the sample answer sheet, use the one on this page.

```
                    Sample Answer Sheet
  1 Ⓐ Ⓑ Ⓒ Ⓓ Ⓔ    5 Ⓐ Ⓑ Ⓒ Ⓓ Ⓔ    9 Ⓐ Ⓑ Ⓒ Ⓓ Ⓔ

  2 Ⓐ Ⓑ Ⓒ Ⓓ Ⓔ    6 Ⓐ Ⓑ Ⓒ Ⓓ Ⓔ   10 Ⓐ Ⓑ Ⓒ Ⓓ Ⓔ

  3 Ⓐ Ⓑ Ⓒ Ⓓ Ⓔ    7 Ⓐ Ⓑ Ⓒ Ⓓ Ⓔ   11 Ⓐ Ⓑ Ⓒ Ⓓ Ⓔ

  4 Ⓐ Ⓑ Ⓒ Ⓓ Ⓔ    8 Ⓐ Ⓑ Ⓒ Ⓓ Ⓔ   12 Ⓐ Ⓑ Ⓒ Ⓓ Ⓔ
```

Instructions to be read (the words in parentheses should not be read aloud):

You are to follow the instructions that I shall read to you. I cannot repeat them.

Look at the samples. Sample 1 has a number and a line beside it. On the line write an A. (Pause 2 seconds.) Now on the sample answer sheet, find number 5 (pause 2 seconds) and darken the space for the letter you just wrote on the line. (Pause 2 seconds.)

Look at Sample 2. (Pause slightly.) Draw a line under the third number. (Pause 2 seconds.) Now look on the sample answer sheet, find the number under which you just drew a line, and darken space B, as in "baker" for that number. (Pause 5 seconds.)

Look at Sample 3. (Pause slightly.) Draw a line under the third letter in the line. (Pause 2 seconds.) Now on your answer sheet find number 9 (pause 2 seconds) and darken the space for the letter under which you drew a line. (Pause 5 seconds.)

Look at the five circles in Sample 4. (Pause slightly.) Each circle has a number and a line in it. Write D, as in "dog," on the blank in the last circle. (Pause 2 seconds.) Now on the sample answer sheet, darken the space for the number-letter combination that is in the circle you just wrote in (pause 5 seconds).

Now look at the sample answer sheet. (Pause slightly.) You should have darkened spaces 4B, 5A, 9A, and 10D on the sample answer sheet. (If the person preparing to take the examination made any mistakes, try to help him see why he made wrong marks.)

Garageman & Motor Vehicle & Tractor-Trailer Operators' Exam

24

Applicants for these positions will take a written test, Examination M/N 91, to measure their ability to understand instructions. The exam will last for approximately two hours, including filling out forms. (See **Who Is Qualified to Apply for Exams?** on pages 5-10 and **Strategies for Standardized Tests,** pages 253-258.)

The job descriptions of the these positions are as follows:

Garageman

Grade: L-5

Salary Range: $26,063 - $36,835 (COLA included)

Persons Eligible to Apply: Open to the general public

Examination Requirements: Applicants must pass the written test and the road test.

Duties: Lubricates, services, and cleans trucks; drives trucks to and from the garage; assists automotive mechanics; cleans garage and washroom.

Qualifications: Ability to service trucks, to understand written instructions, and to fill out forms; ability to work independently and to help mechanics.

Motor Vehicle Operator

Grade: L-5

Salary Range: $26,063 - $36,835 (COLA included)

Persons Eligible to Apply: Open to the general public

Examination Requirements: Must pass the written test and road test.

Duties: Operates trucks and performs related work.

Qualifications: At least one year's experience in driving trucks of at least 5-ton capacity or buses of 24-passenger capacity or over. Ability to drive safely and with a satisfactory driving record; to drive under local driving conditions; to follow instructions and to prepare trip and other reports. Experience in driving pickups, vans, jeeps, step-in vans, etc. does not qualify.

Tractor-Trailer Operator

Grade: L-6

Salary Range: $27,619 - $37,827 (COLA included)

Persons Eligible to Apply: Open to the general public

Examination Requirements: Applicants must pass the written test and road test.

Duties: Operates heavy-duty tractor-trailers and performs related work.

Qualifications: Must have at least one year's experience in driving trucks of at least 5-ton capacity or buses of 24-passenger capacity or over, of which at least 6 months' experience must be in driving tractor-trailers.

T0352 000000

U.S. Postal Service
Sample Questions for Test 91

SQ 91

The sample questions in this booklet show the kinds of questions that you will find in the written test. By reading and answering these questions, you will find out how to answer the questions in the test and about how hard the questions will be.

Read the questions carefully. Be sure you know what the questions are about and then answer the questions in the way you are told to do. If you are told the answer to a question, be sure you understand why the answer is right.

Here are the sample questions for you to answer.

Question 1 is about picture 1, below. Look at the picture.

Picture 1

1. How many vehicles are shown in the picture?

(Write your answer for question 1 here.)

GO ON TO THE NEXT PAGE

Question 2 and 3 are about picture 2, below. Look at the picture.

Picture 2

2. Who is sitting on the motorcycle?

(Write your answer for question 2 here.)

3. What is the policeman probably doing?

(Write your answer for question 3 here.)

Questions 4 and 5 are about picture 3 below. Look at the picture.

Picture 3

4. What is happening in this picture?

(Write your answer for question 4 here.)

5. Show the positions of the truck and the passenger car by drawing boxes like those shown below. (Your boxes will not be in the same positions as these.)

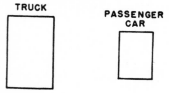

Draw your boxes in the space below.

GO ON TO THE NEXT PAGE

Questions 6 and 7 are about pictures of oilcans. Each picture has a letter. You are to tell what each picture shows by writing a short description of the picture on the answer line that goes with the question.

Now look at picture X.

6. What does picture X show?

(Write your answer for question 6 here.)

Picture X shows two oilcans. So you should have written something like "two oilcans" on the line under question 6.

Now look at picture Y.

7. What does picture Y show?

(Write your answer for question 7 here.)

Question 8 is filling in a chart. You are given the following information to put in the chart.

Truck, license number 48-7128, had its oil changed last at speedometer reading 96,005. Truck, license number 858-232, was greased last at speedometer reading 89,564.

Look at the chart below. The information for the first truck has already been filled in. For question 8, fill in the information for the other truck. You are to show in the proper columns the license number of the truck, the kind of service, and the speedometer reading when serviced.

CHART

Truck License Number	Kind of Service	Speedometer Reading When Serviced
48-7128	Oil Change	96,005

(For question 8, write the information for the second truck in the proper columns above.)

GO ON TO THE NEXT PAGE

Question 9 and 10 are about words that might appear on traffic signs.

In questions like 9, there is one numbered line and then, just below that line, four other lines which are lettered A, B, C, and D. Read the first line. Then read the other four lines. Decide which line—A, B, C, or D—means most nearly the same as the first line in the question. Write the letter of the line that means the same as the numbered line in the answer space.

Here is an example.

9. Speed Limit—20 Miles

   A) Do not exceed 20 Miles per Hour

   B) Railroad Crossing

   C) No Turns

   D) Dangerous Intersection   --
                                (Write letter of answer here for question 9.)

The first line says "Speed Limit—20 Miles." Line A says "Do Not Exceed 20 Miles per Hour." B says "Railroad Crossing." C says "No Turns." D says "Dangerous Intersection." The line that says almost the same thing as the first line is line A. That is, the one that most nearly means "Speed Limit—20 Miles" is "Do not Exceed 20 Miles per Hour." The answer to question 9 is A. You should have marked A on the answer line for question 9.

Here is another example.

10. Dead End

   A) Merging Traffic

   B) No U-Turns

   C) Turn on Red

   D) No Through Traffic   --
                            (Write your answer here for question 10.)

GO ON TO THE NEXT PAGE

After you answer questions like the ones you have just finished, you will be asked other questions to see how well you understand what you have written. To answer the next questions, you will use the information that you wrote for the first 10 questions. Mark your answers to the next questions on the sample answer sheet on the next page.

The sample answer sheet has spaces that look like these:

1 Ⓐ Ⓑ Ⓒ Ⓓ Ⓔ

2 Ⓐ Ⓑ Ⓒ Ⓓ Ⓔ

If you wanted to mark D for your answer to question 1, you would mark it like this:

1 Ⓐ Ⓑ Ⓒ ● Ⓔ

If you wanted to mark C for your answer to question 2, you would mark it like this:

2 Ⓐ Ⓑ ● Ⓓ Ⓔ

Each of the questions in the next part is about something you should have written on your answer lines.

In answering the next questions you may look back to what you have already written as often as you wish. You may look back while you are marking the sample answer sheet. In the actual test, the pictures and their questions will be taken away from you before you mark the answer sheet, but you will keep what you wrote about the pictures while marking the answer sheet. So for this practice, try not to look at the pictures but look at what you wrote about them.

Answer each of the following questions by darkening completely space A, B, C, D, or E beside the number that you are told in the question. Mark all your answers on the sample answer sheet.

Question 11 is about question 1. Use what you wrote under question 1 to answer question 11. Mark your answer on the sample answer sheet.

11. For number 1 on the sample answer sheet,
    mark space A if only one vehicle is shown in the picture
    mark space B if only two vehicles are shown in the picture
    mark space C if only three vehicles are shown in the picture
    mark space D if only four vehicles are shown in the picture
    mark space E if only five vehicles are shown in the picture

If you look at the answer you gave for question 1, you will see that you wrote that three vehicles were shown in the picture. The question above tells you to mark space C on the sample answer sheet if only three vehicles are shown. So you should have marked space C for number 11 on the sample answer sheet.

Question 12 below is about question 2, and question 13 below is about question 3.

12. For number 12 on the sample answer sheet, mark space
    A if a policeman is sitting on the motorcycle
    B if a man in overalls is sitting on the motorcycle
    C if a boy in a sport shirt is sitting on the motorcycle
    D if a nurse is sitting on the motorcycle
    E if a man with a white beard is sitting on the motorcycle

Be sure to mark your answer on the sample answer sheet.

13. For number 13 on the sample answer sheet, mark space
    A if the policeman is probably fixing a tire
    B if the policeman is probably using a telephone
    C if the policeman is probably taking off his cap
    D if the policeman is probably blowing a whistle
    E if the policeman is probably writing a "ticket"

GO ON TO THE NEXT PAGE

Question 14 below is about question 4, and question 15 below is about question 5.

14. For number 14 on the sample answer sheet, mark space
   A if a bus is passing a fire truck
   B if a motorcycle is hitting a fence
   C if a truck is backing up to a platform
   D if a passenger car is getting gas
   E if a passenger car is hitting a truck

15. Look at the boxes you drew for question 5. For number 15 on the sample answer sheet, mark space

   A if a truck is on a ramp and a passenger car is on the street
   B if a truck is to the rear of a passenger car
   C if the front bumpers of a passenger car and a truck are in line
   D if a passenger car is to the rear of a truck
   E if a motorcycle is between a truck and a passenger car

Question 16 below is about question 6 under picture X, and question 17 below is about question 7 under picture Y.

16. For number 16 on the sample answer sheet, mark space

   A if there is only one oilcan in picture X
   B if there are only two oilcans in picture X
   C if there are only three oilcans in picture X
   D if there are only four oilcans in picture X
   E if there are only five oilcans in picture X

17. For number 17 on the sample answer sheet, mark space
   A if there is only one oilcan in picture Y
   B if there are only two oilcans in picture Y
   C if there are only three oilcans in picture Y
   D if there are only four oilcans in picture Y
   E if there are only five oilcans in picture Y

Question 18 below is about the chart you filled in. For this question, mark on the sample answer sheet the letter of the suggested answer—A, B, C, D, or E— that answers the question best.

18. What is the license number of the truck that was greased? (Look at what you wrote on the chart. Don't answer from memory.)
   A) 89,564
   B) 48-7128
   C) 858-232
   D) 96,005

For number 19 on the sample answer sheet, mark the space that has the same letter as the letter you wrote on the answer line for question 9.

For number 20 on the sample answer sheet, mark the space that has the same letter as the letter you wrote on the answer line for question 10.

(See the correct answers on page 175.)

Correct Answers

Sample Questions

11.	C	16.	B
12.	A	17.	D
13.	E	18.	C
14.	E	19.	A
15.	D	20.	D

Maintenance Mechanic Exam

25

The test for maintenance mechanic consists of two parts: Part I, a multiple-choice test dealing with basic mechanics, electricity, and electronics and with the use of hand and portable power tools and test equipment; and Part II, a multiple-choice test dealing with basic mathematical computations, reading, comprehension, and how to follow verbal instructions. Each part of the exam takes about four hours. (See **Who is Qualified to Apply for Exam?** pages 5-10.)

For the reading comprehension and multiple-choice test, see **Analyzing Examination 710**—*Clerical and Verbal Abilities,* pages 155-163; **Reading Comprehension,** pages 177-180; and **Strategies for Standardized Tests,** pages 253-258.)

As an applicant, you must have knowledge of basic mechanics, basic electricity, basic electronics, safety procedures, and equipment; you must know how to perform basic and complex mathematical computations, apply theory, detect patterns, use reference materials, communicate orally and in writing, use hand and power tools, use shop power equipment, and use technical drawings and test equipment.

If you are hired, you'll perform preventive maintenance and repair work at the journeyman level on the mechanical, electrical, electronic, pneumatic, or hydraulic controls and on the operating mechanisms of mail processing equipment.

T0478 00 00 00   **United States Postal Service**   SG-924

Maintenance Mechanic

STUDY CAREFULLY BEFORE YOU GO TO THE EXAMINATION ROOM

Sample Questions

Part I

The purpose of this booklet is to illustrate the types of questions you will see in Examination M/N 924. It also shows you how the questions are to be answered.

Examination M/N 924 measures the knowledge and ability areas which are described in this booklet. First read the definition to get a general idea of the test content. Then answer the sample questions on the sample answer sheet.

The suggested answers to each question are lettered. Select the *best* answer, and make a heavy pencil mark in the space on the sample answer sheet by darkening the space of the best answer to that question. Each mark must be dense black. Each mark must cover more than half of the area of the space, and must not extend into neighboring spaces. If the answer to sample 1 is B, you would mark the sample answer sheet like this:

Record your answers to each sample question. Then compare your answers with those given in the correct answers to sample questions.

85280

The following categories are covered by Examination M/N 924:

1. **Knowledge of basic mechanics** refers to the theory of operation, terminology, usage, and characteristics of basic mechanical principles as they apply to such things as gears, pulleys, cams, pawls, power transmissions, linkages, fasteners, chains, sprockets, and belts; and including hoisting, rigging, roping, and pneumatic and hydraulic devices.

2. **Knowledge of lubrication materials and procedures** refers to the terminology, characteristics, storage, preparation, disposal, and usage techniques involved with lubrication materials such as oils, greases, and other types of lubricants.

3. **Knowledge of basic electricity** refers to the theory, terminology, usage, and characteristics of basic electrical principles such as Ohm's Law, Kirchoff's Law, and magnetism, as they apply to such things as AC-DC circuitry and hardware, relays, switches, and circuit breakers.

4. **Knowledge of basic electronics** refers to the theory, terminology, usage, and characteristics of basic electronic principles concerning such things as solid-state devices, vacuum tubes, coils, capacitors, resistors, and basic logic circuitry.

5. **Knowledge of safety procedures and equipment** refers to the knowledge of industrial hazards (e.g., mechanical, chemical, electrical, electronic) and procedures and techniques established to avoid injuries to self and others such as lock-out devices, protective clothing, and waste disposal techniques.

6. **Ability to apply theoretical knowledge to practical applications** refers to the ability to recall specific theoretical knowledge and apply it to mechanical, electrical, or electronic maintenance applications such as inspection, troubleshooting, equipment repair and modification, preventive maintenance, and installation of electrical equipment.

7. **Ability to use hand tools** refers to the knowledge of, and proficiency with, various hand tools. This ability involves the safe and efficient use and maintenance of such tools as screwdrivers, wrenches, hammers, pliers, chisels, punches, taps, dies, rules, gauges, and alignment tools.

8. **Ability to use portable power tools** refers to the knowledge of, and proficiency with, various power tools. This ability involves the safe and efficient use and maintenance of power tools such as drills, saws, sanders, and grinders.

9. **Ability to solder** refers to the knowledge of, and the ability to apply safely and effectively, the appropriate soldering techniques.

10. **Ability to use test equipment** refers to the knowledge of, and proficiency with, various types of mechanical, electrical, and electronic test equipment such as VOMS, oscilloscopes, circuit tracers, amprobes, and RPM meters.

(Author's Note: See **Strategies for Standardized Tests,** *multiple choice,* pages 253-254 and review any books about basic mechanics, basic electricity, and basic electronics.)

1. The primary function of a take-up pulley in a belt conveyor is to

   A) carry the belt on the return trip
   B) track the belt
   C) maintain proper belt tension
   D) change the direction of the belt
   E) regulate the speed of the belt

2. Which device is used to transfer power and rotary mechanical motion from one shaft to another?

   A) bearing
   B) lever
   C) idler roller
   D) gear
   E) bushing

3. What special care is required in the storage of hard steel roller bearings? They should be

   A) cleaned and spun dry with compressed air
   B) oiled once a month
   C) stored in a humid place
   D) wrapped in oiled paper
   E) stored at temperatures below 90° F

4. Which is the correct method to lubricate a roller chain?

   A) use brush to apply lubricant while chain is in motion
   B) use squirt can to apply lubricant while chain is in motion
   C) use brush to apply lubricant while chain is not in motion
   D) soak chain in pan of lubricant and hang to allow excess to drain
   E) chains do not need lubrication

5. A circuit has two resistors of equal value in series. The voltage and current in the circuit are 20 volts and 2 amps respectively. What is the value of *each* resistor?

   A) 5 ohms
   B) 10 ohms
   C) 15 ohms
   D) 20 ohms
   E) Not enough information given

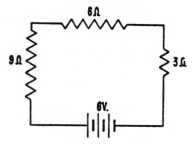

Figure III-A-22

6. Which of the following circuits is shown in Figure III-A-22?

   A) series circuit
   B) parallel circuit
   C) series, parallel circuit
   D) solid state circuit
   E) none of the above

7. What is the total net capacitance of two 60-farad capacitors connected in series?

   A) 30 F
   B) 60 F
   C) 90 F
   D) 120 F
   E) 360 F

8. If two 30-mH inductors are connected in series, what is the total net inductance of the combination?

   A) 15 mH
   B) 20 mH
   C) 30 mH
   D) 45 mH
   E) 60 mH

Figure 75-25-1

9. Crowbars, light bulbs, and vacuum bags are to be stored in the cabinet shown in Figure 75-25-1. Considering the balance of weight, what would be the safest arrangement?

A) top drawer   — crowbars
   middle drawer   — light bulbs
   bottom drawer   — vacuum bag

B) top drawer   — crowbars
   middle drawer   — vacuum bag
   bottom drawer   — light bulbs

C) top drawer   — vacuum bag
   middle drawer   — crowbars
   bottom drawer   — light bulbs

D) top drawer   — vacuum bag
   middle drawer   — light bulbs
   bottom drawer   — crowbars

E) top drawer   — light bulbs
   middle drawer   — vacuum bag
   bottom drawer   — crowbars

10. Contaminants have caused bearings to fail prematurely. Which pair of the items listed below should be kept away from the bearings?

A) dirt and oil
B) grease and water
C) oil and grease
D) dirt and moisture
E) water and oil

11. The electrical circuit term *open circuit* refers to a closed loop being opened. When an ohmmeter is connected into this type of circuit, one can expect the meter to

A) read infinity
B) read infinity and slowly return to *zero*
C) read *zero*
D) read *zero* and slowly return to infinity
E) none of the above

12. Which is most appropriate for pulling a heavy load?

A) electric lift
B) fork lift
C) tow conveyor
D) dolly
E) pallet truck

13. In order to operate a breast drill, in which direction should you turn it?

A) clockwise
B) counterclockwise
C) up and down
D) back and forth
E) right, then left

14. Which is the correct tool for tightening or loosening a water pipe?

A) slip joint pliers
B) household pliers
C) monkey wrench
D) water pump pliers
E) pipe wrench

15. What is one purpose of a chuck key?

A) open doors
B) remove drill bits
C) remove screws
D) remove set screws
E) unlock chucks

16. When smoke is generated as a result of using a portable electric drill for cutting holes into a piece of angle iron, one should

    A) use a fire watch
    B) cease the drilling operation
    C) use an exhaust fan to remove smoke
    D) use a prescribed coolant solution to reduce friction
    E) call the fire department

17. The primary purpose of soldering is to

    A) melt solder to a molten state
    B) heat metal parts to the right temperature to be joined
    C) join metal parts by melting the parts
    D) harden metal
    E) join metal parts

18. Which of the following statements is correct of a soldering gun?

    A) tip is not replaceable
    B) cannot be used in cramped places
    C) heats only when trigger is pressed
    D) not rated by the number of watts they use
    E) has no light

19. What unit of measurement is read on a dial torque wrench?

    A) pounds
    B) inches
    C) centimeters
    D) foot-pounds
    E) degrees

20. Which instrument is used to test insulation breakdown of a conductor?

    A) ohmmeter
    B) ammeter
    C) megger
    D) wheatstone bridge
    E) voltmeter

(See the correct answers on page 183.)

Correct Answers

Sample Questions

Part I

1.	C	11.	A
2.	D	12.	E
3.	D	13.	A
4.	D	14.	E
5.	A	15.	B
6.	A	16.	D
7.	A	17.	E
8.	E	18.	C
9.	E	19.	D
10.	D	20.	C

T0472 00 00 00

United States Postal Service

SG-912

Maintenance Mechanic

Sample Questions

Part II

STUDY CAREFULLY BEFORE YOU GO TO THE EXAMINATION ROOM

The purpose of this booklet is to illustrate the types of questions you will see in Examination M/N 912. It also shows you how the questions are to be answered.

At the beginning of each set of sample questions you will find the definition of a question category which the test measures. First read the definition to get a general idea of the test content. Then answer the sample questions on the sample answer sheet at the bottom of the page.

The suggested answers to each question are lettered. Select the *best* answer, and make a heavy pencil mark in the space on the sample answer sheet by darkening the space of the best answer to that question. Each mark must be dense black. Each mark must cover more than half of the area of the space, and must not extend into neighboring spaces. If the answer to sample 1 is B, you would mark the sample answer sheet like this:

Record your answers to each sample question. Then compare your answers with those given in the correct answers to sample questions.

During the test, directions for answering questions in the last category will be given orally, either by a cassette tape or by the examiner. You are to listen closely to the directions and follow them. To practice for this part of the test you might have a friend read the directions to you while you mark your answers on the sample answer sheet.

85280

Ability to perform basic mathematical computations refers to the ability to perform basic calculations such as addition, subtraction, multiplication, and division with whole numbers, fractions, and decimals. Perform the computations required by each problem. Decide which answer (A, B, C, D, or E) is correct and mark it on the sample answer sheet. If the correct answer is not provided, mark E (none of the above).

Author's Note: See **Strategies for Standardized Tests,** *solving mathematics problems,* pages 255-257, and review any books about basic mechanics, basic electricity, and basic electronics.

1) 23 + 34 =

A) 46
B) 47
C) 56
D) 57
E) 66

2) 2.6 − .5 =

A) 2.0
B) 2.1
C) 3.1
D) 3.3
E) none of the above

3) ½ of ¼ =

A) $\frac{1}{12}$
B) ⅛
C) ¼
D) ½
E) 8

4) 168 ÷ 8 =

A) 20
B) 22
C) 24
D) 26
E) none of the above

```
        SAMPLE
     ANSWER SHEET
  1 Ⓐ Ⓑ Ⓒ Ⓓ Ⓔ

  2 Ⓐ Ⓑ Ⓒ Ⓓ Ⓔ

  3 Ⓐ Ⓑ Ⓒ Ⓓ Ⓔ

  4 Ⓐ Ⓑ Ⓒ Ⓓ Ⓔ
```

```
    CORRECT ANSWERS
  TO SAMPLE QUESTIONS
  1 Ⓐ Ⓑ Ⓒ ● Ⓔ

  2 Ⓐ ● Ⓒ Ⓓ Ⓔ

  3 Ⓐ ● Ⓒ Ⓓ Ⓔ

  4 Ⓐ Ⓑ Ⓒ Ⓓ ●
```

Ability to perform more complex mathematics refers to the ability to perform calculations such as basic algebra, geometry, scientific notation, and number conversions, as applied to mechanical, electrical, and electronic applications. For each problem, decide which is the correct answer (i.e., A, B, C, D, E) and mark it on the sample answer sheet. If the correct answer is not provided mark E (none of the above).

1) Simplify the following expression in terms of amps:

$$563 \times 10^{-6}$$

A) 563,000,000 amps
B) 563,000 amps
C) .563 amps
D) .000563 amps
E) .000000563 amps

2) Solve the power equation

$P = I^2 R$ for R

A) $R = EI$
B) $R = I^2 P$
C) $R = PI$
D) $R = P/I^2$
E) $R = E/I$

3) The product of 3 kilo ohms times 3 micro ohms is

A) 6×10^{-9} ohms
B) 6×10^{-3} ohms
C) 9×10^{3} ohms
D) 9×10^{-6} ohms
E) 9×10^{-3} ohms

```
        SAMPLE
    ANSWER SHEET

    1 Ⓐ Ⓑ Ⓒ Ⓓ Ⓔ

    2 Ⓐ Ⓑ Ⓒ Ⓓ Ⓔ

    3 Ⓐ Ⓑ Ⓒ Ⓓ Ⓔ
```

```
    CORRECT ANSWERS
  TO SAMPLE QUESTIONS

    1 Ⓐ Ⓑ Ⓒ ● Ⓔ

    2 Ⓐ Ⓑ Ⓒ ● Ⓔ

    3 Ⓐ Ⓑ Ⓒ Ⓓ ●
```

Ability to detect patterns refers to the ability to observe and analyze qualitative and quantitative factors such as number progressions, spatial relationships, and auditory and visual patterns. This includes combining information and determining how a given set of numbers, objects, or sounds are related to each other. Solve each problem below and mark the correct answer on the sample answer sheet on the next page.

1) Select from the drawings of objects labeled A, B, C, and D the one that would have the top, front, and right views shown in the drawing at the left.

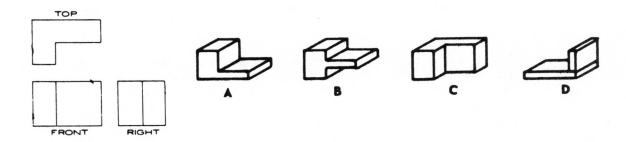

2) In the problem below there is at the left a drawing of a flat piece of paper and at the right four figures labeled A, B, C, and D. When the paper is bent on the dotted lines, it will form one of the figures at the right. Decide which figure can be formed from the flat piece.

In each of the sample questions, look at the symbols in the first two boxes. Something about the three symbols in the first box makes them alike; something about the two symbols in the other box with the question mark makes them alike. Look for some characteristic that is common to all symbols in the same box, yet makes them different from the symbols in the other box. Among the five answer choices, find the symbol that can best be substituted for the question mark, because it is *like* the symbols in the second box, and, *for the same reason*, different from those in the first box.

3.

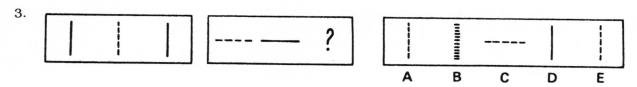

In the sample question 3, all the symbols in the first box are vertical lines. The second box has two lines, one broken and one solid. Their *likeness* to each other consists of their being horizontal; and their being horizontal makes them *different* from the vertical lines in the other box. The answer must be the only one of the five lettered choices that is a horizontal line, either broken or solid. *Note:* There is not supposed to be a *series* or progression in these symbol questions. If you look for a progression in the first box and try to find the missing figure to fill out a similar progression in the second box, you will be wasting time. Remember to look for a *likeness* within each box and a *difference* between the two boxes. Now answer sample questions 4 and 5.

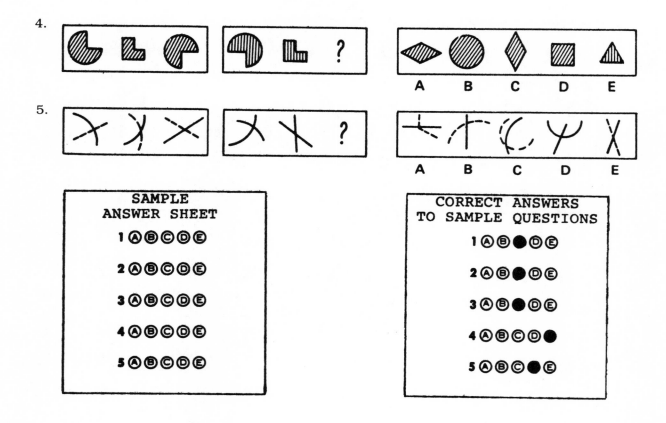

Ability to use written reference materials refers to the ability to locate, read, and comprehend text material such as handbooks, manuals, bulletins, directives, checklists, and route sheets. Read the following paragraph, determine the answer which is most nearly correct (A, B, C, D, or E), and mark it on the sample answer sheet.

1) "Prior to 1870, a conveyor that made use of rollers was developed for transporting clay. This construction substituted rolling friction at the idler bearing points for the sliding friction of the slider bed. A primitive type of troughing belt conveyor was developed about the same time for the handling of grain. This design was improved during the latter part of the century when the troughing idler was developed."

Author's Note: See Analyzing Examination 710, *Clerical and Verbal Abilities*, pages 155-163, and **Reading Comprehension**, pages 253-254.

According to the above paragraph, which of the following statements is *most* nearly correct?

A) The troughing belt conveyor was developed about 1870 to handle clay and grain.

B) Rolling friction construction was replaced by the sliding friction construction prior to 1870.

C) In the late nineteenth century, conveyors were improved with the development of the troughing idler.

D) The troughing idler, a significant design improvement for the conveyors, was developed in the early nineteenth century.

E) Conveyor belts were invented and developed in the 1800's.

```
+-----------------------------+      +-----------------------------+
|          SAMPLE             |      |      CORRECT  ANSWER        |
|       ANSWER SHEET          |      |    TO  SAMPLE  QUESTION     |
|                             |      |                             |
|                             |      |                             |
|      1 Ⓐ Ⓑ Ⓒ Ⓓ Ⓔ          |      |      1 Ⓐ Ⓑ ● Ⓓ Ⓔ          |
|                             |      |                             |
|                             |      |                             |
+-----------------------------+      +-----------------------------+
```

Ability to use technical drawings refers to the ability to read and comprehend technical materials such as diagrams, schematics, flow charts, and blueprints. For each problem, decide which is the correct answer.

1) In Figure 3-8-6, what is the measurement of dimension F?

A) 1 ¾ inches
B) 2 ¼ inches
C) 2 ½ inches
D) 3 ¾ inches
E) none of the above

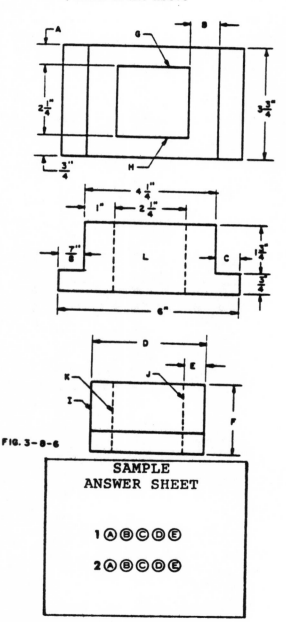

FIG. 3-8-6

2) In Figure 612.160-57, what is the current flow through R_3 when V = 50 volts, R_1 = 25 ohms, R_2 = 25 ohms, R_3, R_4, and R_5 each equal 50 ohms, and the current through the entire circuit totals one amp?

A) 0.5 amp
B) 5.0 amps
C) 5.0 milliamps
D) 50.0 milliamps
E) none of the above

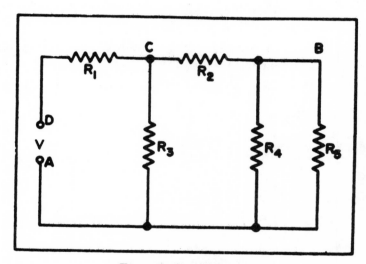

Fig. 612.160--57

SAMPLE
ANSWER SHEET

1 Ⓐ Ⓑ Ⓒ Ⓓ Ⓔ

2 Ⓐ Ⓑ Ⓒ Ⓓ Ⓔ

CORRECT ANSWER
TO SAMPLE QUESTION

1 Ⓐ Ⓑ ● Ⓓ Ⓔ

2 ● Ⓑ Ⓒ Ⓓ Ⓔ

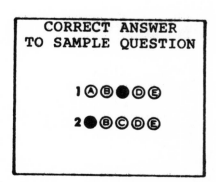

Ability to follow instructions refers to the ability to comprehend and execute written and oral instructions such as work orders, checklists, route sheets, and verbal directions and instructions. The previous questions tested your ability to follow written instructions. The remaining items test your ability to follow instructions given verbally.

You will be told to follow directions by writing in a test booklet and then on an answer sheet. The test booklet will have lines of material like the five samples:

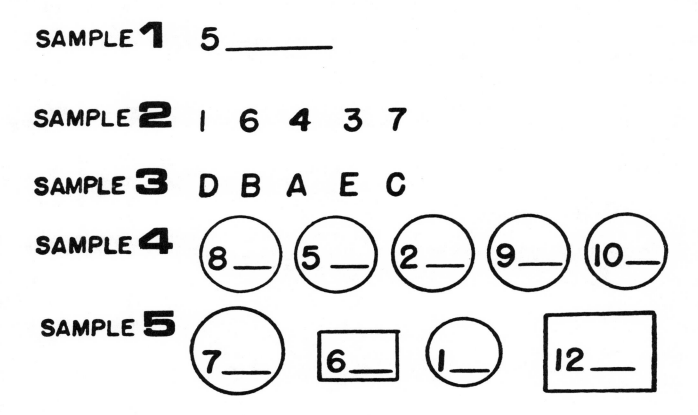

To practice this test, have somebody read the instructions to you and you follow the instructions. When he or she tells you to darken the space on the sample answer sheet, use the one on this page.

Instructions to be read (the words in parentheses should not be read aloud).

You are to follow the instructions that I shall read to you. I cannot repeat them.

Look at the samples. Sample 1 has a number and a line beside it. On the line write an A. (Pause 2 seconds.) Now on the sample answer sheet, find number 5 (pause 2 seconds) and darken the space for the letter you just wrote on the line. (Pause 2 seconds.)

Look at sample 2. (Pause slightly.) Draw a line under the third number. (Pause 2 seconds.) Now look on the sample answer sheet, find the number under which you just drew a line and darken space B as in baker for that number. (Pause 5 seconds.)

Look at sample 3. (Pause slightly.) Draw a line under the third letter in the line. (Pause 2 seconds). Now on your answer sheet, find number 9 (pause 2 seconds) and darken the space for the letter which you drew a line. (Pause 5 seconds.)

Look at the five circles in sample 4. (Pause slightly.) Each circle has a number and a line in it. Write D as in dog on the blank in the last circle. (Pause 2 seconds.) Now on the sample answer sheet, darken the space for the number-letter combination in the box or circle in which you just wrote. (Pause 5 seconds.)

Look at sample 5. (Pause slightly.) There are two circles and two boxes of different sizes with numbers in them. (Pause slightly.) If 4 is more than 2 and if 5 is less than 3, write A in the smaller circle. (Pause slightly.) Otherwise, write C in the larger box. (Pause 2 seconds.) Now on the sample answer sheet, darken the space for the number-letter combination in the box or circle in which you just wrote. (Pause 5 seconds.)

Now look at the sample answer sheet. (Pause slightly.) You should have darkened spaces 4B, 5A, 9A, 10D, and 12C on the sample answer sheet. (If the person preparing to take the examination made any mistakes, try to help him see why he made the wrong marks.)

Electronics Technician Exam

The exam for electronics technician is broken down into two parts: Part I deals with basic mechanics, basic electricity, and basic electronics; Part II deals with mathematical computations and how to follow instructions. (See **Who Is Qualified to Apply for Exams?** pages 5-10 and **Strategies for Standardized Tests,** *multiple choice* and *vocabulary tests* and *solving mathematics problems,* pages 253-257.)

For the reading comprehension part of the test (Part II), see **Reading Comprehension,** pages 177-180.

If you are hired as an electronics technician, you'll carry out what the post office calls "well-documented phases of maintenance, testing, and troubleshooting and knowledge of solid state electronics." To do this job, you must have the knowledge of basic mechanics, basic electricity, and basic electronics, and you should be familiar with such things as gears, pulleys, linkages, belts, magnetism, switches, circuit breakers, coils, capacitors, and resistors.

As an applicant, you must be able to solve problems in basic algebra and geometry, understand scientific notation, and number conversions as applied to mechanical, electrical, and electronic problems. You must also have knowledge of industrial hazards (mechanical, chemical, electrical, and electronic), and understand devices, protective clothing, and waste disposal techniques.

T0474 00 00 00   **SQ-914**

United States Postal Service

Electronics Technician

STUDY CAREFULLY BEFORE YOU GO TO THE EXAMINATION ROOM

Sample Questions

Part I

The purpose of this booklet is to illustrate the types of questions you will see in Examination M/N 914. It also shows you how the questions are to be answered.

Examination M/N 914 measures the knowledge and ability areas which are described in this booklet. First read the definition to get a general idea of the test content. Then answer the sample questions on the sample answer sheet.

The suggested answers to each question are lettered. Select the *best* answer, and make a heavy pencil mark in the space on the sample answer sheet by darkening the space of the best answer to that question. Each mark must be dense black. Each mark must cover more than half of the area of the space, and must not extend into neighboring spaces. If the answer to sample 1 is B, you would mark the sample answer sheet like this:

Record your answers to each sample question. Then compare your answers with those given in the correct answers to sample questions.

The following categories are covered by Examination M/N 914:

1. **Knowledge of basic mechanics** refers to the theory of operation, terminology, usage, and characteristics of basic mechanical principles as they apply to such things as gears, pulleys, cams, pawls, power transmissions, linkages, fasteners, chains, sprockets, and belts; and including hoisting, rigging, roping, pneumatic and hydraulic devices.

2. **Knowledge of basic electricity** refers to the theory, terminology, usage, and characteristics of basic electrical principles such as Ohm's Law, Kirchoff's Law, and magnetism, as they apply to such things as AC-DC circuitry and hardware, relays, switches, and circuit breakers.

3. **Knowledge of basic electronics** refers to the theory, terminology, usage, and characteristics of basic electronic principles concerning such things as solid-state devices, vacuum tubes, coils, capacitors, resistors, and basic logic circuitry.

4. **Knowledge of digital electronics** refers to the terminology, characteristics, symbology, and operation of digital components as used in such things as logic gates, registers, adders, counters, memories, encoders, and decoders.

5. **Knowledge of safety procedures and equipment** refers to the terminology, usage, and characteristics of digital memory storage/processing devices such as core memory, input-output peripherals, and to familiarity with programming concepts.

6. **Knowledge of safety procedures and equipment** refers to the knowledge of industrial hazards (e.g., mechanical, chemical, electrical, electronic) and procedures and techniques established to avoid injuries to self and others such as lock-out devices, protective clothing, and waste disposal techniques.

7. **Ability to apply theoretical knowledge to practical applications** refers to the ability to recall specific theoretical knowledge and apply it to mechanical, electrical, or electronic maintenance applications such as inspection, troubleshooting, equipment repair and modification, preventive maintenance, and installation of electrical equipment.

8. **Ability to use hand tools** refers to the knowledge of, and proficiency with, various hand tools. This ability involves the safe and efficient use and maintenance of such tools as screwdrivers, wrenches, hammers, pliers, chisels, punches, taps, dies, rules, gauges, and alignment tools.

9. **Ability to use portable power tools** refers to the knowledge of, and proficiency with, various power tools. This ability involves the safe and efficient use and maintenance of power tools such as drills, saws, sanders, and grinders.

10. **Ability to solder** refers to the knowledge of, and the ability to safely and effectively apply, the appropriate soldering techniques.

11. **Ability to use test equipment** refers to the knowledge of, and proficiency with, various types of mechanical, electrical, and electronic test equipment, such as VOMs, oscilloscopes, circuit tracers, amprobes, and RPM meters.

Author's Note: See **Strategies for Standardized Tests,** *multiple-choice test techniques,* pages 253-257, and review any books about basic mechanics, basic electricity, and basic electronics.

1. The primary function of a take-up pulley in a belt conveyor is to

   A) carry the belt on the return trip
   B) track the belt
   C) maintain proper belt tension
   D) change the direction of the belt
   E) regulate the speed of the belt

2. Which device is used to transfer power and rotary mechanical motion from one shaft to another?

   A) bearing
   B) lever
   C) idler roller
   D) gear
   E) bushing

3. A circuit has two resistors of equal value in series. The voltage and current in the circuit are 20 volts and 2 amps respectively. What is the value of *each* resistor?

   A) 5 ohms
   B) 10 ohms
   C) 20 ohms
   D) not enough information given

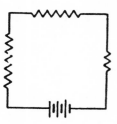

Figure III-A-22

4. Which of the following circuits is shown in Figure III-A-22?

   A) series circuit
   B) parallel circuit
   C) series, parallel circuit
   D) solid state circuit
   E) none of the above

5. What is the total net capacitance of two 60-farad capacitors connected in series?

   A) 30 farads
   B) 60 farads
   C) 90 farads
   D) 120 farads
   E) 360 farads

6. If two 30-mH inductors are connected in series, what is the total net inductance of the combination?

   A) 15 mH
   B) 20 mH
   C) 30 mH
   D) 45 mH
   E) 60 mH

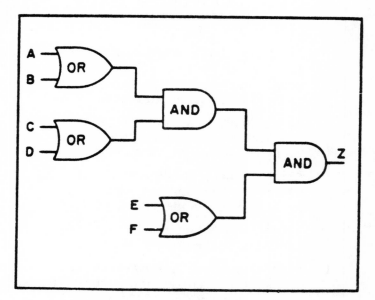

Figure 79-4-17B

7. Select the Boolean equation that matches the circuit diagram in Figure 79-4-17B.

   A) $Z = AB + CD + EF$
   B) $Z = (A+B)(C+D)(E+F)$
   C) $Z = A + B + C + D + EF$
   D) $Z = ABCD(E+F)$

8. In pure binary the decimal number 6 would be expressed as

A) 001
B) 011
C) 110
D) 111

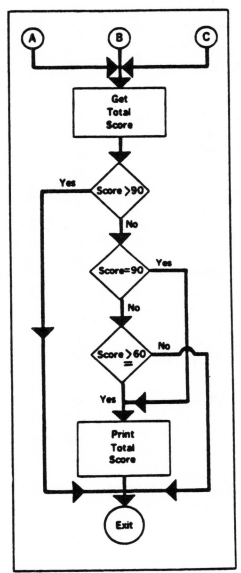

FIGURE 75-8-11

Figure 75-25-1

9. In Figure 75-8-11, which of the following scores will be printed?

A) all scores > 90 and < 60
B) all scores < 90
C) all scores < 90 and > 60 ·
D) all scores < 60

10. Crowbars, light bulbs, and vacuum bags are to be stored in the cabinet shown in Figure 75-25-1. Considering the balance of weight, what would be the safest arrangement?

A) top drawer   — crowbars
    middle drawer   — light bulbs
    bottom drawwer   — vacuum bag

B) top drawer   — crowbars
    middle drawer   — vacuum bag
    bottom drawer   — light bulbs

C) top drawer   — vacuum bag
    middle drawer   — crowbars
    bottom drawer   — light bulbs

D) top drawer   — vacuum bag
    middle drawer   — light bulbs
    bottom drawer   — crowbars

E) top drawer   — light bulbs
    middle drawer   — vacuum bag
    bottom drawer   — crowbars

11. Which is most appropriate for pulling a heavy load?

   A) electric lift
   B) fork lift
   C) tow conveyor
   D) dolly
   E) pallet truck

12. The electrical circuit term *open circuit* refers to a closed loop being opened. When an ohmmeter is connected into this type of circuit, one can expect the meter to

   A) read infinity
   B) read infinity and a slowly return to *zero*
   C) read *zero*
   D) read *zero* and slowly return to infinity
   E) none of the above

13. Contaminants have caused bearings to fail prematurely. Which pair of the items listed below should be kept away from bearings?

   A) dirt and oil
   B) grease and water
   C) oil and grease
   D) dirt and moisture
   E) water and oil

14. In order to operate a breast drill, in which direction should you turn it?

   A) clockwise
   B) counterclockwise
   C) up and down
   D) back and forth
   E) right, then left

15. Which is the correct tool for tightening or loosening a water pipe?

   A) slip joint pliers
   B) household pliers
   C) monkey wrench
   D) water pump pliers
   E) pipe wrench

16. What is the purpose of a chuck key?

   A) open doors
   B) remove drill bits
   C) remove screws
   D) remove chucks
   E) remove set screws

17. When smoke is generated as a result of cutting holes into a piece of angle iron using a portable electric drill, one should

   A) use a fire watch
   B) cease the drilling operation
   C) use an exhaust fan to remove smoke
   D) use a prescribed coolant solution to reduce friction
   E) call the fire department

18. The primary purpose of soldering is to

   A) melt solder to a molten state
   B) heat metal parts to the right temperature to be joined
   C) join metal parts by melting the parts
   D) to harden the metal
   E) join metal parts

19. Which of the following statements is correct about a soldering gun?

   A) tip is not replaceable
   B) cannot be used in cramped places
   C) heats only when trigger is pressed
   D) not rated by the number of watts they use
   E) has no light

20. What unit of measurement is read on a dial torque wrench?

   A) pounds
   B) inches
   C) centimeters
   D) foot-pounds
   E) degrees

21. Which instrument is used to test insulation breakdown of a conductor?

   A) ohmmeter
   B) ammeter
   C) megger
   D) wheatstone bridge
   E) voltmeter

(See the correct answers on page 217.)

Correct Answers

Sample Questions

Part I

1.	C	11.	E
2.	D	12.	A
3.	A	13.	D
4.	A	14.	A
5.	A	15.	E
6.	E	16.	B
7.	B	17.	D
8.	C	18.	E
9.	C	19.	C
10.	E	20.	D
		21.	C

T0472 00 00 00   SQ-912

United States Postal Service
Electronics Technician

Sample Questions
Part II

Author's Note: Part II of the electronic exam is the same as Part II of the maintenance mechanic exam. See **Maintenance Mechanic Exam,** pages 202-210. For the reading comprehension part of the test (Part II), see **Analyzing Examination 710**—*Clerical and Verbal Abilities*, pages 155-163 and **Reading Comprehension,** pages 253-254.

Automotive Mechanic Examination

27

Automotive Mechanic

Grade: L-6

Salary Range: $27,619 - $37,827

Persons Eligible to Apply: Open to the general public

Examination Requirement: Applicants must pass Examination V/N 940. The test and completion of forms will require approximately 1 1/2 hours. Competitions must score 70, exclusive of veteran preference points, to be eligible. (See **Who Is Qualified to Apply for Exams?** on pages 5-10 and **Veterans in the U.S. Postal Service,** pages 29-32.)

To make a high score on this test, read books on tools and shop equipment, brakes, steering and suspension systems, automatic transmissions and torque converters, manual transmissions, and rear axles.

To qualify as an automotive mechanic in the U.S. Postal Service you must know how to diagnose mechanical and operating difficulties of vehicles; adjust and tune engines and clean fuel pumps, carburetors, and radiators.

You must also know how to regulate timing and make other necessary adjustments to maintain trucks that are in service in proper operating condition. In addition, you must know how to repair and replace automotive electrical equipment such as generators, starters, ignition systems, distributors, and wiring; install new spark plugs; conduct road tests of vehicles after repairs, noting performance of engine, clutch, transmission, brakes, and other parts.

As an automotive mechanic, you may also perform any of the following duties: remove, disassemble, and install entire engines; overhaul transmissions, rear end assemblies, and braking systems; straighten frames and axles; make road calls to obtain emergency repairs; and make required truck inspections.

Author's Note: See **Strategies for Standardized Tests,** *multiple-choice test techniques,* pages 253-257, and review any books about basic mechanics, basic electricity, and basic electronics.

U.S. Postal Service

Automotive Mechanic Exam

Sample Questions for Examination V/N 940

The following samples show the types of questions that will be used in the written automotive mechanic examination. They will show how the questions are to be answered by those who take the test and the approximate difficulty of the test. Read the directions below; then look over these questions carefully and try to answer them. Record your answers on the sample answer sheet. Then check your answers with the correct answers.

Each sample question has a number of suggested answers, lettered A, B, C, etc. Decide which one is the *best* answer to the question. Then on the sample answer sheet, find the answer space numbered to correspond with the number of the question and *blacken* the space lettered the same as the suggested answer you consider best.

Here are the sample questions for you to answer on the sample answer sheet.

1. During a cylinder leakage test, what is indicated when air escapes through the radiator from two adjacent cylinders?

   A) Leaking intake valves
   B) Worn piston rings
   C) Burnt exhaust valves
   D) Defective cylinder head gasket
   E) Worn cylinder walls

2. Which of the following would cause a soft, spongy brake pedal?

   A) Master cylinder not returning to proper stop
   B) A brake disc with excessive runout
   C) Out-of-round brake drums
   D) Air in the hydraulic system
   E) Bent brake shoe hold-down pins

3. What is wrong during a compression test, if a low compression reading goes up after a small amount of oil is squirted into a spark plug hole?

   A) Cracked cylinder head
   B) A burnt valve
   C) Worn rings
   D) A blown cylinder head gasket
   E) Valves adjusted too tightly

4. For which of the following should a torque wrench be used?

   A) Measuring engine torque at a specific engine r.p.m.
   B) Tightening automatic transmission valve body bolts
   C) Checking a hydraulic lifter clearance in its bore
   D) Measuring distributor point gap to check swell
   E) Correctly identifying threads per inch on large-diameter bolts

5. Which of the following conditions will result when a brake drum is out of round?

   A) A spongy pedal
   B) A pulsating pedal
   C) A hard pedal
   D) A high pedal
   E) A low pedal

6. A vacuum gauge connected to a well-tuned engine should show a steady reading between which of the following during engine idle?

   A) 5" - 9"
   B) 10" - 13"
   C) 14" - 22"
   D) 23" - 27"
   E) 28" - 30"

7. Which one of the following emission control systems is common to all automobiles and light trucks manufactured at the present time in the United States?

A) CAS — Cleaner Air System
B) CCS — Controlled Combustion System
C) ImCo — Improved Combustion
D) PCV — Positive Crankcase Ventilation
E) AIR — Air Injection Reaction

8. A PCV valve is controlled by which of the following?

A) Throttle linkage
B) Engine temperature
C) Exhaust pressure or flow
D) Engine vacuum
E) Valve lifter or rocker arm

9. Which of the following is used to adjust the up-and-down clearance between an I-beam or solid front axle and the steering knuckle?

A) King pin bushings
B) King pin
C) Draw key
D) Thrust bearing
E) Spacer shims

Gear	Normal Application
Neutral	No Clutches - No Bands
First	Front Clutch - One-way Clutch
Second	Front Clutch - Front Band
Third	Front Clutch - Rear Clutch
Low	Front Clutch - Rear Band
Reverse	Rear Clutch - Rear Band

Fig. 613.180-10

10. Using Figure 613.180-10, determine which unit is defective when the vehicle will not move in *Drive* or *Low* but moves in *Reverse*.

A) Rear band
B) Front clutch
C) Front band
D) One-way clutch
E) Rear clutch

11. In an automatic transmission, which of the following is part of a planetary gear set?

A) Pinion
B) Stator support
C) Modulator
D) Impeller
E) Rotor support

12. The front band of an automatic transmission is applied through which of the following?

A) Front clutch.
B) One-way clutch
C) Input shaft bushing
D) Servo lever
E) Sun gear

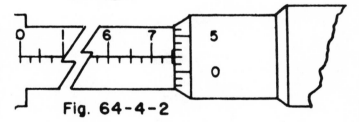

Fig. 64-4-2

13. The reading shown in Fig. 64-4-2 is

A) 0.722
B) 0.742
C) 0.752
D) 0.7112
E) 1.6722

Correct Answers

1. D
2. D
3. C
4. B
5. B
6. C
7. D

8. D
9. E
10. B
11. A
12. D
13. C

Other Jobs That Require Passing Tests

28

(For the exam for the following positions, see pages 233-245.)

Area Maintenance Specialist

Grade: L-7

Salary Range: $28,211 - $38,869 (COLA included)

Persons Eligible to Apply: Open to the general public

Examination Requirements: Applicants must pass the two-part Examination M/N 931. A rating of 70, exclusive of veterance preference points, must be attained on the examination. Total qualifications will be evaluated on the basis of the results of the written test and the review panel's evaluation.

Duties: Installs, maintains, repairs, removes, and disposes of postal equipment as appropriate at post offices within the geographic area served by the area maintenance office to which he or she is assigned. Installs, moves, or repairs post office screen-line equipment, lock boxes, furniture, and mechanical equipment.

Qualifications: Knowledge of basic mechanics, basic electricity, and basic electronics. Knowledge of safety equipment and procedures, carpentry, plumbing, and painting. Ability to perform basic mathematical computations and to apply theoretical knowledge to practical situations such as in the preventive maintenance and installation of electrical equipment. Ability to communicate orally and in writing. Ability to use portable power tools and shop power equipment.

Technician Area Maintenance

Grade: L-8

Salary Range: $33,125 - $40,017 (COLA included)

Persons Eligible to Apply: Open to the general public

Examination Requirements: Applicants must pass the two-part Examination M/N 931. A rating of 70, exclusive of veteran preference points, must be attained on the examination. Total qualifications will be evaluated on the basis of the results of the written test and the review panel's evaluation.

Duties: Installs, maintains, repairs, removes, and disposes of postal equipment as appropriate at post offices within the geographical area served by the area maintenance office to which he or she is assigned.

Qualifications: Same as those for the area maintenance specialist.

Assistant Engineman

Grade: L-5

Salary Range: $26,063 - $36,835 (COLA included)

Persons Eligible to Apply: Open to the general public

Examination Requirements: Applicants must pass the two-part Examination M/N 931. A rating of 70, exclusive of veteran preference points, must be attained on the examination. Total qualifications will be evaluated on the basis of the results of the written test and the review panel's evaluation.

Duties: Assists an engineer or journeyman mechanic in the operation and maintenance of air conditioning, heating, electrical, plumbing, ventilating, and other systems and equipment.

Qualifications: Same as those for engineman.

Blacksmith-Welder

Grade: L-6

Salary Range: $27,619 - $37,627 (COLA included)

Persons Eligible to Apply: Open to the general public

Examination Requirements: Applicants must pass the two-part Examination M/N 931. A rating of 70, exclusive of veteran preference points, must be attained on the examination. The total qualifications will be evaluated on the basis of the results of the written test and the review panel's evaluation.

Duties: Fabricates or repairs metal items in forge and on anvil; performs welding and brazing operations.

Qualifications: Knowledge of basic mechanics, safety procedures, and cleaning materials and procedures; and knowledge of metals and metallurgy. Ability to perform basic mathematics computations. Ability to detect patterns that pertain to observing and analyzing qualitative and quantitative factors such as number progressions, spatial relationships, and auditory and visual patterns. Ability to use written reference materials, to follow instructions, and to work under pressure. Ability to communicate orally and in writing. Ability to work at heights such as ladders, catwalks, walkways, scaffolds, vert-a-lifts, and platforms. Ability to use portable power tools, shop power equipment; ability to apply safely and effectively the appropriate gas and electric cutting, welding and brazing techniques and procedures. (Also see **Who Is Qualified to Apply for Exams?**)

Building Maintenance Custodian

Grade: L-4

Salary Range: $24,599 - $35,949 (COLA included)

Persons Eligible to Apply: Open to the general public

Examination Requirements: Applicants must pass the two-part Examination M/N 931. A rating of 70, exclusive of veteran preference points, must be attained on the examination. Total qualifications will be evaluated on the basis of the results of the written test and the review panel's evaluation.

Duties: Serves as the principal maintenance service employee in a postal facility where no maintenance service employee of a higher level is provided. Performs the normal laboring, cleaning, and maintenance activities required to keep the postal building, equipment, and grounds in proper condition.

Qualifications: Knowledge of basic mechanics, safety procedures and equipment, and cleaning materials and procedures. Ability to perform basic mathematical computations; to use written reference materials; to follow instructions; to communicate orally and in writing. Ability to use hand tools and portable power tools; to work at heights such as ladders, catwalks, walkways, scaffolds, and platforms.

Desirable Qualification Factors: Knowledge of basic electricity and of heating, ventilation, and air-conditioning (HVAC) equipment operation. Knowledge of plumbing that pertains to the terminology, materials, techniques, and procedures used in plumbing applications such as installing pipe and tubing, making joints, repairing flush and float valves, and cleaning drains. Ability to observe and analyze qualitative and quantitative factors such as number progressions, spatial relationships, and auditory and visual patterns. These include combining information and determining how one given set of numbers, objects, or sounds is related to another.

Building Equipment Mechanic

Grade: L-7

Salary Range: $28,211 - $38,869 (COLA included)

Persons Eligible to Apply: Open to the general public

Examination Requirements: Applicants must pass the two-part Examination M/N 931. A rating of 70, exclusive of veteran preference points, must be attained on the examination. Total qualifications will be evaluated on the basis of the results of the written test and the review panel's evaluation.

Duties: Performs troubleshooting and complex maintenance work throughout the building and building equipment systems. Maintains and operates a large automated air-conditioning system and a large heating system.

Qualifications: Knowledge of basic mechanics, basic electricity, and basic electronics. Knowledge of safety pro-

cedures and equipment; lubrication materials and procedures; refrigeration, heating, ventilation, and air conditioning (HVA); and the National Electrical Code (NEC). Ability to perform basic mathematical computations; and to apply theoretical knowledge to practical situations. Ability to use written reference materials; to communicate knowledge orally and in writing; to follow instructions; to work from heights; to use hand tools, portable power tools, and shop power equipment. Ability to use technical drawings, testing equipment, and soldering techniques.

Carpenter

Grade: L-6

Salary Range: $27,619 - $37,827 (COLA included)

Persons Eligible to Apply: Open to the general public

Examination Requirements: Applicants must pass the two-part Examination M/N 931. A rating of 70, exclusive of veteran preference points, must be attained on the examination. Total qualifications will be evaluated on the basis of the results of the written test and the review panel's evaluation.

Duties: Performs carpentry in the fabrication of new work and in repairing or adding existing structures and equipment.

Qualifications: Knowledge of basic mechanics, such as gears, pulleys, cams, pawls, power transmissions, linkages, fasteners, chain sprockets, and belts, and hoisting, rigging, roping, pneumatic, and hydraulic devices. Knowledge of safety procedures and equipment (mechanical, chemical, electrical, electronic) such as lockout devices, protective clothing, and waste disposal techniques; carpentry. Ability to perform basic mathematical computations; to detect patterns such as number of progressions, spatial relationships, and auditory and visual patterns. Ability to use written reference materials; to communicate orally and in writing; to follow instructions; to work from heights such as ladders and catwalks. Ability to use hand and portable power tools; to use shop power equipment such as bench grinders, drill presses, and table and band saws.

Elevator Mechanic

Grade: L-7

Salary Range: $28,211 - $38,869 (COLA included)

Persons Eligible to Apply: Open to the general public

Examination Requirements: Applicants must pass the two-part Examination M/N 931. A rating of 70, exclusive of veteran preference points, must be attained on the examination. Total qualifications will be evaluated on the basis of the results of the written test and the review panel's evaluation.

Duties: Maintains, repairs, and inspects mechanical, hydraulic, and electric elevators and lifts as well as their related component parts.

Qualifications: Knowledge of basic mechanics, basic electricity, and basic electronics. Knowledge of elevator equipment pertaining to equipment operation, safety considerations, and operating characteristics of hydraulic and electric traction elevator equipment, including roping, controllers, and dispatchers. Knowledge of National Electric Code (NEC), especially to basic knowledge and familiarity with the techniques and procedures specified in the NEC as they apply to electrical installations such as circuit protection, wiring, conduit, power, and lighting circuits. Ability to perform basic mathematical computations; ability to perform more complex mathematics with regard to calculations in basic algebra, geometry, scientific notation, and number conversions, as used in mechanical, electrical, and electronic applications.

Engineman

Grade: L-6

Salary Range: $27,619 - $37,827 (COLA included)

Persons Eligible to Apply: Open to the general public

Examination Requirements: Applicants must pass the two-part Examination M/N 931. A rating of 70, exclusive of veteran preference points, must be attained on the examination. Total qualifications will be evaluated on the basis of the results of the written test and the review panel's evaluation.

Duties: Checks systematically for proper operation and services; makes repairs on equipment associated with the air-conditioning, heating, ventilating, refrigerating, temperature control, and water and sewage systems. Checks, services, and performs routine repairs on equipment associated with electrical, elevator, and other building systems.

Qualifications: Knowledge of basic mechanics, basic electricity, safety procedures and equipment, lubrication materials and procedures, refrigeration, heating, ventilating, plumbing, and other maintenance jobs. Ability to use hand and portable power tools and shop power equipment. Ability to use various types of mechanical, electrical, and electronic test equipment such as VOMS, circuit tracers, amprobes, and RPM meters.

General Mechanic

Grade: L-5

Salary Range: $26,063 - $36,635 (COLA included)

Persons Eligible to Apply: Open to the general public

Examination Requirements: Applicants must pass the two-part Examination M/N 931. A rating of 70, exclusive of veteran preference points, must be attained on the examination. Total qualifications will be evaluated on the basis of the results of the written test and the review panel's valuation.

Duties: Performs maintenance work not requiring full journeyman skills and knowledge on various types of building, mail handling, and related equipment.

Qualifications: Knowledge of basic mechanics, basic electricity, safety procedures and equipment, lubrication materials and procedures; knowledge of cleaning materials and procedures. Ability to perform basic mathematical computations; to work with hand tools, portable power tools, and shop power equipment; to use written reference materials and follow instructions. Ability to communicate orally and in writing. Ability to work at heights such as ladders, catwalks, walkways, scaffolds, vert-a-lifts, and platforms.

Desirable Qualification Factors: Knowledge of carpentry, plumbing, and painting. Ability to observe and analyze qualitative and quantitative factors such as number progressions, spatial relationships, and auditory and visual patterns. These include combining information and determining how one given set of numbers, objects, or sounds is related to another.

Industrial Equipment Mechanic

Grade: L-6

Salary Range: $27,619 - $37,827 (COLA included)

Persons Eligible to Apply: Open to the general public

Examination Requirements: Applicants must pass the two-part Examination M/N 931. A rating of 70, exclusive of veteran preference points, must be attained on the examination. Total qualifications will be evaluated on the basis of the results of the written test and the review panel's evaluation.

Duties: Maintains, repairs, overhauls, and inspects battery-operated industrial equipment.

Qualifications: Knowledge of basic mechanics, basic electricity, and basic electronics. Knowledge of safety equipment and procedures; knowledge of lubrication materials and procedures. Ability to perform mathematical computations and to apply theoretical knowledge to practical situations. Ability to use hand tools, portable power tools and shop power equipment. Ability to use written reference materials and to follow instructions. Ability to communicate orally and in writing. Ability to use test equipment and to solder.

Desirable Qualification Factors: Knowledge of cleaning materials and procedures, as in the techniques involved in application and removal of cleaning materials such as alcohol, solvents, detergents, and degreasers. Ability to observe and analyze qualitative factors such as number progressions, spatial relationships, and auditory and visual patterns. These include combining information and determining how one given set of numbers, objects, or sounds is related to another.

Letter Box Mechanic

Grade: L-6

Salary Range: $27,619 - $37,827 (COLA included)

Persons Eligible to Apply: Open to the general public

Examination Requirements: Applicants must pass the two-part Examination M/N 931. A rating of 70, exclusive of veteran preference points, must be attained on the examination. Total qualifications will be evaluated on the basis of the results of the written test and the review panel's evaluation.

Duties: Performs major repair and overhaul work on street letter boxes using power and hand tools and welding equipment for cutting, shaping, bending, and attaching metal material.

Qualifications: Knowledge of safety procedures and equipment, and cleaning materials and procedures. Knowledge of painting that pertains to the terminology, materials, techniques, and procedures used in painting such as surface preparation, application procedures, and use of protective and identifying materials (e.g., enamels, varnishes, plastics, stains, sealants, decals) and painting equipment. Ability to cut and weld as it pertains to the knowledge of and ability to apply safely and effectively the appropriate gas and electric cutting, welding, and brazing techniques and procedures used in equipment and machine maintenance applications. Ability to use written reference materials and to follow instructions; ability to use hand tools, portable power tools, and shop power equipment. Ability to communicate orally and in writing.

Desirable Qualification Factors: Knowledge of basic mechanics, metals, and metallurgy. Knowledge of mechanics as it refers to the theory of operation, terminology, use, and characteristics of basic mechanical principles when applied to such things as fasteners, hoisting, rigging, and roping devices. Knowledge of metals and metallurgy as it refers to the terminology, working properties, and other characteristics of metals used in equipment and machine maintenance applications such as heat treating, tempering, machining, bending, and inspecting.

Machinist

Grade: L-7

Salary Range: $28,211 - $38,869 (COLA included)

Persons Eligible to Apply: Open to the general public

Examination Requirements: Applicants must pass the two-part Examination M/N 931. A rating of 70, exclusive of veteran preference points, must be attained on the examination. Total qualifications will be evaluated on the basis of the results of the written test and the review panel's evaluation.

Duties: Maintains machine parts used in the repair and overhaul of various types of post office equipment; dismantles, repairs, assembles, and installs equipment as required.

Qualifications: Knowledge of basic mechanics, basic electricity, safety procedures, and equipment; knowledge of lubrication materials and procedures, metals, and metallurgy. Ability to perform basic mathematical computations; to perform more complex mathematics; to apply theoretical knowledge to practical situations. Ability to detect patterns as they pertain to number progressions, spatial relationships, and auditory and visual patterns. Ability to work with visual patterns. Ability to work at heights such as ladders, catwalks, walkways, scaffolds, vert-a-lifts, and platforms. Ability to use hand tools, portable power tools, and shop power equipment. Ability to use test equipment and to cut and weld.

Maintenance Electrician

Grade: L-6

Salary Range: $27,619 - $37,827 (COLA included)

Persons Eligible to Apply: Open to the general public

Examination Requirements: Applicants must pass the two-part Examination M/N 931. A rating of 70, exclusive of veteran preference points, must be attained on the examination. Total qualifications will be evaluated on the basis of the results of the written test and the review panel's evaluation.

Duties: Repairs, tests, and maintains electric wiring, switches, motors, and related equipment.

Qualifications: Knowledge of basic mechanics, basic electricity, and basic electronics. Knowledge of the National Electrical Code (NEC); familiarity with the techniques and procedures specified in the NEC as they apply to electrical installations such as circuit protection, wiring, conduit, power, and lighting circuits. Ability to perform basic mathematical computations, to apply theoretical knowledge to practical situations, to use written reference materials. Ability to use hand tools, portable power tools, and shop power equipment; to use test equipment and to solder.

Desirable Qualification Factors: Ability to perform more complex mathematics pertaining to calculations in basic algebra, geometry, scientific notation, and number conversions, as used in mechanical, electrical, and electronic applications. Ability to observe and analyze qualitative and quantitative factors such as number progressions, spatial relationships, and auditory and visual patterns. These include combining information and determining how one given set of numbers, objects, or sounds is related to another.

Mechanic Helper

Grade: L-4

Salary Range: $24,599 - $35,949 (COLA included)

Persons Eligible to Apply: Open to the general public

Examination Requirements: Applicants must pass the two-part Examination M/N 931. A rating of 70, exclusive of veteran preference points, must be attained on the examination. Total qualifications will be evaluated on the basis of the results of the written test and the review panel's evaluation.

Duties: Performs independently, a variety of simple nontechnical and semi-skilled tasks which are incidental to recognized trades or crafts, or similar maintenance repair functions. Assists craftsmen and mechanics in performance of maintenance tasks which require skill and knowledge of the function.

Qualifications: Knowledge of basic mechanics, safety procedures and equipment, lubrication materials and procedures, and cleaning materials and procedures. Ability to perform basic mathematical computations and to use written reference materials; ability to work at heights such as ladders, catwalks, walkways, scaffolds, vert-a-lifts, and platforms; ability to use hand tools, portable power tools, and shop power equipment.

Desirable Qualification Factors: Knowledge of basic electricity; ability to apply theoretical knowledge to practical applications; ability to observe and analyze qualitative and quantitative factors such as number progressions, spatial relationships, and auditory and visual patterns. These include combining information and determining how one set of numbers, objects, or sounds is related to another. Ability to use test equipment such as VOMs, amprobes, and RPM meters.

Painter

Grade: L-6

Salary Range: $27,619 - $37,827 (COLA included)

Persons Eligible to Apply: Open to the general public

Examination Requirements: Applicants must pass the two-part Examination M/N 931. A rating of 70, exclusive of veteran preference points, must be attained on the examination. Total qualifications will be evaluated on the basis of the results of the written test and the review panel's evaluation.

Duties: Performs painting and finishing duties related to the maintenance and repair of buildings, furniture, and equipment.

Qualifications: Knowledge of basic mechanics, safety procedures and equipment, and cleaning materials and procedures. Knowledge of painting that pertains to the terminology, materials, techniques, and procedures used in painting, including surface preparation, application procedures, use of protective and identifying materials (e.g., enamels, varnishes, plastics, stains, sealants, decals), and painting equipment. Ability to use written reference materials and to follow instructions; ability to work without immediate supervision. Ability to work at heights such as ladders, catwalks, walkways, scaffolds, vert-a-lifts, and platforms. Ability to communicate orally and in writing.

Desirable Qualification Factors: Ability to use portable power tools such as drills, saws, sanders, and grinders. Ability to use shop power equipment such as bench grinders, drill presses, and table and band saws.

Plumber

Grade: L-6

Salary Range: $27,619 - $37,827 (COLA included)

Persons Eligible to Apply: Open to the general public

Examination Requirements: Applicants must pass the two-part Examination M/N 931. A rating of 70, exclusive of veteran preference points, must be attained on the examination. Total qualifications will be evaluated on the basis of the results of the written test and the review panel's evaluation.

Duties: Performs plumbing work involved in the maintenance, repair, and replacement of plumbing fixtures, equipment, supply and disposal systems, and heating systems.

Qualifications: Knowledge of plumbing techniques and procedures, basic mechanics, safety equipment and procedures, lubrication materials and procedures. Knowledge of metals and metallurgy, such as heat treating, tempering, machining, bending, and inspecting; knowledge of heating, ventilating and air-conditioning (HVAC) equipment operation such as safety considerations, startup, shutdown, and mechanical and electrical operating characteristics of HVAC equipment. Ability to communicate orally and in writing; ability to use written reference materials and to follow instructions; ability to work at heights such as on ladders, catwalks, walkways, scaffolds, vert-a-lifts, and platforms. Ability to use portable power tools and shop power equipment.

Postal Machines Mechanic

Grade: L-6

Salary Range: $27,619 - $37,827 (COLA included)

Persons Eligible to Apply: Open to the general public

Examination Requirements: Applicants must pass the two-part Examination M/N 931. A rating of 70, exclusive of veteran preference points, must be attained on the examination. The total qualifications will be evaluated on the basis of the results of the written test and the review panel's evaluation.

Duties: Inspects, maintains, repairs, and overhauls canceling machines, wire- and cord-tying machines, meter machines, and other postal equipment.

Qualifications: Knowledge of basic mechanics, basic electricity, and basic electronics. Knowledge of safety equipment and procedures; knowledge of lubrication materials and procedures. Ability to perform mathematical computations and to apply theoretical knowledge to practical situations. Ability to use hand tools, portable power tools, and shop power equipment. Ability to use written reference materials and to follow instructions. Ability to communicate orally and in writing. Ability to use test equipment and to solder.

Desirable Qualification Factors: Knowledge of cleaning materials and procedures, as in application and removal of cleaning materials such as alcohol, solvents, detergents, and degreasers. Ability to observe and analyze qualitative and quantitative factors such as number progressions, spatial relationships, and auditory and visual patterns. These include combining information and determining how one given set of numbers, objects, or sounds is related to another.

Stationary Engineer

Grade: L-7

Salary Range: $28,211 - $38,869 (COLA included)

Persons Eligible to Apply: Open to the general public

Examination Requirements: Applicants must pass the two-part Examination M/N 931. A rating of 70, exclusive of veteran preference points, must be attained on the examination. Total qualifications will be evaluated on the basis of the results of the written test and the review panel's evaluation.

Duties: Maintains and operates automated air-conditioning and steam heating systems for a large postal installation.

Qualifications: Knowledge of AC-DC circuitry and hardware, relays, switches, pneumatic and hydraulic devices, punches, gages, alignment tools, and HVAC equipment such as chillers, direct expansion units, and heating equipment. Knowledge of various instruments such as ohmmeter, ammeter, voltmeter, screw pitch gage, and amplifier band. General knowledge of basic mechanics, basic electricity, and basic electronics.

United States Postal Service
Sample Questions

The following positions use Test M/N 931:

Area Maintenance Specialist	**Letter Box Mechanic**
Area Maintenance Technician	**Machinist**
Assistant Engineman	**Maintenance Electrician**
Blacksmith-Welder	**Mason**
Building Equipment Mechanic	**Mechanic Helper**
Building Maintenance Custodian	**Oiler, MPE**
Carpenter	**Painter**
Elevator Mechanic	**Painter/Finisher**
Engineman	**Plumber**
Fireman	**Postal Machines Mechanic**
Fireman-Laborer	**Postal Maintenance Trainee**
General Mechanic	**Scale Mechanic**
Industrial Equipment Mechanic	**Stationary Engineer**

The examination, which is known as Examination M/N 931, is given to applicants for the above positions. This exam consists of Parts I, Following Oral Instructions, and Part II, which involves basic mechanics, basic electricity, and basic electronics. (See **Who Is Qualified to Apply for Exams,** pages 5-10; **Vocabulary, Spelling & Reading Comprehension,** pages 169-180; **Analyzing Examination 710,** pages 155-163; and **Strategies for Standardized Tests,** *multiple choice, vocabulary,* and *solving mathematics problems,* pages 253-258.) An applicant's total qualifications will be evaluated based on the results of the written rest and the review panel evaluation.

(For job descriptions of the above positions, see pages 223-231.)

The purpose of this booklet is to illustrate the types of questions that will be used in Test M/N 931. The samples will also show how the questions in the test are to be answered.

Test M/N 931 measures 16 Knowledge, Skills, and Abilities (KSAs) used by a variety of maintenance positions. Exhibit A lists the actual KSAs that are measured. However, not all KSAS that are measured in this test are scored for every position listed. The qualification standard for each position lists the KSAs required for the position. Only those questions that measure KSAs required for the position(s) for which you are applying will be scored for the position(s).

The suggested answers to each question are lettered A, B, C, etc. Select the *best* answer and make a heavy pencil mark in the corresponding space on the sample answer sheet. Each mark must be dense black. Each mark must cover more than half the space and must not extend into neighboring spaces. If the answer to Sample 1 is B, you would make the sample answer sheet like this:

After recording your answers, compare them with those in the correct answers to sample questions. If they do not agree, carefully reread the questions that were missed to get a clear understanding of what each question is asking.

During the test, directions for answering questions in Part I will be given orally, either by a cassette tape or by the examiner. You are to listen closely to the directions and follow them. To practice for this part of the test you might have a friend read the direction to you while you mark your answers on the sample answer sheet. Directions for answering questions in Part II will be completely described in the test booklet.

STUDY CAREFULLY BEFORE YOU GO TO THE EXAMINATION ROOM

PART I

In Part I of the test, you will be told to follow directions by writing in a test booklet and then on an answer sheet. The test booklet will have lines of material like the following five samples.

SAMPLE 1.   5 _____

SAMPLE 2.   1 6 4 3 7

SAMPLE 3.   D B A E C

SAMPLE 4.   (8__) (5__) (2__) (9__) (10__)

SAMPLE 5.   (7__) [6__] (1__) [12__]

To practice this test, have someone read the instructions on the next page to you and you follow the instructions. When they tell you to darken the space on the sample answer sheet, use the one on this page.

Instructions to be read (the words in parentheses should not be read aloud).

You are to follow the instructions that I shall read to you. I cannot repeat them.

Look at the samples. Sample 1 has a number and a line beside it. On the line write an A. (Pause 2 seconds.) Now on the sample answer sheet, find numbers 5 (pause 2 seconds) and darken the space for the letter you just wrote on the line. (Pause 2 seconds.)

Look at Sample 2. (Pause slightly.) Draw a line under the third number. (Pause 2 seconds.) Now look on the sample answer sheet, find the number under which you just drew a line and darken space B as in baker for that number. (Pause 5 seconds.)

Look at Sample 3. (Pause slightly.) Draw a line under the third letter in the line. (Pause 2 seconds.) Now on your sample answer sheet, find number 9 (pause 2 seconds) and darken the space for the letter under which you drew a line. (Pause 5 seconds.)

Look at the five circles in Sample 4. (Pause slightly.) Each circle has a number and a line in it. Write D as in dog on the blank in the last circle. (Pause 2 seconds.) Now on the sample answer sheet, darken the space for the number-letter combination that is in the circle you just wrote in. (Pause 5 seconds.)

Look at Sample 5. (Pause slightly.) There are two circles and two boxes of different sizes with numbers in them. (Pause slightly.) If 4 is more than 2 and if 5 is less than 3, write A in the smaller circle. (Pause slightly.) Otherwise write C in the larger box. (Pause 2 seconds.) Now on the sample answer sheet, darken the space for the number-letter combination in the circle or box in which you just wrote. (Pause 5 seconds.)

Now look at the sample answer sheet. (Pause slightly.) You should have darkened spaces 4B, 5A, 9A, 10D, and 12C on the sample answer sheet. (If the person preparing to take the examination made any mistakes, try to help him or her understand why the answers are wrong.)

Author's Note: See **Strategies for Standardized Tests,** *multiple-choice test techniques,* pages 253-257, and review any books about basic mechanics, basic elecitrity, and basic electronics.

Part II

1. Which device is used to transfer power and rotary mechanical motion from one shaft to another?

   A) bearing
   B) lever
   C) idler roller
   D) gear
   E) bushing

2. Lead anchors are usually mounted in

   A) steel paneling
   B) drywall construction
   C) masonry construction
   D) wood construction
   E) gypsum board

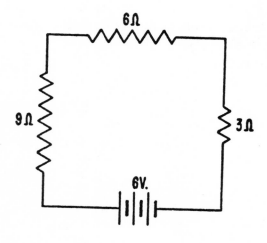

Figure III-A-22

3. Which of the following circuits is shown in Figure III-A-22?

   A) series circuit
   B) parallel circuit
   C) series, parallel circuit
   D) solid state circuit
   E) none of the above

4. Which component would *best* simulate the actions of the photocell in Figure 24-3-1?

   A) variable resistor
   B) variable capacitor
   C) variable inductor
   D) autotransformer
   E) battery

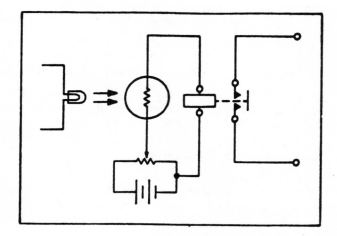

Figure 24-3-1

5. The semi-conductor materials contained in a transistor are designated by the letter(s)

   A) Q
   B) N, P
   C) CR
   D) M, P, M
   E) none of the above

6. Which of the following circuits or devices always has inductance?

   A) rectifier
   B) coil
   C) current limiter
   D) condenser
   E) filter

7. Crowbars, light bulbs, and vacuum bags are to be stored in the cabinet shown in Figure 75-25-1. Considering the balance of weight, what would be the safest arrangement?

A) top drawer   — crowbars
    middle drawer   — light bulbs
    bottom drawer   — vacuum bags

B) top drawer   — crowbars
    middle drawer   — vacuum bags
    bottom drawer   — light bulbs

C) top drawer   — vacuum bags
    middle drawer   — crowbars
    bottom drawer   — light bulbs

D) top drawer   — vacuum bags
    middle drawer   — light bulbs
    bottom drawer   — crowbars

E) top drawer   — light bulbs
    middle drawer   — vacuum bags
    bottom drawer   — crowbars

Figure 75-25-1

8. Which is most appropriate for pulling a heavy load?

A) electric lift
B) fork lift
C) tow conveyor
D) dolly
E) pallet truck

9. What measuring device is illustrated in Figure 75-26-1?

A) screw pitch gage
B) vernier calipers
C) inside calipers
D) outside calipers
E) outside micrometer

Figure 75-26-1

10. A screw pitch gage can be used for

A) determining the pitch and number of internal threads
B) measuring the number of gages available for use
C) measuring the depth of a screw hole
D) checking the thread angle
E) cleaning the external threads

11. What measuring device is illustrated in Figure 75-20-17?

A) screw pitch gage
B) vernier caliper
C) inside calipers
D) outside calipers
E) outside micrometer

Figure 75-20-17

12. One characteristic of the breast drill is that it

A) is gearless
B) is hand operated
C) has a 3 ¼ hp motor
D) has 4 speeds
E) is steam powered

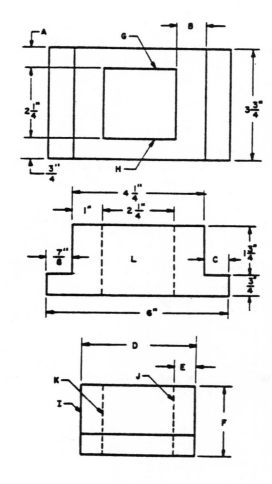

Figure 3-8-6

13. In Figure 3-8-6, what is the measurement of dimension F?

A) 1 ¾ inches
B) 2 ¼ inches
C) 2 ½ inches
D) 3 ¾ inches
E) none of the above

14. The device pictured in Figure 36 is in a rest position. Which position, if any, is the normal closed?

A) A
B) B
C) C
D) devices of this sort have no normal closed position
E) the normal closed is not shown in this diagram

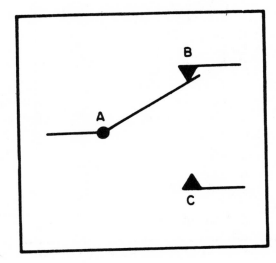

Figure 36

15. Which of the following test equipment would most likely be used in determining amplifier band width?

A) clamp-on ammeter
B) tube tester
C) watt meter
D) frequency analyzer
E) sweep frequency generator

16. Which instrument is used to test insulation breakdown of a conductor?

A) ohmmeter
B) ammeter
C) megger
D) wheatstone bridge
E) voltmeter

17. The primary purpose of soldering is to

A) melt solder to a molten state
B) heat metal parts to the right temperature to be joined
C) join metal parts by melting the parts
D) harden metal
E) join metal parts

18. Which of the following statements is correct of a soldering gun?

A) tip is not replaceable
B) cannot be used in cramped places
C) heats only when trigger is pressed
D) not rated by the number of watts they use
E) has no light

19. Contaminants have caused bearings to fail prematurely. Which pair of the items listed below should be kept away from bearings?

A) dirt and oil
B) grease and water
C) oil and grease
D) dirt and moisture
E) water and oil

20. The electrical circuit term *open circuit* refers to a closed loop being opened. When an ohmmeter is connected into this type of circuit, one can expect the meter to

A) read infinity
B) read infinity and slowly return to *zero*
C) read *zero*
D) read *zero* and slowly return to infinity
E) none of the above

21. A change from refrigerant vapor to liquid while the temperature stays constant results in a

A) latent pressure loss
B) sensible heat loss
C) sensible pressure loss
D) latent heat loss
E) super heat loss

22. The mediums normally used in condensing refrigerants are

A) air and water
B) air and vapor
C) water and gas
D) liquid and vapor
E) vapor and gas

23. Most condenser problems are caused by

   A) high head pressure
   B) high suction pressure
   C) low head pressure
   D) low suction pressure
   E) line leaks

24. Most air conditioners with motors of 1 horsepower, or less, operate on which type of source?

   A) 110-volt, single-phase
   B) 110-volt, three-phase
   C) 220-volt, single-phase
   D) 220-volt, three-phase
   E) 220-440-volt, three-phase

25. 2.6 − .5 =

   A) 2.0
   B) 2.1
   C) 3.1
   D) 3.3
   E) None of the above

26. ½ of ¼ is

   A) $\frac{1}{12}$
   B) ⅛
   C) ¼
   D) ½
   E) 8

27. A drawing of a certain large building is 10 inches by 15 inches. On this drawing, 1 inch represents 5 feet. If the same drawing had been made 20 inches by 30 inches, 1 inch on the drawing would represent

   A) 2 1/2 feet
   B) 3 ⅓ feet
   C) 5 feet
   D) 7 1/2 feet
   E) 10 feet

28. In a shipment of bearings, 51 were defective. This is 30 percent of the total number of bearings ordered. What was the total number of bearings ordered?

   A) 125
   B) 130
   C) 153
   D) 171
   E) None of the above

Author's Note: To answer the questions that follow, see **Analyzing Examination 710,** *Reading Comprehension,* pages 163-164 and **Reading Comprehension,** pages 177-180.

In sample questions 29 below, select the statement which is most nearly correct according to the paragraph.

"Without accurate position descriptions, it is difficult to have proper understanding of who is to do what and when. As the organization obtains newer and different equipment and as more and more data are accumulated to help establish proper preventive maintenance routines, the organization will change. When changes occur, it is important that the organization charts and the position descriptions are updated to reflect them."

29. According to the above paragraph, which of the following statements is most nearly correct?

   A) Job descriptions should be general in nature to encourage job flexibility.
   B) The organizational structure is not dependent upon changes in preventive maintenance routines.
   C) As long as supervisory personnel are aware of organizational changes, there is no need to constantly update the organization chart.
   D) Organizational changes can result from procurement of new, advanced equipment.
   E) Formal job descriptions are not needed for an office to function on a day-to-day basis. The supervisor knows who is to do what and when.

30. A small crane was used to raise the heavy part. Raise *most* nearly means

    A) lift   D) deliver
    B) drag   E) guide
    C) drop

31. Short *most* nearly means

    A) tall   D) heavy
    B) wide   E) dark
    C) brief

In each of the sample questions below, look at the symbols in the first two boxes. Something about the three symbols in the first box makes them alike; something about the two symbols in the other box with the question mark makes them alike. Look for some characteristics that is common to all symbols in the same box, yet makes them different from the symbols in the other box. Among the five answer choices, find the symbol that can best be substituted for the question mark, because it is *like* the symbols in the second box, and, *for the same reason*, different from those in the first box.

32.

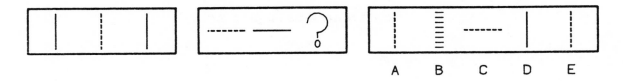

In the sample question above, all the symbols in the first box are vertical lines. The second box has two lines, one broken and one solid. Their *likeness* to each other consists in their being horizontal; and their being horizontal makes them *different* from the vertical lines in the other box. The answer must be the only one of the five lettered choices that is a horizontal line, either broken or solid. NOTE: There is not supposed to be a series of progression in these symbol questions. If you look for a progression in the first box and the second box, you will be wasting time. Remember, look for a *likeness* within each box and a *difference* between the two boxes. Now do sample question 33.

33.

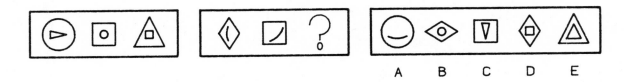

In sample question 34 below, there is at the left a drawing of a flat piece of paper and at the right, four figures labeled A, B, C, and D. When the paper is rolled, it will form one of the figures at its right. Decide which figure can be formed from the flat piece. Then on the answer sheet darken the space which has the same letter as your answer.

34.

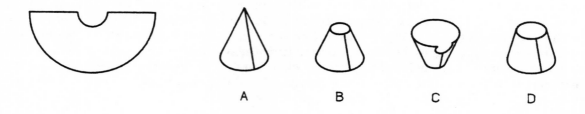

A   B   C   D

(See the correct answers on page 225.)

Exhibit A

Test M/N 931 covers the following Knowledge, Skills, and Abilities:

(1) **Knowledge of basic mechanics** refers to the theory of operation, terminology, usage, and characteristics of basic mechanical principles as they apply to such things as gears, pulleys, cams, pawls, power transmissions, linkages, fasteners, chains, sprockets, and belts; and including hoisting, rigging, roping, pneumatics, and hydraulic devices.

(2) **Knowledge of basic electricity** refers to the theory, terminology, usage, and characteristics of basic electrical principles such as Ohm's Law, Kirchoff's Law, and magnetism, as they apply to such things as AC-DC circuitry and hardware, relays, switches, and circuit breakers.

(3) **Knowledge of basic electronics** refers to the theory, terminology, usage, and characteristics of basic electronic principles concerning such things as solid state devices, vacuum tubes, coils, capacitors, resistors, and basic logic circuity.

(5) **Knowledge of safety procedures and equipment** refers to the knowledge of industrial hazards (e.g., mechanical, chemical, electrical, electronic) and procedures and techniques established to avoid injuries to self and others such as lock-out devices, protective clothing, and waste disposal techniques.

(12) Knowledge of refrigeration refers to the theory, terminology, usage, and characteristics of refrigeration principles as they apply to such things as the refrigeration cycle, compressors, condensers, receivers, evaporators, metering devices, and refrigerant oils.

(13) **Knowledge of heating, ventilation, and air conditioning (HVAC) equipment operation** refers to the knowledge of equipment operation such as safety considerations, start-up, shut-down, and mechanical/electrical operating characteristics of HVAC equipment (e.g., chillers, direct expansion units, window units, heating equipment). This does not include the knowledge of refrigeration.

(19) **Ability to perform basic mathematical computations** refers to the ability to perform basic calculations such as addition, subtraction, multiplication and division with whole numbers, fractions and decimals.

(20) **Ability to perform more complex mathematics** refers to the ability to perform calculations such as basic algebra, geometry, scientific notation, and number conversions, as applied to mechanical, electrical and electronic applications.

(21) **Ability to apply theoretical knowledge to practical applications** refers to mechanical, electrical and electronic maintenance applications such as inspection, troubleshooting equipment repair and modification, preventive maintenance, and installation of electrical equipment.

(22) **Ability to detect patterns** refers to the ability to observe and analyze qualitative factors such as number progressions, spatial relationships, and auditory and visual patterns. This includes combining information and determining how a given set of numbers, objects, or sounds are related to each other.

(23) **Ability to use written reference materials** refers to the ability to locate, read, and comprehend text material such as handbooks, manuals, bulletins, directives, and checklists and route sheets.

(26) **Ability to follow instructions** refers to the ability to comprehend and execute written and oral instructions such as work orders, checklists, route sheets, and verbal directions and instructions.

(31) **Ability to use hand tools** refers to knowledge of, and proficiency with, various hand tools. This ability involves the safe and efficient use and maintenance of such tools as screwdrivers, wrenches, hammers, pliers, chisels, punches, taps, dies, rules, gauges, and alignment tools.

(35) **Ability to use technical drawings** refers to the ability to read and comprehend technical materials such as diagrams, schematics, flow charts, and blueprints.

(36) **Ability to use test equipment** refers to the knowledge of, and proficiency with, various types of mechanical, electrical and electronic test equipment such as VOMS, oscilloscopes, circuit tracers, amprobes, and tachometers.

(37) **Ability to solder** refers to the knowledge of, and the ability to safely and effectively apply, the appropriate soldering techniques.

Correct Answers

Sample Questions

Part I

1.	D	18.	C
2.	C	19.	D
3.	A	20.	A
4.	A	21.	D
5.	B	22.	A
6.	B	23.	A
7.	E	24.	A
8.	E	25.	B
9.	C	26.	B
10.	A	27.	A
11.	E	28.	E
12.	B	29.	D
13.	C	30.	A
14.	B	31.	C
15.	D	32.	C
16.	C	33.	A
17.	E	34.	B

Numbers & Mathematics

30

Numbers and mathematics play an important part in our lives. Still, many people are afraid of mathematical subjects, believing that they are difficult and that only the talented can learn and master them.

To do well in math, you must master the basic rules and principles of arithmetic and algebraic operations. To solve math problems you must work step by step and remember the symbols, equations, and formulas for each branch of mathematics.

Here are some of the symbols used in math:

$+$, $-$, $\times$, and $\div$ refer to addition, subtraction, multiplication, and division, respectively. Parentheses and brackets are also used to indicate multiplication. Example $(8)(9)$ means 8×9. If a multiplication sign is not needed, the product of x and y is written as xy. Division is usually indicated not by a $\div$ but by a bar. **Example:** x divided by y is written x/y or a/b.

Some of the other math symbols are as follows:

$=$ means equal to
$\equiv$ means identical to
$>$ means greater than
$<$ means less than

$y \sim x$ means approximately equal, or equal in value, but not identical.
$|$ means "when" or "if." Example $a = 10|b$ *equals 15 means* "a equals 10 when b equals 15."

An exponent is a small figure placed above and to the right of a symbol:

$4^3 = 4 \times 4 \times 4$
$x^3 y^3 = xxxyyy.$

Sometimes small figures or letters are used as subscripts, but they have no value or meaning: The numbers in 1 and 2 in $a_1 + a_2$ *merely differentiate a_1 from another, a_2.*

Improving Mathematical Ability

At least three major factors can improve mathematical ability:

- Memory
- Strategies
- Practice

Memory. Scientists say that the memory has an unlimited capacity. We have incredible brains that record, retain, and replay every bit of information on all subjects, including mathematical problems, formulas, and solutions.

Techniques. Mathematicians have developed simple techniques in solving mathematical problems, particularly in addition, subtraction, multiplication, and division. Those who use these techniques are also good at other mathematical subjects such as algebra and calculus, because we also use addition, subtraction, multiplication, and division in those subjects.

247

Practice. A boxer shadow boxes; a basketball player takes practice shots; a singer (or nonsinger) sings even in the bathroom. Everyone who wants to excel in something does it, for it has been proved that "practice makes perfect." Above and beyond these three factors, one of the best ways to learn math is to have the will and determination to learn the formulas and procedures for solving problems.

Simple Techniques You Can Use

Here are some techniques in addition, subtraction, multiplication, and division.

Addition:

Techniques in addition may be divided into the following categories.

1. Simple left-to-right addition
2. 10 packets
3. Multiples
4. Splitting numbers

$$\begin{array}{r} 45 \\ 34 \\ \hline 79 \end{array}$$

Simple left-to-right addition. In the above problem, two numbers, 45 and 34, are to be added together. The solution is called the "sum."

If the problem is as simple as this, and requires no "carrying," you can simply add the numbers (starting with the first digits) from left to right—not from right to left, as is taught in school. Example: $4 + 3 = 7$; $5 + 4 = 9$. Thus the answer is 79. It's much simpler and faster to add from left to right, if there's no "carrying" involved.

An error in "carrying" is the most common mistake in addition. People either forget to carry the number or forget to add the number being carried.

The secret is to avoid carrying; think of another way. Imagine that you're adding 85 and 57. If you follow the usual procedure, you work in the following number:

$$\begin{array}{r} 85 \\ +67 \\ \hline 152 \end{array}$$

In other words, $5 + 7 = 12$; put down 2 and carry 1; $8 + 6 = 14 + 1 = 15$. The answer is 152. If you eliminate carrying, the procedure is as follows:

$$\begin{array}{r} 85 \\ +67 \\ \hline 12 \\ 14 \\ \hline 152 \end{array}$$

In this case, write 12, the sum of the digits in the right-hand column, under the numbers being added (5 and 7). Then write 14, the sum of the digits in the left-hand column (8 and 6), one place to the right, and add the two sums for a total of 152.

10-packets. When you add long columns of numbers, you can use the 10-packet system, which is merely the linking of numbers to give you a series of 10-packets.

58
71
42
95
51
89
22
55

When adding these numbers, do not mumble to yourself, "8 plus 1 = 9, plus 2 = 11, plus 5 = 16, plus 1 = 17," and so on. There is an easier way. Link the numbers that add up to 10, giving you a series of 10-packets. Make a check mark to indicate the 10-packet and write down the "extra" or leftover number, which is added to the next 10-packet.

For instance, in adding the right-hand column of the numbers given above, add 8 + 1 + 2 = 11, make a check next to 2, and write 1 (the leftover) to the right; 1 + 5 + 1 + 9 = 16, make a check next to 9 and write 6 (the leftover) on its right; 6 + 2 + 5 = 13; make a check next to 5 and write 3 (the leftover) to the right. Hence 10 + 10 + 10 (three 10-packets) = 30 + 3 (the leftover) = 33. Carry the 3 to the left-hand column; 3 + 5 + 7 = 15; put a check before 7, write 5 (the leftover) to the left. Continue adding, following the same procedure. This is how it is done:

3
58
5√ 71
42 √1
8√ 95
3√ 51
1√ 89 √6
22
55 √3
———
483

Multiples. If you have a long column to add, count the various numbers in the column and multiply each number by the number of times it is repeated.

5
8
7
3
3
9
5
6
8
7
3
8

In the example above, there are two 5's, three 8's, two 7's, three 3's, one 9, and one 6.

Thus the solution is as follows:

$$2 \times 5 = 10$$
$$3 \times 8 = 24$$
$$2 \times 7 = 14$$
$$3 \times 3 = 9$$
$$1 \times 9 = 9$$
$$1 \times 6 = 6$$

Now use the 10-packet system to solve the problem more easily. The correct answer is 72.

Splitting the Numbers. Splitting numbers is simply dividing a difficult addition problem into small units to make it easier to add.

$$498$$
$$362$$
$$381$$

In this case, the splitting should be done in this manner:

```
   49          8
   36          2
   38          1
  ----        ---
  123         11
  +11
  ----
 1241
```

Thus the correct answer is 1241.

Subtraction

There are two major techniques for easier and faster subtraction:
1. Adding
2. Splitting the numbers

Simple subtraction:

```
   26
  - 5
  ----
   21
```

If the subtraction is as simple as this, you can subtract from left to right instead of from right to left.

Adding:

```
   62
  -37
  ----
```

In this example, however, you have a problem: you cannot subtract 7 from 2. In this situation, you usually do what you are taught in school: you *borrow*, as if you were borrowing money from a friend. So instead of subtracting 7 from 2, you add 10 to 2 to make it 12. Now what does the 6 become? The system says it becomes 5. Why? Because you borrowed 10 instead of 1.

Here's the solution. 12 (originally 2) − 7 = 5; 5 (originally 6) − 3 = 2. The answer is 25.

Here's another way to do this. The number 62 is 60 + 2 but you may consider it as 50 + 12; that is, you may consider "sixty-two" as "fifty-twelve."

$$
\begin{array}{rr}
5 & (12) \\
-3 & 7 \\
\hline
2 & 5
\end{array}
$$

Thus the correct answer is 25.

Splitting Numbers. You can also divide difficult subtraction into smaller units to make it easier, as you do in addition.

Take this example:

$$
\begin{array}{r}
597 \\
-359 \\
\hline
\end{array}
$$

Split these numbers as follows:

$$
\begin{array}{rr}
59 & 17 \\
-36 & -9 \\
\hline
23 & 8
\end{array}
$$

When splitting the numbers, you add 10 to 7 (because 7 is smaller than 9) and add 1 to the number in the next column (5). The correct answer is 238.

This may seem harder at first because you're not used to it, but with practice, you'll usually be able to do the subtraction mentally, without the trouble of writing it out.

Other Methods. If you're subtracting 100, 1,000, 10,000, 100,000, or 1,000,000, don't work from right to left. Start subtracting from the left as follows:

$$
\begin{array}{r}
100 \\
-51 \\
\hline
\end{array}
$$

Subtract 5 from 9, which leaves 4; subtract 1 from 10, which leaves 9. The correct answer is 49.

$$
\begin{array}{r}
10,000 \\
-532 \\
\hline
\end{array}
$$

To subtract 532 from 10,000, subtract 0 from 9, which leaves 9; 5 from 9, which leaves 4; 3 from 9, leaving 6, and 2 from 10 (adding 10 to 0), leaving 8. The correct answer is 9468.

As you can see in the above examples, you work from left to right. Always subtract 1 from each digit, working from left to right, but add 10 to the last digit of the number from which you subtract. Notice, too, that you subtract the lower number only from the zeros and not from the 1, which is part of the 10 that you added. Add zeros to the number up to the farthest-left zero of the higher number which is 0532.

Multiplication

In multiplication, you can use three techniques to arrive at fast solutions:
1. Multiplying by 5
2. Multiplying by 10
3. Multiplying by 11

Multiplying by 5. To multiply a number by five, simply multiply it by 10 and divide the result by 2. To multiply 45,760 by 5, multiply it by 10 and then divide by 2. That is, 45,760 times 10 equals 457,600, which when divided by 2, equals 228,800.

Multiplying by 10. To multiply any number by 10, simply add a zero; to multiply any number by 100, add two zeros. Thus 580 times 10 equals 5,800; 857 times 100 equals 85,700.

Multiplying by 11. If you want to multiply a two-digit number by 11, add the two digits together and place the sum of those digits in the middle of the number. To multiply 81 by 11, for example, split 8 and 1 and place 9, the sum of 8 and 1, between them. The correct answer is 891.

If the digits total more than 10, add 1 to the left hand digit. For example, if you multiply 87 by 11, split 87 into 8 and 7, totaling 15. Then add 1 to the 8 for a total of 9 and insert the 5 between 9 and 7. The answer is 957.

Division

There are at least three shortcuts to easier division.
1. Division by 2
2. Division by 5
3. Division by 10

Division by 2. If you want to divide a number by 2, you can use "group vision." Split the group of digits into small groups, as you did in addition and subtraction. To divide 8,306,422 by 2, split the number in the following manner:

$$8 \quad 30 \quad 6 \quad 42 \quad 2$$

As you can see, the numbers can be divided easily by 2. The solution is 4,153,211.

Division by 5. To divide any number by 5, first divide it by 10 and then multiply by 2. For instance, 636 divide by 10 equals 63.6. When 63.6 is multiplied by 2, the answer is 127.2.

Division by 10 or 100. To divide a number by 10, put a decimal point before the last digit. (If the last digit is a zero, then you don't need the decimal point. Simply remove the zero. To divide 4,630 by 10 for example, put a decimal point before the final zero, making it 463.0. To divide 3,731 by 10, put a decimal point before 1, making it 373.1. To divide a number by 100, put a decimal point before the last two digits; 7,356 divided by 100 is 73.56. You must move any commas involved in the process.

Strategies for Standardized Tests

31

Standardized tests, prepared in standard patterns and ways, are time tested. That is, a time limit is set for each test. For example, Part A should be finished in five minutes and Part B should be finished in six.

There are strategies you can use to attack the questions. A test is a game; if you take a standardized test, you are a football quarterback and the testmaker is the opposing team: you read the defense, anticipating what kind of defense the opponent has formed and deciding what to do, whether to throw the ball to a wide receiver or give it to a fullback for a touchdown. If you aren't sure, at least make a guess.

Since postal tests are standardized, you can become an exam expert and make a high score on any test once you master the types of questions which have been asked in past years.

I. Multiple-Choice Test Strategies

One of the most common types of examination is the multiple-choice test, in which you select one correct answer from four or five choices. Some questions contain more than one correct answer.

Here are some strategies you can use in answering multiple-choice tests.

■ **Tactic 1:** Answer the sample questions for practice.

■ **Tactic 2:** Answer the easy questions first and the tough questions last.

■ **Tactic 3:** Evaluate the questions and see how they are designed. For example, questions within each test usually progress in difficulty from easy to hard.

■ **Tactic 4:** Search for hints. Some clues will help you find the right answer. Testmakers, for instance, usually use correct grammar in the correct answers and sometimes use incorrect grammar in the wrong answers without knowing it, because of their speed in preparing the other answers.

- **Tactic 5:** If you're sure of a correct answer, select it and don't look for any traps.

- **Tactic 6:** If you can't figure out the correct answer to a question, pick one. Make a little mark alongside the number with your pencil, and tell yourself, "I shall return!" (That is, if you have the time to do so.)

- **Tactic 7:** Be on the lookout for choices like "all of the above" and "none of the above"; usually they are not the right answers. If the first three choices are right, for instance, and if the fourth is wrong, and if the fifth is "all of the above," don't select number 4 or 5. Choose among 1, 2, and 3.

- **Tactic 8:** Watch out for sentences that contain words such as *all, only, none, never, always, usually, generally*. Often these words are traps; they do not belong to the correct answers. Unless you're sure that it's the right answer. don't select it.

- **Tactic 9:** Most often, two out of the four or five choices are obvious wrong answers; so eliminate them first. In other words, eliminate the answers which are clearly wrong until you come to a point where you are to choose between the two best choices.

- **Tactic 10.** Follow your first hunch on a particular answer; don't change it unless you're certain that you're making the right move.

- **Tactic 11:** When two answers have opposite meanings, usually one of them is the right answer; when two answers express the same thing, usually one of the pair is the right answer.

- **Tactic 12:** Guess if you don't know the answer, but be careful when the test score is calculated by subtracting the wrong answers from the right answers.

II. Vocabulary Test Strategies

- **Tactic 1**: Words are divided into simple words, so study the roots, prefixes, and suffixes. (Also see **Vocabulary, Spelling, and Reading Comprehension**, pages 169-172.) *Anthropology,* for example, can be divided into two roots: *anthropo* and *logy;* anthropo means "man" and *logy* means "study of"; thus anthropology means "study of man."

- **Tactic 2:** Watch out for traps. For example, if the question and one of the answers sound alike or look alike, it may be a trap, and most often it's not the right answer.

- **Tactic 3:** Eliminate wrong parts of speech. If the word you are to define is a noun, the correct answer will be a noun; if it's a verb, the answer will be a verb. If you aren't sure whether a word is a noun or a verb, place "the" before the word. If it looks or sounds right, it's a noun. Place "to" before a word that may be a verb. If it sounds okay, it's a verb.

- **Tactic 4:** Read a lot and look up every unfamiliar word in the dictionary. Learning vocabulary is a continuing education.

III. Solving Mathematics Problems

You can find the answers to math problems, no matter how complicated they are, by addition, subtraction, multiplication, and division, or by conversion of millimeters into centimeters, ounces into pounds, and so on. First, though, you must know whether you're going east or west. If you don't know, you're lost.

■ **Tactic 1:** The first time you're faced with a math problem, figure out how you're going to solve it. You must know the following:

- What you are supposed to find out.
- The given numbers.
- The principles or formulas needed to solve the problems.

■ **Tactic 2:** Write the numbers carefully. Be extra careful in writing 0 so that it doesn't look like a 6 or 8, and vice versa. Don't write a 3 that looks like a 5 or a 1 that looks like a 7, or vice versa. The columns should be in straight lines so that you don't make mistakes in addition or subtraction.

■ **Tactic 3:** Be sure to check the units of measurement. If they are not in the proper units, convert them into the correct units, such as millimeters into centimeters, ounces into pounds, or kilometers into miles. Don't try to add pounds to ounces, for example.

■ **Tactic 4:** Use diagrams such as squares, triangles and other shapes as much as possible. Label all the given numbers if such diagrams are needed to simplify solving.

■ **Tactic 5:** In solving any problem, particularly in a multiple-choice math test, don't glance at the choices (A, B, C, D, E) before you work on the problem. Work on the problem first, and when you have an answer, see if it matches any of the given numbers. It's like comparing your numbers with the numbers in a lottery; if your numbers don't match the winning numbers, you didn't win and you must try another time. So if your answer is not among the choices, it's not the correct answer.

■ **Tactic 6:** If you don't really know how to solve the problem, you'd better guess; that's better than leaving the question unanswered. Use the following elimination system:

- First eliminate the least probable answers.
- Eliminate the lowest and highest values among the remaining answers.
- Then select the most likely answer from the answers that remain.

Math Test techniques

Thomas F. Ewald, a former college instructor, gives the following advice on multiplication problems:

Solve the following multiplication problem:

$$3453 \times 4376 =$$

A) 15,112,432   C) 15,110,328
B) 15,121,324   D) 15,432,222

How long did it take you? If it took more than five seconds, you need this technique!

Take the last digit of each of the numbers to be multiplied against each other; now find the product of these two digits (that is, multiply them against each other): $3 \times 6 = 18$. Now notice the last digit of the correct answer above, Answer C. (You did get the right answer, didn't you?) It's 8. What was the last digit of the simple problem we just did (3×6)? That was also 8. It's not a coincidence. It will happen every time! As long as only one answer is given with the correct last digit, it's easy to pick the right answer!

If more than one answer ends in the correct digit, you'll have to do the actual multiplication. Also, my advice won't work if "none of the above" is given as an option. But it will help some of the time and can save precious seconds, or even minutes.

On some tests, such as the SAT, speed is extra important. Tactics like the one above helped me achieve a perfect score on the math portion of the SAT! It can be done!

Other Uses of the Technique

I tried Ewald's technique and it worked. I found out that you can also use this technique in solving *addition, subtraction,* and *division* problems.

For example, you are asked to add the following numbers:

388
359
159
312
746
324
———

A) 3727
B) 2288
C) 1789
D) 4725

In solving addition problems, (also see **Numbers and Mathematics,** pages 247-252), add the last digits of the numbers. In the above example, $8 + 9 + 9 + 2 + 6 + 4 = 38$. Now stop adding, and take the last digit of the answer (which is 8). Compare it with the last digits of the answers given as choices. In this case, *B* is the correct answer because 2288 ends with the number 8.

Follow the same rule with subtraction. Take the last digit of the answer (subtract only the last digits, for example, $9 - 4 = 5$) and compare it with the last digits of the answers given as choices.

In division, however, the number that is to be chosen as the correct answer is the *first* digit of your answer, not the last. As soon as you get the first digit of the answers, stop dividing and compare that digit with the *first* digits of the four answers given as choices. If it is the same *first* digit of any of the choices, that choice is the answer! If there are at least two choices with the same first digits, continue solving until you get two digits, and so on.

If "none of the above" is among the choices, you can select it if the last digit of the answer doesn't match the last digit of any of the answers given as choices in *multiplication, addition,* and *subtraction.* If "none of the above" option is given in a *division* problem, pick it if the first digit of your answer doesn't match the first digit of any of the answers given as choices.

Examination 715 **32**

(Sample Typing Test for Mark-Up Clerk)

Examination 715 is a computer administered and scored exam. Applicants are assisted with the start-up of the exam and with the exam instructions. You do *not* need prior experience on a computer terminal to take this test.

The exam contains a list of seven digit mail codes each consisting of four letters and three numbers just as you see in the sample items below. To pass this test, applicants must show that they can type these codes on the computer terminal at a rate of 14 correct lines per minute. Credit is given only for correctly typed lines. Practice for the exam by typing the sample provided below.

Type each line as shown in the exercise using lower case or capital letters. When you reach the end of a line, single space and begin typing the next line. When you reach the end of the sample items, simply begin again with the first line and continue to type until the five minutes have elapsed.

See whether you can copy it three times in a five-minute timing. Now count the number of lines you typed correctly and divide this number by five to determine your per minute score.

In the examination you will have five minutes in which to type the test material. Keep in mind that in order to pass the test you must type both rapidly and accurately.

Sample Test Copy

KATZ204
CURR907
ADAM101
BONN530
GORD223
OWEN241
SCHN421
HALL375
LOGU779
ROSE995
USHER963
MART895
KATA854
SHAN289
JAME409
CHER103
LINC510
MOSI521
NORM486
SALY541
MCNE326
PATS293
PRIN815
KAPL337
DUNN919

Practice Typing Test

Work—5 Minutes

As the Post Office instructs, type each line as shown in the exercise using lower case or capital letters. It's easier for you to use the upper case because you won't have to hit the "shift" key every time to capitalize any letter. Just set the Caps lock, and that's it. Type the sample material below in five minutes. When you reach the end of the sample items, simply begin again with the first line and continue to type until the five minutes have elapsed. See whether you can copy it three times in a five-minute timing. Afterwards, count the number of lines you typed correctly and divide this number by five to determine your per minute store. In order to pass the test, you must type both quickly and accurately. However, before typing the sample codes below, learn the technique for fast and accurate typing of the items. Also, see why these codes are typed by mark-up clerks.

Typing Techniques. When you type the line, MARC891. vou divide the line into two parts: MAR-891. First, type the letters MARC and then 891. As you type the lines below, you'll notice that you'll gain your own rhythm. That is, you type the lines as if you were hearing music. Or better still, listen to a radio station playing music.

Actually as a mark-up clerk, you'll be typing these codes. The codes as shown below representing the first four letters of a family name or last name and the first three number of a street or a P.O. box address. These codes are used by mark-up clerks to enter names and addresses of people moving to other addresses. Change of address cards are sent by letter carriers within a certain area consisting of several Post Offices to so-called Computerized Forwarding System Units of a Postal Sectional Center, such as the Royal Oak Post Office. In the Royal Oak area, letter carriers from associate Post Offices send their Change-of-address cards and all mail to be forwarded to the CFS Unit of the Royal Oak Post Office which is on the corner of American Way and Minnesota St. in Troy, Michigan. In the Detroit area, letter carriers from the associate Post Offices send their mail and change-of-address cards to the U.S. Postal Service building on Fort Street in Detroit, Michigan. Clerks in CFS units enter these addresses into the systems. Once entered, when a mark-up clerk keys the codes such as HARR541, the computer will generate labels, automatically attached to letters passing by through a mini-conveyor in front of a clerk's typing the codes on the computer terminal. Other mail, with unknown forwarding addresses are returned to senders. The computer also attaches the corresponding label for mail with notes: "Return to Sender." That's why

mark-up clerks should type rapidly and accurately "to process" more mails to be forwarded to new addresses.

Now, type the example test below:

HARR541
BAUT215
REYE041
ALVE915
POOL412
MARC286
CART316
REYE981
PAJA315
BURN886
WOOD451
ASIR199
CLAR773
CRUZ839
DERR321
MARV315
PADI315
NATI384
MARR310
RAVA938
ABDU336
MANG991
CORR327
MARR387
LEON447

As indicated above, you must type the above lines at least three times in five minutes.

460 Rural Carrier Associate Exam

Applicant Instructions

YOU MUST BRING THE FOLLOWING TO BE ADMITTED:

Completed Sample Answer Sheet

Admission Card/Notice

Photo ID and

2 Sharpened No. 2 Pencils

LATECOMERS WILL NOT BE ADMITTED.

UNITED STATES POSTAL SERVICE

These instructions will prepare you for the exam. Please take time to **carefully read ALL of the instructions. THIS IS YOUR RESPONSIBILITY.** You should read all of the instructions and complete the required items even if you have taken a Postal exam before. **We are providing you with:**

1. *A SAMPLE ANSWER SHEET TO FILL OUT AT HOME.* This will enable you to complete the Answer Sheet in the exam room.

2. *WHAT YOU CAN EXPECT DURING THE ACTUAL TEST PART OF THE EXAM SESSION.*

3. *SAMPLE QUESTIONS FOR PRACTICE.* So that you will be familiar with the type of questions on the test, sample questions are included for practice.

4. *HOW THE FOUR PARTS OF THE TEST WILL BE SCORED.*

To fill out the Sample Answer Sheet, you will need:

This booklet,

Sample Answer Sheet,

Your Admission Card/Notice,

No. 2 pencil,

Social Security card,

ZIP Code for current address and

ZIP+4 Code for current address.

In the exam room, you will be given 15 minutes to copy your work from the Sample Answer Sheet to the Answer Sheet. The test will begin soon thereafter. **You will not have time in the exam room to become familiar with these instructions.**

The Answer Sheet will be given to you in the exam room. It is processed by a high-speed scanner. It is important that you precisely complete the grids on the Sample Answer Sheet. This is so you will know exactly how to fill out the Answer Sheet in the exam room.

You are responsible for correctly completing the Sample Answer Sheet. When you report to take the test, you must bring it with you.

Your Sample Answer Sheet will be checked for accurate and total completion. You may not have time to fix any errors or complete items not filled out before the session starts. Only those who have a properly completed Sample Answer Sheet will be admitted. Those who still have an incomplete Sample Answer Sheet by the time the exam starts will NOT be admitted.

THE FOLLOWING INSTRUCTIONS EXPLAIN HOW TO FILL OUT EACH GRID ON THE SAMPLE ANSWER SHEET.

Examples of correct and incorrect marks are:

CORRECT MARKS

INCORRECT MARKS

1 NAME. Use your full, legal name when completing this grid. Use the same name every time you take a postal exam. Use of a nickname could result in a delay in processing the result.

GRID 1 is divided into three parts: **Last Name, First Name and MI** (Middle Initial). Each part is surrounded by a border. **Each part of your name must be entered ONLY in the place for that part.**

Last Name. Enter your last name one letter to a box. **You must start with the first square box to the left.**

If you are a **JR, SR, III or IV,** this should be included as a part of your last name. After entering your last name, **skip a box** and enter the correct letters.

To help you complete the grids correctly, you will use the **E D G E** of the Admission Card/Notice or the envelope as a guide. Place the Admission Card/Notice or envelope on top of GRID 1 so that the edge is to the LEFT of the first column. For **example,** when the last name is "HALL III":

Last Name

EDGE

(**If you are left handed,** place the edge to the RIGHT of the first column.)

For the letter in the box, find the matching circle in the column below and darken that circle.

Next, move the edge **with one hand** so that it is against the **next** column. Darken the circle **with the other hand** for that letter.

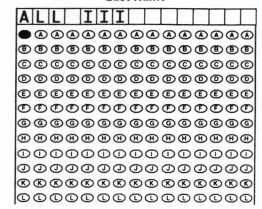

Last Name

EDGE

Then proceed until you have darkened the circle for each letter you have entered in a box.

If your name has the letter "O" in it, make sure to darken the circle that comes after "N". Do not mistake the letter "Q" for the letter "O".

When you come to a blank box, do nothing.

The following is an **example of a completed grid** when the last name is "HALL III":

Last Name

First Name. Enter your first name one letter to a box. **You must start with the first box after the border line.**

As you did for **Last Name,** take the edge and place it on top of this grid against the first column.

Find the matching circle below and darken that circle. Next, move the edge so it is against the next column. Darken the circle for that letter. Then proceed until you have darkened the circle for each letter you have entered in a box.

Do not mistake the letter "Q" for the letter "O".

When you come to a blank box, do nothing.

MI (Middle Initial). Enter your middle initial and darken the circle for the letter. If you do not have a middle initial, do not enter anything in the box or darken a circle.

2 SOCIAL SECURITY NUMBER. Look at your Social Security Number card. Compare the number with the one on the Admission Card/Notice. If the number on the Admission Card/Notice is not correct, draw a line through it and make the correction.

Enter your correct Social Security Number in GRID 2 on the Sample Answer Sheet.

Using the edge, darken the matching numerical circles.

3 BIRTH DATE. For GRID 3, in the box labeled "MM", enter the two numbers for your birth month, one number to a box. If you were born in January through September, you would enter a "0" in the first box and the number for the month in the second box. Using the edge, darken the matching circles.

In the box labeled "DD", enter the two numbers for your day of birth, one number to a box. If your day of birth is from one to nine, enter a "0" in the first box and the number for the day in the second box. Using the edge, darken the matching circles.

In the box labeled "YY", enter the last two numbers of the year in which you were born, one number to a box. Do not use the current year. Using the edge, darken the matching circles.

WHEN YOU FINISH GRID 3, YOU SHOULD HAVE ENTERED AND GRIDDED SIX NUMBERS.

4 LEAD OFFICE/INSTALLATION FINANCE NUMBER. Look at the Admission Card/Notice. On it there is a six digit number and the name of the office for which you have applied. With your pencil, enter this number in GRID 4, one number to a box. Using the edge, darken the matching numerical circles.

5 JOB CHOICE. Do nothing with GRID 5.

6 TEST SERIES. Do nothing with GRID 6.

7 EXAM DATE. Look at the Admission Card/Notice for the date you are scheduled to take this exam. For GRID 7, in the box labeled "MM", enter the two numbers for the exam month, one number to a box. If the exam is in January through September, you would

enter a "0" in the first box and the number for the month in the second box. Using the edge, darken the matching circles.

In the box labeled "DD", enter the two numbers for your day of exam, one number to a box. If your day of exam is from one to nine, enter a "0" in the first box and the number for the day in the second box. Using the edge, darken the matching circles.

In the box labeled "YY", enter the last two numbers of the year of the exam, one number to a box. Using the edge, darken the matching circles.

WHEN YOU FINISH GRID 7, YOU SHOULD HAVE ENTERED AND GRIDDED SIX NUMBERS.

8 YOUR CHOICE OF INSTALLATIONS. If a sheet was NOT supplied for choosing installations, do nothing with GRID 8. If the installation for which you have applied has an Area Register, a sheet was supplied from which you must choose one to three offices. For each office you choose, circle its number on the sheet. Then darken the circle in GRID 8 for the number of each office you chose. You must not darken more than three circles. It is your responsibility to make sure the circles you grid are your choices. Once you have gridded the circles on the Answer Sheet in the exam room, your choices cannot be changed.

9 VETERAN PREFERENCE. If you are not eligible to claim Veteran Preference, do nothing with GRID 9. The following is an explanation of the different types of Veteran Preference:

5 Points (tentative). This preference is usually given to honorably separated veterans who served on active duty in the Armed Forces of the United States under one of the following conditions:

a. During a declared war (the last one was World War II); or

b. During the period April 28, 1952 to July 1, 1955; or

c. During the period February 1, 1955 through October 14, 1976 for which any part of more than 180 consecutive days was served. (An initial period of active duty for training under the 6-month Reserve or National Guard Program does not count.)

d. In any campaign or expedition for which a campaign badge was authorized.

Veterans who served in Southwest Asia or in the surrounding contiguous waters or air space on or after August 2, 1990 AND who were awarded the

Southwest Asia Service Medal can claim five points.

10 Points - Compensable (Less than 30%). This preference is given to honorably separated veterans who served on active duty in the Armed Forces at any time and have a service-connected disability for which compensation is provided at 10% or more, but less than 30%.

10 Points - Compensable (30% or more). This preference is given to honorably separated veterans who served on active duty in the Armed Forces at any time and have a service-connected disability for which compensation is provided at 30% or more.

10 Points (other). This preference is claimed by a variety of people:

a. Veterans who were awarded the Purple Heart; or

b. Veterans who have a recognized service-connected disability for which no compensation is received or a recognized nonservice-connected disability; or

c. Until remarried, the widow or widower of an honorably separated veteran, provided the deceased veteran served in active duty during a war, or the veteran died while in the Armed Forces; or

d. Spouses of certain veterans with a service-connected disability; or

e. Mothers of certain deceased or disabled veterans.

Darken only one circle in GRID 9 if you wish to claim Veteran Preference. Do not darken more than one circle. Points claimed will be added to your score ONLY if you pass the exam with a score of 70 or better.

10 EXAM TYPE. In GRID 10, darken the circle for "Entrance". Do not darken the other circle.

11 SPECIAL INSTRUCTIONS. If you do not have "DELAYED" or "REOPENED" stamped on your Admission Card/Notice, do nothing with GRID 11. This grid is only for people who are taking this exam because they either:

a. missed an opportunity to take the exam when last opened to the public because they were on active military duty, **"DELAYED"** status OR

b. entitled to 10 point Veteran Preference, **"REOPENED"** status.

Grid the circle labeled **"3"** for **"DELAYED"**, or the circle labeled **"4"** for **"REOPENED."**

12 LEAD OFFICE (Name). Look at the right side of the Admission Card/Notice for the name of the installation for which you are applying. Print the name in the block labeled: "Lead Office/Installation (Please Print)". Print the two letter abbreviation for the state in the block labeled "State."

Sign your name in the block labeled "Signature."

13 PRINT YOUR CITY AND STATE. Turn to Page 2 of the Sample Answer Sheet. Print the city and state of your current mailing address.

14 STREET ADDRESS. This is for the one line address that will be used to deliver your test result. If you pass and later your score is reached for consideration, the address you grid will be used to notify you. The address you grid **must** meet Postal standards. Study the following examples:

1234 MAIN ST APT 999

45678 MADISON BLVD S

33 1/2 IVY DR SW

4329-02 MONTGOMERY PL

2342 NW SMITH RD

RR 2 BOX 50

PO BOX 4502

You must use the correct shortened format for your one line address. Also, such an address will be easier and quicker to grid.

This grid is different from the other ones because it contains numbers, special symbols and letters. Enter your one line address in the boxes. **You must start with the first box to the left.** Skip a blank box where there needs to be a space. By using the edge and starting with the first column to the left, darken the circles.

Do not mistake the letter "Q" for the letter "O".

When you come to a blank box, do nothing.

15 ZIP (Code). You must have your correct ZIP Code to complete this grid. An incorrect ZIP Code will result in a delay in sending your rating to you. Your ZIP Code is found on magazines, utility bills and other business mail you receive at home. Enter your correct five digit ZIP Code in the boxes. Then use the edge to darken the matching numerical circles.

16 +4 (Code). You must have your correct ZIP+4 Code to complete this grid. Your ZIP+4 is usually found on mail you receive at home. This four digit number appears after the five digit ZIP Code. Enter this number in GRID 16. Use the edge and darken the numerical circles.

FOR GRIDS 17, 18 AND 19, read the General Instructions for the RESEARCH QUESTIONNAIRE on Page 2 of the Sample Answer Sheet.

17 SEX. Darken the appropriate circle in GRID 17.

18 DISABILITY CODE. If you do not have a disability, enter 0 in the first box and 5 in the second box in GRID 18. Code "05" indicates "No Disability." Using the edge, darken the numerical circles.

A disability refers to a physical or mental disability or history of such disability which is likely to cause difficulty in obtaining, maintaining, or advancing in employment. On Page 4, you will find a list of various disabilities. Each of the disabilities has a number. If you have a disability, read the list carefully and select the code that best describes your disability. If you have multiple disabilities, choose the code for the one that is most disabling. Enter the two numbers of the disability code in the boxes at the top of GRID 18. If your disability is not listed, enter zero in the first column and six in the second column. Using the edge, darken the numerical circles.

19 RACIAL AND NATIONAL ORIGIN. This grid is for the collection of your racial and national origin. Darken the circle for the category that applies to you. If you are of mixed racial and/or national origin, you should identify yourself by the one category for which you most closely associate yourself by darkening the appropriate circle in GRID 19.

Checking your work. After you have finished, go back and check your work. For a letter or number in a box, you should have only one circle darkened in the column found directly below. Make sure that you have completed all items as requested.

After checking your work, go back to Page 1 of the Sample Answer Sheet. In the upper left corner is the United States Postal Service eagle. Draw a circle around the eagle.

Get someone else to check your work. Since the scanner that reads the Answer Sheet only picks up what is gridded, you should have someone else check your work. Let them tell you if you made a mistake so that you can correct it. This will help make sure that you do the best job you possibly can on the Answer Sheet in the exam room.

SAMPLE ANSWER SHEET
for
TEST 460

USE NO. 2 PENCIL ONLY

1 In the boxes below, print your last name, first name and middle initial in the proper sections as indicated, one letter per box. Below each box, blacken the oval which is lettered the same as the letter in the box. For each blank letter box, do not blacken any of the ovals.

Last Name   **First Name**   **MI**

(Ovals A through Z for each letter box)

2 Social Security Number

(Ovals 0 through 9)

3 Birth Date

MM	DD	YY

(Ovals 0 through 9)

4 Lead Office/ Installation Finance Number

(Ovals 0 through 9)

5 DO NOT WRITE IN THIS AREA

6 Test Series

DO NOT COMPLETE

(Ovals 0 through 9)

7 Exam Date

MM	DD	YY

(Ovals 0 through 9)

8 Your choice of installations where you want to be considered (not more than 3)

① ② ③ ④ ⑤ ⑥ ⑦ ⑧ ⑨ ⑩
⑪ ⑫ ⑬ ⑭ ⑮ ⑯ ⑰ ⑱ ⑲ ⑳
㉑ ㉒ ㉓ ㉔ ㉕ ㉖ ㉗ ㉘ ㉙ ㉚
㉛ ㉜ ㉝ ㉞ ㉟ ㊱ ㊲ ㊳ ㊴ ㊵
㊶ ㊷ ㊸ ㊹ ㊺ ㊻ ㊼ ㊽ ㊾ ㊿

9 Veteran Preference

○ 5 points (tentative)
○ 10 points-Compensable (Less than 30%)
○ 10 points-Compensable (30% or more)
○ 10 points (other)

10 Exam Type

○ Entrance
○ In Service

11 Special Instructions

① ② ③ ④ ⑤ ⑥ ⑦ ⑧ ⑨ ⑩ ⑪ ⑫ ⑬ ⑭ ⑮ ⑯ ⑰ ⑱ ⑲ ⑳ ㉑ ㉒ ㉓ ㉔

12 Lead Office/Installation (Please Print)   State   Signature

13 Print your city and state →

14 In the boxes below, print your street address or post office box (one letter, number, or symbol per box).

15 ZIP

16 +4

(grids of filled-in ovals for numbers 0–9, blank, /, and letters A–Z for address, ZIP, and +4 fields)

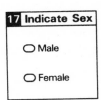

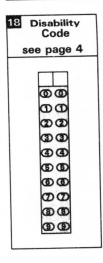

RESEARCH QUESTIONNAIRE
General Instructions

The U.S. Postal Service wants to make sure that its part in the recruitment and hiring of postal employees is fair for everyone. To do this we need your answers to the three questions below. Your responses are voluntary. Please answer each of the questions to the best of your ability. Your answers will be used for research purposes only and to help assure equal employment opportunity. Please provide accurate information. Your cooperation is important. Completely darken the oval corresponding to your response choice.

17 Indicate Sex

○ Male

○ Female

18 Disability Code
see page 4

19 The categories below are designed to identify your basic racial and national origin category. If you are of mixed racial and/or national origin, indicate the category with which you most closely identify yourself.

Name of Category	Definition of Category
○ American Indian or Alaskan Native	A person having origins in any of the original peoples of North America, and who maintains cultural identification through community recognition or tribal affiliation.
○ Asian or Pacific Islander	A person having origins in any of the original peoples of the Far East, Southeast Asia, the Indian subcontinent, or the Pacific Islands. This area includes, for example China, India, Japan, Korea, the Philippine Islands, Samoa, and Vietnam.
○ Black, not of Hispanic Origin	A person having origins in any of the black racial groups of Africa. Does not include persons of Mexican, Puerto Rican, Cuban, Central or South American, or other Spanish cultures or origins (see Hispanic).
○ Hispanic	A person of Mexican, Puerto Rican, Cuban, Central or South American, or other Spanish cultures or origins. Does not include persons of Portuguese culture or origin.
○ White, not of Hispanic Origin	A person having origins in any of the original peoples of Europe, North Africa, or the Middle East. Does not include persons of Mexican, Puerto Rican, Cuban, Central or South American, or other Spanish cultures or origins (see Hispanic). Also includes persons not included in other categories.

DID YOU READ **ALL** OF THE
INSTRUCTIONS?

THANK YOU FOR FOLLOWING THE
DIRECTIONS AND COMPLETING
THE SAMPLE ANSWER SHEET.

THE UNITED STATES POSTAL SERVICE IS
AN EQUAL OPPORTUNITY EMPLOYER.

Disability Code Listing

CODE	GENERAL	CODE	PARTIAL PARALYSIS (continued)
01	Disability Not Reported	66	Both arms, any part
05	No Disability	67	One side of body, including one arm and one leg
06	Disability Not Listed on This Form	68	Three or more major parts of the body (arms and legs)

CODE	SPEECH IMPAIRMENTS	CODE	COMPLETE PARALYSIS
13	Severe speech malfunction or inability to speak, hearing is normal. Example: defects of articulation (unclear language sounds); stuttering; aphasia; laryngectomy (removal of the voice box).		(Because of a brain, nerve, or muscle problem, including palsy and cerebral palsy, there is complete loss of ability to move or use a part of the body, including legs, arms and/or trunk.)
		70	One hand

CODE	HEARING IMPAIRMENTS	CODE	
15	Hard of hearing; correctable by hearing aid	71	Both hands
16	Total deafness with understandable speech	72	One arm
17	Total deafness with inability to speak clearly	73	Both arms
		74	One leg

CODE	VISION IMPAIRMENTS	CODE	
		75	Both legs
22	Can read ordinary size print with glasses, but with loss of peripheral (side) vision	76	Lower half of body, including legs
		77	One side of body, including one arm and one leg
23	Cannot read ordinary size print; not correctable by glasses	78	Three or more major parts of the body (arms and legs)
24	Blind in one eye		OTHER IMPAIRMENTS
25	Blind in both eyes	80	Heart disease with no restriction or limitation of activity (history of heart problem with complete recovery)

CODE	MISSING EXTREMITIES	CODE	
27	One hand	81	Heart disease with restriction or limitation of activity
28	One arm		
29	One foot	82	Convulsive disorder (e.g., epilepsy)
32	One leg		
33	Both hands or arms	83	Blood disease (e.g., sickle cell disease, leukemia, hemophilia)
34	Both feet or legs		
35	One hand or arm and one foot or leg	84	Diabetes
36	One hand or arm and both feet or legs		
37	Both hands or arms and one foot or leg	86	Pulmonary or respiratory (e.g., tuberculosis, emphysema, asthma)
38	Both hands or arms and both feet or legs		

CODE	NONPARALYTIC ORTHOPEDIC IMPAIRMENTS	CODE	
	(Because of chronic pain, stiffness, or weakness in bones or joints, there is some loss of ability to move or use a part of the body.)	87	Kidney dysfunctioning (e.g., use of an artificial kidney machine)
44	One or both hands	88	Cancer (history of cancer with complete recovery)
45	One or both feet		
46	One or both arms		
47	One or both legs	89	Cancer (undergoing surgical and/or medical treatment)
48	Hip or pelvis		
49	Back	92	Severe distortion of limbs and/or spine (e.g., dwarfism, kyphosis — severe distortion of back, etc.)
57	Any combination of two or more parts of the body		

CODE	PARTIAL PARALYSIS	CODE	
	(Because of a brain, nerve, or muscle problem, including palsy and cerebral palsy, there is some loss of ability to move or use a part of the body, including legs, arms, and/or trunk.)	93	Disfigurement of face, hands, or feet (e.g., distortion of features on skin, such as those caused by burns, gunshot injuries, and birth defects, gross facial birth marks, club feet, etc.)
61	One hand		MENTAL RETARDATION/EMOTIONAL PROBLEMS
62	One arm, any part	90	A chronic and lifelong condition involving a limited ability to learn, to be educated and to be trained for useful productive employment as certified by a State Vocational Rehabilitation Agency.
63	One leg, any part	91	Mental or emotional illness (history of treatment for mental or emotional problems)
64	Both hands		
65	Both legs, any part	94	Learning Disability

Sample Questions
460 Rural Carrier Associate Exam
U.S. Postal Service

TEST INSTRUCTIONS

During the test session, it will be your responsibility to pay close attention to what the examiner has to say and to follow all instructions. One of the purposes of the test is to see how quickly and accurately you can work. Therefore, each part of the test will be carefully timed. You will not START until being told to do so. Also, when you are told to STOP, you must immediately STOP answering the questions. When you are told to work on a particular part of the examination, regardless of which part, you are to work on that part ONLY. If you finish a part before time is called, you may review your answers for that part, but you will not go on or back to any other part. Failure to follow ANY directions given to you by the examiner may be grounds for disqualification. Instructions read by the examiner are intended to ensure that each applicant has the same fair and objective opportunity to compete in the examination.

SAMPLE QUESTIONS

Study carefully before the examination.

The following questions are like the ones that will be on the test. Study these carefully. This will give you practice with the different kinds of questions and show you how to mark your answers.

Part A: Address Checking

In this part of the test, you will have to decide whether two addresses are alike or different. If the two addresses are exactly *Alike* in every way, darken circle A for the question. If the two addresses are *Different* in any way, darken circle D for the question.

Mark your answers to these sample questions on the Sample Answer Grid at the right.

1...2134 S 20th St   2134 S 20th St

Since the two addresses are exactly alike, mark A for
question 1 on the Sample Answer Grid.

2...4608 N Warnock St   4806 N Warnock St

3...1202 W Girard Dr   1202 W Girard Rd

4...Chappaqua NY 10514   Chappaqua NY 10514

5...2207 Markland Ave   2207 Markham Ave

Sample Answer Grid		
1	Ⓐ	Ⓓ
2	Ⓐ	Ⓓ
3	Ⓐ	Ⓓ
4	Ⓐ	Ⓓ
5	Ⓐ	Ⓓ

The correct answers to questions 2 to 5 are: 2D, 3D, 4A, and 5D.

(See *Techniques for Address-Checking Test* on pages 77-81.)

Your score on Part A of the actual test will be based on the number of wrong answers as well as on the number of right answers. Part A is scored right answers minus wrong answers. Random guessing should not help your score. For the Part A test, you will have six minutes to answer as many of the 95 questions as you can. It will be to your advantage to work as quickly and as accurately as possible. You will not be expected to be able to answer all the questions in the time allowed.

Part B: Memory for Addresses

In this part of the test, you will have to memorize the locations (A, B, C, D, or E) of 25 addresses shown in five boxes, like those below. For example, "Sardis" is in Box C, "6800-6999 Table" is in Box B, etc. (The addresses in the actual test will be different.)

A	B	C	D	E
4700-5599 Table	6800-6999 Table	5600-6499 Table	6500-6799 Table	4400-4699 Table
Lismore	Kelford	Joel	Tatum	Ruskin
5600-6499 West	6500-6799 West	6800-6999 West	4400-4699 West	4700-5599 West
Hesper	Musella	Sardis	Porter	Nathan
4400-4699 Blake	5600-6499 Blake	6500-6799 Blake	4700-5599 Blake	6800-6999 Blake

Study the locations of the addresses for five minutes. As you study, silently repeat these to yourself. Then cover the boxes and try to answer the questions below. Mark your answers for each question by darkening the circle as was done for questions 1 and 2.

1. Musella
2. 4700-5599 Blake
3. 4700-5599 Table
4. Tatum
5. 4400-4699 Blake
6. Hesper
7. Kelford
8. Nathan
9. 6500-6799 Blake
10. Joel
11. 4400-4699 Blake
12. 6500-6799 West
13. Porter
14. 6800-6999 Blake

Sample Answer Grid

The correct answers for questions 3 to 14 are: 3A, 4D, 5A, 6A, 7B, 8E, 9C, 10C, 11A, 12B, 13D, and 14E.

(See *Memory-for-Address Test: Tips & Strategies* on pages 107-112.)

During the examination, you will have three practice exercises to help you memorize the location of addresses shown in five boxes. After the practice exercises, the actual test will be given. Part B is scored right answers minus one-fourth of the wrong answers. Random guessing should not help your score. But, if you can eliminate one or more alternatives, it is to your advantage to guess. For the Part B test, you will have five minutes to answer as many of the 88 questions as you can. It will be to your advantage to work as quickly and as accurately as you can. You will not be expected to be able to answer all the questions in the time allowed.

Part C: Number Series

For each *Number Series* question there is at the left a series of numbers which follow some definite order and at the right five sets of two numbers each. You are to look at the numbers in the series at the left and find out what order they follow. Then decide what the next two numbers in that series would be if the same order were continued. Mark your answers on the Sample Answer Grid.

    1. 1 2 3 4 5 6 7 . . . .   A) 1 2   B) 5 6   C) 8 9   D) 4 5   E) 7 8

The numbers in this series are increasing by 1. If the series were continued for two more numbers, it would read: 1 2 3 4 5 6 7 8 9. Therefore the correct answer is 8 and 9 and you should have darkened C for question 1.

    2. 15 14 13 12 11 10 9 . . . .   A) 2 1   B) 17 16   C) 8 9   D) 8 7   E) 9 8

The numbers in this series are decreasing by 1. If the series were continued for two more numbers, it would read: 15 14 13 12 11 10 9 8 7. Therefore the correct answer is 8 and 7 and you should have darkened D for question 2.

    3. 20 20 21 21 22 22 23 . . . .   A) 23 23   B) 23 24   C) 19 19   D) 22 23   E) 21 22

Each number in this series is repeated and then increased by 1. If the series were continued for two more numbers, it would read: 20 20 21 21 22 22 23 23 24. Therefore the correct answer is 23 and 24 and you should have darkened B for question 3.

    4. 17 3 17 4 17 5 17 . . . .   A) 6 17   B) 6 7   C) 17 6   D) 5 6   E) 17 7

This series is the number 17 separated by numbers increasing by 1, beginning with the number 3. If the series were continued for two more numbers, it would read: 17 3 17 4 17 5 17 6 17. Therefore the correct answer is 6 and 17 and you should have darkened A for question 4.

    5. 1 2 4 5 7 8 10 . . . .   A) 11 12   B) 12 14   C) 10 13   D) 12 13   E) 11 13

The numbers in this series are increasing first by 1 (plus 1) and then by 2 (plus 2). If the series were continued for two more numbers, it would read: 1 2 4 5 7 8 10 (plus 1) *11* and (plus 2) *13*. Therefore the correct answer is 11 and 13 and you should have darkened E for question 5.

Now read and work sample questions 6 through 10 and mark your answers on the Sample Answer Grid.

    6. 21 21 20 20 19 19 18 . . . .   A) 18 18   B) 18 17   C) 17 18   D) 17 17   E) 18 19

    7. 1 22 1 23 1 24 1 . . . .   A) 26 1   B) 25 26   C) 25 1   D) 1 26   E) 1 25

    8. 1 20 3 19 5 18 7 . . . .   A) 8 9   B) 8 17   C) 17 10   D) 17 9   E) 9 18

    9. 4 7 10 13 16 19 22 . . . .   A) 23 26   B) 25 27   C) 25 26   D) 25 28   E) 24 27

   10. 30 2 28 4 26 6 24 . . . .   A) 23 9   B) 26 8   C) 8 9   D) 26 22   E) 8 22

(See **Number Series Test** on pages 135-138.)

	Sample Answer Grid			
6 Ⓐ Ⓑ Ⓒ Ⓓ Ⓔ	8 Ⓐ Ⓑ Ⓒ Ⓓ Ⓔ	9 Ⓐ Ⓑ Ⓒ Ⓓ Ⓔ	10 Ⓐ Ⓑ Ⓒ Ⓓ Ⓔ
7 Ⓐ Ⓑ Ⓒ Ⓓ Ⓔ			

The correct answers to sample questions 6 to 10 are: 6B, 7C, 8D, 9D and 10E. Explanations follow.

6. Each number in the series repeats itself and then decreases by 1 or minus 1; *21* (repeat) *21* (minus 1) *20* (repeat) *20* (minus 1) *19* (repeat) *19* (minus 1) *18* (repeat) *?* (minus 1) *?*

7.   The number 1 is separated by numbers which begin with 22 and increased by 1; *1 22 1* (increase 22 by 1) *23 1* (increase 23 by 1) *24 1* (increase 24 by 1) *?*

8. This is best explained by two alternating series -- one series starts with 1 and increases by 2 or plus 2; the other series starts with 20 and decreases by 1 or minus 1.

1	^	*3*	^	*5*	^	*7*	^	*?*
	20		*19*		*18*		*?*	

9. This series of numbers increases by 3 (plus 3) beginning with the first number -- *4 7 10 13 16 19 22 ? ?*

10. Look for two alternating series -- one series starts with 30 and decreases by 2 (minus 2); the other series starts with 2 and increases by 2 (plus 2).

Now try questions 11 to 15.

11. 5 6 20 7 8 19 9 . . . . A) 10 18   B) 18 17   C) 10 17   D) 18 19   E) 10 11

12. 4 6 9 11 14 16 19 . . . . A) 21 24   B) 22 25   C) 20 22   D) 21 23   E) 22 24

13. 8 8 1 10 10 3 12 . . . . A) 13 13   B) 12 5   C) 12 4   D) 13 5   E) 4 12

14. 10 12 50 15 17 50 20 . . . . A) 50 21   B) 21 50   C) 50 22   D) 22 50   E) 22 24

15. 20 21 23 24 27 28 32 33 38 39 . A) 45 46   B) 45 52   C) 44 45   D) 44 49   E) 40 46

	Sample Answer Grid			
11 Ⓐ Ⓑ Ⓒ Ⓓ Ⓔ	13 Ⓐ Ⓑ Ⓒ Ⓓ Ⓔ	14 Ⓐ Ⓑ Ⓒ Ⓓ Ⓔ	15 Ⓐ Ⓑ Ⓒ Ⓓ Ⓔ
12 Ⓐ Ⓑ Ⓒ Ⓓ Ⓔ			

The correct answers to the sample questions above are: 11A, 12A, 13B, 14D and 15A.

It will be to your advantage to answer every question in Part C that you can, since your score on this part of the test will be based on the number of questions that you answer correctly. Answer first those questions which are easiest for you. For the Part C test, you will have 20 minutes to answer as many of the 24 questions as you can.

(See **Number Series Test** on pages 135-138.)

Part D: Following Oral Instructions

In this part of the test, you will be told to follow directions by writing in a test booklet and then on an answer sheet. The test booklet will have lines of material like the following five samples:

SAMPLE 1.   5 __

SAMPLE 2.   1   6   4   3   7

SAMPLE 3.   D   B   A   E   C

SAMPLE 4.   (8 __) (5 __) (2 __) (9 __) (10 __)

SAMPLE 5.   (7 __) [6 __] (1 __) [12 __]

To practice this part of the test, tear off page 11. Then have somebody read the instructions to you and you follow the instructions. When he or she tells you to darken the space on the Sample Answer Grid, use the one on this page.

Sample Answer Grid			
1 Ⓐ Ⓑ Ⓒ Ⓓ Ⓔ	4 Ⓐ Ⓑ Ⓒ Ⓓ Ⓔ	7 Ⓐ Ⓑ Ⓒ Ⓓ Ⓔ	10 Ⓐ Ⓑ Ⓒ Ⓓ Ⓔ
2 Ⓐ Ⓑ Ⓒ Ⓓ Ⓔ	5 Ⓐ Ⓑ Ⓒ Ⓓ Ⓔ	8 Ⓐ Ⓑ Ⓒ Ⓓ Ⓔ	11 Ⓐ Ⓑ Ⓒ Ⓓ Ⓔ
3 Ⓐ Ⓑ Ⓒ Ⓓ Ⓔ	6 Ⓐ Ⓑ Ⓒ Ⓓ Ⓔ	9 Ⓐ Ⓑ Ⓒ Ⓓ Ⓔ	12 Ⓐ Ⓑ Ⓒ Ⓓ Ⓔ

Your score for part D will be based on the number of questions that you answer correctly. Therefore, if you are not sure of an answer, it will be to your advantage to guess. Part D will take about 25 minutes.

KEEP THESE INSTRUCTIONS FOR FUTURE REFERENCE. YOUR PARTICIPATION AND COOPERATION IN THIS POSTAL EXAM IS APPRECIATED.

Instructions to be read (the words in parentheses should NOT be read aloud)

You are to follow the instructions that I shall read to you. I cannot repeat them.

Look at the samples. Sample 1 has a number and a line beside it. On the line write A as in ace. (Pause 2 seconds.) Now on the Sample Answer Grid, find the number 5 (pause 2 seconds) and darken the letter you just wrote on the line. (Pause 2 seconds.)

Look at Sample 2. (Pause slightly.) Draw a line under the third number. (Pause 2 seconds.) Now look on the Sample Answer Grid, find the number under which you just drew a line and darken B as in boy. (Pause 5 seconds.)

Look at the letters in Sample 3. (Pause slightly.) Draw a line under the third letter in the line. (Pause 2 seconds.) Now on your Sample Answer Grid, find number 9 (pause 2 seconds) and darken the letter under which you drew a line. (Pause 5 seconds.)

Look at the five circles in Sample 4. (Pause slightly.) Each circle has a number and a line in it. Write D as in dog on the line in the last circle. (Pause 2 seconds.) Now on the Sample Answer Grid, darken the number-letter combination that is in the circle you just wrote in. (Pause 5 seconds.)

Look at Sample 5. (Pause slightly.) There are two circles and two boxes of different sizes with numbers in them. (Pause slightly.) If 4 is more than 2 and if 5 is less than 3, write A as in ace in the smaller circle. (Pause slightly.) Otherwise write C as in car in the larger box. (Pause 2 seconds.) Now on the Sample Grid, darken the number-letter combination in the box or circle in which you just wrote. (Pause 5 seconds.)

Now look at the Sample Answer Grid. (Pause slightly.) You should have darkened 4B, 5A, 9A, 10D, and 12C on the Sample Answer Grid. (If the person preparing to take the examination made any mistakes, try to help him or her see why he or she made the wrong marks.)

## 34

10 Practice Tests (RCA 460 Exam)

5 Address-Checking Practice Tests
5 Memory-for-Address Practice Tests

(See Techniques for Address-Checking Test on pages 77-81.)
(See Memory-for-Address Test: Tips & Strategies on pages 107-112.)

(Note: Exam 460 is exclusively for Rural Carrier Associates.)

Address-Checking Practice Test

Work—6 Minutes

These addresses are like the ones in the address-checking test.

Decide whether the two addresses are *Alike* or *Different*. If they are *Alike,* darken or mark space A; if they are *Different,* darken space D. Mark the answers on the answer sheet to the right. Work as fast as you can without making too any errors. Work exactly 6 minutes.

ANSWER SHEET

			Test A	Test B
1.	1405 Hickory Rd NW	1504 Hickory Rd NW	1 ⒶⒹ	1 ⒶⒹ
2.	1354 Central Park W	1354 Central Park W	2 ⒶⒹ	2 ⒶⒹ
3.	500 Court Rd NE	500 Court RD NW	3 ⒶⒹ	3 ⒶⒹ
4.	East Point, MI 48021	East Pointe, MI 48031	4 ⒶⒹ	4 ⒶⒹ
5.	35016 S Main St	35015 S Main St	5 ⒶⒹ	5 ⒶⒹ
6.	Bay Pines, FL 33503	Bay Pines, FL 33503	6 ⒶⒹ	6 ⒶⒹ
7.	3653 Peasant Run Ave	3653 Pleasant Run Ave	7 ⒶⒹ	7 ⒶⒹ
8.	154 S Washington Sq	154 N Washington Sq	8 ⒶⒹ	8 ⒶⒹ
9.	3531 McWeeney Rd	3531 McWeeney Rd	9 ⒶⒹ	9 ⒶⒹ
10.	7535 Cedar Ln	7535 Cedar St	10 ⒶⒹ	10 ⒶⒹ
11.	Meridian, Idaho 83645	Meridian, Idaho 83345	11 ⒶⒹ	11 ⒶⒹ
12.	Manson, NC 27553	Manson, NC 27553	12 ⒶⒹ	12 ⒶⒹ
13.	2105 W 18th Ave	2103 W 18th Ave	13 ⒶⒹ	13 ⒶⒹ
14.	3153 Carter Dr	3157 Carter Dr	14 ⒶⒹ	14 ⒶⒹ
15.	98354 Hopeville Ln	98354 Hopeville Ln	15 ⒶⒹ	15 ⒶⒹ
16.	15315 N Audrey Rd	15815 N Audrey Rd	16 ⒶⒹ	16 ⒶⒹ
17.	31543 Stony Brook	31543 Stony Brook	17 ⒶⒹ	17 ⒶⒹ
18.	Southfield, MI 48075	Southfield, MI 48073	18 ⒶⒹ	18 ⒶⒹ
19.	11359 N Tulipe St	11359 S Tulipe St	19 ⒶⒹ	19 ⒶⒹ
20.	31547 Country Club Rd	31547 Country Club Rd	20 ⒶⒹ	20 ⒶⒹ
21.	80329 Guillian Rdg	80329 Guillian Rdg	21 ⒶⒹ	21 ⒶⒹ
22.	93178 Herschel Plaza	98178 Hershel Plaza	22 ⒶⒹ	22 ⒶⒹ
23.	5462 Audobon Ct	5462 Audobon Ct	23 ⒶⒹ	23 ⒶⒹ
24.	89354 Ocean Blvd	19354 Ocean Blvd	24 ⒶⒹ	24 ⒶⒹ
25.	77331 SW Teppert St	77381 SW Teppert St	25 ⒶⒹ	25 ⒶⒹ
26.	315 Bensen Pky	315 Bensen Pky	26 ⒶⒹ	26 ⒶⒹ
27.	20361 Alexander St	20361 Alexander Ave	27 ⒶⒹ	27 ⒶⒹ
28.	3154 S Colorado Rd	3154 N Colorado Rd	28 ⒶⒹ	28 ⒶⒹ
29.	9156 N Placid Ln	9156 S Placid Ln	29 ⒶⒹ	29 ⒶⒹ
30.	1120 Kenilworth Ct	1120 Kenilworth Ct	30 ⒶⒹ	30 ⒶⒹ
31.	87104 Tulip Pky	87104 Tulip Rd	31 ⒶⒹ	31 ⒶⒹ
32.	2465 Cornplakes Sq	2465 Cornplakes Sq	32 ⒶⒹ	32 ⒶⒹ
33.	9037 Delaware Ave	9038 Delaware Ave	33 ⒶⒹ	33 ⒶⒹ
34.	3154 N Lancaster	3154 N Lancaster	34 ⒶⒹ	34 ⒶⒹ
35.	3698 Stonybrook Sq	3698 Stonybrook Sq	35 ⒶⒹ	35 ⒶⒹ
36.	3154 E Jefferson St	3154 E Jefferson St	36 ⒶⒹ	36 ⒶⒹ
37.	8634 19th Ave SW	8634 19th Ave SE	37 ⒶⒹ	37 ⒶⒹ
38.	2654 Avenue NW	3645 Avenue NW	38 ⒶⒹ	38 ⒶⒹ
39.	3545 Monticello Ct	3545 Montecello Ct	39 ⒶⒹ	39 ⒶⒹ
40.	46017 Thunder Hill	46017 Thunder Hill	40 ⒶⒹ	40 ⒶⒹ

Go on to the next number on the next page.

41. 8761 Woodridge Ave	8761 Woodrige Rd	41 Ⓐ Ⓓ	41 Ⓐ Ⓓ
42, 11253 Lovers Ln	11253 Lovers Ln	42 Ⓐ Ⓓ	42 Ⓐ Ⓓ
43. 7718 Rolling Hills NW	7718 Rolling Hills SE	43· Ⓐ Ⓓ	43 Ⓐ Ⓓ
44. 3838 Edgecom View	3383 Edgecom View	44 Ⓐ Ⓓ	44 Ⓐ Ⓓ
45. 7634 5th Ave S	7634 5th Ave S	45· Ⓐ Ⓓ	45 Ⓐ Ⓓ
46. 1873 7th St SW	1878 7th St SW	46· Ⓐ Ⓓ	46 Ⓐ Ⓓ
47. 3838 Oceanside Blvd	3838 Oceanside Blvd	47 Ⓐ Ⓓ	47 Ⓐ Ⓓ
48. 9835 Frescot Ct E	9835 Frescot CT W	48 Ⓐ Ⓓ	48 Ⓐ Ⓓ
49. 43735 Belleview N	43735 Belleview N	49 Ⓐ Ⓓ	49 Ⓐ Ⓓ
50. 3549 Eastland Dr E	3549 Eastland Dr W	50 Ⓐ Ⓓ	50 Ⓐ Ⓓ
51. 860 Rolling Acres W	860 Rolling Acres W	51 Ⓐ Ⓓ	51 Ⓐ Ⓓ
52. 9117 Surf St	9117 Surf St	52 Ⓐ Ⓓ	52 Ⓐ Ⓓ
53. 3938 Woodridge Ct	3938 Woodridge Ct	53 Ⓐ Ⓓ	53 Ⓐ Ⓓ
54. 9304 Yarbu St	9304 Yarbugh St	54 Ⓐ Ⓓ	54 Ⓐ Ⓓ
55. 11397 Edgeman Blvd S	11395 Edgeman Blvd S	55 Ⓐ Ⓓ	55 Ⓐ Ⓓ
56. 62660 High Noon Rd	62669 High Noon Rd	56 Ⓐ Ⓓ	56 Ⓐ Ⓓ
57. 2951 Lamaro Cove	2551 Lamaro Cove	57 Ⓐ Ⓓ	57 Ⓐ Ⓓ
58. 5066 Laurel Cir	5066 Laurel Cir	58 Ⓐ Ⓓ	58 Ⓐ Ⓓ
59. Ashburn, Virginia 22111	Ashburne, Virginia 22111	59 Ⓐ Ⓓ	59 Ⓐ Ⓓ
60. 1703 Allensville St	1708 Allensville St	60 Ⓐ Ⓓ	60 Ⓐ Ⓓ
61. 58356 Deerfield Cir	58356 Deerfield Cir	61 Ⓐ Ⓓ	61 Ⓐ Ⓓ
62. 3259 Rolling Stone Ct	3259 Rolling Stone Ct	62 Ⓐ Ⓓ	62 Ⓐ Ⓓ
63. 9306 High St SW	9307 High St SW	63 Ⓐ Ⓓ	63 Ⓐ Ⓓ
64. 305 Kentucky Ave	305 Kentucky Ave	64 Ⓐ Ⓓ	64 Ⓐ Ⓓ
65. 2548 Redesco Rd	2548 Redesco Sq	65 Ⓐ Ⓓ	65 Ⓐ Ⓓ
66. 2088 N Melendreso St	2089 N Melendreso St	66 Ⓐ Ⓓ	66 Ⓐ Ⓓ
67. 5983 Aroma Blvd	5983 Aroma Blvd	67 Ⓐ Ⓓ	67 Ⓐ Ⓓ
68. 3784 Lincoln Ave	3785 Lincoln Ave	68 Ⓐ Ⓓ	68 Ⓐ Ⓓ
69. 7835 Malcom Rd	7838 Malcom Rd	69 Ⓐ Ⓓ	69 Ⓐ Ⓓ
70. 2549 Montgomery Ave	2549 Montgomery Cir	70 Ⓐ Ⓓ	70 Ⓐ Ⓓ
71. 250 Virginia St W	250 Virginia St W	71 Ⓐ Ⓓ	71 Ⓐ Ⓓ
72. 13286 E Ausburn St	13286 W Ausburne St	72 Ⓐ Ⓓ	72 Ⓐ Ⓓ
73. 934 Lenoxin Cir SW	934 Lenoxin Cir SW	73 Ⓐ Ⓓ	73 Ⓐ Ⓓ
74. 1035 Lovers Ln W	1085 Lovers Ln W	74 Ⓐ Ⓓ	74 Ⓐ Ⓓ
75. 937 W Waterford Rd	937 W Waterford Rd	75 Ⓐ Ⓓ	75 Ⓐ Ⓓ
76. 3087 E Bellevue Hill	3087 W Bellevue Hill	76 Ⓐ Ⓓ	76 Ⓐ Ⓓ
77. 6943 6th Ave N	6948 6th Ave N	77 Ⓐ Ⓓ	77 Ⓐ Ⓓ
78 . 2052 Hubert Ave	2052 Hubert Ave	78 Ⓐ Ⓓ	78 Ⓐ Ⓓ
79. 983 SW Campbell Rd	983 SW Campbell Rd	79 Ⓐ Ⓓ	79 Ⓐ Ⓓ
80. 4088 4th Ave W	4088 4th Ave SE	80 Ⓐ Ⓓ	80 Ⓐ Ⓓ
81. 22011 Crossroad Ave	22011 Crossroad Ave	81 Ⓐ Ⓓ	81 Ⓐ Ⓓ
82. 1342 Northwest St	1342 Northeast St	82 Ⓐ Ⓓ	82 Ⓐ Ⓓ
83. 2057 Tender Rd	2057 Tender Rd	83 Ⓐ Ⓓ	83 Ⓐ Ⓓ
84. 3522 Bleeker Cove	3522 Bleeker Cove	84 Ⓐ Ⓓ	84 Ⓐ Ⓓ
85. 3154 Pittsburg Ct	3134 Pitsburg Ct	85 Ⓐ Ⓓ	85 Ⓐ Ⓓ
86. 5497 Gilmore Sq	5495 Gilmore Sq	86 Ⓐ Ⓓ	86 Ⓐ Ⓓ
87. 3921 Melendres Ave	3921 Melendres Ave	87 Ⓐ Ⓓ	87 Ⓐ Ⓓ
88. 5834 SW 7th Ave	5835 SW 7th Ave	88 Ⓐ Ⓓ	88 Ⓐ Ⓓ
89. 8640 Cherry Hill	8640 Cherry Hill	89 Ⓐ Ⓓ	89 Ⓐ Ⓓ

Go on to the next number on the next page.

90. 306 Calihan Ave E	306 Calihan Ave W	90 Ⓐ Ⓓ	90 Ⓐ Ⓓ
91. 3040 Makiling Ct	3040 Makiling Sq	91 Ⓐ Ⓓ	91 Ⓐ Ⓓ
92. 1555 Rectory Pl	1555 Rectory Pl	92 Ⓐ Ⓓ	92 Ⓐ Ⓓ
93. 3056 Bradley Ave	3056 Bradley Ave	93 Ⓐ Ⓓ	93 Ⓐ Ⓓ
94. 3054 Gangho Cir W	3054 Gangho Cir E	94 Ⓐ Ⓓ	94 Ⓐ Ⓓ
95. 97711 Acres Rd	97711 Acres Rd	95 Ⓐ Ⓓ	95 Ⓐ Ⓓ

STOP

If you finish before the time is up, check your answers for Part A.

Do not go to any other part.

(See the correct answers on the next page.

Correct Answers

Address-Checking Test

1. D	25. D	49. A	73. A
2. A	26. A	50. D	74. D
3. D	27. D	51. A	75. A
4. D	28. D	52. A	76. D
5. D	29. D	53. A	77. D
6. A	30. A	54. D	78. A
7. D	31. D	55. D	79. A
8. D	32. A	56. D	80. D
9. A	33. D	57. D	81. A
10. D	34. A	58. A	82. D
11. D	35. A	59. D	83. A
12. A	36. A	60. D	84. A
13. D	37. D	61. A	85. D
14. D	38. D	62. A	86. D
15. A	39. D	63. D	87. A
16. D	40. A	64. A	88. D
17. A	41. D	65. D	89. A
18. D	42. A	66. D	90. D
19. D	43. D	67. A	91. D
20. A	44. D	68. D	92. A
21. A	45. A	69. D	93. A
22. D	46. D	70. D	94. D
23. A	47. A	71. A	95. A
24. D	48. D	72. D	

Address-Checking Practice Test

Work—6 Minutes

These addresses are like the ones in the adress-checking test.

Decide whether the two addresses are *Alike* or *Different.* If they are Alike, darken or mark space A; if they are *Different,* darken space D. Mark the answers on the answer sheet to the right. Work as fast as you can without making too many errors. Work exactly 6 minutes.

ANSWER SHEET

		Test A	Test B
1. 1545 Harrison Ave	1543 Harrison Ave	1 Ⓐ Ⓓ	1 Ⓐ Ⓓ
2. 94375 Forrest Pl SW	94375 Forrest Pl SW	2 Ⓐ Ⓓ	2 Ⓐ Ⓓ
3. 3598 Lassie Rd W	3598 Lassie Rd W	3 Ⓐ Ⓓ	3 Ⓐ Ⓓ
4. 5071 Nesika Bay Sq	5077 Nesika Bay SQ	4 Ⓐ Ⓓ	4 Ⓐ Ⓓ
5. 3857 Blackberry Ln E	5857 Blackberry Ln W	5 Ⓐ Ⓓ	5 Ⓐ Ⓓ
6. 3547 Sherman Oaks St	3547 Sherman Oaks St	6 Ⓐ Ⓓ	6 Ⓐ Ⓓ
7. 9763 Clay Pky W	8653 Ckay Pkwy W	7 Ⓐ Ⓓ	7 Ⓐ Ⓓ
8. 308 S Lincolnside Dr	308 S Lincolnside Dr	8 Ⓐ Ⓓ	8 Ⓐ Ⓓ
9. 836 Sundae Sq N	836 Sundae Sq S	9 Ⓐ Ⓓ	9 Ⓐ Ⓓ
10. 3547 E Brighton Rd	3547 E Brighton Rd	10 Ⓐ Ⓓ	10 Ⓐ Ⓓ
11. 9836 W Falkner St	9836 E Falkner St	11 Ⓐ Ⓓ	11 Ⓐ Ⓓ
12. 5945 Stevens Rd	4945 Stevens Rd	12 Ⓐ Ⓓ	12 Ⓐ Ⓓ
13. 9003 Underwood St	9003 Underwood St	13 Ⓐ Ⓓ	13 Ⓐ Ⓓ
14. 4846 Blanchard Ave	4846 Glanchard Ave	14 Ⓐ Ⓓ	14 Ⓐ Ⓓ
15. 93658 Mt. Elena Sq	93658 Mt. Elena Dr	15 Ⓐ Ⓓ	15 Ⓐ Ⓓ
16. 354 W Boston Way	354 E Boston Way	16 Ⓐ Ⓓ	16 Ⓐ Ⓓ
17. 1919 Sievers Pky	1919 Stevers Pkwy	17 Ⓐ Ⓓ	17 Ⓐ Ⓓ
18. 3785 Apache Drum Rd	3785 Apache Dr Rd	18 Ⓐ Ⓓ	18 Ⓐ Ⓓ
19. 301 Bryan Ct	301 Bryan Ct	19 Ⓐ Ⓓ	19 Ⓐ Ⓓ
20. 9381 Agatha Pass Way	9331 Agatha Pass Way	20 Ⓐ Ⓓ	20 Ⓐ Ⓓ
21. 3547 Brownsville St	3547 Bronsville St	21 Ⓐ Ⓓ	21 Ⓐ Ⓓ
22. 3078 13th Ave SW	3073 13th Ave SW	22 Ⓐ Ⓓ	22 Ⓐ Ⓓ
23. 234 Creol Pass	234 Creole Pass	23 Ⓐ Ⓓ	23 Ⓐ Ⓓ
24. 7878 Burnett Dr	7878 Burnett Dr	24 Ⓐ Ⓓ	24 Ⓐ Ⓓ
25. 235 Dixon	235 Dixon	25 Ⓐ Ⓓ	25 Ⓐ Ⓓ
26. 9478 Wicker Way	9478 Wicker Way	26 Ⓐ Ⓓ	26 Ⓐ Ⓓ
27. 3054 17th St	3054 17th St	27 Ⓐ Ⓓ	27 Ⓐ Ⓓ
28. 37854 Bonn Ave	37854 Bonn Ave	28 Ⓐ Ⓓ	28 Ⓐ Ⓓ
29. 9076 Bingham Dr	9076 Bighan Dr	29 Ⓐ Ⓓ	29 Ⓐ Ⓓ
30. 3175 Walnut	3175 Walnut	30 Ⓐ Ⓓ	30 Ⓐ Ⓓ
31. 347 Bridgeview Ave	347 Bridgeview Rd	31 Ⓐ Ⓓ	31 Ⓐ Ⓓ
32. 9048 3rd Avenue SE	9048 3rd Avenue SE	32 Ⓐ Ⓓ	32 Ⓐ Ⓓ
33. 3250 Grant S	3250 Grant W	33 Ⓐ Ⓓ	33 Ⓐ Ⓓ
34. 1867 Pinecone Creek	1867 Pinecone Creek	34 Ⓐ Ⓓ	34 Ⓐ Ⓓ
35. 3065 Simon Blvd	3065 Simon Blvd	35 Ⓐ Ⓓ	35 Ⓐ Ⓓ
36. 3545 Armstrong Rd	3545 Armstrong Rdg	36 Ⓐ Ⓓ	36 Ⓐ Ⓓ
37. 16459 Rudolf Rdg	16459 Rudolf Rdg	37 Ⓐ Ⓓ	37 Ⓐ Ⓓ
38. 3649 Campbell Way	3669 Campbell Way	38 Ⓐ Ⓓ	38 Ⓐ Ⓓ
39. 3965 Simon Ave	9363 Simon Ave	39 Ⓐ Ⓓ	39 Ⓐ Ⓓ
40. 3548 Walnut Rd	3548 Walnut Rd	40 Ⓐ Ⓓ	40 Ⓐ Ⓓ

Go on to the next nmber on the next page.

41. 35646 W Armstrong St	35648 W Armstrong Sq	41	Ⓐ Ⓓ	41	Ⓐ Ⓓ
42. 3759 N Ford	3759 N Ford	42	Ⓐ Ⓓ	42	Ⓐ Ⓓ
43. 3584 Rose S	3584 Rose N	43	Ⓐ Ⓓ	43	Ⓐ Ⓓ
44. 40647 S Philips	40647 S Philips	44	Ⓐ Ⓓ	44	Ⓐ Ⓓ
45. 4657 Scotts Bluff	4657 Scotts Bluff	45	Ⓐ Ⓓ	45	Ⓐ Ⓓ
46. 9486 Beechnut St	9486 Beechnut Ct	46	Ⓐ Ⓓ	46	Ⓐ Ⓓ
47. 7786 Maleroy Ct	7788 Maleroy Ct	47	Ⓐ Ⓓ	47	Ⓐ Ⓓ
48. 36547 Keyport Rd	36547 Keyport Rd	48	Ⓐ Ⓓ	48	Ⓐ Ⓓ
49. 6458 47th Ave W	6458 47th Ave W	49	Ⓐ Ⓓ	49	Ⓐ Ⓓ
50. 308 King Dr	308 King Dr	50	Ⓐ Ⓓ	50	Ⓐ Ⓓ
51. 5496 Franklin Cove	5496 Franklin Cove	51	Ⓐ Ⓓ	51	Ⓐ Ⓓ
52. 8745 Cactus Ave	8745 Cactus Ave S	52	Ⓐ Ⓓ	52	Ⓐ Ⓓ
53. 35648 W Glenn	35648 S. Glenn	53	Ⓐ Ⓓ	53	Ⓐ Ⓓ
54. 8475 E Cherokee	8475 E Cherokee	54	Ⓐ Ⓓ	54	Ⓐ Ⓓ
55. 48757 Roxbury Sq	48757 Roxbury Sq	55	Ⓐ Ⓓ	55	Ⓐ Ⓓ
56. 9475 Lawrence Ct	9473 Lawrence Ct	56	Ⓐ Ⓓ	56	Ⓐ Ⓓ
57. 35548 Bauxite Sq	35548 Bauxite Sq	57	Ⓐ Ⓓ	57	Ⓐ Ⓓ
58. 3756 Pearl Bay	3756 Pearl Bay	58	Ⓐ Ⓓ	58	Ⓐ Ⓓ
59. 30657 Plymouth Rock	30655 Plymouth Rock	59	Ⓐ Ⓓ	59	Ⓐ Ⓓ
60. 9486 Pleasant Rdg	9486 Pleasant Rd	60	Ⓐ Ⓓ	60	Ⓐ Ⓓ
61. 32875 Clifton Blvd	32875 Clifton Blvd	61	Ⓐ Ⓓ	61	Ⓐ Ⓓ
62. 307 Paramount W	307 Paramount W	62	Ⓐ Ⓓ	62	Ⓐ Ⓓ
63. 9468 Cottonwood Cove	9463 Cottonwood Sq	63	Ⓐ Ⓓ	63	Ⓐ Ⓓ
64. 3757 E Atchinson	3757 E Atchinson	64	Ⓐ Ⓓ	64	Ⓐ Ⓓ
65. 3756 Sheridan St	3758 Sheridan St	65	Ⓐ Ⓓ	65	Ⓐ Ⓓ
66. 5476 Bloomfield Rd	5476 Bloomfield Rd	66	Ⓐ Ⓓ	66	Ⓐ Ⓓ
67. 396547 Highland	396547 Highland	67	Ⓐ Ⓓ	67	Ⓐ Ⓓ
68. 5430 Shellfield SW	5430 Shellfield SW	68	Ⓐ Ⓓ	68	Ⓐ Ⓓ
69. 37546 Taft Ave E	37546 Taft Ave W	69	Ⓐ Ⓓ	69	Ⓐ Ⓓ
70. 307 Panama Park	307 Panama Park	70	Ⓐ Ⓓ	70	Ⓐ Ⓓ
71. 68456 Bayview St.	68456 Bayview St	71	Ⓐ Ⓓ	71	Ⓐ Ⓓ
72. 305 Ballard Sq E	305 Ballard Sq E	72	Ⓐ Ⓓ	72	Ⓐ Ⓓ
73. 38656 Rose Rd	38656 Rose Rd	73	Ⓐ Ⓓ	73	Ⓐ Ⓓ
74. 9357 Armstrong Ave	9357 Armstrong Ave	74	Ⓐ Ⓓ	74	Ⓐ Ⓓ
75. 3547 Madonna Way	3547 Madonna Way	75	Ⓐ Ⓓ	75	Ⓐ Ⓓ
76. 39658 Victor Sq	39658 Victor Sq	76	Ⓐ Ⓓ	76	Ⓐ Ⓓ
77. 458 N Hermosillo Ct	458 N Hemosillo Ct	77	Ⓐ Ⓓ	77	Ⓐ Ⓓ
78. 3233 Teppert	3233 Teppert	78	Ⓐ Ⓓ	78	Ⓐ Ⓓ
79. 3065 Salty Bay Sq	3063 Salty Bay Sq	79	Ⓐ Ⓓ	79	Ⓐ Ⓓ
80. 9654 Audubon Blvd	9654 Audubon Blvd	80	Ⓐ Ⓓ	80	Ⓐ Ⓓ
81. 3054 Sleepy Hollow	3054 Sleep Holly	81	Ⓐ Ⓓ	81	Ⓐ Ⓓ
82. 3258 Pine Way St	3253 Pine Way St	82	Ⓐ Ⓓ	82	Ⓐ Ⓓ
83. 3547 Bums Ct W	3547 Bums Ct W	83	Ⓐ Ⓓ	83	Ⓐ Ⓓ
84. 30645 Mountainside View	30643 Mountainside View	84	Ⓐ Ⓓ	84	Ⓐ Ⓓ
85. 354 Carlson St W	354 Carlson St W	85	Ⓐ Ⓓ	85	Ⓐ Ⓓ
86. 659 Brooks Shield N	659 Brooks Shield N	86	Ⓐ Ⓓ	86	Ⓐ Ⓓ
87. 3645 Stevens Rd	3647 Stevesn Rd W	87	Ⓐ Ⓓ	87	Ⓐ Ⓓ
88. 3547 Alderwood W	3547 Alderwood W	88	Ⓐ Ⓓ	88	Ⓐ Ⓓ
89. 3543 Pineapple Cove	3543 Pineapple Cove	89	Ⓐ Ⓓ	89	Ⓐ Ⓓ

Go on the next number on the next page.

90. 3540 Francisco Sq	3540 Francisco Sq	90 Ⓐ Ⓓ	90 Ⓐ Ⓓ
91. 6486 Pleasan Rd	8486 Pleasant Sq	91 Ⓐ Ⓓ	91 Ⓐ Ⓓ
92. 3547 Sutter Ave	3547 Sutter Ave	92 Ⓐ Ⓓ	92 Ⓐ Ⓓ
93. 3547 Mango Sq	3547 Mango Sq	93 Ⓐ Ⓓ	93 Ⓐ Ⓓ
94. 54 5 Marina Dr	545 Marina St	94 Ⓐ Ⓓ	94 Ⓐ Ⓓ
95. 65406 Marine Way	65406 Marine Way	95 Ⓐ Ⓓ	95 Ⓐ Ⓓ

STOP

If you finish before the time is up, check your answers for Part A

)   **Do not go to any other part.**

(See the correct answers on the next page.)

Correct Answers

Address-Checking Test

1. D	25. A	49. A	73. A
2. A	26. A	50. A	74. A
3. A	27. A	51. A	75. A
4. D	28. A	52. D	76. A
5. D	29. D	53. D	77. D
6. A	30. A	54. A	78. A
7. D	31. D	55. A	79. D
8. A	32. A	56. D	80. A
9. D	33. D	57. A	81. D
10. A	34. A	58. A	82. D
11. D	35. A	59. D	83. A
12. D	36. D	60. D	84. D
13. A	37. A	61. A	85. A
14. D	38. D	62. A	86. A
15. D	39. D	63. D	87. D
16. D	40. A	64. A	88. A
17. D	41. D	65. D	89. A
18. D	42. A	66. A	90. A
19. A	43. D	67. A	91. D
20. D	44. A	68. A	92. A
21. D	45. A	69. D	93. A
22. D	46. D	70. A	94. D
23. D	47. D	71. A	95. A
24. A	48. A	72. A	

Address-Checking Practice Test

Work—6 Minutes

These addresses are like the ones in the address-checking test.

Decide whether the two addresses are *Alike* or *Different*. If they are *Alike,* darken or mark space A; if they are *Different,* darken space D. Mark the answers on the answer sheet to the right. Work as fast as you can without making too many errors. Work Exactly 6 minutes.

			Test A	Test B
1.	3854 Carson S	3854 Carson S	1 Ⓐ Ⓓ	1 Ⓐ Ⓓ
2.	9046 Los Padres Cir	9048 Los Padres Cir	2 Ⓐ Ⓓ	2 Ⓐ Ⓓ
3.	354 S Luverne Rd	354 S Luverne Rd	3 Ⓐ Ⓓ	3 Ⓐ Ⓓ
4.	3548 Kimberly Sq	3548 Kimberly Sq	4 Ⓐ Ⓓ	4 Ⓐ Ⓓ
5.	253 Larami Rd N	258 Larami Rd N	5 Ⓐ Ⓓ	5 Ⓐ Ⓓ
6.	9461 S Audubon	9461 S Audubon	6 Ⓐ Ⓓ	6 Ⓐ Ⓓ
7.	3547 La Cross Dr	3547 La Cross Dr	7 Ⓐ Ⓓ	7 Ⓐ Ⓓ
8.	547 Salty Bay Rd	547 Salty Bay Rd	8 Ⓐ Ⓓ	8 Ⓐ Ⓓ
9.	36548 Harrison Cir	36543 Harrison Cir	9 Ⓐ Ⓓ	9 Ⓐ Ⓓ
10.	547 S Gregory Park	547 S Gregory Park	10 Ⓐ Ⓓ	10 Ⓐ Ⓓ
11.	658 S Salem Ln	658 S Salem Ln	11 Ⓐ Ⓓ	11 Ⓐ Ⓓ
12.	7845 S Liberty Pl	7845 N Liberty Pl	12 Ⓐ Ⓓ	12 Ⓐ Ⓓ
13.	745 Olympic Way	745 Olympic Way	13 Ⓐ Ⓓ	13 Ⓐ Ⓓ
14.	5478 Monterrey Rd	5478 Monterrey Rd	14 Ⓐ Ⓓ	14 Ⓐ Ⓓ
15	986 S Ocean Blvd	986 N Ocean Blvd	15 Ⓐ Ⓓ	15 Ⓐ Ⓓ
16.	389 S Placid Plaza	389 N Placid Plaza	16 Ⓐ Ⓓ	16 Ⓐ Ⓓ
17.	9475 Olympic Cove	7475 Olympic Cove	17 Ⓐ Ⓓ	17 Ⓐ Ⓓ
18.	346 S Blanchard Ct	346 S Blanchard Ct	18 Ⓐ Ⓓ	18 Ⓐ Ⓓ
19.	8764 Jensen Way	3764 Jensen Way	19 Ⓐ Ⓓ	19 Ⓐ Ⓓ
20.	3754 Hayes Point	8754 Hayes Point	20 Ⓐ Ⓓ	20 Ⓐ Ⓓ
21.	8457 Galveston Blvd	8457 Galveston Hwy	21 Ⓐ Ⓓ	21 Ⓐ Ⓓ
22.	8475 NE Wilmoth	8475 NE Wilmont	22 Ⓐ Ⓓ	22 Ⓐ Ⓓ
23.	3503 O'Neal Rd	3503 O'Neal Rd	23 Ⓐ Ⓓ	23 Ⓐ Ⓓ
24.	1057 S Pierce Ct	1057 N Pierce Ct	24 Ⓐ Ⓓ	24 Ⓐ Ⓓ
25.	3854 Monroe NW	3854 Monroe NW	25 Ⓐ Ⓓ	25 Ⓐ Ⓓ
26.	79845 Bonn Blvd	79845 Bonn Blvd	26 Ⓐ Ⓓ	26 Ⓐ Ⓓ
27.	3015 Holiday Inn Dr	3015 Holiday Inn Dr	27 Ⓐ Ⓓ	27 Ⓐ Ⓓ
28.	4961 Warner St	8961 Warner St	28 Ⓐ Ⓓ	28 Ⓐ Ⓓ
29.	5488 Wellington Way	5488 Wellington Way	29 Ⓐ Ⓓ	29 Ⓐ Ⓓ
30.	466 S Terrace	466 S Terrace	30 Ⓐ Ⓓ	30 Ⓐ Ⓓ
31.	4466 Jackson Rd W	4466 Jackson Rd E	31 Ⓐ Ⓓ	31 Ⓐ Ⓓ
32.	4455 Concord Blvd	4455 Concord Pky	32 Ⓐ Ⓓ	32 Ⓐ Ⓓ
33.	776 Symington St	767 Symington St	33 Ⓐ Ⓓ	33 Ⓐ Ⓓ
34.	8811 Carver Cove	8811 Carver Cove	34 Ⓐ Ⓓ	34 Ⓐ Ⓓ
35.	8835 Joplin Ct	8885 Joplin Ct	35 Ⓐ Ⓓ	35 Ⓐ Ⓓ
36.	9947 S Lighthouse Ln	9947 S Lighthouse Ln	36 Ⓐ Ⓓ	36 Ⓐ Ⓓ
37.	6649 Main St	6649 Main St	37 Ⓐ Ⓓ	37 Ⓐ Ⓓ
38.	9488 32nd Ave S	9483 32nd Ave S	38 Ⓐ Ⓓ	38 Ⓐ Ⓓ
39.	1143 S Greenbriar Ct	1149 S Greenbriar Ct	39 Ⓐ Ⓓ	39 Ⓐ Ⓓ
40.	766 Hazel Park	766 Hazel Park	40 Ⓐ Ⓓ	40 Ⓐ Ⓓ

Go on to the next number on the next page.

#	Address	Address	#		#	
41.	8976 S Lester	8976 S Lester	41	Ⓐ Ⓓ	41	Ⓐ Ⓓ
42.	389 Hubert Rd	389 Hubert Rd	42	Ⓐ Ⓓ	42	Ⓐ Ⓓ
43.	8881 Melvin Way	8881 Melvin Way	43	Ⓐ Ⓓ	43	Ⓐ Ⓓ
44.	76459 Ronald St	76459 Ronald Dr	44	Ⓐ Ⓓ	44	Ⓐ Ⓓ
45.	3887 Saint Peter Dr	3887 Saint Peter Dr	45	Ⓐ Ⓓ	45	Ⓐ Ⓓ
46.	4152 Melrose Park	4152 Melrose Park	46	Ⓐ Ⓓ	46	Ⓐ Ⓓ
47.	4648 Crestwood N	4643 Crestwood N	47	Ⓐ Ⓓ	47	Ⓐ Ⓓ
48.	37647 Stables St	37647 Stables Rd	48	Ⓐ Ⓓ	48	Ⓐ Ⓓ
49.	3754 S Belair Blvd	3754 S Belaire Blvd	49	Ⓐ Ⓓ	49	Ⓐ Ⓓ
50.	370 E Essex St	370 W Essex St	50	Ⓐ Ⓓ	50	Ⓐ Ⓓ
51.	3654 S Mathews	3654 S Mathew	51	Ⓐ Ⓓ	51	Ⓐ Ⓓ
52.	94745 Severance Ct	94745 Severance Ct	52	Ⓐ Ⓓ	52	Ⓐ Ⓓ
53.	4538 Wheeler Way	4538 Wheeler Way	53	Ⓐ Ⓓ	53	Ⓐ Ⓓ
54.	794 Norfolk Ave	794 Norfolk Ave	54	Ⓐ Ⓓ	54	Ⓐ Ⓓ
55.	578 7th Ave NW	578 7th Ave SW	55	Ⓐ Ⓓ	55	Ⓐ Ⓓ
56.	3904 12th St. SW	3904 12th St SE	56	Ⓐ Ⓓ	56	Ⓐ Ⓓ
57.	3547 S Wendover	3547 S Wendover	57	Ⓐ Ⓓ	57	Ⓐ Ⓓ
58.	448 E Lincoln Sq	448 E Lincoln Sq	58	Ⓐ Ⓓ	58	Ⓐ Ⓓ
59.	354 St. Peter St E	354 St Peter St E	59	Ⓐ Ⓓ	59	Ⓐ Ⓓ
60.	3308 Essex Ct	3308 Essex Ct	60	Ⓐ Ⓓ	60	Ⓐ Ⓓ
61.	947 E Amherst	947 W Amherst	61	Ⓐ Ⓓ	61	Ⓐ Ⓓ
62.	7987 Elizabeth Ln	7987 Elizabeth Ln	62	Ⓐ Ⓓ	62	Ⓐ Ⓓ
63.	3649 Montrose Rd	3649 Montrose Rd	63	Ⓐ Ⓓ	63	Ⓐ Ⓓ
64.	396 Montreal Pl	3946 Montreal Pl	64	Ⓐ Ⓓ	64	Ⓐ Ⓓ
65.	4497 Clayton Ct	4497 Clayton St	65	Ⓐ Ⓓ	65	Ⓐ Ⓓ
66.	436 Ontario Way	486 Ontario Way	66	Ⓐ Ⓓ	66	Ⓐ Ⓓ
67.	94876 S Olmstead	94876 N Olmstead	67	Ⓐ Ⓓ	67	Ⓐ Ⓓ
68.	3540 Brooks Shield	3540 Brooks Shield	68	Ⓐ Ⓓ	68	Ⓐ Ⓓ
69.	9887 Cortland Dr	9837 Cortland Dr	69	Ⓐ Ⓓ	69	Ⓐ Ⓓ
70.	397 S Hamilton Ln	397 S Hamilton Ln	70	Ⓐ Ⓓ	70	Ⓐ Ⓓ
71.	547 E Vernon	547 S Vernon	71	Ⓐ Ⓓ	71	Ⓐ Ⓓ
72.	7845 S Perry Dr	7845 N Perry Dr	72	Ⓐ Ⓓ	72	Ⓐ Ⓓ
73.	4457 Old Hickory	4487 Old Hickory	73	Ⓐ Ⓓ	73	Ⓐ Ⓓ
74.	5645 N Dolomite Dr	5645 S Dolomite Dr	74	Ⓐ Ⓓ	74	Ⓐ Ⓓ
75.	3540 S Hampstead Pl	3540 S Hampstead Pl	75	Ⓐ Ⓓ	75	Ⓐ Ⓓ
76.	35489 E Clinton Sq	85489 E Clinton Sq	76	Ⓐ Ⓓ	76	Ⓐ Ⓓ
77.	3548 Bush Hwy	3548 Bush Hwy	77	Ⓐ Ⓓ	77	Ⓐ Ⓓ
78.	3540 S Kendall	3540 S Kendall	78	Ⓐ Ⓓ	78	Ⓐ Ⓓ
79.	3540 Battlecreek Rd	354 Battlecreeek Rd	79	Ⓐ Ⓓ	79	Ⓐ Ⓓ
80.	5469 Bismark Park	5489 Bismark Park	80	Ⓐ Ⓓ	80	Ⓐ Ⓓ
81.	84645 Pocahontas Hwy	84645 Pocahontas Hwy	81	Ⓐ Ⓓ	81	Ⓐ Ⓓ
82.	3954 Wasbash Rd	3854 Wasbash Rd	82	Ⓐ Ⓓ	82	Ⓐ Ⓓ
83.	4965 Bancroft Pky	4965 Gancroft Pky	83	Ⓐ Ⓓ	83	Ⓐ Ⓓ
84.	3547 S Windsor Ave	3547 S Windsor Ave	84	Ⓐ Ⓓ	84	Ⓐ Ⓓ
85.	6947 Hiawatha Way	6947 Hiawatha Way	85	Ⓐ Ⓓ	85	Ⓐ Ⓓ
86.	3540 E Lucerne Dr	3540 E Lucerne Dr	86	Ⓐ Ⓓ	86	Ⓐ Ⓓ
87.	4645 Marshall Park	4645 Marshal Park	87	Ⓐ Ⓓ	87	Ⓐ Ⓓ
88.	3545 Janet Pl	3548 Janet Pl	88	Ⓐ Ⓓ	88	Ⓐ Ⓓ
89.	9943 Lucern Way	9943 Lucern Way	89	Ⓐ Ⓓ	89	Ⓐ Ⓓ

Go on to the next number on the next page.

90. 3369 S Laverne Rd	3369 S Laverne St	90 Ⓐ Ⓓ	90 Ⓐ Ⓓ
91. 6536 Sta. Ana Rd	6536 Sta. Ana St	91 Ⓐ Ⓓ	91 Ⓐ Ⓓ
92. 7659 5th Ave SW	7659 5th Ave SE	92 Ⓐ Ⓓ	92 Ⓐ Ⓓ
93. 36450 S Marshall	36450 S Marshall	93 Ⓐ Ⓓ	93 Ⓐ Ⓓ
94. 4783 Randolph Hwy	4783 Randolf Hwy	94 Ⓐ Ⓓ	94 Ⓐ Ⓓ
95. 6459 Bismark Cove	6459 Bismark Cove	95 Ⓐ Ⓓ	95 Ⓐ Ⓓ

STOP

If you finish before the time is up, check your answers for Part A.

Do not go to any other part.

(See the correct answers on the next page.)

Correct Answers

Address-Checking Test

1. A	25. A	49. D	73. D
2. D	26. A	50. D	74. D
3. A	27. A	51. D	75. A
4. A	28. D	52. A	76. D
5. D	29. A	53. A	77. A
6. A	30. A	54. A	78. A
7. A	31. D	55. D	79. D
8. A	32. D	56. D	80. D
9. D	33. D	57. A	81. A
10. A	34. A	58. A	82. D
11. A	35. D	59. A	83. D
12. D	36. A	60. A	84. A
13. A	37. A	61. D	85. A
14. A	38. D	62. A	86. A
15. D	39. D	63. A	87. D
16. D	40. A	64. D	88. D
17. D	41. A	65. D	89. A
18. A	42. A	66. D	90. D
19. D	43. A	67. D	91. D
20. D	44. D	68. A	92. D
21. D	45. A	69. D	93. A
22. D	46. A	70. A	94. D
23. A	47. D	71. D	95. A
24. D	48. D	72. D	

Address-Checking Practice Test

Work—6 Minutes

These addresses are like the ones in the address-checking test.

Decide whether the two addresses are *Alike* or *Different*. if they are *Alike*, darken or mark space A; if they are *Different* darken Space D. Mark the answers on the answer sheet to the right. Work as fast as you can without making too many errors. Work exactly 6 minutes.

		Test A	Test B
1. 3540 Willow SW	3540 Willo SE	1 Ⓐ Ⓓ	1 Ⓐ Ⓓ
2. 3548 Santa Cruz Bay	3548 Santa Cruz Bay	2 Ⓐ Ⓓ	2 Ⓐ Ⓓ
3. 9375 Hollister Rd	9375 Hollister St	3 Ⓐ Ⓓ	3 Ⓐ Ⓓ
4. 65499 Grandview Dr	65499 Grandview Dr	4 Ⓐ Ⓓ	4 Ⓐ Ⓓ
5. 385 Evangeline St	385 Evangeline St	5 Ⓐ Ⓓ	5 Ⓐ Ⓓ
6. 9354 Briarcliff View	9354 Briarcliff View	6 Ⓐ Ⓓ	6 Ⓐ Ⓓ
7. 39547 Memphis Rd	39547 Memphis St	7 Ⓐ Ⓓ	7 Ⓐ Ⓓ
8. 1978 Briarwood Cir	1978 Briarwood Cir	8 Ⓐ Ⓓ	8 Ⓐ Ⓓ
9. 3954 Peppermint	3954 Peppermint	9 Ⓐ Ⓓ	9 Ⓐ Ⓓ
10. 3549 Woodward Ave	3549 Woodward Ave	10 Ⓐ Ⓓ	10 Ⓐ Ⓓ
11. 23323 Teppert St	23328 Teppert St	11 Ⓐ Ⓓ	11 Ⓐ Ⓓ
12. 4488 Campbell	4488 Campbell	12 Ⓐ Ⓓ	12 Ⓐ Ⓓ
13. 8745 S Copper Creek	8745 N Copper Creek	13 Ⓐ Ⓓ	13 Ⓐ Ⓓ
14. 865 12th Mile S	865 12th Mile S	14 Ⓐ Ⓓ	14 Ⓐ Ⓓ
15. 647 Morning Breeze	647 Morning Breese	15 Ⓐ Ⓓ	15 Ⓐ Ⓓ
16. 9481 Bownsville Cove	9481 Brownsville Cove	16 Ⓐ Ⓓ	16 Ⓐ Ⓓ
17. 1054 Gainsville Rd	1054 Gainsville Rd	17 Ⓐ Ⓓ	17 Ⓐ Ⓓ
18. 6493 Parker Cir	6493 Parker Cir	18 Ⓐ Ⓓ	18 Ⓐ Ⓓ
19. 9454 Alexandria St	9454 Alexandra Dr	19 Ⓐ Ⓓ	19 Ⓐ Ⓓ
20. 7845 Crescent View	7845 Crescent View	20 Ⓐ Ⓓ	20 Ⓐ Ⓓ
21. 9450 Darwin St	9450 Darwin Sq	21 Ⓐ Ⓓ	21 Ⓐ Ⓓ
22. 390 Pandora Rd	390 Pandora Rd	22 Ⓐ Ⓓ	22 Ⓐ Ⓓ
23. 5403 Gilbert St	5408 Gilbert St	23 Ⓐ Ⓓ	23 Ⓐ Ⓓ
24. 38545 Santa Fe Cir	33545 Santa Fe Cir	24 Ⓐ Ⓓ	24 Ⓐ Ⓓ
25. 3054 S Daytona St	3054 S Daytona St	25 Ⓐ Ⓓ	25 Ⓐ Ⓓ
26. 9467 Guadalupe Loop	9467 Guadalupe Loop	26 Ⓐ Ⓓ	26 Ⓐ Ⓓ
27. 10545 Tallahasse Ln	10548 Tallsahasse Ln	27 Ⓐ Ⓓ	27 Ⓐ Ⓓ
28. 54065 Redfield SW	54065 Redfield SW	28 Ⓐ Ⓓ	28 Ⓐ Ⓓ
29. 8351 Greenfield Sq	3351 Greenfield Sq	29 Ⓐ Ⓓ	29 Ⓐ Ⓓ
30. 8354 52nd Ave S	8354 52nd Ave S	30 Ⓐ Ⓓ	30 Ⓐ Ⓓ
31. 8540 Sleepy Hollow	8540 Sleepy Hollow	31 Ⓐ Ⓓ	31 Ⓐ Ⓓ
32. 3954 Hubert Dr	3954 Hubert Dr	32 Ⓐ Ⓓ	32 Ⓐ Ⓓ
33. 5482 Durhamn Rd	5482 Durham Rd	33 Ⓐ Ⓓ	33 Ⓐ Ⓓ
34. 9354 Maleroy	9354 Maleroy	34 Ⓐ Ⓓ	34 Ⓐ Ⓓ
35. 3367 Franklin S	3367 Franklin N	35 Ⓐ Ⓓ	35 Ⓐ Ⓓ
36. 3954 E Beechnut	3954 E Beechnut	36 Ⓐ Ⓓ	36 Ⓐ Ⓓ
37. 9461 Falcon Crest	9461 Falcon Crest	37 Ⓐ Ⓓ	37 Ⓐ Ⓓ
38. 94564 Carver Pl	94564 Carver Pl	38 Ⓐ Ⓓ	38 Ⓐ Ⓓ
39. 7735 Keyport Point	7733 Keyport Point	39 Ⓐ Ⓓ	39 Ⓐ Ⓓ
40. 9454 Scotts Bluff N	9454 Scotts Bluff S	40 Ⓐ Ⓓ	40 Ⓐ Ⓓ

Go on to the next number on the next page.

41.	3300 Boston Harbor	3300 Boston Harbor	41 Ⓐ Ⓓ	41 Ⓐ Ⓓ
42.	93547 St John	93547 St John	42 Ⓐ Ⓓ	42 Ⓐ Ⓓ
43.	9476 Eagle View	9476 Eagle View	43 Ⓐ Ⓓ	43 Ⓐ Ⓓ
44.	3054 Blanchard Dr	3054 Blanchard Cir	44 Ⓐ Ⓓ	44 Ⓐ Ⓓ
45.	3377 Alderwood Ln	3377 Alderwood Ln	45 Ⓐ Ⓓ	45 Ⓐ Ⓓ
46.	5667 Sievers Rd	5661 Sievers Rd	46 Ⓐ Ⓓ	46 Ⓐ Ⓓ
47.	9457 S Burnett	9457 N Burnett	47 Ⓐ Ⓓ	47 Ⓐ Ⓓ
48.	6573 Dixon Rd	6573 Dixon Rd	48 Ⓐ Ⓓ	48 Ⓐ Ⓓ
49.	8477 Covington Ln	8477 Covington Ln	49 Ⓐ Ⓓ	49 Ⓐ Ⓓ
50.	3549 E Amhurst Creek	3549 W Amherst Creek	50 Ⓐ Ⓓ	50 Ⓐ Ⓓ
51.	9474 Melbourne Ave	9474 Melborne Ave	51 Ⓐ Ⓓ	51 Ⓐ Ⓓ
52.	3549 Granite View	3549 Gratite View	52 Ⓐ Ⓓ	52 Ⓐ Ⓓ
53.	3047 Diamond Crest	3047 Diamond Crest	53 Ⓐ Ⓓ	53 Ⓐ Ⓓ
54.	39540 Central Plaza	30540 Central Plaza	54 Ⓐ Ⓓ	54 Ⓐ Ⓓ
55.	3540 Blake Rd	3540 Blake Rd	55 Ⓐ Ⓓ	55 Ⓐ Ⓓ
56.	3054 Cooper SW	3054 Cooper SE	56 Ⓐ Ⓓ	56 Ⓐ Ⓓ
57.	745 Knoll Hwy	745 Knoll Hwy	57 Ⓐ Ⓓ	57 Ⓐ Ⓓ
58.	5400 Birmingham Park	5400 Biningham Park	58 Ⓐ Ⓓ	58 Ⓐ Ⓓ
59.	3954 Grant Pl	3954 Grant Pl	59 Ⓐ Ⓓ	59 Ⓐ Ⓓ
60.	45451 7th Ave SW	45451 7th Ave SE	60 Ⓐ Ⓓ	60 Ⓐ Ⓓ
61.	3054 Bridgeview St	3054 Bridgeview St	61 Ⓐ Ⓓ	61 Ⓐ Ⓓ
62.	3954 Armistice	3954 Armistice	62 Ⓐ Ⓓ	62 Ⓐ Ⓓ
63.	541 S Averley	541 N Averley	63 Ⓐ Ⓓ	63 Ⓐ Ⓓ
64.	3005 Flint SW	8005 Flint SW	64 Ⓐ Ⓓ	64 Ⓐ Ⓓ
65.	39651 Chrysler Rd	39651 Chrysler Rd	65 Ⓐ Ⓓ	65 Ⓐ Ⓓ
66.	3301 Ford Pky	3301 Ford Pky	66 Ⓐ Ⓓ	66 Ⓐ Ⓓ
67.	7731 Armstrong Dr	7731 Armstrong Dr	67 Ⓐ Ⓓ	67 Ⓐ Ⓓ
68.	33901 King St	33907 King Sq	68 Ⓐ Ⓓ	68 Ⓐ Ⓓ
69.	310 Amapola Rd	310 Anapola Rd	69 Ⓐ Ⓓ	69 Ⓐ Ⓓ
70.	3016 Straton Lake	3016 Straton Lake	70 Ⓐ Ⓓ	70 Ⓐ Ⓓ
71.	3011 Belmont Way	3011 Belmont Way	71 Ⓐ Ⓓ	71 Ⓐ Ⓓ
72.	318 S Marine	318 N Marine	72 Ⓐ Ⓓ	72 Ⓐ Ⓓ
73.	3105 N Foster Ave	3105 N Foster Ave	73 Ⓐ Ⓓ	73 Ⓐ Ⓓ
74.	3016 Knottingham	3016 Knottingham	74 Ⓐ Ⓓ	74 Ⓐ Ⓓ
75.	7861 Bell St	7861 Bell St	75 Ⓐ Ⓓ	75 Ⓐ Ⓓ
76.	3810 Jerriman S	3810 Jerriman N	76 Ⓐ Ⓓ	76 Ⓐ Ⓓ
77.	3106 Knickerbocker	3106 Knickerbocker	77 Ⓐ Ⓓ	77 Ⓐ Ⓓ
78.	1154 R Johnston	1154 R Johnston	78 Ⓐ Ⓓ	78 Ⓐ Ⓓ
79.	31545 Dorchester	31545 Darchester	79 Ⓐ Ⓓ	79 Ⓐ Ⓓ
80.	3154 Ft. Hamilton	3154 Ft Hamilton	80 Ⓐ Ⓓ	80 Ⓐ Ⓓ
81.	3190 S Boulder	3190 S Boulder	81 Ⓐ Ⓓ	81 Ⓐ Ⓓ
82.	3106 NW 157th St	8315 SW 157th St	82 Ⓐ Ⓓ	82 Ⓐ Ⓓ
83.	3154 Evergreen	3154 Evergreen	83 Ⓐ Ⓓ	83 Ⓐ Ⓓ
84.	3154 Rosengarden	3154 Rosengarden	84 Ⓐ Ⓓ	84 Ⓐ Ⓓ
85.	3965 Lumberville N	3965 Lumberville S	85 Ⓐ Ⓓ	85 Ⓐ Ⓓ
86.	316 Markham S	316 Markam S	86 Ⓐ Ⓓ	86 Ⓐ Ⓓ
87.	3188 Warnock Creek	3188 Warnock Creek	87 Ⓐ Ⓓ	87 Ⓐ Ⓓ
88.	3110 Kessler Nook	3110 Kessler Nook	88 Ⓐ Ⓓ	88 Ⓐ Ⓓ
89.	3388 Ovington Park	3388 Ovington Park	89 Ⓐ Ⓓ	89 Ⓐ Ⓓ

Go on to the next number on the next page.

90.	3100 Catalina Cir	3100 Catalina Cir	90 Ⓐ Ⓓ	90 Ⓐ Ⓓ
91.	9615 Dorchester	9615 Darchester	91 Ⓐ Ⓓ	91 Ⓐ Ⓓ
92.	3110 Blake E	3110 Blake S	92 Ⓐ Ⓓ	92 Ⓐ Ⓓ
93.	3174 Empire St	8174 Empire St	93 Ⓐ Ⓓ	93 Ⓐ Ⓓ
94.	1947 Hampton Ave	1847 Hampton Ave	94 Ⓐ Ⓓ	94 Ⓐ Ⓓ
95.	31054 Hancock	31054 Hamcock	95 Ⓐ Ⓓ	95 Ⓐ Ⓓ

STOP

If you finish before the time is up, check your answers for Part A.

Do not go to any other part.

(See the correct answers on the next page.)

Correct Answers

Address-Checking Test

1. D		49. A	73. A
2. A	25. A	50. D	74. A
3. D	26. A	51. D	75. A
4. A	27. D	52. D	76. D
5. A	28. A	53. A	77. A
6. A	29. D	54. D	78. A
7. D	30. A	55. A	79. D
8. A	31. A	56. D	80. A
9. A	32. A	57. A	81. A
10. A	33. D	58. D	82. D
11. D	34. A	59. A	83. A
12. A	35. D	60. D	84. A
13. D	36. A	61. A	85. D
14. A	37. A	62. A	86. D
15. D	38. A	63. D	87. A
16. D	39. D	64. D	88. A
17. A	40. D	65. A	89. A
18. A	41. A	66. A	90. A
19. D	42. A	67. A	91. D
20. A	43. A	68. D	92. D
21. D	44. D	69. D	93. D
22. A	45. A	70. A	94. D
23. D	46. D	71. A	95. D
24. D	47. D	72. D	
	48. A		

Address-Checking Practice Test

Work—6 Minutes

These addresses are like the ones in the address-checking test.

Decide whether the two addresses are *Alike* or *Different*. If they are *Alike*, darken or mark space A; if they are *Different*, darken space D. Mark the answers on the answer sheet to the right. Work as fast as you can without making too many errors. Work exactly 6 minutes.

#	Address 1	Address 2	Test A	Test B
1.	76386 Island Park	76386 Island Park	1 Ⓐ Ⓓ	1 Ⓐ Ⓓ
2.	3540 S Hotel Rd	9540 S Hotel Rd	2 Ⓐ Ⓓ	2 Ⓐ Ⓓ
3.	3964 Missouri Ct	3964 Misouri Ct	3 Ⓐ Ⓓ	3 Ⓐ Ⓓ
4.	93645 Harness St	93647 Harness St	4 Ⓐ Ⓓ	4 Ⓐ Ⓓ
5.	3540 Raffles Blvd	3540 Raffles Blvd	5 Ⓐ Ⓓ	5 Ⓐ Ⓓ
6.	350 N Westminster	350 N Westminster	6 Ⓐ Ⓓ	6 Ⓐ Ⓓ
7.	3064 Columbia Dr	3064 Columbia Dr	7 Ⓐ Ⓓ	7 Ⓐ Ⓓ
8.	5400 Cordelia NW	5400 Cordelia NE	8 Ⓐ Ⓓ	8 Ⓐ Ⓓ
9.	1649 Kauai Rd	1649 Kauai Rd	9 Ⓐ Ⓓ	9 Ⓐ Ⓓ
10.	3540 Cadiz Way	3540 Cadiz Way	10 Ⓐ Ⓓ	10 Ⓐ Ⓓ
11.	3889 Stockbridge S	3839 Stockbridge S	11 Ⓐ Ⓓ	11 Ⓐ Ⓓ
12.	4401 E Cadiz Ln	4401 S Cadiz Ln	12 Ⓐ Ⓓ	12 Ⓐ Ⓓ
13.	35400 Morris Ave	35400 Morris Ave	13 Ⓐ Ⓓ	13 Ⓐ Ⓓ
14.	3054 Hampton Rd	3054 Hanpton Rd	14 Ⓐ Ⓓ	14 Ⓐ Ⓓ
15.	3358 Marina Rd	3353 Marina Rd	15 Ⓐ Ⓓ	15 Ⓐ Ⓓ
16.	30658 Windmill Ave	30658 Windmill Ave	16 Ⓐ Ⓓ	16 Ⓐ Ⓓ
17.	7883 Markham Way	7883 Markhan Way	17 Ⓐ Ⓓ	17 Ⓐ Ⓓ
18.	30654 Warnock St	30654 Warnock St	18 Ⓐ Ⓓ	18 Ⓐ Ⓓ
19.	5400 Berkshire Sq	5400 Berkshire Sq	19 Ⓐ Ⓓ	19 Ⓐ Ⓓ
20.	9365 Columbia Dr	9365 Columbia Ave	20 Ⓐ Ⓓ	20 Ⓐ Ⓓ
21.	8835 Doughty Hwy	8835 Doughty Hwy	21 Ⓐ Ⓓ	21 Ⓐ Ⓓ
22.	3047 Jerriman Pky	3047 Jerriman Pky	22 Ⓐ Ⓓ	22 Ⓐ Ⓓ
23.	6589 Nautilus Castle	6539 Nautilus Castle	23 Ⓐ Ⓓ	23 Ⓐ Ⓓ
24.	4054 Red Light	4058 Red Light	24 Ⓐ Ⓓ	24 Ⓐ Ⓓ
25.	385 S Blue Moon	385 S Blue Moon	25 Ⓐ Ⓓ	25 Ⓐ Ⓓ
26.	3054 Green Lagoon	3058 Green Lagoon	26 Ⓐ Ⓓ	26 Ⓐ Ⓓ
27.	3064 Kalamazoo Rd	3064 Kalamazoo St	27 Ⓐ Ⓓ	27 Ⓐ Ⓓ
28.	6540 Catalunia Dr	6540 Catalunia Dr	28 Ⓐ Ⓓ	28 Ⓐ Ⓓ
29.	9463 Delaware Creek	9469 Delaware Creek	29 Ⓐ Ⓓ	29 Ⓐ Ⓓ
30.	3054 LaSalle Village	3054 LaSale Village	30 Ⓐ Ⓓ	30 Ⓐ Ⓓ
31.	5405 Hamilton Way	5405 Hamilton Way	31 Ⓐ Ⓓ	31 Ⓐ Ⓓ
32.	5481 Montana Dr	5481 Montana Dr	32 Ⓐ Ⓓ	32 Ⓐ Ⓓ
33.	8954 Doughty Way	8957 Doughty Hwy	33 Ⓐ Ⓓ	33 Ⓐ Ⓓ
34.	3054 Christy St	3054 Christy St	34 Ⓐ Ⓓ	34 Ⓐ Ⓓ
35.	3437 Glendale Rd	5437 Glendale St	35 Ⓐ Ⓓ	35 Ⓐ Ⓓ
36.	43065 7th Ave W	40368 7th Ave W	36 Ⓐ Ⓓ	36 Ⓐ Ⓓ
37.	3054 MacDonald Vlg	3054 MacDonald Vlg	37 Ⓐ Ⓓ	37 Ⓐ Ⓓ
38.	30547 Keating E	30547 Keating W	38 Ⓐ Ⓓ	38 Ⓐ Ⓓ
39.	3054 Carter Dr	3057 Carter Dr	39 Ⓐ Ⓓ	39 Ⓐ Ⓓ
40.	3068 E Evanston	3063 Evanston	40 Ⓐ Ⓓ	40 Ⓐ Ⓓ

Go on to the next number on the next page.

41. 64506 Pittmar Dr	64506 Pittmar Dr	41 Ⓐ Ⓓ	41 Ⓐ Ⓓ
42. 3540 Chamber Ln	3540 Chamber Ln	42 Ⓐ Ⓓ	42 Ⓐ Ⓓ
43. 3954 Central Sq	3954 Central Sq	43 Ⓐ Ⓓ	43 Ⓐ Ⓓ
44. 944 S Apple Rdge	944 S Apple Rdg	44 Ⓐ Ⓓ	44 Ⓐ Ⓓ
45. 4867 Tripp Rd	4887 Tripp Rd	45 Ⓐ Ⓓ	45 Ⓐ Ⓓ
46. 1469 Brayton Cir	1469 Brytom Cir	46 Ⓐ Ⓓ	46 Ⓐ Ⓓ
47. 4954 Crestlane Rd	4954 Crestlane Rd	47 Ⓐ Ⓓ	47 Ⓐ Ⓓ
48. 3054 Wilmington Pl	3054 Wilmington Pl	48 Ⓐ Ⓓ	48 Ⓐ Ⓓ
49. 7697 Brooklyn Bridge	7697 Brooklyn Bridge	49 Ⓐ Ⓓ	49 Ⓐ Ⓓ
50. 85349 Williston St	85349 Williston St	50 Ⓐ Ⓓ	50 Ⓐ Ⓓ
51. 5831 Medford Dr	5831 Melford Dr	51 Ⓐ Ⓓ	51 Ⓐ Ⓓ
52. 9485 Tuyvesant Way	9485 Tuysevent Way	52 Ⓐ Ⓓ	52 Ⓐ Ⓓ
53. 5948 Briarcliff St	5948 Briarcliff St	53 Ⓐ Ⓓ	53 Ⓐ Ⓓ
54. 4057 59th St W	4057 59th St E	54 Ⓐ Ⓓ	54 Ⓐ Ⓓ
55. 57849 Prince Rd	57849 Prince Rd	55 Ⓐ Ⓓ	55 Ⓐ Ⓓ
56. 4857 Welch Sq	4857 Welch Sq	56 Ⓐ Ⓓ	56 Ⓐ Ⓓ
57. 59846 Interlaken	53846 Interlaken	57 Ⓐ Ⓓ	57 Ⓐ Ⓓ
58. 3857 Rugby St	3857 Rugby St	58 Ⓐ Ⓓ	58 Ⓐ Ⓓ
59. 4395 Boutinville	4395 Boutinville	59 Ⓐ Ⓓ	59 Ⓐ Ⓓ
60. 294 76th Ave SW	294 76th Ave SW	60 Ⓐ Ⓓ	60 Ⓐ Ⓓ
61. 8823 Pleasant Run	8828 Pleasant Run	61 Ⓐ Ⓓ	61 Ⓐ Ⓓ
62. 4867 Old Coral Rd	4867 Old Coral Rd	62 Ⓐ Ⓓ	62 Ⓐ Ⓓ
63. 4856 Chessnut Way	4356 Chessnut Way	63 Ⓐ Ⓓ	63 Ⓐ Ⓓ
64. 475 Penn Sq	475 Penn Sq	64 Ⓐ Ⓓ	64 Ⓐ Ⓓ
65. 4057 Mountainville	4057 Mountainville	65 Ⓐ Ⓓ	65 Ⓐ Ⓓ
66. 4005 Bryant Rd	4008 Bryant Rd	66 Ⓐ Ⓓ	66 Ⓐ Ⓓ
67. 4481 Carmen Cove	4482 Carmen Cove	67 Ⓐ Ⓓ	67 Ⓐ Ⓓ
68. 497 S Elmhurst	497 S Elmhurst	68 Ⓐ Ⓓ	68 Ⓐ Ⓓ
69. 3751 Spring Valley	3751 Spring Valley	69 Ⓐ Ⓓ	69 Ⓐ Ⓓ
70. 4477 Sycamore Rd	4477 Sycamore St	70 Ⓐ Ⓓ	70 Ⓐ Ⓓ
71. 8845 Massachusettes	8848 Massachusettes	71 Ⓐ Ⓓ	71 Ⓐ Ⓓ
72. 405 SE Griffin Way	405 SW Griffin Way	72 Ⓐ Ⓓ	72 Ⓐ Ⓓ
73. 4054 Crossroad Pky	4054 Crossroad Pky	73 Ⓐ Ⓓ	73 Ⓐ Ⓓ
74. 4976 Kempner Dr	4976 Kempner Sq	74 Ⓐ Ⓓ	74 Ⓐ Ⓓ
75. 9451 Stephenway Hwy	9451 Stephenway Pky	75 Ⓐ Ⓓ	75 Ⓐ Ⓓ
76. 8830 Runyon Way	8830 Runyon Way	76 Ⓐ Ⓓ	76 Ⓐ Ⓓ
77. 7740 Sedgewick St	7740 Sedgewick St	77 Ⓐ Ⓓ	77 Ⓐ Ⓓ
78. 8847 Upper Loop Dr	8347 Upper Loop Dr	78 Ⓐ Ⓓ	78 Ⓐ Ⓓ
79. 3754 Westchester Rd	3754 Westchester Rd	79 Ⓐ Ⓓ	79 Ⓐ Ⓓ
80. 9973 Bisbee Creek	9973 Bisbeek Creek	80 Ⓐ Ⓓ	80 Ⓐ Ⓓ
81. 4956 Kneeland Way S	4956 Kneeland Way S	81 Ⓐ Ⓓ	81 Ⓐ Ⓓ
82. 6947 LeRoy Rdg	6947 LeRoy Brdg	82 Ⓐ Ⓓ	82 Ⓐ Ⓓ
83. 4954 Honeybee Cir	4954 Honebee Cir	83 Ⓐ Ⓓ	83 Ⓐ Ⓓ
84. 7745 Kneeland Ct	7745 Kneeland Ct	84 Ⓐ Ⓓ	84 Ⓐ Ⓓ
85. 3354 Upperhill Way	3354 Uppperhill Hwy	85 Ⓐ Ⓓ	85 Ⓐ Ⓓ
86. 46549 Moseman Rd	46549 Moseman Rd	86 Ⓐ Ⓓ	86 Ⓐ Ⓓ
87. 449 17th Ave SW	449 17th Ave SE	87 Ⓐ Ⓓ	87 Ⓐ Ⓓ
88. 5478 Curtis Way	5478 Curtis Way	88 Ⓐ Ⓓ	88 Ⓐ Ⓓ
89. 54854 Gedney Rd	54854 Gedney Rd	89 Ⓐ Ⓓ	89 Ⓐ Ⓓ

Go on to the next number on the next page.

90. 68893 Hudson Bay	68893 Hudson Bay	90	Ⓐ Ⓓ	90	Ⓐ Ⓓ
91. 44054 Palmer Rd	44054 Palmer Rd	91	Ⓐ Ⓓ	91	Ⓐ Ⓓ
92. 9943 Evangeline Sq	9943 Evangeline Sq	92	Ⓐ Ⓓ	92	Ⓐ Ⓓ
93. 4467 Lorezo Rd	4467 Lorenzo Rd	93	Ⓐ Ⓓ	93	Ⓐ Ⓓ
94. 9947 Robbin W	9847 Robbin W	94	Ⓐ Ⓓ	94	Ⓐ Ⓓ
95. 4471 S Lawton Sq	4471 N Lawton Sq	95	Ⓐ Ⓓ	95	Ⓐ Ⓓ

If you finish before the time is up, check your answers for Part A.

STOP

If you finish before the time is up, check your answers for Part A.

Do not go to any other part.

(See the correct answers on the next page.)

Correct Answers

Address-Checking Test

1. A	25. A	49. A	73. A
2. D	26. D	50. A	74. D
3. D	27. D	51. D	75. D
4. D	28. A	52. D	76. A
5. A	29. D	53. A	77. A
6. A	30. D	54. D	78. D
7. A	31. A	55. A	79. A
8. D	32. A	56. A	80. D
9. A	33. D	57. D	81. A
10. A	34. A	58. A	82. D
11. D	35. D	59. A	83. D
12. D	36. D	60. A	84. A
13. A	37. A	61. D	85. D
14. D	38. D	62. A	86. A
15. D	39. D	63. D	87. D
16. A	40. D	64. A	88. A
17. D	41. A	65. A	89. A
18. A	42. A	66. D	90. A
19. A	43. A	67. D	91. A
20. D	44. A	68. A	92. A
21. A	45. D	69. A	93. D
22. A	46. D	70. D	94. D
23. D	47. A	71. D	95. D
24. D	48. A	72. D	

Memory-for-Address Test

Work—3 Minutes

Answer each question on a piece of paper to show the letter of the box in which the address belongs.

Try to remember the location of as many addresses as you can. If you are not sure of an address, guess. Work only three minutes.

A	B	C	D	E
1800-2499 Wood Lott 7500-8799 Lang Dushore 6400-6599 James	2200-3199 Wood Vanna 8600-9299 Lang Jeriel 5400-6299 James	1200-1599 Wood Ekron 7400-9399 Lang Levering 6100-6499 James	3100-3699 Wood Viborg 8000-8299 Lang Valley 5500-5899 James	2700-2799 Wood Lycan 5600-9999 Lang Danby 4500-4699 James

1. 1800-2499 Wood
2. 2700-2799 Wood
3. Danby
4. 8600-9299 Lang
5. Lott
6. 6400-6599 James
7. Vanna
8. 6100-6499 James
9. 8000-8299 Lang
10. Levering
11. 5600-9999 Lang
12. 8600-9299 Lang
13. Lott
14. 4500-4699 James
15. Ekron
16. 5500-5899 James
17. Jeriel
18. Dushore
19. 6400-6599 James
20. Viborg
21. 7500-8799 Lang
22. Danby
23. 4500-4699 James
24. 5500-5899 James

25. 2200-3199 Wood
26. Viborg
27. 7500-8799 Lang
28. Lycan
29. 5600-9999 Lang
30. 2200-3199 Wood
31. Levering
32. 2700-2799 Wood
33. 5500-5899 James
34. Vanna
35. 4500-4699 James
36. Dushore
37. 7500-8799 Lang
38. 6400-6599 James
39. 2700-2799 Wood
40. Valley
41. 8600-9299 Lang
42. Lycan
43. Vanna
44. 8000-8299 Lang
45. 2700-2799 Wood
46. Valley
47. Dushore
48. 7500-8799 Lang

49. Levering
50. 6400-6599 James
51. 5600-9999 Lang
52. 4500-4699 James
53. Jeriel
54. 7400-9399 Lang
55. Dushore
56. 3100-3699 Wood
57. 2200-3199 Wood
58. Valley
59. 6400-6599 James
60. Danby
61. 7400-9399 Lang
62. 5500-5899 James
63. Jeriel
64. 2200-3199 Wood
65. Viborg
66. 8000-8299 Lang
67. Ekron
68. 5400-6299 James
69. 5600-9999 Lang
70. 6400-6599 James
71. 2700-2799 Wood
72. Valley

73. Lott
74. Danby
75. 1800-2499 Wood
76. 8600-9299 Lang
77. 6100-6499 James
78. Lycan
79. 5400-6299 James
80. 6100-6499 James
81. Vanna
82. 7400-9399 Lang
83. 3100-3699 Wood
84. 4500-4699 James
85. 2200-3199 Wood
86. 6400-6599 james
87. Ekron
88. 8600-9299 Lang

STOP

When the time is up, go on to the next page for the correct answers.

(**Author's Note:** The sample test above is known as the memory-for-address test in the 470 Battery Test and the 460 Rural Carrier Associate Exam. This Part B is considered as a practice test. You'll be allowed to look at the names and addresses in the boxes, as you are instructed to answer as many questions as possible in three minutes. In the next part, however, you will be asked to answer all the 88 questions in five minutes and you won't be allowed to look at the names and addresses. During the three-minute practice test, answer only a few questions. Spend most of the three minutes in memorizing the placement of numbers and names (just the first two numbers of each address and the first syllables of names, combining two syllables into one. Now, answer a few questions and memorize the names and addresses in preparation for the next part. (**See Memory-for-Address Test: Tips & Strategies, pages 107-112.**)

Correct Answers

Memory-for-Address Test

1. A	31. C	61. C
2. E	32. E	62. D
3. E	33. D	63. B
4. B	34. B	64. B
5. A	35. E	65. D
6. A	36. A	66. D
7. B	37. A	67. C
8. C	38. A	68. B
9. D	39. E	69. E
10. C	40. D	70. A
11. E	41. B	71. E
12. B	42. E	72. D
13. A	43. B	73. A
14. E	44. D	74. E
15. C	45. E	75. A
16. D	46. D	76. B
17. B	47. A	77. C
18. A	48. A	78. E
19. A	49. C	79. B
20. D	50. A	80. C
21. A	51. E	81. B
22. E	52. E	82. C
23. E	53. B	83. D
24. D	54. C	84. E
25. B	55. A	85. B
26. D	56. D	86. A
27. A	57. B	87. C
28. E	58. D	88. B
29. E	59. A	
30. B	60. E	

Memory-for-Address Test

Work—5 Minutes

This is the section that counts.

Decide in which box each name or address belongs. Don't look back at the boxes with the addresses in them. Work 5 minutes. For each question, mark the answers on the answer sheet to the right.

ANSWER SHEET

1. Ekron
2. 4500-4699 James
3. 1800-2499 Wood
4. Dushore
5. 8600-9299 Lang
6. 5400-5899 James
7. Levering
8. 6400-6599 James
9. Viborg
10. 2200-3199 Wood
11. 5400-6299 James
12. Lycan
13. 6400-6599 James
14. 8000-8299 Lang
15. 8600-9299 Lang
16. Dushore
17. 1200-1599 Wood
18. Levering
19. 8600-9299 Lang
20. 1200-1599 Wood
21. Danby
22. 2700-2799 Wood
23. Vanna
24. 6400-6599 James
25. Levering
26. 3100-3699 Wood
27. Lott
28. 1800-2499 Wood
29. 7400-9399 Lang
30. Jeriel
31. 5400-6299 James
32. 4500-4699 James
33. 5600-9999 Lang
34. 7400-9399 Lang
35. 8600-9299 Lang
36. Viborg
37. 5600-9999 Lang
38. Jeriel
39. 1800-2499 Wood
40. 8000-8299 Lang

	Test A	Test B
1	Ⓐ Ⓑ Ⓒ Ⓓ Ⓔ	Ⓐ Ⓑ Ⓒ Ⓓ Ⓔ
2	Ⓐ Ⓑ Ⓒ Ⓓ Ⓔ	Ⓐ Ⓑ Ⓒ Ⓓ Ⓔ
3	Ⓐ Ⓑ Ⓒ Ⓓ Ⓔ	Ⓐ Ⓑ Ⓒ Ⓓ Ⓔ
4	Ⓐ Ⓑ Ⓒ Ⓓ Ⓔ	Ⓐ Ⓑ Ⓒ Ⓓ Ⓔ
5	Ⓐ Ⓑ Ⓒ Ⓓ Ⓔ	Ⓐ Ⓑ Ⓒ Ⓓ Ⓔ
6	Ⓐ Ⓑ Ⓒ Ⓓ Ⓔ	Ⓐ Ⓑ Ⓒ Ⓓ Ⓔ
7	Ⓐ Ⓑ Ⓒ Ⓓ Ⓔ	Ⓐ Ⓑ Ⓒ Ⓓ Ⓔ
8	Ⓐ Ⓑ Ⓒ Ⓓ Ⓔ	Ⓐ Ⓑ Ⓒ Ⓓ Ⓔ
9	Ⓐ Ⓑ Ⓒ Ⓓ Ⓔ	Ⓐ Ⓑ Ⓒ Ⓓ Ⓔ
10	Ⓐ Ⓑ Ⓒ Ⓓ Ⓔ	Ⓐ Ⓑ Ⓒ Ⓓ Ⓔ
11	Ⓐ Ⓑ Ⓒ Ⓓ Ⓔ	Ⓐ Ⓑ Ⓒ Ⓓ Ⓔ
12	Ⓐ Ⓑ Ⓒ Ⓓ Ⓔ	Ⓐ Ⓑ Ⓒ Ⓓ Ⓔ
13	Ⓐ Ⓑ Ⓒ Ⓓ Ⓔ	Ⓐ Ⓑ Ⓒ Ⓓ Ⓔ
14	Ⓐ Ⓑ Ⓒ Ⓓ Ⓔ	Ⓐ Ⓑ Ⓒ Ⓓ Ⓔ
15	Ⓐ Ⓑ Ⓒ Ⓓ Ⓔ	Ⓐ Ⓑ Ⓒ Ⓓ Ⓔ
16	Ⓐ Ⓑ Ⓒ Ⓓ Ⓔ	Ⓐ Ⓑ Ⓒ Ⓓ Ⓔ
17	Ⓐ Ⓑ Ⓒ Ⓓ Ⓔ	Ⓐ Ⓑ Ⓒ Ⓓ Ⓔ
18	Ⓐ Ⓑ Ⓒ Ⓓ Ⓔ	Ⓐ Ⓑ Ⓒ Ⓓ Ⓔ
19	Ⓐ Ⓑ Ⓒ Ⓓ Ⓔ	Ⓐ Ⓑ Ⓒ Ⓓ Ⓔ
20	Ⓐ Ⓑ Ⓒ Ⓓ Ⓔ	Ⓐ Ⓑ Ⓒ Ⓓ Ⓔ
21	Ⓐ Ⓑ Ⓒ Ⓓ Ⓔ	Ⓐ Ⓑ Ⓒ Ⓓ Ⓔ
22	Ⓐ Ⓑ Ⓒ Ⓓ Ⓔ	Ⓐ Ⓑ Ⓒ Ⓓ Ⓔ
23	Ⓐ Ⓑ Ⓒ Ⓓ Ⓔ	Ⓐ Ⓑ Ⓒ Ⓓ Ⓔ
24	Ⓐ Ⓑ Ⓒ Ⓓ Ⓔ	Ⓐ Ⓑ Ⓒ Ⓓ Ⓔ
25	Ⓐ Ⓑ Ⓒ Ⓓ Ⓔ	Ⓐ Ⓑ Ⓒ Ⓓ Ⓔ
26	Ⓐ Ⓑ Ⓒ Ⓓ Ⓔ	Ⓐ Ⓑ Ⓒ Ⓓ Ⓔ
27	Ⓐ Ⓑ Ⓒ Ⓓ Ⓔ	Ⓐ Ⓑ Ⓒ Ⓓ Ⓔ
28	Ⓐ Ⓑ Ⓒ Ⓓ Ⓔ	Ⓐ Ⓑ Ⓒ Ⓓ Ⓔ
29	Ⓐ Ⓑ Ⓒ Ⓓ Ⓔ	Ⓐ Ⓑ Ⓒ Ⓓ Ⓔ
30	Ⓐ Ⓑ Ⓒ Ⓓ Ⓔ	Ⓐ Ⓑ Ⓒ Ⓓ Ⓔ
31	Ⓐ Ⓑ Ⓒ Ⓓ Ⓔ	Ⓐ Ⓑ Ⓒ Ⓓ Ⓔ
32	Ⓐ Ⓑ Ⓒ Ⓓ Ⓔ	Ⓐ Ⓑ Ⓒ Ⓓ Ⓔ
33	Ⓐ Ⓑ Ⓒ Ⓓ Ⓔ	Ⓐ Ⓑ Ⓒ Ⓓ Ⓔ
34	Ⓐ Ⓑ Ⓒ Ⓓ Ⓔ	Ⓐ Ⓑ Ⓒ Ⓓ Ⓔ
35	Ⓐ Ⓑ Ⓒ Ⓓ Ⓔ	Ⓐ Ⓑ Ⓒ Ⓓ Ⓔ
36	Ⓐ Ⓑ Ⓒ Ⓓ Ⓔ	Ⓐ Ⓑ Ⓒ Ⓓ Ⓔ
37	Ⓐ Ⓑ Ⓒ Ⓓ Ⓔ	Ⓐ Ⓑ Ⓒ Ⓓ Ⓔ
38	Ⓐ Ⓑ Ⓒ Ⓓ Ⓔ	Ⓐ Ⓑ Ⓒ Ⓓ Ⓔ
39	Ⓐ Ⓑ Ⓒ Ⓓ Ⓔ	Ⓐ Ⓑ Ⓒ Ⓓ Ⓔ
40	Ⓐ Ⓑ Ⓒ Ⓓ Ⓔ	Ⓐ Ⓑ Ⓒ Ⓓ Ⓔ

Go on to the next number on the next page.

41.	Danby	41 Ⓐ Ⓑ Ⓒ Ⓓ Ⓔ	41 Ⓐ Ⓑ Ⓒ Ⓓ Ⓔ
42.	5400-6299 James	42 Ⓐ Ⓑ Ⓒ Ⓓ Ⓔ	42 Ⓐ Ⓑ Ⓒ Ⓓ Ⓔ
43.	Ekron	43 Ⓐ Ⓑ Ⓒ Ⓓ Ⓔ	43 Ⓐ Ⓑ Ⓒ Ⓓ Ⓔ
44.	8000-8299 Lang	44 Ⓐ Ⓑ Ⓒ Ⓓ Ⓔ	44 Ⓐ Ⓑ Ⓒ Ⓓ Ⓔ
45.	Lott	45 Ⓐ Ⓑ Ⓒ Ⓓ Ⓔ	45 Ⓐ Ⓑ Ⓒ Ⓓ Ⓔ
46.	5500-9999 Lang	46 Ⓐ Ⓑ Ⓒ Ⓓ Ⓔ	46 Ⓐ Ⓑ Ⓒ Ⓓ Ⓔ
47.	Ekron	47 Ⓐ Ⓑ Ⓒ Ⓓ Ⓔ	47 Ⓐ Ⓑ Ⓒ Ⓓ Ⓔ
48.	8000-8299 Lang	48 Ⓐ Ⓑ Ⓒ Ⓓ Ⓔ	48 Ⓐ Ⓑ Ⓒ Ⓓ Ⓔ
49.	5400-6299 James	49 Ⓐ Ⓑ Ⓒ Ⓓ Ⓔ	49 Ⓐ Ⓑ Ⓒ Ⓓ Ⓔ
50.	2200-3199 Wood	50 Ⓐ Ⓑ Ⓒ Ⓓ Ⓔ	50 Ⓐ Ⓑ Ⓒ Ⓓ Ⓔ
51.	Valley	51 Ⓐ Ⓑ Ⓒ Ⓓ Ⓔ	51 Ⓐ Ⓑ Ⓒ Ⓓ Ⓔ
52.	1800-2499 Wood	52 Ⓐ Ⓑ Ⓒ Ⓓ Ⓔ	52 Ⓐ Ⓑ Ⓒ Ⓓ Ⓔ
53.	7500-8799 Lang	53 Ⓐ Ⓑ Ⓒ Ⓓ Ⓔ	53 Ⓐ Ⓑ Ⓒ Ⓓ Ⓔ
54.	8000-8299 Lang	54 Ⓐ Ⓑ Ⓒ Ⓓ Ⓔ	54 Ⓐ Ⓑ Ⓒ Ⓓ Ⓔ
55.	Levering	55 Ⓐ Ⓑ Ⓒ Ⓓ Ⓔ	55 Ⓐ Ⓑ Ⓒ Ⓓ Ⓔ
56.	8000-8299 Lang	56 Ⓐ Ⓑ Ⓒ Ⓓ Ⓔ	56 Ⓐ Ⓑ Ⓒ Ⓓ Ⓔ
57.	5500-5899 James	57 Ⓐ Ⓑ Ⓒ Ⓓ Ⓔ	57 Ⓐ Ⓑ Ⓒ Ⓓ Ⓔ
58.	3100-3699 Wood	58 Ⓐ Ⓑ Ⓒ Ⓓ Ⓔ	58 Ⓐ Ⓑ Ⓒ Ⓓ Ⓔ
59.	5400-6299 James	59 Ⓐ Ⓑ Ⓒ Ⓓ Ⓔ	59 Ⓐ Ⓑ Ⓒ Ⓓ Ⓔ
60.	3100-3699 Wood	60 Ⓐ Ⓑ Ⓒ Ⓓ Ⓔ	60 Ⓐ Ⓑ Ⓒ Ⓓ Ⓔ
61.	4500-4699 James	61 Ⓐ Ⓑ Ⓒ Ⓓ Ⓔ	61 Ⓐ Ⓑ Ⓒ Ⓓ Ⓔ
62.	2700-2799 Wood	62 Ⓐ Ⓑ Ⓒ Ⓓ Ⓔ	62 Ⓐ Ⓑ Ⓒ Ⓓ Ⓔ
63.	1200-1599 Wood	63 Ⓐ Ⓑ Ⓒ Ⓓ Ⓔ	63 Ⓐ Ⓑ Ⓒ Ⓓ Ⓔ
64.	Valley	64 Ⓐ Ⓑ Ⓒ Ⓓ Ⓔ	64 Ⓐ Ⓑ Ⓒ Ⓓ Ⓔ
65.	7500-8799 Lang	65 Ⓐ Ⓑ Ⓒ Ⓓ Ⓔ	65 Ⓐ Ⓑ Ⓒ Ⓓ Ⓔ
66.	6100-6499 James	66 Ⓐ Ⓑ Ⓒ Ⓓ Ⓔ	66 Ⓐ Ⓑ Ⓒ Ⓓ Ⓔ
67.	8000-8299 Lang	67 Ⓐ Ⓑ Ⓒ Ⓓ Ⓔ	67 Ⓐ Ⓑ Ⓒ Ⓓ Ⓔ
68.	5600-9999 Lang	68 Ⓐ Ⓑ Ⓒ Ⓓ Ⓔ	68 Ⓐ Ⓑ Ⓒ Ⓓ Ⓔ
69.	Levering	69 Ⓐ Ⓑ Ⓒ Ⓓ Ⓔ	69 Ⓐ Ⓑ Ⓒ Ⓓ Ⓔ
70.	7400-9399 Lang	70 Ⓐ Ⓑ Ⓒ Ⓓ Ⓔ	70 Ⓐ Ⓑ Ⓒ Ⓓ Ⓔ
71.	Valley	71 Ⓐ Ⓑ Ⓒ Ⓓ Ⓔ	71 Ⓐ Ⓑ Ⓒ Ⓓ Ⓔ
72.	5400-6299 James	72 Ⓐ Ⓑ Ⓒ Ⓓ Ⓔ	72 Ⓐ Ⓑ Ⓒ Ⓓ Ⓔ
73.	3100-3699 Wood	73 Ⓐ Ⓑ Ⓒ Ⓓ Ⓔ	73 Ⓐ Ⓑ Ⓒ Ⓓ Ⓔ
74.	6400-6599 James	74 Ⓐ Ⓑ Ⓒ Ⓓ Ⓔ	74 Ⓐ Ⓑ Ⓒ Ⓓ Ⓔ
75.	5400-6299 James	75 Ⓐ Ⓑ Ⓒ Ⓓ Ⓔ	75 Ⓐ Ⓑ Ⓒ Ⓓ Ⓔ
76.	2200-3199 Wood	76 Ⓐ Ⓑ Ⓒ Ⓓ Ⓔ	76 Ⓐ Ⓑ Ⓒ Ⓓ Ⓔ
77.	5600-9999 Lang	77 Ⓐ Ⓑ Ⓒ Ⓓ Ⓔ	77 Ⓐ Ⓑ Ⓒ Ⓓ Ⓔ
78.	Dushore	78 Ⓐ Ⓑ Ⓒ Ⓓ Ⓔ	78 Ⓐ Ⓑ Ⓒ Ⓓ Ⓔ
79.	3100-3699 Wood	79 Ⓐ Ⓑ Ⓒ Ⓓ Ⓔ	79 Ⓐ Ⓑ Ⓒ Ⓓ Ⓔ
80.	2200-3199 Wood	80 Ⓐ Ⓑ Ⓒ Ⓓ Ⓔ	80 Ⓐ Ⓑ Ⓒ Ⓓ Ⓔ
81.	8600-9299 Lang	81 Ⓐ Ⓑ Ⓒ Ⓓ Ⓔ	81 Ⓐ Ⓑ Ⓒ Ⓓ Ⓔ
82.	Lycan	82 Ⓐ Ⓑ Ⓒ Ⓓ Ⓔ	82 Ⓐ Ⓑ Ⓒ Ⓓ Ⓔ
83.	7400-9399 Lang	83 Ⓐ Ⓑ Ⓒ Ⓓ Ⓔ	83 Ⓐ Ⓑ Ⓒ Ⓓ Ⓔ
84.	5600-9999 Lang	84 Ⓐ Ⓑ Ⓒ Ⓓ Ⓔ	84 Ⓐ Ⓑ Ⓒ Ⓓ Ⓔ
85.	7400-9399 Lang	85 Ⓐ Ⓑ Ⓒ Ⓓ Ⓔ	85 Ⓐ Ⓑ Ⓒ Ⓓ Ⓔ
86.	4500-4699 James	86 Ⓐ Ⓑ Ⓒ Ⓓ Ⓔ	86 Ⓐ Ⓑ Ⓒ Ⓓ Ⓔ
87.	8600-9299 Lang	87 Ⓐ Ⓑ Ⓒ Ⓓ Ⓔ	87 Ⓐ Ⓑ Ⓒ Ⓓ Ⓔ
88.	Viborg	88 Ⓐ Ⓑ Ⓒ Ⓓ Ⓔ	88 Ⓐ Ⓑ Ⓒ Ⓓ Ⓔ

Go on to the next number on the next page.

STOP

If you finish before the time is up,

go back and check your answers.

(See the correct answers on the next page.)

Correct Answers

Memory-for-Address Test

1.	C	31.	B	61.	E
2.	E	32.	E	62.	E
3.	A	33.	E	63.	C
4.	A	34.	C	64.	D
5.	B	35.	B	65.	A
6.	B	36.	D	66.	C
7.	C	37.	E	67.	D
8.	A	38.	B	68.	E
9.	D	39.	A	69.	C
10.	B	40.	D	70.	C
11.	B	41.	E	71.	D
12.	E	42.	B	72.	B
13.	A	43.	C	73.	D
14.	D	44.	D	74.	A
15.	B	45.	A	75.	B
16.	A	46.	E	76.	B
17.	C	47.	C	77.	E
18.	C	48.	D	78.	A
19.	B	49.	B	79.	D
20.	C	50.	B	80.	B
21.	E	51.	D	81.	B
22.	E	52.	A	82.	E
23.	B	53.	A	83.	C
24.	A	54.	D	84.	E
25.	C	55.	C	85.	C
26.	D	56.	D	86.	E
27.	A	57.	D	87.	B
28.	A	58.	D	88.	D
29.	C	59.	B		
30.	B	60.	D		

Memory-for-Address Test

Work—3 Minutes

Answer each question on a piece of paper to show the letter of the box in which the address belongs.
Try to remember the location of as many addresses as you can. If you are not sure of an address, guess.
Work only three minutes.

A	B	C	D	E
1500-2599 Blake Cathy 5500-8799 Beach Baker 3400-6599 Walker	1200-3599 Blake Cedar 4600-9599 Beach Forter 1400-2299 Walker	3200-1899 Blake Halstead 6400-9599 Beach Winter 5500-6499 Walker	2100-3599 Blake Hotel 7000-8599 Beach Central 1500-1899 Walker	3500-2999 Blake Tatum 7500-9999 Beach River 2500-4999 Walker

1. 5500-8799 Beach
2. Winter
3. 3200-1899 Blake
4. River
5. 3500-2999 Blake
6. 1400-2299 Walker
7. Baker
8. 3200-1899 Blake
9. 2500-4999 Walker
10. Halsted
11. 700-8599 Beach
12. 5500-4999 Walker
13. Cedar
14. 4600-9599 Beach
15. Cathy
16. 2100-3599 Blake
17. 7500-9999 Beach
18. 4600-9599 Beach
19. 7000-8599 Beach
20. 3400-6599 Walker
21. 3200-1899 Blake
22. Halsted
23. 3500-2999 Blake
24. 1400-2299 Walker

25. 6400-9599 Beach
26. 5500-6499 Walker
27. 3500-2999 Blake
28. Halsted
29. 1400-2299 Walker
30. 1500-2599 Blake
31. Forter
32. 7000-8599 Beach
33. Tatum
34. 3200-1899 Blake
35. Cedar
36. 7000-8599 Beach
37. Winter
38. 1200-3599 Blake
39. Central
40. 4600-9599 Beach
41. Hotel
42. 7500-9999 Beach
43. 1400-2299 Walker
44. 1500-2599 Blake
45. 2100-3599 Blake
46. 7500-9999 Beach
47. 6400-9599 Beach
48. River

49. 7500-9999 Beach
50. 1500-2599 Blake
51. 1200-3599 Blake
52. 1500-1899 Walker
53. 3500-299 Blakel
54. Baker
55. Cedar
56. 1400-2299 Walker
57. 2100-3599 Blake
58. 4600-9599 Beach
59. Cathy
60. 2500-4999 Walker
61. 1200-3599 Blake
62. Forter
63. 3400-6599 Walker
64. 7000-8599 Beach
65. 1400-2299 Walker
66. 3500-2999 Blake
67. Baker
68. 1500-2599 Blake
69. Halsted
70. 5500-6499 Walker
71. 7500-9999 Beach
72. 1200-3599 Blake

73. River
74. 7000-8599 Beach
75. 1400-2299 Walker
76. 3400-6599 Walker
77. Cedar
78. Hotel
79. 3400-6599 Walker
80. Halsted
81. 1200-3599 Blake
82. 5500-6499 Walker
83. 7500-9999 Beach
84. Forter
85. Winter
86. 1500-2599 Blake
87. 3400-6599 Walker
88. 7000-8599 Beach

STOP

When the time is up, go on to the next page for the correct answers.

(**Author's Note:** The sample test above is known as the memory-for-address test in the 470 Battery Test and the 460 Rural Carrier Associate Exam. This Part B is considered as a practice test. You'll be allowed to look at the names and addresses in the boxes, as you are instructed to answer as many questions as possible in three minutes. In the next part, however, you will be asked to answer all the 88 questions in five minutes and you won't be allowed to look at the names and addresses. During the three-minute practice test, answer only a few questions. Spend most of the three minutes in memorizing the placement of numbers and names (just the first two numbers of each address and the first syllables of names, combining two syllables into one. Now, answer a few questions and memorize the names and addresses in preparation for the next part. (**See Memory-for-Address Test: Tips & Strategies, pages 107-112.**)

Correct Answers

Memory-for-Address Test

1. A	31. B	61. B
2. C	32. D	62. B
3. C	33. E	63. A
4. E	34. C	64. D
5. E	35. B	65. B
6. B	36. D	66. E
7. A	37. C	67. A
8. C	38. B	68. A
9. E	39. D	69. C
10. C	40. B	70. C
11. D	41. D	71. E
12. E	42. E	72. B
13. B	43. B	73. E
14. B	44. A	74. E
15. A	45. D	75. B
16. D	46. E	76. A
17. E	47. C	77. B
18. B	48. E	78. D
19. D	49. E	79. A
20. A	50. A	80. C
21. C	51. B	81. B
22. C	52. D	82. C
23. E	53. E	83. E
24. B	54. A	84. B
25. C	55. B	85. C
26. C	56. B	86. A
27. E	57. D	87. A
28. C	58. B	88. D
29. B	59. A	
30. A	60. E	

Memory-for-Address Test

Work—5 Minutes

This is the section that counts.

Decide in which box each name or address belongs. Don't look back at the boxes with the addresses in them. Work 5 minutes. For each question, mark the answers on the answer sheet to the right.

ANSWER SHEET

	Test A	Test B
1. 7500-9999 Beach	1 Ⓐ Ⓑ Ⓒ Ⓓ Ⓔ	1 Ⓐ Ⓑ Ⓒ Ⓓ Ⓔ
2. Cathy	2 Ⓐ Ⓑ Ⓒ Ⓓ Ⓔ	2 Ⓐ Ⓑ Ⓒ Ⓓ Ⓔ
3. 2100-3599 Blake	3 Ⓐ Ⓑ Ⓒ Ⓓ Ⓔ	3 Ⓐ Ⓑ Ⓒ Ⓓ Ⓔ
4. 7500-9999 Beach	4 Ⓐ Ⓑ Ⓒ Ⓓ Ⓔ	4 Ⓐ Ⓑ Ⓒ Ⓓ Ⓔ
5. 3400-6599 Walker	5 Ⓐ Ⓑ Ⓒ Ⓓ Ⓔ	5 Ⓐ Ⓑ Ⓒ Ⓓ Ⓔ
6. Halsted	6 Ⓐ Ⓑ Ⓒ Ⓓ Ⓔ	6 Ⓐ Ⓑ Ⓒ Ⓓ Ⓔ
7. 1400-2299 Walker	7 Ⓐ Ⓑ Ⓒ Ⓓ Ⓔ	7 Ⓐ Ⓑ Ⓒ Ⓓ Ⓔ
8. Tatum	8 Ⓐ Ⓑ Ⓒ Ⓓ Ⓔ	8 Ⓐ Ⓑ Ⓒ Ⓓ Ⓔ
9. 3200-1899 Blake	9 Ⓐ Ⓑ Ⓒ Ⓓ Ⓔ	9 Ⓐ Ⓑ Ⓒ Ⓓ Ⓔ
10. River	10 Ⓐ Ⓑ Ⓒ Ⓓ Ⓔ	10 Ⓐ Ⓑ Ⓒ Ⓓ Ⓔ
11. 3400-6599 Walker	11 Ⓐ Ⓑ Ⓒ Ⓓ Ⓔ	11 Ⓐ Ⓑ Ⓒ Ⓓ Ⓔ
12. 7000-8599 Beach	12 Ⓐ Ⓑ Ⓒ Ⓓ Ⓔ	12 Ⓐ Ⓑ Ⓒ Ⓓ Ⓔ
13. Winter	13 Ⓐ Ⓑ Ⓒ Ⓓ Ⓔ	13 Ⓐ Ⓑ Ⓒ Ⓓ Ⓔ
14. 4600-9599 Beach	14 Ⓐ Ⓑ Ⓒ Ⓓ Ⓔ	14 Ⓐ Ⓑ Ⓒ Ⓓ Ⓔ
15. 6400-9599 Beach	15 Ⓐ Ⓑ Ⓒ Ⓓ Ⓔ	15 Ⓐ Ⓑ Ⓒ Ⓓ Ⓔ
16. Cathy	16 Ⓐ Ⓑ Ⓒ Ⓓ Ⓔ	16 Ⓐ Ⓑ Ⓒ Ⓓ Ⓔ
17. 2100-3599 Blake	17 Ⓐ Ⓑ Ⓒ Ⓓ Ⓔ	17 Ⓐ Ⓑ Ⓒ Ⓓ Ⓔ
18. 7000-8599 Beach	18 Ⓐ Ⓑ Ⓒ Ⓓ Ⓔ	18 Ⓐ Ⓑ Ⓒ Ⓓ Ⓔ
19. Cedar	19 Ⓐ Ⓑ Ⓒ Ⓓ Ⓔ	19 Ⓐ Ⓑ Ⓒ Ⓓ Ⓔ
20. 1400-2299 Walker	20 Ⓐ Ⓑ Ⓒ Ⓓ Ⓔ	20 Ⓐ Ⓑ Ⓒ Ⓓ Ⓔ
21. River	21 Ⓐ Ⓑ Ⓒ Ⓓ Ⓔ	21 Ⓐ Ⓑ Ⓒ Ⓓ Ⓔ
22. 2100-3599 Blake	22 Ⓐ Ⓑ Ⓒ Ⓓ Ⓔ	22 Ⓐ Ⓑ Ⓒ Ⓓ Ⓔ
23. 5500-6499 Walker	23 Ⓐ Ⓑ Ⓒ Ⓓ Ⓔ	23 Ⓐ Ⓑ Ⓒ Ⓓ Ⓔ
24. 2100-3599 Blake	24 Ⓐ Ⓑ Ⓒ Ⓓ Ⓔ	24 Ⓐ Ⓑ Ⓒ Ⓓ Ⓔ
25. 7500-9999 Beach	25 Ⓐ Ⓑ Ⓒ Ⓓ Ⓔ	25 Ⓐ Ⓑ Ⓒ Ⓓ Ⓔ
26. Winter	26 Ⓐ Ⓑ Ⓒ Ⓓ Ⓔ	26 Ⓐ Ⓑ Ⓒ Ⓓ Ⓔ
27. 4600-9599 Beach	27 Ⓐ Ⓑ Ⓒ Ⓓ Ⓔ	27 Ⓐ Ⓑ Ⓒ Ⓓ Ⓔ
28. 3200-1899 Blake	28 Ⓐ Ⓑ Ⓒ Ⓓ Ⓔ	28 Ⓐ Ⓑ Ⓒ Ⓓ Ⓔ
29. Central	29 Ⓐ Ⓑ Ⓒ Ⓓ Ⓔ	29 Ⓐ Ⓑ Ⓒ Ⓓ Ⓔ
30. Forter	30 Ⓐ Ⓑ Ⓒ Ⓓ Ⓔ	30 Ⓐ Ⓑ Ⓒ Ⓓ Ⓔ
31. 7500-9999 Beach	31 Ⓐ Ⓑ Ⓒ Ⓓ Ⓔ	31 Ⓐ Ⓑ Ⓒ Ⓓ Ⓔ
32. 2100-3599 Blake	32 Ⓐ Ⓑ Ⓒ Ⓓ Ⓔ	32 Ⓐ Ⓑ Ⓒ Ⓓ Ⓔ
33. 1500-2599 Blake	33 Ⓐ Ⓑ Ⓒ Ⓓ Ⓔ	33 Ⓐ Ⓑ Ⓒ Ⓓ Ⓔ
34. 7000-8599 Beach	34 Ⓐ Ⓑ Ⓒ Ⓓ Ⓔ	34 Ⓐ Ⓑ Ⓒ Ⓓ Ⓔ
35. 7500-9999 Beach	35 Ⓐ Ⓑ Ⓒ Ⓓ Ⓔ	35 Ⓐ Ⓑ Ⓒ Ⓓ Ⓔ
36. 1500-1899 Walker	36 Ⓐ Ⓑ Ⓒ Ⓓ Ⓔ	36 Ⓐ Ⓑ Ⓒ Ⓓ Ⓔ
37. 5500-8799 Beach	37 Ⓐ Ⓑ Ⓒ Ⓓ Ⓔ	37 Ⓐ Ⓑ Ⓒ Ⓓ Ⓔ
38. Hotel	38 Ⓐ Ⓑ Ⓒ Ⓓ Ⓔ	38 Ⓐ Ⓑ Ⓒ Ⓓ Ⓔ
39. 1200-3599 Blake	39 Ⓐ Ⓑ Ⓒ Ⓓ Ⓔ	39 Ⓐ Ⓑ Ⓒ Ⓓ Ⓔ
40. River	40 Ⓐ Ⓑ Ⓒ Ⓓ Ⓔ	40 Ⓐ Ⓑ Ⓒ Ⓓ Ⓔ

Go on to the next number on the next page.

41. 2500-4999 Walker	41 Ⓐ Ⓑ Ⓒ Ⓓ Ⓔ	41 Ⓐ Ⓑ Ⓒ Ⓓ Ⓔ
42. Forter	42 Ⓐ Ⓑ Ⓒ Ⓓ Ⓔ	42 Ⓐ Ⓑ Ⓒ Ⓓ Ⓔ
43. Central	43 Ⓐ Ⓑ Ⓒ Ⓓ Ⓔ	43 Ⓐ Ⓑ Ⓒ Ⓓ Ⓔ
44. 1400-2299 Walker	44 Ⓐ Ⓑ Ⓒ Ⓓ Ⓔ	44 Ⓐ Ⓑ Ⓒ Ⓓ Ⓔ
45. 7500-9999 Beach	45 Ⓐ Ⓑ Ⓒ Ⓓ Ⓔ	45 Ⓐ Ⓑ Ⓒ Ⓓ Ⓔ
46. 2100-3599 Blake	46 Ⓐ Ⓑ Ⓒ Ⓓ Ⓔ	46 Ⓐ Ⓑ Ⓒ Ⓓ Ⓔ
47. 6400-9599 Beach	47 Ⓐ Ⓑ Ⓒ Ⓓ Ⓔ	47 Ⓐ Ⓑ Ⓒ Ⓓ Ⓔ
48. Halsted	48 Ⓐ Ⓑ Ⓒ Ⓓ Ⓔ	48 Ⓐ Ⓑ Ⓒ Ⓓ Ⓔ
49. Baker	49 Ⓐ Ⓑ Ⓒ Ⓓ Ⓔ	49 Ⓐ Ⓑ Ⓒ Ⓓ Ⓔ
50. 1200-3599 Blake	50 Ⓐ Ⓑ Ⓒ Ⓓ Ⓔ	50 Ⓐ Ⓑ Ⓒ Ⓓ Ⓔ
51. 1500-1899 Walker	51 Ⓐ Ⓑ Ⓒ Ⓓ Ⓔ	51 Ⓐ Ⓑ Ⓒ Ⓓ Ⓔ
52. 1400-2299 Walker	52 Ⓐ Ⓑ Ⓒ Ⓓ Ⓔ	52 Ⓐ Ⓑ Ⓒ Ⓓ Ⓔ
53. 3200-1899 Blake	53 Ⓐ Ⓑ Ⓒ Ⓓ Ⓔ	53 Ⓐ Ⓑ Ⓒ Ⓓ Ⓔ
54. Central	54 Ⓐ Ⓑ Ⓒ Ⓓ Ⓔ	54 Ⓐ Ⓑ Ⓒ Ⓓ Ⓔ
55. 4600-9599 Beach	55 Ⓐ Ⓑ Ⓒ Ⓓ Ⓔ	55 Ⓐ Ⓑ Ⓒ Ⓓ Ⓔ
56. Tatum	56 Ⓐ Ⓑ Ⓒ Ⓓ Ⓔ	56 Ⓐ Ⓑ Ⓒ Ⓓ Ⓔ
57. Baker	57 Ⓐ Ⓑ Ⓒ Ⓓ Ⓔ	57 Ⓐ Ⓑ Ⓒ Ⓓ Ⓔ
58. 5500-6499 Walker	58 Ⓐ Ⓑ Ⓒ Ⓓ Ⓔ	58 Ⓐ Ⓑ Ⓒ Ⓓ Ⓔ
59. 3400-6599 Walker	59 Ⓐ Ⓑ Ⓒ Ⓓ Ⓔ	59 Ⓐ Ⓑ Ⓒ Ⓓ Ⓔ
60. 6400-9599 Beach	60 Ⓐ Ⓑ Ⓒ Ⓓ Ⓔ	60 Ⓐ Ⓑ Ⓒ Ⓓ Ⓔ
61. Halsted	61 Ⓐ Ⓑ Ⓒ Ⓓ Ⓔ	61 Ⓐ Ⓑ Ⓒ Ⓓ Ⓔ
62. 5500-6499 Walker	62 Ⓐ Ⓑ Ⓒ Ⓓ Ⓔ	62 Ⓐ Ⓑ Ⓒ Ⓓ Ⓔ
63. 7500-9999 Beach	63 Ⓐ Ⓑ Ⓒ Ⓓ Ⓔ	63 Ⓐ Ⓑ Ⓒ Ⓓ Ⓔ
64. Forter	64 Ⓐ Ⓑ Ⓒ Ⓓ Ⓔ	64 Ⓐ Ⓑ Ⓒ Ⓓ Ⓔ
65. 3500-2999 Blake	65 Ⓐ Ⓑ Ⓒ Ⓓ Ⓔ	65 Ⓐ Ⓑ Ⓒ Ⓓ Ⓔ
66. 3400-6599 Walker	66 Ⓐ Ⓑ Ⓒ Ⓓ Ⓔ	66 Ⓐ Ⓑ Ⓒ Ⓓ Ⓔ
67. Cedar	67 Ⓐ Ⓑ Ⓒ Ⓓ Ⓔ	67 Ⓐ Ⓑ Ⓒ Ⓓ Ⓔ
68. 7500-9999 Beach	68 Ⓐ Ⓑ Ⓒ Ⓓ Ⓔ	68 Ⓐ Ⓑ Ⓒ Ⓓ Ⓔ
69. River	69 Ⓐ Ⓑ Ⓒ Ⓓ Ⓔ	69 Ⓐ Ⓑ Ⓒ Ⓓ Ⓔ
70. 6400-9599 Beach	70 Ⓐ Ⓑ Ⓒ Ⓓ Ⓔ	70 Ⓐ Ⓑ Ⓒ Ⓓ Ⓔ
71. 3500-2999 Blake	71 Ⓐ Ⓑ Ⓒ Ⓓ Ⓔ	71 Ⓐ Ⓑ Ⓒ Ⓓ Ⓔ
72. 1400-2299 Walker	72 Ⓐ Ⓑ Ⓒ Ⓓ Ⓔ	72 Ⓐ Ⓑ Ⓒ Ⓓ Ⓔ
73. Winter	73 Ⓐ Ⓑ Ⓒ Ⓓ Ⓔ	73 Ⓐ Ⓑ Ⓒ Ⓓ Ⓔ
74. 1400-2299 Walker	74 Ⓐ Ⓑ Ⓒ Ⓓ Ⓔ	74 Ⓐ Ⓑ Ⓒ Ⓓ Ⓔ
75. 3400-6599 Walker	75 Ⓐ Ⓑ Ⓒ Ⓓ Ⓔ	75 Ⓐ Ⓑ Ⓒ Ⓓ Ⓔ
76. 6400-9599 Beach	76 Ⓐ Ⓑ Ⓒ Ⓓ Ⓔ	76 Ⓐ Ⓑ Ⓒ Ⓓ Ⓔ
77. Tatum	77 Ⓐ Ⓑ Ⓒ Ⓓ Ⓔ	77 Ⓐ Ⓑ Ⓒ Ⓓ Ⓔ
78. 1200-3599 Blake	78 Ⓐ Ⓑ Ⓒ Ⓓ Ⓔ	78 Ⓐ Ⓑ Ⓒ Ⓓ Ⓔ
79. 7500-9999 Beach	79 Ⓐ Ⓑ Ⓒ Ⓓ Ⓔ	79 Ⓐ Ⓑ Ⓒ Ⓓ Ⓔ
80. Forter	80 Ⓐ Ⓑ Ⓒ Ⓓ Ⓔ	80 Ⓐ Ⓑ Ⓒ Ⓓ Ⓔ
81. River	81 Ⓐ Ⓑ Ⓒ Ⓓ Ⓔ	81 Ⓐ Ⓑ Ⓒ Ⓓ Ⓔ
82. 5500-8799 Beach	82 Ⓐ Ⓑ Ⓒ Ⓓ Ⓔ	82 Ⓐ Ⓑ Ⓒ Ⓓ Ⓔ
83. 2100-3599 Blake	83 Ⓐ Ⓑ Ⓒ Ⓓ Ⓔ	83 Ⓐ Ⓑ Ⓒ Ⓓ Ⓔ
84. 1400-2299 Walker	84 Ⓐ Ⓑ Ⓒ Ⓓ Ⓔ	84 Ⓐ Ⓑ Ⓒ Ⓓ Ⓔ
85. 7500-9999 Beach	85 Ⓐ Ⓑ Ⓒ Ⓓ Ⓔ	85 Ⓐ Ⓑ Ⓒ Ⓓ Ⓔ
86. Baker	86 Ⓐ Ⓑ Ⓒ Ⓓ Ⓔ	86 Ⓐ Ⓑ Ⓒ Ⓓ Ⓔ
87. 1200-3599 Blake	87 Ⓐ Ⓑ Ⓒ Ⓓ Ⓔ	87 Ⓐ Ⓑ Ⓒ Ⓓ Ⓔ
88. 2500-49999 Walker	88 Ⓐ Ⓑ Ⓒ Ⓓ Ⓔ	88 Ⓐ Ⓑ Ⓒ Ⓓ Ⓔ

Go on to the next number on the next page.

STOP

If you finish before the time is up,

go back and check your answers.

(See the correct answers on the next page.)

Correct Answers

Memory-for-Address Test

1.	E	31.	E	61.	C
2.	A	32.	D	62.	C
3.	D	33.	A	63.	E
4.	E	34.	D	64.	B
5.	A	35.	E	65.	E
6.	C	36.	D	66.	A
7.	B	37.	A	67.	B
8.	E	38.	D	68.	E
9.	C	39.	B	69.	E
10.	E	40.	E	70.	C
11.	A	41.	E	71.	E
12.	D	42.	B	72.	B
13.	C	43.	D	73.	C
14.	B	44.	B	74.	B
15.	C	45.	E	75.	A
16.	A	46.	D	76.	C
17.	D	47.	C	77.	E
18.	D	48.	C	78.	B
19.	B	49.	A	79.	E
20.	B	50.	B	80.	B
21.	E	51.	D	81.	E
22.	D	52.	B	82.	A
23.	C	53.	C	83.	D
24.	D	54.	D	84.	B
25.	E	55.	B	85.	E
26.	C	56.	E	86.	A
27.	B	57.	A	87.	B
28.	C	58.	C	88.	E
29.	D	59.	A		
30.	B	60.	C		

Memory-for-Address Test

Work—3 Minutes

Answer each question on a piece of paper to show the letter of the box in which the address belongs.
Try to remember the location of as many addresses as you can. If you are not sure of an address, guess.
Work only three minutes.

A	B	C	D	E
1200-2599 Drake Weber 1500-1799 Palmer Dewey 4400-6599 Pine	2400-3599 Drake Baker 3600-4599 Palmer Madison 1400-2599 Pine	3200-5599 Drake Hillside 1640-2599 Palmer Dexter 4500-6599 Pine	2100-3599 Drake Ceres 6000-7599 Palmer Bayview 4200-5999 Pine	1700-2599 Drake Girard 3500-9999 Palmer Herald 3400-4599 Pine

1. Hillside
2. 2100-3599 Drake
3. 3500-9999 Palmer
4. 3600-4599 Palmer
5. 4500-6599 Pine
6. 1500-1799 Palmer
7. 3200-5599 Drake
8. Madison
9. 6000-7599 Palmer
10. 1400-2599 Pine
11. 3400-4599 Pine
12. 2400-3599 Drake
13. Dewey
14. Baker
15. 1700-2599 Drake
16. 1400-2599 Pine
17. 4400-6599 Pines
18. 3200-5599 Drake
19. 1500-1799 Palmer
20. Hillside
21. Ceres
22. 2400-3599 Drake
23. 4400-6599 Pine
24. Girard

25. 1640-2599 Palmer
26. 3200-5599 Drake
27. Baker
28. 3500-9999 Palmer
29. 4400-6599 Pine
30. Weber
31. 1400-2599 Pine
32. 2400-3599 Drake
33. 3400-4599 Pine
34. Dewey
35. 3600-4599 Palmer
36. 4400-6599 Pine
37. 2100-3599 Drake
38. 3400-4599 Pine
39. Baker
40. 1200-2599 Drake
41. 2400-3599 Drake
42. Madison
43. 6000-7599 Palmer
44. 2400-3599 Drake
45. Dexter
46. 1700-2599 Drake
47. Madison
48. Bayview

49. 3500-9999 Palmer
50. 4400-6599 Pine
51. 1640-2599 Palmer
52. 3600-4599 Palmer
53. 1700-2599 Drake
54. 2400-3599 Drake
55. 1400-2599 Pine
56. 4400-6599 Pine
57. Baker
58. 3600-4599 Palmer
59. 4400-6599 Pine
60. 3600-4599 Palmer
61. 3500-9999 Palmer
62. Dewey
63. 4200-5999 Pine
64. Hillside
65. 3200-5599 Drake
66. Dewey
67. 4400-6599 Pine
68. 1200-2599 Drake
69. Herald
70. Dexter
71. 2100-3599 Drake
72. 1700-2599 Drake

73. Bayview
74. 2400-3599 Drake
75. 1400-2599 Pine
76. Weber
77. Hillside
78. 4500-6599 Pine
79. 3500-9999 Palmer
80. 1400-2599 Pine
81. 3200-5599 Drake
82. 1500-1799 Palmer
83. 2100-3599 Drake
84. 1640-2599 Palmer
85. Ceres
86. 3600-4599 Palmer
87. Girard
88. 3200-5599 Drake

STOP

When the time is up, go on to the next page for the correct answers.

(**Author's Note:** The sample test above is known as the memory-for-address test in the 470 Battery Test and the 460 Rural Carrier Associate Exam. This Part B is considered as a practice test. You'll be allowed to look at the names and addresses in the boxes, as you are instructed to answer as many questions as possible in three minutes. In the next part, however, you will be asked to answer all the 88 questions in five minutes and you won't be allowed to look at the names and addresses. During the three-minute practice test, answer only a few questions. Spend most of the three minutes in memorizing the placement of numbers and names (just the first two numbers of each address and the first syllables of names, combining two syllables into one. Now, answer a few questions and memorize the names and addresses in preparation for the next part. (**See Memory-for-Address Test: Tips & Strategies, pages 107-112.**)

Correct Answers

Memory-for-Address Test

1. C	31. B	61. E
2. D	32. B	62. A
3. E	33. E	63. D
4. B	34. A	64. C
5. C	35. B	65. C
6. A	36. A	66. A
7. C	37. D	67. A
8. B	38. E	68. A
9. D	39. B	69. E
10. B	40. A	70. C
11. E	41. B	71. D
12. B	42. B	72. E
13. A	43. D	73. D
14. B	44. B	74. B
15. E	45. C	75. B
16. B	46. E	76. A
17. A	47. B	77. C
18. C	48. D	78. C
19. A	49. E	79. E
20. C	50. A	80. B
21. D	51. C	81. C
22. B	52. B	82. A
23. A	53. E	83. D
24. E	54. B	84. C
25. C	55. B	85. D
26. C	56. A	86. B
27. B	57. B	87. E
28. E	58. B	88. C
29. A	59. A	
30. A	60. B	

Memory-for-Address Test

Work—5 Minutes

This is the section that counts.

Decide in which box each name or address belongs. Don't look back at the boxes with the addresses in them. Work 5 minutes. For each question, mark the answers on the answer sheet to the right.

ANSWER SHEET

		Test A	Test B
1.	1700-2599 Drake	1 Ⓐ Ⓑ Ⓒ Ⓓ Ⓔ	1 Ⓐ Ⓑ Ⓒ Ⓓ Ⓔ
2.	Bayview	2 Ⓐ Ⓑ Ⓒ Ⓓ Ⓔ	2 Ⓐ Ⓑ Ⓒ Ⓓ Ⓔ
3.	1500-1799 Palmer	3 Ⓐ Ⓑ Ⓒ Ⓓ Ⓔ	3 Ⓐ Ⓑ Ⓒ Ⓓ Ⓔ
4.	4200-4599 Pine	4 Ⓐ Ⓑ Ⓒ Ⓓ Ⓔ	4 Ⓐ Ⓑ Ⓒ Ⓓ Ⓔ
5.	Baker	5 Ⓐ Ⓑ Ⓒ Ⓓ Ⓔ	5 Ⓐ Ⓑ Ⓒ Ⓓ Ⓔ
6.	1640-2599 Palmer	6 Ⓐ Ⓑ Ⓒ Ⓓ Ⓔ	6 Ⓐ Ⓑ Ⓒ Ⓓ Ⓔ
7.	Girard	7 Ⓐ Ⓑ Ⓒ Ⓓ Ⓔ	7 Ⓐ Ⓑ Ⓒ Ⓓ Ⓔ
8.	4400-6599 Pine	8 Ⓐ Ⓑ Ⓒ Ⓓ Ⓔ	8 Ⓐ Ⓑ Ⓒ Ⓓ Ⓔ
9.	2100-3599 Drake	9 Ⓐ Ⓑ Ⓒ Ⓓ Ⓔ	9 Ⓐ Ⓑ Ⓒ Ⓓ Ⓔ
10.	2400-3599 Drake	10 Ⓐ Ⓑ Ⓒ Ⓓ Ⓔ	10 Ⓐ Ⓑ Ⓒ Ⓓ Ⓔ
11.	Herald	11 Ⓐ Ⓑ Ⓒ Ⓓ Ⓔ	11 Ⓐ Ⓑ Ⓒ Ⓓ Ⓔ
12.	4200-5999 Pine	12 Ⓐ Ⓑ Ⓒ Ⓓ Ⓔ	12 Ⓐ Ⓑ Ⓒ Ⓓ Ⓔ
13.	3600-4599 Palmer	13 Ⓐ Ⓑ Ⓒ Ⓓ Ⓔ	13 Ⓐ Ⓑ Ⓒ Ⓓ Ⓔ
14.	Hillside	14 Ⓐ Ⓑ Ⓒ Ⓓ Ⓔ	14 Ⓐ Ⓑ Ⓒ Ⓓ Ⓔ
15.	2400-3599 Drake	15 Ⓐ Ⓑ Ⓒ Ⓓ Ⓔ	15 Ⓐ Ⓑ Ⓒ Ⓓ Ⓔ
16.	4400-6599 Pine	16 Ⓐ Ⓑ Ⓒ Ⓓ Ⓔ	16 Ⓐ Ⓑ Ⓒ Ⓓ Ⓔ
17.	Ceres	17 Ⓐ Ⓑ Ⓒ Ⓓ Ⓔ	17 Ⓐ Ⓑ Ⓒ Ⓓ Ⓔ
18.	3500-9999 Palmer	18 Ⓐ Ⓑ Ⓒ Ⓓ Ⓔ	18 Ⓐ Ⓑ Ⓒ Ⓓ Ⓔ
19.	4400-6599 Pine	19 Ⓐ Ⓑ Ⓒ Ⓓ Ⓔ	19 Ⓐ Ⓑ Ⓒ Ⓓ Ⓔ
20.	3600-4599 Palmer	20 Ⓐ Ⓑ Ⓒ Ⓓ Ⓔ	20 Ⓐ Ⓑ Ⓒ Ⓓ Ⓔ
21.	6000-7599 Palmer	21 Ⓐ Ⓑ Ⓒ Ⓓ Ⓔ	21 Ⓐ Ⓑ Ⓒ Ⓓ Ⓔ
22.	1700-2599 Drake	22 Ⓐ Ⓑ Ⓒ Ⓓ Ⓔ	22 Ⓐ Ⓑ Ⓒ Ⓓ Ⓔ
23.	1400-2599 Pine	23 Ⓐ Ⓑ Ⓒ Ⓓ Ⓔ	23 Ⓐ Ⓑ Ⓒ Ⓓ Ⓔ
24.	Dexter	24 Ⓐ Ⓑ Ⓒ Ⓓ Ⓔ	24 Ⓐ Ⓑ Ⓒ Ⓓ Ⓔ
25.	4200-5999 Pine	25 Ⓐ Ⓑ Ⓒ Ⓓ Ⓔ	25 Ⓐ Ⓑ Ⓒ Ⓓ Ⓔ
26.	Baker	26 Ⓐ Ⓑ Ⓒ Ⓓ Ⓔ	26 Ⓐ Ⓑ Ⓒ Ⓓ Ⓔ
27.	1400-2599 Pine	27 Ⓐ Ⓑ Ⓒ Ⓓ Ⓔ	27 Ⓐ Ⓑ Ⓒ Ⓓ Ⓔ
28.	1640-2599 Palmer	28 Ⓐ Ⓑ Ⓒ Ⓓ Ⓔ	28 Ⓐ Ⓑ Ⓒ Ⓓ Ⓔ
29.	Herald	29 Ⓐ Ⓑ Ⓒ Ⓓ Ⓔ	29 Ⓐ Ⓑ Ⓒ Ⓓ Ⓔ
30.	4500-6599 Pine	30 Ⓐ Ⓑ Ⓒ Ⓓ Ⓔ	30 Ⓐ Ⓑ Ⓒ Ⓓ Ⓔ
31.	3200-5599 Drake	31 Ⓐ Ⓑ Ⓒ Ⓓ Ⓔ	31 Ⓐ Ⓑ Ⓒ Ⓓ Ⓔ
32.	4200-5999 Pine	32 Ⓐ Ⓑ Ⓒ Ⓓ Ⓔ	32 Ⓐ Ⓑ Ⓒ Ⓓ Ⓔ
33.	2400-3599 Drake	33 Ⓐ Ⓑ Ⓒ Ⓓ Ⓔ	33 Ⓐ Ⓑ Ⓒ Ⓓ Ⓔ
34.	1640-2599 Palmer	34 Ⓐ Ⓑ Ⓒ Ⓓ Ⓔ	34 Ⓐ Ⓑ Ⓒ Ⓓ Ⓔ
35.	Dexter	35 Ⓐ Ⓑ Ⓒ Ⓓ Ⓔ	35 Ⓐ Ⓑ Ⓒ Ⓓ Ⓔ
36.	1400-2599 Pine	36 Ⓐ Ⓑ Ⓒ Ⓓ Ⓔ	36 Ⓐ Ⓑ Ⓒ Ⓓ Ⓔ
37.	3400-4599 Pine	37 Ⓐ Ⓑ Ⓒ Ⓓ Ⓔ	37 Ⓐ Ⓑ Ⓒ Ⓓ Ⓔ
38.	1500-1799 Palmer	38 Ⓐ Ⓑ Ⓒ Ⓓ Ⓔ	38 Ⓐ Ⓑ Ⓒ Ⓓ Ⓔ
39.	3600-4599 Palmer	39 Ⓐ Ⓑ Ⓒ Ⓓ Ⓔ	30 Ⓐ Ⓑ Ⓒ Ⓓ Ⓔ
40.	1500-1799 Palmer	40 Ⓐ Ⓑ Ⓒ Ⓓ Ⓔ	40 Ⓐ Ⓑ Ⓒ Ⓓ Ⓔ

Go on to the next number on the next page.

41. Ceres	41 Ⓐ Ⓑ Ⓒ Ⓓ Ⓔ	41 Ⓐ Ⓑ Ⓒ Ⓓ Ⓔ	
42. Madison	42 Ⓐ Ⓑ Ⓒ Ⓓ Ⓔ	42 Ⓐ Ⓑ Ⓒ Ⓓ Ⓔ	
43. Girard	43 Ⓐ Ⓑ Ⓒ Ⓓ Ⓔ	43 Ⓐ Ⓑ Ⓒ Ⓓ Ⓔ	
44. 3600-4599 Palmer	44 Ⓐ Ⓑ Ⓒ Ⓓ Ⓔ	44 Ⓐ Ⓑ Ⓒ Ⓓ Ⓔ	
45. 4400-6599 Pine	45 Ⓐ Ⓑ Ⓒ Ⓓ Ⓔ	45 Ⓐ Ⓑ Ⓒ Ⓓ Ⓔ	
46. 3200-5599 Drake	46 Ⓐ Ⓑ Ⓒ Ⓓ Ⓔ	46 Ⓐ Ⓑ Ⓒ Ⓓ Ⓔ	
47. 1700-2599 Drake	47 Ⓐ Ⓑ Ⓒ Ⓓ Ⓔ	47 Ⓐ Ⓑ Ⓒ Ⓓ Ⓔ	
48. 3400-4599 Pine	48 Ⓐ Ⓑ Ⓒ Ⓓ Ⓔ	48 Ⓐ Ⓑ Ⓒ Ⓓ Ⓔ	
49. 4500-6599 Pine	49 Ⓐ Ⓑ Ⓒ Ⓓ Ⓔ	49 Ⓐ Ⓑ Ⓒ Ⓓ Ⓔ	
50. 3600-4599 Palmer	50 Ⓐ Ⓑ Ⓒ Ⓓ Ⓔ	50 Ⓐ Ⓑ Ⓒ Ⓓ Ⓔ	
51. 4400-6599 Pine	51 Ⓐ Ⓑ Ⓒ Ⓓ Ⓔ	51 Ⓐ Ⓑ Ⓒ Ⓓ Ⓔ	
52. 2100-3599 Drake	52 Ⓐ Ⓑ Ⓒ Ⓓ Ⓔ	52 Ⓐ Ⓑ Ⓒ Ⓓ Ⓔ	
53. 1640-2599 Palmer	53 Ⓐ Ⓑ Ⓒ Ⓓ Ⓔ	53 Ⓐ Ⓑ Ⓒ Ⓓ Ⓔ	
54. Dewey	54 Ⓐ Ⓑ Ⓒ Ⓓ Ⓔ	54 Ⓐ Ⓑ Ⓒ Ⓓ Ⓔ	
55. Madison	55 Ⓐ Ⓑ Ⓒ Ⓓ Ⓔ	55 Ⓐ Ⓑ Ⓒ Ⓓ Ⓔ	
56. 1500-1799 Palmer	56 Ⓐ Ⓑ Ⓒ Ⓓ Ⓔ	56 Ⓐ Ⓑ Ⓒ Ⓓ Ⓔ	
57. 2100-3599 Drake	57 Ⓐ Ⓑ Ⓒ Ⓓ Ⓔ	57 Ⓐ Ⓑ Ⓒ Ⓓ Ⓔ	
58. Herald	58 Ⓐ Ⓑ Ⓒ Ⓓ Ⓔ	58 Ⓐ Ⓑ Ⓒ Ⓓ Ⓔ	
59. 1640-2599 Palmer	59 Ⓐ Ⓑ Ⓒ Ⓓ Ⓔ	59 Ⓐ Ⓑ Ⓒ Ⓓ Ⓔ	
60. Dexter	60 Ⓐ Ⓑ Ⓒ Ⓓ Ⓔ	60 Ⓐ Ⓑ Ⓒ Ⓓ Ⓔ	
61. 1400-2599 Pine	61 Ⓐ Ⓑ Ⓒ Ⓓ Ⓔ	61 Ⓐ Ⓑ Ⓒ Ⓓ Ⓔ	
62. 2100-3599 Drake	62 Ⓐ Ⓑ Ⓒ Ⓓ Ⓔ	62 Ⓐ Ⓑ Ⓒ Ⓓ Ⓔ	
63. Herald	63 Ⓐ Ⓑ Ⓒ Ⓓ Ⓔ	63 Ⓐ Ⓑ Ⓒ Ⓓ Ⓔ	
64. 3200-5599 Drake	64 Ⓐ Ⓑ Ⓒ Ⓓ Ⓔ	64 Ⓐ Ⓑ Ⓒ Ⓓ Ⓔ	
65. 4500-6599 Pine	65 Ⓐ Ⓑ Ⓒ Ⓓ Ⓔ	65 Ⓐ Ⓑ Ⓒ Ⓓ Ⓔ	
66. 6000-7599 Palmer	66 Ⓐ Ⓑ Ⓒ Ⓓ Ⓔ	66 Ⓐ Ⓑ Ⓒ Ⓓ Ⓔ	
67. 1640-2599 Palmer	67 Ⓐ Ⓑ Ⓒ Ⓓ Ⓔ	67 Ⓐ Ⓑ Ⓒ Ⓓ Ⓔ	
68. 4500-6599 Pine	68 Ⓐ Ⓑ Ⓒ Ⓓ Ⓔ	68 Ⓐ Ⓑ Ⓒ Ⓓ Ⓔ	
69. Dewey	69 Ⓐ Ⓑ Ⓒ Ⓓ Ⓔ	69 Ⓐ Ⓑ Ⓒ Ⓓ Ⓔ	
70. 1200-2599 Drake	70 Ⓐ Ⓑ Ⓒ Ⓓ Ⓔ	70 Ⓐ Ⓑ Ⓒ Ⓓ Ⓔ	
71. 3500-9999 Palmer	71 Ⓐ Ⓑ Ⓒ Ⓓ Ⓔ	71 Ⓐ Ⓑ Ⓒ Ⓓ Ⓔ	
72. 1700-2599 Drake	72 Ⓐ Ⓑ Ⓒ Ⓓ Ⓔ	72 Ⓐ Ⓑ Ⓒ Ⓓ Ⓔ	
73. 4200-5999 Pine	73 Ⓐ Ⓑ Ⓒ Ⓓ Ⓔ	73 Ⓐ Ⓑ Ⓒ Ⓓ Ⓔ	
74. Madison	74 Ⓐ Ⓑ Ⓒ Ⓓ Ⓔ	74 Ⓐ Ⓑ Ⓒ Ⓓ Ⓔ	
75. 1200-2599 Drake	75 Ⓐ Ⓑ Ⓒ Ⓓ Ⓔ	75 Ⓐ Ⓑ Ⓒ Ⓓ Ⓔ	
76. Hillside	76 Ⓐ Ⓑ Ⓒ Ⓓ Ⓔ	76 Ⓐ Ⓑ Ⓒ Ⓓ Ⓔ	
77. 3600-4599 Palmer	77 Ⓐ Ⓑ Ⓒ Ⓓ Ⓔ	77 Ⓐ Ⓑ Ⓒ Ⓓ Ⓔ	
78. Bayview	78 Ⓐ Ⓑ Ⓒ Ⓓ Ⓔ	78 Ⓐ Ⓑ Ⓒ Ⓓ Ⓔ	
79. 3600-4599 Palmer	79 Ⓐ Ⓑ Ⓒ Ⓓ Ⓔ	79 Ⓐ Ⓑ Ⓒ Ⓓ Ⓔ	
80. 2100-3599 Drake	80 Ⓐ Ⓑ Ⓒ Ⓓ Ⓔ	80 Ⓐ Ⓑ Ⓒ Ⓓ Ⓔ	
81. 4400-6599 Pine	81 Ⓐ Ⓑ Ⓒ Ⓓ Ⓔ	81 Ⓐ Ⓑ Ⓒ Ⓓ Ⓔ	
82. 1640-2599 Palmer	82 Ⓐ Ⓑ Ⓒ Ⓓ Ⓔ	82 Ⓐ Ⓑ Ⓒ Ⓓ Ⓔ	
83. 1700-2599 Drake	83 Ⓐ Ⓑ Ⓒ Ⓓ Ⓔ	83 Ⓐ Ⓑ Ⓒ Ⓓ Ⓔ	
84. Madison	84 Ⓐ Ⓑ Ⓒ Ⓓ Ⓔ	84 Ⓐ Ⓑ Ⓒ Ⓓ Ⓔ	
85. 4500-6599 Pine	85 Ⓐ Ⓑ Ⓒ Ⓓ Ⓔ	85 Ⓐ Ⓑ Ⓒ Ⓓ Ⓔ	
86. Girard	86 Ⓐ Ⓑ Ⓒ Ⓓ Ⓔ	86 Ⓐ Ⓑ Ⓒ Ⓓ Ⓔ	
87. 2400-3599 Drake	87 Ⓐ Ⓑ Ⓒ Ⓓ Ⓔ	87 Ⓐ Ⓑ Ⓒ Ⓓ Ⓔ	
88. Dewey	88 Ⓐ Ⓑ Ⓒ Ⓓ Ⓔ	88 Ⓐ Ⓑ Ⓒ Ⓓ Ⓔ	

Go on to the next number on the next page.

STOP

If you finish before the time is up,

go back and check your answers.

(See the correct answers on the next page.)

Correct Answers

Memory-for-Address Test

1. E	31. C	61. B
2. D	32. D	62. D
3. A	33. B	63. E
4. D	34. C	64. C
5. B	35. C	65. C
6. C	36. B	66. D
7. E	37. E	67. C
8. A	38. A	68. C
9. D	39. B	69. A
10. B	40. A	70. A
11. E	41. D	71. E
12. D	42. B	72. E
13. B	43. E	73. D
14. C	44. B	74. B
15. B	45. A	75. A
16. A	46. C	76. C
17. D	47. E	77. B
18. E	48. E	78. D
19. A	49. C	79. B
20. B	50. B	80. D
21. D	51. A	81. A
22. E	52. D	82. C
23. B	53. C	83. E
24. C	54. A	84. B
25. D	55. B	85. C
26. B	56. A	86. E
27. B	57. D	87. B
28. C	58. E	88. A
29. E	59. C	
30. C	60. C	

Memory-for-Address Test
Work—3 Minutes

Answer each question on a piece of paper to show the letter of the box in which the address belongs.
Try to remember the location of as many addresses as you can. If you are not sure of an address, guess.
Work only three minutes.

A	B	C	D	E
1500-2399 Bell Cadiz 5500-8599 Carter Wilton 3300-3589 Huber	2500-3599 Bell Windell 1600-2499 Carter Vernon 8100-8499 Huber	2200-2699 Bell Madison 3700-9899 Carter Atlantic 6500-6499 Huber	3400-3699 Bell Alden 7099-8999 Carter Lucy 4400-5399 Huber	7200-8799 Bell Livonia 4500-9999 Carter Perry 3500-4699 Huber

1. 2500-3599 Bell
2. 7099-8999 Carter
3. Lucy
4. Wilton
5. 3500-4699 Huber
6. 1600-2499 Carter
7. Lucy
8. 3500-4699 Huber
9. 2500-3599 Bell
10. 1600-2499 Carter
11. Alden
12. 3400-3699 Bell
13. 1600-2499 Carter
14. 3700-9899 Carter
15. 8100-8499 Huber
16 Perry
17. Madison
18. 2500-3599 Bell
19. 3300-3589 Huber
20. 3700-9899 Carter
21. 2500-3599 Bell
22. 1600-2499 Carter
23. 7200-8799 Bell
24. 7099-8999 Carter

25. Livonia
26. 4400-5399 Hubert
27. Windell
28. 1500-2399 Bell
29. 2200-2699 Bell
30. 5500-8599 Carter
31. 4500-9999 Carter
32. 8100-8499 Huber
33. 7099-9899 Carter
34. 7200-8799 Bell
35. Madison
36. Vernon
37. 3400-3699 Bell
38. Windell
39. 3300-3589 Huber
40. 5500-8599 Carter
41. 2500-3599 Bell
42. 3400-3699 Bell
43. Lucy
44. 7200-8799 Bell
45. 3500-6499 Huber
46. 8100-8499 Huber
47. Windell
48. 2200-2699 Bell

49. Cadiz
50. Vernon
51. 3700-9899 Carter
52. Lucy
53. 3500-4699 Huber
54. 6500-6499 Huber
55. 3400-3699 Bell
56. 3300-3589 Huber
57. 7099-8999 Carter
58. 4500-9999 Carter
59. Vernon
60. 2200-2699 Bell
61. 7099-8999 Carter
62. 4500-9999 Carter
63. 2200-2699 Bell
64. 3700-9899 Carter
65. 4400-5399 Huber
66. 5500-8599 Carter
67. 3400-3699 Bell
68 . 4500-9999 Carter
69. 2500-3599 Bell
70. Atlantic
71. 3300-3589 Huber
72. Alden

73. 7200-8799 Bell
74. Lucy
75. 2200-2699 Bell
76. Vernon
77. 7099-8999 Carter
78. 6500-6499 Huber
79. 4400-5399 Huber
80. 7200-8799 Bell
81. 2500-3599 Bell
82. 8100-8499 Huber
83. Alden
84. 3400-3699 Bell
85. 3500-4699 Huber
86. 1500-2399 Bell
87. Atlantic
88. 1600-2499 Carter

STOP

When the time is up, go on to the next page for the correct answers.

(**Author's Note:** The sample test above is known as the memory-for-address test in the 470 Battery Test and the 460 Rural Carrier Associate Exam. This Part B is considered as a practice test. You'll be allowed to look at the names and addresses in the boxes, as you are instructed to answer as many questions as possible in three minutes. In the next part, however, you will be asked to answer all the 88 questions in five minutes and you won't be allowed to look at the names and addresses. During the three-minute practice test, answer only a few questions. Spend most of the three minutes in memorizing the placement of numbers and names (just the first two numbers of each address and the first syllables of names, combining two syllables into one. Now, answer a few questions and memorize the names and addresses in preparation for the next part. (**See Memory-for-Address Test: Tips & Strategies, pages 107-112.**)

Correct Answers

Memory-for-Address Test

1. B	31. E	61. D
2. D	32. B	62. E
3. D	33. D	63. C
4. A	34. E	64. C
5. E	35. C	65. D
6. B	36. B	66. A
7. D	37. D	67. D
8. E	38. B	68. E
9. B	39. A	69. B
10. B	40. A	70. C
11. D	41. B	71. A
12. D	42. D	72. D
13. B	43. D	73. E
14. C	44. E	74. D
15. B	45. E	75. C
16. E	46. B	76. B
17. C	47. B	77. D
18. B	48. C	78. C
19. A	49. A	79. D
20. C	50. B	80. E
21. B	51. C	81. B
22. B	52. D	82. B
23. E	53. E	83. D
24. D	54. C	84. D
25. E	55. D	85. E
26. D	56. A	86. A
27. B	57. D	87. C
28. A	58. E	88. B
29. C	59. B	
30. A	60. C	

Memory-for-Address Test

Work—5 Minutes

This is the section that counts.

Decide in which box each name or address belongs. Don't look back at the boxes with the addresses in them. Work 5 minutes. For each question, mark the answers on the answer sheet to the right.

ANSWER SHEET

	Test A	Test B
1. 7200-8799 Bell	1 Ⓐ Ⓑ Ⓒ Ⓓ Ⓔ	1 Ⓐ Ⓑ Ⓒ Ⓓ Ⓔ
2. Atlantic	2 Ⓐ Ⓑ Ⓒ Ⓓ Ⓔ	2 Ⓐ Ⓑ Ⓒ Ⓓ Ⓔ
3. 1500-2399 Bell	3 Ⓐ Ⓑ Ⓒ Ⓓ Ⓔ	3 Ⓐ Ⓑ Ⓒ Ⓓ Ⓔ
4. 4400-5399 Huber	4 Ⓐ Ⓑ Ⓒ Ⓓ Ⓔ	4 Ⓐ Ⓑ Ⓒ Ⓓ Ⓔ
5. Livonia	5 Ⓐ Ⓑ Ⓒ Ⓓ Ⓔ	5 Ⓐ Ⓑ Ⓒ Ⓓ Ⓔ
6. 1600-2499 Carter	6 Ⓐ Ⓑ Ⓒ Ⓓ Ⓔ	6 Ⓐ Ⓑ Ⓒ Ⓓ Ⓔ
7. Madison	7 Ⓐ Ⓑ Ⓒ Ⓓ Ⓔ	7 Ⓐ Ⓑ Ⓒ Ⓓ Ⓔ
8. 3300-3589 Huber	8 Ⓐ Ⓑ Ⓒ Ⓓ Ⓔ	8 Ⓐ Ⓑ Ⓒ Ⓓ Ⓔ
9. 1600-2499 Carter	9 Ⓐ Ⓑ Ⓒ Ⓓ Ⓔ	9 Ⓐ Ⓑ Ⓒ Ⓓ Ⓔ
10. Perry	10 Ⓐ Ⓑ Ⓒ Ⓓ Ⓔ	10 Ⓐ Ⓑ Ⓒ Ⓓ Ⓔ
11. 4400-5399 Huber	11 Ⓐ Ⓑ Ⓒ Ⓓ Ⓔ	11 Ⓐ Ⓑ Ⓒ Ⓓ Ⓔ
12. 4500-9999 Carter	12 Ⓐ Ⓑ Ⓒ Ⓓ Ⓔ	12 Ⓐ Ⓑ Ⓒ Ⓓ Ⓔ
13. 2500-3599 Bell	13 Ⓐ Ⓑ Ⓒ Ⓓ Ⓔ	13 Ⓐ Ⓑ Ⓒ Ⓓ Ⓔ
14. Vernon	14 Ⓐ Ⓑ Ⓒ Ⓓ Ⓔ	14 Ⓐ Ⓑ Ⓒ Ⓓ Ⓔ
15. 3300-3589 Huber	15 Ⓐ Ⓑ Ⓒ Ⓓ Ⓔ	15 Ⓐ Ⓑ Ⓒ Ⓓ Ⓔ
16. 3400-3699 Bell	16 Ⓐ Ⓑ Ⓒ Ⓓ Ⓔ	16 Ⓐ Ⓑ Ⓒ Ⓓ Ⓔ
17. 4500-9999 Carter	17 Ⓐ Ⓑ Ⓒ Ⓓ Ⓔ	17 Ⓐ Ⓑ Ⓒ Ⓓ Ⓔ
18. 4400-5399 Huber	18 Ⓐ Ⓑ Ⓒ Ⓓ Ⓔ	18 Ⓐ Ⓑ Ⓒ Ⓓ Ⓔ
19. Madison	19 Ⓐ Ⓑ Ⓒ Ⓓ Ⓔ	19 Ⓐ Ⓑ Ⓒ Ⓓ Ⓔ
20. Wilton	20 Ⓐ Ⓑ Ⓒ Ⓓ Ⓔ	20 Ⓐ Ⓑ Ⓒ Ⓓ Ⓔ
21. 5500-8599 Carter	21 Ⓐ Ⓑ Ⓒ Ⓓ Ⓔ	21 Ⓐ Ⓑ Ⓒ Ⓓ Ⓔ
22. 3700-9899 Carter	22 Ⓐ Ⓑ Ⓒ Ⓓ Ⓔ	22 Ⓐ Ⓑ Ⓒ Ⓓ Ⓔ
23. 7200-8799 Bell	23 Ⓐ Ⓑ Ⓒ Ⓓ Ⓔ	23 Ⓐ Ⓑ Ⓒ Ⓓ Ⓔ
24. Atlantic	24 Ⓐ Ⓑ Ⓒ Ⓓ Ⓔ	24 Ⓐ Ⓑ Ⓒ Ⓓ Ⓔ
25. 3300-3589 Huber	25 Ⓐ Ⓑ Ⓒ Ⓓ Ⓔ	25 Ⓐ Ⓑ Ⓒ Ⓓ Ⓔ
26. 3500-4699 Huber	26 Ⓐ Ⓑ Ⓒ Ⓓ Ⓔ	26 Ⓐ Ⓑ Ⓒ Ⓓ Ⓔ
27. 1500-2399 Bell	27 Ⓐ Ⓑ Ⓒ Ⓓ Ⓔ	27 Ⓐ Ⓑ Ⓒ Ⓓ Ⓔ
28. 7099-8999 Carter	28 Ⓐ Ⓑ Ⓒ Ⓓ Ⓔ	28 Ⓐ Ⓑ Ⓒ Ⓓ Ⓔ
29. 3500-4699 Huber	29 Ⓐ Ⓑ Ⓒ Ⓓ Ⓔ	29 Ⓐ Ⓑ Ⓒ Ⓓ Ⓔ
30. 3700-9899 Carter	30 Ⓐ Ⓑ Ⓒ Ⓓ Ⓔ	30 Ⓐ Ⓑ Ⓒ Ⓓ Ⓔ
31. Vernon	31 Ⓐ Ⓑ Ⓒ Ⓓ Ⓔ	31 Ⓐ Ⓑ Ⓒ Ⓓ Ⓔ
32. 3300-3589 Huber	32 Ⓐ Ⓑ Ⓒ Ⓓ Ⓔ	32 Ⓐ Ⓑ Ⓒ Ⓓ Ⓔ
33. Alden	33 Ⓐ Ⓑ Ⓒ Ⓓ Ⓔ	33 Ⓐ Ⓑ Ⓒ Ⓓ Ⓔ
34. 3500-4699 Huber	34 Ⓐ Ⓑ Ⓒ Ⓓ Ⓔ	34 Ⓐ Ⓑ Ⓒ Ⓓ Ⓔ
35. Windell	35 Ⓐ Ⓑ Ⓒ Ⓓ Ⓔ	35 Ⓐ Ⓑ Ⓒ Ⓓ Ⓔ
36. 6500-6499 Huber	36 Ⓐ Ⓑ Ⓒ Ⓓ Ⓔ	36 Ⓐ Ⓑ Ⓒ Ⓓ Ⓔ
37. 3400-3699 Bell	37 Ⓐ Ⓑ Ⓒ Ⓓ Ⓔ	37 Ⓐ Ⓑ Ⓒ Ⓓ Ⓔ
38. 1600-2499 Carter	38 Ⓐ Ⓑ Ⓒ Ⓓ Ⓔ	38 Ⓐ Ⓑ Ⓒ Ⓓ Ⓔ
39. Atlantic	39 Ⓐ Ⓑ Ⓒ Ⓓ Ⓔ	39 Ⓐ Ⓑ Ⓒ Ⓓ Ⓔ
40. 8100-8499 Huber	40 Ⓐ Ⓑ Ⓒ Ⓓ Ⓔ	40 Ⓐ Ⓑ Ⓒ Ⓓ Ⓔ

Go on to the next number on the next page.

41. 3400-3699 Bell	41 Ⓐ Ⓑ Ⓒ Ⓓ Ⓔ	41 Ⓐ Ⓑ Ⓒ Ⓓ Ⓔ
42. 3700-9899 Carter	42 Ⓐ Ⓑ Ⓒ Ⓓ Ⓔ	42 Ⓐ Ⓑ Ⓒ Ⓓ Ⓔ
43. Alden	43 Ⓐ Ⓑ Ⓒ Ⓓ Ⓔ	43 Ⓐ Ⓑ Ⓒ Ⓓ Ⓔ
44. Wilton	44 Ⓐ Ⓑ Ⓒ Ⓓ Ⓔ	44 Ⓐ Ⓑ Ⓒ Ⓓ Ⓔ
45. 7099-8999 Carter	45 Ⓐ Ⓑ Ⓒ Ⓓ Ⓔ	45 Ⓐ Ⓑ Ⓒ Ⓓ Ⓔ
46. 8100-8499 Huber	46 Ⓐ Ⓑ Ⓒ Ⓓ Ⓔ	46 Ⓐ Ⓑ Ⓒ Ⓓ Ⓔ
47. 4500-9999 Carter	47 Ⓐ Ⓑ Ⓒ Ⓓ Ⓔ	47 Ⓐ Ⓑ Ⓒ Ⓓ Ⓔ
48. 7200-8799 Bell	48 Ⓐ Ⓑ Ⓒ Ⓓ Ⓔ	48 Ⓐ Ⓑ Ⓒ Ⓓ Ⓔ
49. Atlantic	49 Ⓐ Ⓑ Ⓒ Ⓓ Ⓔ	49 Ⓐ Ⓑ Ⓒ Ⓓ Ⓔ
50. Windell	50 Ⓐ Ⓑ Ⓒ Ⓓ Ⓔ	50 Ⓐ Ⓑ Ⓒ Ⓓ Ⓔ
51. 3300-3589 Huber	51 Ⓐ Ⓑ Ⓒ Ⓓ Ⓔ	51 Ⓐ Ⓑ Ⓒ Ⓓ Ⓔ
52. 3400-3699 Bell	52 Ⓐ Ⓑ Ⓒ Ⓓ Ⓔ	52 Ⓐ Ⓑ Ⓒ Ⓓ Ⓔ
53. 6500-6499 Huber	53 Ⓐ Ⓑ Ⓒ Ⓓ Ⓔ	53 Ⓐ Ⓑ Ⓒ Ⓓ Ⓔ
54. Lucy	54 Ⓐ Ⓑ Ⓒ Ⓒ Ⓔ	54 Ⓐ Ⓑ Ⓒ Ⓓ Ⓔ
55. 4400-5399 Huber	55 Ⓐ Ⓑ Ⓒ Ⓓ Ⓔ	55 Ⓐ Ⓑ Ⓒ Ⓓ Ⓔ
56. 2200-2699 Bell	56 Ⓐ Ⓑ Ⓒ Ⓓ Ⓔ	56 Ⓐ Ⓑ Ⓒ Ⓓ Ⓔ
57. Perry	57 Ⓐ Ⓑ Ⓒ Ⓓ Ⓔ	57 Ⓐ Ⓑ Ⓒ Ⓓ Ⓔ
58. 4400-5399 Huber	58 Ⓐ Ⓑ Ⓒ Ⓓ Ⓔ	58 Ⓐ Ⓑ Ⓒ Ⓓ Ⓔ
59. 6500-6499 Huber	59 Ⓐ Ⓑ Ⓒ Ⓓ Ⓔ	59 Ⓐ Ⓑ Ⓒ Ⓓ Ⓔ
60. 7200-8799 Bell	60 Ⓐ Ⓑ Ⓒ Ⓓ Ⓔ	60 Ⓐ Ⓑ Ⓒ Ⓓ Ⓔ
61. 4400-5399 Huber	61 Ⓐ Ⓑ Ⓒ Ⓓ Ⓔ	61 Ⓐ Ⓑ Ⓒ Ⓓ Ⓔ
62. 6500-6499 Huber	62 Ⓐ Ⓑ Ⓒ Ⓓ Ⓔ	62 Ⓐ Ⓑ Ⓒ Ⓓ Ⓔ
63. 3400-3699 Bell	63 Ⓐ Ⓑ Ⓒ Ⓓ Ⓔ	63 Ⓐ Ⓑ Ⓒ Ⓓ Ⓔ
64. Livonia	64 Ⓐ Ⓑ Ⓒ Ⓓ Ⓔ	64 Ⓐ Ⓑ Ⓒ Ⓓ Ⓔ
65. 3700-9899 Carter	65 Ⓐ Ⓑ Ⓒ Ⓓ Ⓔ	65 Ⓐ Ⓑ Ⓒ Ⓓ Ⓔ
66. Vernon	66 Ⓐ Ⓑ Ⓒ Ⓓ Ⓔ	66 Ⓐ Ⓑ Ⓒ Ⓓ Ⓔ
67. 3700-9899 Carter	67 Ⓐ Ⓑ Ⓒ Ⓓ Ⓔ	67 Ⓐ Ⓑ Ⓒ Ⓓ Ⓔ
68. 2500-3599 Bell	68 Ⓐ Ⓑ Ⓒ Ⓓ Ⓔ	68 Ⓐ Ⓑ Ⓒ Ⓓ Ⓔ
69. 3400-3699 Bell	69 Ⓐ Ⓑ Ⓒ Ⓓ Ⓔ	69 Ⓐ Ⓑ Ⓒ Ⓓ Ⓔ
70. 5500-8599 Carter	70 Ⓐ Ⓑ Ⓒ Ⓓ Ⓔ	70 Ⓐ Ⓑ Ⓒ Ⓓ Ⓔ
71. 1600-2499 Carter	71 Ⓐ Ⓑ Ⓒ Ⓓ Ⓔ	71 Ⓐ Ⓑ Ⓒ Ⓓ Ⓔ
72. Atlantic	72 Ⓐ Ⓑ Ⓒ Ⓓ Ⓔ	72 Ⓐ Ⓑ Ⓒ Ⓓ Ⓔ
73. 3300-3589 Huber	73 Ⓐ Ⓑ Ⓒ Ⓓ Ⓔ	73 Ⓐ Ⓑ Ⓒ Ⓓ Ⓔ
74. 7099-8999 Carter	74 Ⓐ Ⓑ Ⓒ Ⓓ Ⓔ	74 Ⓐ Ⓑ Ⓒ Ⓓ Ⓔ
75. 4500-9999 Carter	75 Ⓐ Ⓑ Ⓒ Ⓓ Ⓔ	75 Ⓐ Ⓑ Ⓒ Ⓓ Ⓔ
76. 2500-3599 Bell	76 Ⓐ Ⓑ Ⓒ Ⓓ Ⓔ	76 Ⓐ Ⓑ Ⓒ Ⓓ Ⓔ
77. 8100-8499 Huber	77 Ⓐ Ⓑ Ⓒ Ⓓ Ⓔ	77 Ⓐ Ⓑ Ⓒ Ⓓ Ⓔ
78. Alden	78 Ⓐ Ⓑ Ⓒ Ⓓ Ⓔ	78 Ⓐ Ⓑ Ⓒ Ⓓ Ⓔ
79. 3300-3589 Huber	79 Ⓐ Ⓑ Ⓒ Ⓓ Ⓔ	79 Ⓐ Ⓑ Ⓒ Ⓓ Ⓔ
80. Lucy	80 Ⓐ Ⓑ Ⓒ Ⓓ Ⓔ	80 Ⓐ Ⓑ Ⓒ Ⓓ Ⓔ
81. 4500-9999 Carter	81 Ⓐ Ⓑ Ⓒ Ⓓ Ⓔ	81 Ⓐ Ⓑ Ⓒ Ⓓ Ⓔ
82. 4400-5399 Huber	82 Ⓐ Ⓑ Ⓒ Ⓓ Ⓔ	82 Ⓐ Ⓑ Ⓒ Ⓓ Ⓔ
83. 6500-6499 Huber	83 Ⓐ Ⓑ Ⓒ Ⓓ Ⓔ	83 Ⓐ Ⓑ Ⓒ Ⓓ Ⓔ
84. 5500-8599 Carter	84 Ⓐ Ⓑ Ⓒ Ⓓ Ⓔ	84 Ⓐ Ⓑ Ⓒ Ⓓ Ⓔ
85. 7099-8999 Carter	85 Ⓐ Ⓑ Ⓒ Ⓓ Ⓔ	85 Ⓐ Ⓑ Ⓒ Ⓓ Ⓔ
86. 4500-9999 Carter	86 Ⓐ Ⓑ Ⓒ Ⓓ Ⓔ	86 Ⓐ Ⓑ Ⓒ Ⓓ Ⓔ
87. 3500-4699 Huber	87 Ⓐ Ⓑ Ⓒ Ⓓ Ⓔ	87 Ⓐ Ⓑ Ⓒ Ⓓ Ⓔ
88. 2500-3599 Bell	88 Ⓐ Ⓑ Ⓒ Ⓓ Ⓔ	88 Ⓐ Ⓑ Ⓒ Ⓓ Ⓔ

Go on to the next number on the next page.

STOP

If you finish before the time is up,

go back and check your answers.

(See the correct answers on the next page.)

Correct Answers

Memory-for-Address Test

1. E	31. B	61. D
2. C	32. A	62. C
3. A	33. D	63. D
4. D	34. E	64. E
5. E	35. B	65. C
6. B	36. C	66. B
7. C	37. D	67. C
8. A	38. B	68. B
9. B	39. C	69. D
10. E	40. B	70. A
11. D	41. D	71. B
12. E	42. C	72. C
13. B	43. D	73. A
14. B	44. A	74. D
15. A	45. D	75. E
16. D	46. B	76. B
17. E	47. E	77. B
18. D	48. E	78. D
19. C	49. C	79. A
20. A	50. B	80. D
21. A	51. A	81. E
22. C	52. D	82. D
23. E	53. C	83. C
24. C	54. D	84. A
25. A	55. D	85. D
26. E	56. C	86. E
27. A	57. E	87. E
28. D	58. D	88. B
29. E	59. C	
30. C	60. E	

Memory-for-Address Test

Work—3 Minutes

Answer each question on a piece of paper to show the letter of the box in which the address belongs.

Try to remember the location of as many addresses as you can. If you are not sure of an address, guess. Work only three minutes.

A	B	C	D	E
1600-2499 Dole Hazel 3500-7599 Barton Utah 3100-3589 Haley	2200-2599 Dole Victory 1700-2499 Barton Calgary 6100-8499 Haley	3200-2799 Dole Donald 7400-9999 Barton Mason 4500-6499 Haley	4400-3099 Dole Regina 6099-8999 Barton Holbrook 4000-5599 Haley	8200-8999 Dole Luverne 1500-2599 Barton Caribou 8500-4999 Haley

1. Hazel
2. 8200-8999 Dole
3. 1700-2499 Barton
4. Holbrook
5. 4400-3099 Dole
6. 1700-2499 Barton
7. 3100-3589 Haley
8. Mason
9. 8500-4999 Haley
10. 4400-3099 Dole
11. 7400-9999 Barton
12. Holbrook
13. 2200-2599 Dole
14. Utah
15. 7400-9999 Barton
16. 4000-5599 Haley
17. 3200-2799 Dole
18. 6100-8499 Haley
19. 1700-2499 Barton
20. 3500-7599 Barton
21. Donald
22. 6099-8999 Barton
23. Luverne
24. 6099-8999 Barton

25. 6100-8499 Haley
26. Regina
27. 1600-2499 Dole
28. Utah
29. 7400-9999 Barton
30. 8500-4999 Haley
31. Hazel
32. 4400-3099 Dole
33. 3100-3589 Haley
34. Mason
35. Caribou
36. 6099-8999 Barton
37. 3200-2799 Dole
38. 1500-2599 Barton
39. Victory
40. Utah
41. 4500-6499 Haley
42. Calgary
43. 6099-89999Barton
44. 2200-2599 Dole
45. 6100-8499 Haley
46. 6099-8999 Barton
47. Luverne
48. 1700-2499 Barton

49. Holbrook
50. 3100-3589 Haley
51. 1500-2599 Barton
52. 1700-2499 Barton
53. 6100-8499 Haley
54. 6099-8999 Barton
55. 8200-8999 Dole
56. 3500-7599 Barton
57. Donald
58. Caribou
59. 2200-2599 Dole
60. 6100-8499 Haley
61. Donald
62. 1700-2499 Barton
63. 4000-5599 Haley
64. Victory
65. 3100-3589 Haley
66. 6099-8999 Barton
67. 2200-2599 Dole
68 . Calgary
69. 4500-6499 Haley
70. 4400-3099 Dole
71. 1500-2599 Barton
72. 6100-8499 Haley

73. Holbrook
74. 7400-9999 Barton
75. 4500-6499 Haley
76. 4400-3099 Dole
77. 1500-2599 Barton
78. 3100-3589 Haley
79. 3200-2799 Dole
80. 6099-8999 Barton
81. Hazel
82. Victory
83. 4500-6499 Haley
84. 8200-8999 Dole
85. 3500-7599 Barton
86. 3200-2799 Dole
87. 1700-2499 Barton
88. 8200-8999 Dole

STOP

When the time is up, go on to the next page for the correct answers.

(**Author's Note:** The sample test above is known as the memory-for-address test in the 470 Battery Test and the 460 Rural Carrier Associate Exam. This Part B is considered as a practice test. You'll be allowed to look at the names and addresses in the boxes, as you are instructed to answer as many questions as possible in three minutes. In the next part, however, you will be asked to answer all the 88 questions in five minutes and you won't be allowed to look at the names and addresses. During the three-minute practice test, answer only a few questions. Spend most of the three minutes in memorizing the placement of numbers and names (just the first two numbers of each address and the first syllables of names, combining two syllables into one. Now, answer a few questions and memorize the names and addresses in preparation for the next part. (**See Memory-for-Address Test: Tips & Strategies, pages 107-112.**)

Correct Answers

Memory-for-Address Test

1. A	31. A	61. C
2. E	32. D	62. B
3. B	33. A	63. D
4. D	34. C	64. B
5. D	35. E	65. A
6. B	36. D	66. D
7. A	37. C	67. B
8. C	38. E	68. B
9. E	39. B	69. C
10. D	40. A	70. D
11. C	41. C	71. E
12. D	42. B	72. B
13. B	43. D	73. D
14. A	44. B	74. C
15. C	45. B	75. C
16. D	46. D	76. D
17. C	47. E	77. E
18. B	48. B	78. A
19. B	49. D	79. C
20. A	50. A	80. D
21. C	51. E	81. A
22. D	52. B	82. B
23. E	53. B	83. C
24. D	54. D	84. E
25. B	55. E	85. A
26. D	56. A	86. C
27. A	57. C	87. B
28. A	58. E	88. E
29. C	59. B	
30. E	60. B	

Memory-for-Address Test

Work—5 Minutes

This is the section that counts.

Decide in which box each name or address belongs. Don't look back at the boxes with the addresses in them. Work 5 minutes. For each question, mark the answers on the answer sheet to the right.

ANSWER SHEET

	Question	Test A	Test B
1.	8200-8999 Dole	1 Ⓐ Ⓑ Ⓒ Ⓓ Ⓔ	1 Ⓐ Ⓑ Ⓒ Ⓓ Ⓔ
2.	Holbrook	2 Ⓐ Ⓑ Ⓒ Ⓓ Ⓔ	2 Ⓐ Ⓑ Ⓒ Ⓓ Ⓔ
3.	3500-7599 Barton	3 Ⓐ Ⓑ Ⓒ Ⓓ Ⓔ	3 Ⓐ Ⓑ Ⓒ Ⓓ Ⓔ
4.	Mason	4 Ⓐ Ⓑ Ⓒ Ⓓ Ⓔ	4 Ⓐ Ⓑ Ⓒ Ⓓ Ⓔ
5.	4000-5599 Haley	5 Ⓐ Ⓑ Ⓒ Ⓓ Ⓔ	5 Ⓐ Ⓑ Ⓒ Ⓓ Ⓔ
6.	1500-2599 Barton	6 Ⓐ Ⓑ Ⓒ Ⓓ Ⓔ	6 Ⓐ Ⓑ Ⓒ Ⓓ Ⓔ
7.	Regina	7 Ⓐ Ⓑ Ⓒ Ⓓ Ⓔ	7 Ⓐ Ⓑ Ⓒ Ⓓ Ⓔ
8.	Utah	8 Ⓐ Ⓑ Ⓒ Ⓓ Ⓔ	8 Ⓐ Ⓑ Ⓒ Ⓓ Ⓔ
9.	1600-2499 Dole	9 Ⓐ Ⓑ Ⓒ Ⓓ Ⓔ	9 Ⓐ Ⓑ Ⓒ Ⓓ Ⓔ
10.	6099-8999 Barton	10 Ⓐ Ⓑ Ⓒ Ⓓ Ⓔ	10 Ⓐ Ⓑ Ⓒ Ⓓ Ⓔ
11.	Calgary	11 Ⓐ Ⓑ Ⓒ Ⓓ Ⓔ	11 Ⓐ Ⓑ Ⓒ Ⓓ Ⓔ
12.	1500-2599 Barton	12 Ⓐ Ⓑ Ⓒ Ⓓ Ⓔ	12 Ⓐ Ⓑ Ⓒ Ⓓ Ⓔ
13.	4000-5599 Haley	13 Ⓐ Ⓑ Ⓒ Ⓓ Ⓔ	13 Ⓐ Ⓑ Ⓒ Ⓓ Ⓔ
14.	Utah	14 Ⓐ Ⓑ Ⓒ Ⓓ Ⓔ	14 Ⓐ Ⓑ Ⓒ Ⓓ Ⓔ
15.	6100-8499 Haley	15 Ⓐ Ⓑ Ⓒ Ⓓ Ⓔ	15 Ⓐ Ⓑ Ⓒ Ⓓ Ⓔ
16.	8200-8999 Dole	16 Ⓐ Ⓑ Ⓒ Ⓓ Ⓔ	16 Ⓐ Ⓑ Ⓒ Ⓓ Ⓔ
17.	3100-3589 Haley	17 Ⓐ Ⓑ Ⓒ Ⓓ Ⓔ	17 Ⓐ Ⓑ Ⓒ Ⓓ Ⓔ
18.	4500-6499 Haley	18 Ⓐ Ⓑ Ⓒ Ⓓ Ⓔ	18 Ⓐ Ⓑ Ⓒ Ⓓ Ⓔ
19.	4400-3099 Dole	19 Ⓐ Ⓑ Ⓒ Ⓓ Ⓔ	19 Ⓐ Ⓑ Ⓒ Ⓓ Ⓔ
20.	3500-7599 Barton	20 Ⓐ Ⓑ Ⓒ Ⓓ Ⓔ	20 Ⓐ Ⓑ Ⓒ Ⓓ Ⓔ
21.	Victory	21 Ⓐ Ⓑ Ⓒ Ⓓ Ⓔ	21 Ⓐ Ⓑ Ⓒ Ⓓ Ⓔ
22.	Caribou	22 Ⓐ Ⓑ Ⓒ Ⓓ Ⓔ	22 Ⓐ Ⓑ Ⓒ Ⓓ Ⓔ
23.	6100-8499 Haley	23 Ⓐ Ⓑ Ⓒ Ⓓ Ⓔ	23 Ⓐ Ⓑ Ⓒ Ⓓ Ⓔ
24.	6099-8999 Barton	24 Ⓐ Ⓑ Ⓒ Ⓓ Ⓔ	24 Ⓐ Ⓑ Ⓒ Ⓓ Ⓔ
25.	1500-2599 Barton	25 Ⓐ Ⓑ Ⓒ Ⓓ Ⓔ	25 Ⓐ Ⓑ Ⓒ Ⓓ Ⓔ
26.	2200-2599 Dole	26 Ⓐ Ⓑ Ⓒ Ⓓ Ⓔ	26 Ⓐ Ⓑ Ⓒ Ⓓ Ⓔ
27.	7400-9999 Barton	27 Ⓐ Ⓑ Ⓒ Ⓓ Ⓔ	27 Ⓐ Ⓑ Ⓒ Ⓓ Ⓔ
28.	Utah	28 Ⓐ Ⓑ Ⓒ Ⓓ Ⓔ	28 Ⓐ Ⓑ Ⓒ Ⓓ Ⓔ
29.	2200-2599 Dole	29 Ⓐ Ⓑ Ⓒ Ⓓ Ⓔ	29 Ⓐ Ⓑ Ⓒ Ⓓ Ⓔ
30.	7400-9999 Barton	30 Ⓐ Ⓑ Ⓒ Ⓓ Ⓔ	30 Ⓐ Ⓑ Ⓒ Ⓓ Ⓔ
31.	1500-2599 Barton	31 Ⓐ Ⓑ Ⓒ Ⓓ Ⓔ	31 Ⓐ Ⓑ Ⓒ Ⓓ Ⓔ
32.	8500-4999 Haley	32 Ⓐ Ⓑ Ⓒ Ⓓ Ⓔ	32 Ⓐ Ⓑ Ⓒ Ⓓ Ⓔ
33.	Donald	33 Ⓐ Ⓑ Ⓒ Ⓓ Ⓔ	33 Ⓐ Ⓑ Ⓒ Ⓓ Ⓔ
34.	3100-3589 Haley	34 Ⓐ Ⓑ Ⓒ Ⓓ Ⓔ	34 Ⓐ Ⓑ Ⓒ Ⓓ Ⓔ
35.	6099-8999 Barton	35 Ⓐ Ⓑ Ⓒ Ⓓ Ⓔ	35 Ⓐ Ⓑ Ⓒ Ⓓ Ⓔ
36.	6099-8999 Barton	36 Ⓐ Ⓑ Ⓒ Ⓓ Ⓔ	36 Ⓐ Ⓑ Ⓒ Ⓓ Ⓔ
37.	Calgary	37 Ⓐ Ⓑ Ⓒ Ⓓ Ⓔ	37 Ⓐ Ⓑ Ⓒ Ⓓ Ⓔ
38.	Caribou	38 Ⓐ Ⓑ Ⓒ Ⓓ Ⓔ	38 Ⓐ Ⓑ Ⓒ Ⓓ Ⓔ
39.	6100-8499 Haley	39 Ⓐ Ⓑ Ⓒ Ⓓ Ⓔ	39 Ⓐ Ⓑ Ⓒ Ⓓ Ⓔ
40.	6099-8999 Barton	40 Ⓐ Ⓑ Ⓒ Ⓓ Ⓔ	40 Ⓐ Ⓑ Ⓒ Ⓓ Ⓔ

Go on to the next number on the next page.

41. 6100-8499 Haley	41 Ⓐ Ⓑ Ⓒ Ⓓ Ⓔ	42 Ⓐ Ⓑ Ⓒ Ⓓ Ⓔ
42. 8200-8999 Dole	42 Ⓐ Ⓑ Ⓒ Ⓓ Ⓔ	43 Ⓐ Ⓑ Ⓒ Ⓓ Ⓔ
43. Regina	43 Ⓐ Ⓑ Ⓒ Ⓓ Ⓔ	44 Ⓐ Ⓑ Ⓒ Ⓓ Ⓔ
44. Holbrook	44 Ⓐ Ⓑ Ⓒ Ⓓ Ⓔ	44 Ⓐ Ⓑ Ⓒ Ⓓ Ⓔ
45. Donald	45 Ⓐ Ⓑ Ⓒ Ⓓ Ⓔ	45 Ⓐ Ⓑ Ⓒ Ⓓ Ⓔ
46. 1500-2599 Barton	46 Ⓐ Ⓑ Ⓒ Ⓓ Ⓔ	46 Ⓐ Ⓑ Ⓒ Ⓓ Ⓔ
47. 1700-2499 Barton	47 Ⓐ Ⓑ Ⓒ Ⓓ Ⓔ	47 Ⓐ Ⓑ Ⓒ Ⓓ Ⓔ
48. 3100-3589 Haley	48 Ⓐ Ⓑ Ⓒ Ⓓ Ⓔ	48 Ⓐ Ⓑ Ⓒ Ⓓ Ⓔ
49. 3200-2799 Dole	49 Ⓐ Ⓑ Ⓒ Ⓓ Ⓔ	49 Ⓐ Ⓑ Ⓒ Ⓓ Ⓔ
50. 6100-8499 Haley	50 Ⓐ Ⓑ Ⓒ Ⓓ Ⓔ	50 Ⓐ Ⓑ Ⓒ Ⓓ Ⓔ
51. 4500-6499 Haley	51 Ⓐ Ⓑ Ⓒ Ⓓ Ⓔ	51 Ⓐ Ⓑ Ⓒ Ⓓ Ⓔ
52. Holbrook	52 Ⓐ Ⓑ Ⓒ Ⓓ Ⓔ	52 Ⓐ Ⓑ Ⓒ Ⓓ Ⓔ
53. 1500-2599 Barton	53 Ⓐ Ⓑ Ⓒ Ⓓ Ⓔ	53 Ⓐ Ⓑ Ⓒ Ⓓ Ⓔ
54. 3100-3589 Haley	54 Ⓐ Ⓑ Ⓒ Ⓓ Ⓔ	54 Ⓐ Ⓑ Ⓒ Ⓓ Ⓔ
55. 7400-9999 Barton	55 Ⓐ Ⓑ Ⓒ Ⓓ Ⓔ	55 Ⓐ Ⓑ Ⓒ Ⓓ Ⓔ
56. 8200-8999 Dole	56 Ⓐ Ⓑ Ⓒ Ⓓ Ⓔ	56 Ⓐ Ⓑ Ⓒ Ⓓ Ⓔ
57. 3100-3589 Haley	57 Ⓐ Ⓑ Ⓒ Ⓓ Ⓔ	57 Ⓐ Ⓑ Ⓒ Ⓓ Ⓔ
58. Regina	58 Ⓐ Ⓑ Ⓒ Ⓓ Ⓔ	58 Ⓐ Ⓑ Ⓒ Ⓓ Ⓔ
59. Luverne	59 Ⓐ Ⓑ Ⓒ Ⓓ Ⓔ	59 Ⓐ Ⓑ Ⓒ Ⓓ Ⓔ
60. 4000-5599 Haley	60 Ⓐ Ⓑ Ⓒ Ⓓ Ⓔ	60 Ⓐ Ⓑ Ⓒ Ⓓ Ⓔ
61. 8200-8999 Dole	61 Ⓐ Ⓑ Ⓒ Ⓓ Ⓔ	61 Ⓐ Ⓑ Ⓒ Ⓓ Ⓔ
62. 2200-2599 Dole	62 Ⓐ Ⓑ Ⓒ Ⓓ Ⓔ	62 Ⓐ Ⓑ Ⓒ Ⓓ Ⓔ
63. 3100-3589 Haley	63 Ⓐ Ⓑ Ⓒ Ⓓ Ⓔ	63 Ⓐ Ⓑ Ⓒ Ⓓ Ⓔ
64. 1600-2499 Dole	64 Ⓐ Ⓑ Ⓒ Ⓓ Ⓔ	64 Ⓐ Ⓑ Ⓒ Ⓓ Ⓔ
65. 7400-9999 Barton	65 Ⓐ Ⓑ Ⓒ Ⓓ Ⓔ	65 Ⓐ Ⓑ Ⓒ Ⓓ Ⓔ
66. 8200-8999 Dole	66 Ⓐ Ⓑ Ⓒ Ⓓ Ⓔ	66 Ⓐ Ⓑ Ⓒ Ⓓ Ⓔ
67. 3100-3589 Haley	67 Ⓐ Ⓑ Ⓒ Ⓓ Ⓔ	67 Ⓐ Ⓑ Ⓒ Ⓓ Ⓔ
68. Caribou	68 Ⓐ Ⓑ Ⓒ Ⓓ Ⓔ	68 Ⓐ Ⓑ Ⓒ Ⓓ Ⓔ
69. 1700-2499 Barton	69 Ⓐ Ⓑ Ⓒ Ⓓ Ⓔ	69 Ⓐ Ⓑ Ⓒ Ⓓ Ⓔ
70. Donald	70 Ⓐ Ⓑ Ⓒ Ⓓ Ⓔ	70 Ⓐ Ⓑ Ⓒ Ⓓ Ⓔ
71. 3100-3589 Haley	71 Ⓐ Ⓑ Ⓒ Ⓓ Ⓔ	71 Ⓐ Ⓑ Ⓒ Ⓓ Ⓔ
72. 1500-2599 Barton	72 Ⓐ Ⓑ Ⓒ Ⓓ Ⓔ	72 Ⓐ Ⓑ Ⓒ Ⓓ Ⓔ
73. 3200-2799 Dole	73 Ⓐ Ⓑ Ⓒ Ⓓ Ⓔ	73 Ⓐ Ⓑ Ⓒ Ⓓ Ⓔ
74. 6100-8499 Haley	74 Ⓐ Ⓑ Ⓒ Ⓓ Ⓔ	74 Ⓐ Ⓑ Ⓒ Ⓓ Ⓔ
75. Mason	75 Ⓐ Ⓑ Ⓒ Ⓓ Ⓔ	75 Ⓐ Ⓑ Ⓒ Ⓓ Ⓔ
76. 3500-7599 Barton	76 Ⓐ Ⓑ Ⓒ Ⓓ Ⓔ	76 Ⓐ Ⓑ Ⓒ Ⓓ Ⓔ
77. 1500-2599 Barton	77 Ⓐ Ⓑ Ⓒ Ⓓ Ⓔ	77 Ⓐ Ⓑ Ⓒ Ⓓ Ⓔ
78. Utah	78 Ⓐ Ⓑ Ⓒ Ⓓ Ⓔ	78 Ⓐ Ⓑ Ⓒ Ⓓ Ⓔ
79. 4400-3099 Dole	79 Ⓐ Ⓑ Ⓒ Ⓓ Ⓔ	79 Ⓐ Ⓑ Ⓒ Ⓓ Ⓔ
80. 4000-5599 Haley	80 Ⓐ Ⓑ Ⓒ Ⓓ Ⓔ	80 Ⓐ Ⓑ Ⓒ Ⓓ Ⓔ
81. 1700-2499 Barton	81 Ⓐ Ⓑ Ⓒ Ⓓ Ⓒ	81 Ⓐ Ⓑ Ⓒ Ⓓ Ⓒ
82. Hazel	82 Ⓐ Ⓑ Ⓒ Ⓓ Ⓔ	82 Ⓐ Ⓑ Ⓒ Ⓓ Ⓔ
83. 3200-2799 Dole	83 Ⓐ Ⓑ Ⓒ Ⓓ Ⓔ	83 Ⓐ Ⓑ Ⓒ Ⓓ Ⓔ
84. 6099-8999 Barton	84 Ⓐ Ⓑ Ⓒ Ⓓ Ⓔ	84 Ⓐ Ⓑ Ⓒ Ⓓ Ⓔ
85. 8500-4999 Haley	85 Ⓐ Ⓑ Ⓒ Ⓓ Ⓔ	85 Ⓐ Ⓑ Ⓒ Ⓓ Ⓔ
86. Calgary	86 Ⓐ Ⓑ Ⓒ Ⓓ Ⓔ	86 Ⓐ Ⓑ Ⓒ Ⓓ Ⓔ
87. 3200-2799 Dole	87 Ⓐ Ⓑ Ⓒ Ⓓ Ⓔ	87 Ⓐ Ⓑ Ⓒ Ⓓ Ⓔ
88. 3100-3589 Haley	88 Ⓐ Ⓑ Ⓒ Ⓓ Ⓔ	88 Ⓐ Ⓑ Ⓒ Ⓓ Ⓔ

Go on to the next number on the next page.

STOP

If you finish before the time is up,

go back and check your answers.

(See the correct answers on the next page.)

Correct Answers

Memory-for-Address Stest

1. E	31. E	61. E
2. D	32. E	62. B
3. A	33. C	63. A
4. C	34. A	64. A
5. D	35. D	65. X
6. E	36. D	66. E
7. D	37. B	67. A
8. A	38. E	68. E
9. A	39. B	69. B
10. D	40. D	70. X
11. B	41. B	71. A
12. E	42. E	72. E
13. D	43. D	73. X
14. A	44. D	74. B
15. B	45. C	75. C
16. E	46. E	76. A
17. A	47. B	77. E
18. C	48. A	78. A
19. D	49. C	79. D
20. A	50. B	80. D
21. B	51. C	81. B
22. E	52. D	82. A
23. B	53. E	83. C
24. D	54. A	84. D
25. E	55. C	85. E
26. B	56. E	86. B
27. C	57. A	87. C
28. A	58. D	88. A
29. B	59. E	
30. C	60. D	

## 35

Postal Test 473/473-C

Part A: Address Checking

The U.S. Postal Service has replaced the 470 Battery Test with the new **Test 473/473-C**, an exam for major entry-level jobs: **City Carriers, Mail Processing Clerks, Mail Handlers,** and **Sales, Services, and Distribution Associates.**

City Carriers: These carriers sort, rack, and tie mail at the post office before they start making deliveries within their route or area of delivery. They also maintain required information, record changes of address. maintain other reports, and forward undeliverable-as-addressed mail. **Test 473** and **473-C** are exactly the same. However, **Test 473 C** is for **City Carriers** only.

Mail Processing Clerks: These clerks operate and maintain automated mail processing equipment or do manual sorting of mail. They collate, bundle, and move processed mail from one location to another.

Mail Handlers: They load and unload mail onto and off trucks and perform duties incidental to the movement and processing of mail. Duties include separating mail sacks to go to different routes or cities; cancel parcel post stamps and operate canceling machines, addressographs, and fork-lifts.

Sales, Services, and Distribution Associates: They do direct sales and customer support services and distribution of mail. The associates must pass an on-the-job training program.

When you pass the test, you'll be listed in the **Register of Eligibles.** But **although 70 is the passing score, you need to score 95-100% on the exams,** to have a better chance of being called for employment. Remember, those on top of the list are the ones who are called first for employment.

This Test 473 requires memorizing numbers, streets, states, and zip codes. What you need to do is know how to do the memorization of these things in a very short time. Remember, this is a timed test. For example, for the Address Checking part, you need to answer 60 questions in 11 minutes; for the **Coding** section of the test, you are to answer 36 questions in 6 minutes. On the actual **Memory** section test, you have to answer 36 questions in seven minutes. Our strategies for memorizing codes and street names will be useful to you.

Parts of Test 473:

The test covers the following parts':

Test Unit	Number of Questions	Time Allowed	Subjects Covered
Part A Address Checking	60	11 minutes	Determine if 2 addresses are alike
Part B Forms Completion	30	15 minutes	Determine if completion of form is correct.
Part C Section 1 - Coding	36	6 minutes	Determine if correct code is assigned to an address.
Section 2 - Memory	36	7 minutes	Use assigned codes for address ranges.
Part D: Identify Job-Related Experiences & Characteristics	236	90 minutes	Identify job-related experiences & characteristics

Part A: Address Checking

Part A of Post Office Test 473 involves 60 questions to be finished in 11 minutes, comparing two rows of addresses as quickly as possible. You have to match the **Corrected List** (left column) of addresses containing numbers, names of streets, city, and state and Zip code, and the **List to be Checked** containing the same items. You must identify in comparing the left and right rows of addresses and Zip codes, if there are **No Errors, if there Errors in the Address Only, Errors in the ZIP Code Only,** or **Errors** in **Both** the address and the Zip codes.

Address Checking Sample Items

A. No Errors   **B. Address Only**   **C. Zip Code Only**   **D. Both**

	Corrected List			List to be Checked	
	Address	ZIP Code		Address	ZIP Code
1'	3540 Willow Ct Sedona, AZ	86351-0001		3540 Willow Ct Sedona, AZ	86451-0001
2.	2163 Jones Dr Palm Desert, CA	92211-2506		2163 Jones St Palm Desert, CA	02211-3640

As mentioned on the previous page, you must determine if there are errors in the rows of addresses and zip codes being compared. If there are no errors in both the addresses and zip codes, meaning they are exactly the same, the answer should be **A (No Errors)**; if there are errors in the **address only,** the answer should be **B (Address Only)**; if there are errors in the **ZIP code only**, the answer should be **C (ZIP Code only);** and if there are errors in **both address and the zip code,** the answer should be **D (Both)**.

Strategies for Answering Address-Checking Items

There are 60 questions to be answered in 11 minutes only. So so you have to compare the two addresses and zip codes quickly but accurately to score high on the exams.

Here are some strategies needed to answer all the questions within the time allocated to the items.

How to Use Your Fingers

In comparing addresses and zip codes (Corrected List and List to Be Checked), you can point at the numbers and streeets with your fingers. Place the little finger of your nonwriting hand on one column of address and the index finger of the same hand on the other column. Move your hand downward as you make comparisons, while your hand hand marks the answers.

How to Do the Comparison

Compare the two addresses (left and right) by one or two eye sweeps of the line. The question sheet and the answer sheet should be lying side by side; the question sheet on your non-writing side, the answer sheet on your writing side. Don't jerk your neck from left to right as you read; just let your eyes do the sweeping. Then hold your pencil in your writing hand and don't move your non-writing hand from the answer sheet. Then move it downward as you mark a circle with two or three strikes by your writing hand. Be sure that the line you are marking corresponds to the question you are answering. (See **How to Mark Circles on the Answer Sheet** on page 33.)

Spellings: Note the spellings of street, city, state, and numbers in the Zip code. There are times that the first address has a zip code such as 48012 and the second address has a ZIP code of 48021.

Differences: Most of the time, there are differences in abbreviations, such as Ave, St, or Rd. Sometimes the first address (left) is abbreviated as St and the second address (right) is Ave, or vice versa. Or maybe the state abbreviation in the **List to Be Checked** is different from that in the **Correct List**.

In a nutshell, here are the ways to compare the addresses and zip codes:

First Way: Compare the two addresses by moving your eyes from left to right. That is, compare the address on the left to the one on the right. Make one or two "eye sweeps" of the addresses. Look at the numbers and street at the left column (**Correct List**) and compare them to the numbers and street at the right column (**List to Be Checked**). As soon as you see an **error or errors (right column), don't compare anymore the name of city and state** of both columns. Instatnly check if the zip codes are the same or not. If the zip codes are the same, then the answer is **B (Address Only). If there are errors in the address and ZIP code,** the anwer is **D (Both).**

Example:

27551 Hickory Dr, Warren, MI   48091 27551 Heckory Dr, Warren, MI 48091

Since there's an error in the address, the answer should be **B**.

Second Way: Compare only the streets and the abbrebiations Rd, St, or Ave of both columns. If they are alike, then compare the street numbers on the left to the numbers on the right. Then compare the city and state of both columns. If they are alike; compare the zip codes. If no errors, answer **A (No errors)** If there are errors in the address and no errors in the Zip code, answer **B (Address only)**. If there are errors in the **ZIP Code only**, the answer is **C (ZIP Code only)**.

3192 Aberdeen Ct	3192 Aberden Ct
Kissimme, FL 34743	Kissimme, FL 34743

In the above example, the answer is **B**.

Third Way: You campare the numbers at the left to the numbers at the right, including the street name, and abbreviation (Rd, etc.) and the state. If there are errors, then compare the zip codes. If there are also errors, answer **D (Both)**. Of course, if addresses and ZIP codes have no errors, the answer is **A (No Errors)**. See an example below of an error in the address.(The answer is **B (Address only)**.

3812 Bourbon Ln	3813 Bourbon Ln
Naperville, IL 60565-2101	Naperville, IL 60566-2101

Fourth Way: Compare the zip codes first; then compare the numbers in the address on the left and the numbers in the address on the right. If you see errors in the address and in the zip code, the answer is **D (Both)**. If there are errors in the **ZIP code only**, the answer is **C (ZIP code only)**.

2401 Bourbon Ln, Naperville, IL 60565   2401 Bourbon, Naperville, IL 60568

In the above example, the answer is C **(ZIP code only)**

Practice Test (Test 473)

Part A: Address Checking

This is a practice test containing 30 items. You have to answer these questions in 5.5 minutes. In the actual test, there are 60 items to be answered in 11 minutes.

What you have to do is compare the addresses and zip codes in each row of the the **List to be Checked** with the **Correct List** (left column). Decide if each block (either address or ZIP code) is correct or incorrect.) Mark any of **A, B, C,** or **D,** for **No Errors,** errors in the **Address Only,** errors in the **ZIP Code Only,** or errors in **Both** the address and Zup code.

A. No Errors   **B. Address Only**   **C. ZIP Code Only**   **D. Both**

	Correct List		List to be Checked		
	Address	ZIP Code	Address	ZIP Code	Answers
1.	3145 Sandra Ln Corona, CA	92879-2109	3145 Sandra Ln Corona, CA	93879-2109	1. C
2.	4402 Asbrook Ln Orlando, FL	32919	4302 Asbrook Ln Orland, FL	32919	2. ____
3.	91201 Old Ham Dr Indianapolis, IN	46228-0122	91201 Old Ham Dr Indianapolis, IN	46228-0128	3. ____
4.	2108 Vasseur Ave Paduca, KY	42003-2102	2108 Basseur Ave Paduca, KY	42003-2102	4. ____
5.	2345 Church Rd Chesterfield, MO	63005	2435 Church Rd Chesterfield, MO	63005	5. ____
6.	21307 Bluebird Ln Naperville, IL	60565-2901	21307 Bluebird Ln Naperville, IL	60565-2801	6. ____
7.	7821 Compass Ln Tampa, FL	33611-0120	7821 Compass Rd Tampa, FL	33611-0120	7. ____
8.	17854 King St New Iberia, LA	70560	17854 King Ln New Iheria, LA	70560	8. ____
9.	3094 Oakview St Worcester, MA	01605-7021	3194 Oakview St Worcester, MA	01605-7022	9. ____
10.	4129 Riverview Ave Saint Paul, MN	55107-1027	4129 Riverview Ave Saint Paul, MN	55107-1027	10. ____
11.	8129 Gladys Ct McDonough, GA	30252-2905	8128 Gladys Ct McDonough, GA	30253-2905	11. ____
12	3451 Belvedere Dr Stratford, CT	06614-2109	3451 Belvedere Dr Stratford, CT	06615-2109	12. ____
13	76095 Gibson Rd San Francisco, CA	94129-2160	76095 Gibson Rd San Francisco, GA	94129-2160	13. ____
14.	30591 San Juan Dr Anchorage, AK	99504-3106	30691 San Juan Dr Anchorage, AK	99504-3106	14. ____
15.	1678 Brookdwood Rd Peoria, IL	61614	1778 Brookwood Rd Peoria, IL	61615	15. ____

A. No Errors   B. Address Only   C. ZIP Code Only   D. Both

Correct List   **List to be Checked**

#	Correct List		List to be Checked		Answer
16.	21595 Packard St Rochester, NY	14609-2102	21895 Packard St Rochester, NY	14608-2102	16.___
17.	28091 Hickory St New Bern, NC	28562	28091 Hickory St New Bern, NC	28562	17.___
18	2121 Rolling Hills Dr Kingsport, TN	37660-8125	2121 Rolling Hills Dr Kingsport, TN	37661-8125	18. __
19	50605 SW Millen Dr Portland, OR	97224-2101	50605 SW Millen Dr Portland, OR	97224-2101	19.___
20.	50672 Armstrong Dr Spartanburg, SC	29301-2106	50673 Armstrong Dr Spartanburg, NC	29301-2108	20.___
21	50618 Peterson Ct Fort Worth, TX	76177-0102	50618 Peterson Ct Fort Worth, TX	76117-0102	21.___
22	87401 Baywood Dr Harrisburgh, PA	17111	87401 Beywood Dr Harrisburgh, PA	17111	22,___
23	3194 Beaver Ave Columbus, OH	43213-2104	3195 Beaver Ave Columbus, OH	43213-2104	23. ___
24.	8254 Sandy Creek Raleigh, NC	27615	8254 Sandy Creek Raleigh, NC	38726	24.___
25.	54902 Bedford Ave Middletown, NY	10940	54902 Bedfort Ave Middletown, NY	10940	25.___
26.	48125 Wisconsin St Middletown, OH	45049-2109	48125 Wisconsin Ln Middletown, OH	45049-2109	26.___
27.	2586 Sky Park Dr Portland, OR	97504	2586 Sky Park Dr Portland, OR	97504	27.___
28.	9321 Hudson Pl Providence, RI	02905-3102	9321 Hudson Pl Providence, RI	0295-3108	28.___
29.	17092 Arlington Dr Johnson City, TN	37601-0120	17092 Arlington Dr Johnson City, TN	37601-0120	29.___
30.	1021 Cypress Brook Cypress, TX	77429	1021 Cypress Brook Cypress, TX	88420	30.___

For answers to the above questions, see page 351 (1st Column)

2 Practice Tests (Postal Test 473)

Part A: Addressing Checking - Test 1

Here's another practice test that contains 30 items to be completed in 5.5 minutes. In the actual test, you have to complete 60 items within 11 minutes.

Compare the addresses and ZIP codes in each row of the **List to be Checked** with the **Correct List** (left) column). You must determine if each block (either addresses or zip codes) is correct or incorrect.) Mark the correct answer, any of the A, B, C, or D. For **No Errors**, mark D; for errors in the **Address Only**, mark B; for **errors in the ZIP Code Only**, mark C. or **errors in Both (the addresses and the ZIP code)**, mark D.

A. No Errors   B. Address Only   C. ZIP Code Only   D. Both

	Correct List		List to be Checked		Answers
	Address	Zip Code	Address	Zip Code	
1.	50278 Bear Hollow Dr Park City, UT	84098-3101	50878 Bear Hollow St Park City, UT	84098-3101	1. ____
2.	89411 Braxton Ct Williamsburg, VA	23185-2183	89411 Braxton Ct Williamsburg, VA	23195-2183	2. ____
3.	2028 Bay Ct Pasadena, TX	77505-0109	2026 Bay Ct Pasadena, TX	77505-0109	3. ____
4.	15982 Townsend Rd Charleston, SC	29406-1102	15982 Townsed Rd Charleston, SC	29406-1102	4. ____
5.	21033 Walnut Dr Hamilton, OH	45011	21933 Walnut Dr Hamilton, OH	45011	5. ____
6.	20931 Greenbriar Dr Goldsboro, NC	27534-0102	20931 Greenbriar Dr Goldsboro, NC	27534-0103	6. ____
7.	50921 Coleridge Rd Rochester, NY	14509-2302	50921 Coleridge Dr Rochester, NY	14509-2303	7. ____
8	29105 Richmond Pl Akron, OH	44303-2109	29105 Richmond Pl Akron, OH	44303-2109	8. ____
9	3422 Dove Dr Los Angeles, CA	90065	4322 Dove Dr Los Angeles, CA	90065	9. ____
10.	24161 Chapman Orange, CA	92868-4120	24161 Chapman Orange, CA	92868-4120	10. ____
11.	70830 Pepperfield Dr Tampa, FL	33624-2309	70330 Pepperfield Dr Tampa, FL	33624-238	11. ____
12	9310 Tuscany Ln Griffin, GA	92868	9310 Tuscany Dr Griffin, GA	92869	12. ____
13.	28014 Madison Ct Champaign, IL	61820-2117	28015 Madison Ct Champaign, IL	61825-2117	13. ____
14.	3815 Shady Grove Rd Rockville, MD	20850-0105	3815 Shady Grove St Rockville, MD	20850-0105	14. ____
15.	35151 Pineview Ct Battle Creek, MI	49017	35151 Pineview Ct Battle Creek, MI	49017	15.

A . No Errors   B. Address Only   C. ZIP Code Only   D. Both

	Correct List		List to Be Checked		
	Address	ZIP Code	Address	Zip Code	Answers
16.	31012 Todd St Ypsilanti, MI	48198	37012 Todd St Ypsilanti, MI	48098	16.____
17.	4109 Mayfair St Waterloo, IA	50701-2131	4109 Mayfair St Waterloo, IA	50701-2131	17.____
18.	72103 Rock Rd Rockville, MD	20852-4121	7203 Rock Rd Rockville, MD	20852-4122	18.____
19.	2130 Randall Ln Bloomfield Hills, MI	48304-0120	2130 Randall Ln Bloomfield Hills, MI	48304-0220	19.____
20.	42591 Scott Loop Honolulu, HI	96818	42591 Scott Loop Honolulu, HI	96818	20.____
21.	2131 Blanchard St Pensacola, FL	32505-2109	2131 Blanchard Dr Pensacola, FL	32505-2709	21.____
22.	7012 Old Ridge PL Atlanta, GA	30327	7013 Old Ridge Dr Atlanta, GA	30827	22.____
23	20831 Princeton Ln Valdosa, GA	30327-2103	20831 Princeton Rd Valdosa, GA	30328-2103	23.____
24	7079 Heatherfield Dr Lafayette, IN	47909-1025	7079 Heatherfield Dr Lafayette, IN	47809-1025	24.____
25	10254 Thompson Rd Newport, KY	41076	10254 Thompson Rd Newport, KY	41076	25.____
26.	40120 Bush Ave Chicopee, MA	01013-5121	40120 Bush Ave Chicopee, MA	01013-5121	26.____
27.	4015 Yonka St Detroit. MI	48234-2120	4016 Yonka St Detroit, MI	48284-2120	27.____
28.	8530 Thompson Ave Waterbury, CT	06708-2109	8530 Thompson Ave Waterbury, CT	06708-2109	28.____
29.	20512 Pershing Ave Dade City, FL	33525-3012	20812 Pershing Cir Dade City, FL	33525-3912	29.____
30.	5021 Jones Wood Rd Monroe, GA	30655	5021 Jones Wood Rd Monroe, GA	30658	30.____

For answers to the above items or questions, see page 351, 2nd Column).

Postal Test 473

Part A: Address Checking - Practice Test 2

As in previous tests, here's another practice test with 30 items that you must answer in 5.5 minutes. Just remember, on the actual test, there will be 60 items or questions to be answered in 11 minutes.

You must compare the addresses and zip codes in each row of the **List To be Checked** (right column) with the **Correct List** (left column). Identify if each block (either addresses or zip code) is correct or incorrect. Mark **A, B, C,** or **D,** for any of the questions: **A - For No Errors; B,** for errors in **the Address Only; C** for errors in the **ZIP Code only;** or **D** for errors in **Both** the address and Zip code.

A. No Errors   **B. Address Only**   **C. ZIP Code Only**   **D. Both**

	Correct List		List to be Checked		
	Address	ZIP Code	Address	ZIP Code	Answers
1.	3182 Teakwood Dr Santa Maria, CA	93455-2102	3182 Teakwood Dr Santa Maria, CA	93455-2102	1.____
2	25911 Sulivan St Waterbury, CT	06708-0125	25911 Sulvan Rd Waterbury, CT	06708-0125	2.____
3	5209 Richmond Way Commerce, GA	30529	5909 Richmond Rd Commerce, GA	30529	3.____
4	30510 Edmonton St Detroit, MI	48204	30510 Edmonton Dr Detroit, MI	48204	4.____
5	2812 Roundtree Blvd Ypsilanti, MI	48197-4102	2812 Roundtree Blvd Ypsilanti, MI	48197-4103	5.____
6	21501 Grand Oak Dr Carbondale, IL	62901-0205	21501 Grand Oak Dr Carbondale, IL	62901-0205	6____
7	2014 Singleton Ave Newport, KY	41076-0326	2014 Singleton Ave Newport, KY	41078-0326	7.____
8	38312 Paradise Way Eustis, FL	32736-0106	38312 Paradise Cir Eustis, FL	32736-0106	8.____
9	3054 Missouri Ave Los Angeles, CA	90025-1256	3054 Missouri Ave Los Angeles, CA	90025-1256	9.____
10.	31561 Winnipig St Brighton, CO	80603-0127	31561 Winnig St Brighton, CO	80803-0127	10.___
11.	301 Shadowbrook Ct Burlington, NC	27215-0220	307 Shadowcrook Ct Burlington, NC	27215-0220	11.____
12.	3157 Glastonburgh Ln Portland, OR	97224-2146	3157 Glastonburg Dr Portland, OR	97224-2146	12.____
13	6725 Manchester Ln Chesapeake, VA	23321	6725 Manhester Rd Chesapeake, VA	23321	13.____
14	12254 Parryville Dr Houston, TX	77041-0109	12254 Perryville Dr Houston, TX	77041-0109	14.____
15.	4254 Westside Dr Olympia, WA	98502-0121	4254 Westside Dr Olympia, WA	98502-0127	15.____

A. No Errors   B. Address Only   C. ZIP Code Only   D. Both

	Correct List		List to be Checked		Answers
	Addresss	ZIP Code	Address	ZIP Code	
16.	3152 Stonebrook Rd Charleston, WV	25314-2109	3152 Stonebrook Rd Charleston, WV	25314-2109	16. ___
17.	214 Peacock Dr Forth Worth, TX	76131-0129	215 Peacock Dr Forth Worth, TX	76137-0129	17. ___
18.	30912 Mallard Dr Pittsburg, PA	15238-2012	30912 Malard Dr Pittsburg, PA	15238-2012	18. ___
19.	3152 Bayham Dr Cincinnaati, OH	45218	3152 Bayham Dr Cincinnati, OH	48218	19. ___
20.	2154 Netherfield Ct Winchester, VA	22602	2154 Netherfield Dr Winchester, VA	22603	20. ___
21.	542 Auburn Dr Madison, WI	53711-0109	542 Auburn Dr Madison, WI	53811-0109	21. ___
22.	50113 NW 32nd Ave Vancouver, WA	98685-2199	50113 NW 33rd Ave Vancouver, WA	98685-2199	22. ___
23.	3452 Castlewood Dr Greenville, SC	29615-2298	3452 Castlewood Dr Greenoak, SC	29615-2298	23. ___
24.	31075 Ottawa St Pittsburg, PA	15211	31075 Ottawa St Pittsburg, PA	15212	24. ___
25.	423 Woodside Dr Oklahoma City, OK	73110-0610	423 Woodside Dr Oklahoma City, OK	73110-0610	25. ___
26..	3154 Kellwood Ct Raleigh, NC	27609-0291	3154 Kellwood Ct Raleigh, SC	27609-0297	26. ___
27.	12540 Rutland Ave Buffalo, NY	14212-0029	12540 Rutlan Ave Buffalo, NY	14212-0028	27. ___
28.	5409 Knoll Crest Ct Boulder, CO	80301-2158	5409 Knoll Court Dr Boulder, CO	80307-2158	28. ___
29.	6789 S Vassar St Wichita, KS	67218	6788 S Vassar St Wichita, KS	78219	29. ___
30	9054 Bramble Way Shreveport, LA	71118-0929	9054 Bramble Way Shreveport, LA	71118-0929	30. ___

For answers to the above questions, see page 351.

Postal Test 473

Part B: Forms Completion

Part B: Forms Completion of **Test 473** involves the identification of information required to fill out or complete a form. A number of forms with several items or questions, will be shown to you by the US Postal Service so that you can identify the data required to complete the form.

You will be answering 30 items or questions to be finished in 16 minutes. Actually, there are no techniques or strategies needed to complete the form. You just have to understand the questions, and think of the correct information to complete it. Just understand the questions, and see to it that you give the right information needed to accomplish the form.

A sample of a form used by the US Post Office is shown below. It's the **Domestic Return Receipt**.

SENDER: *COMPLETE THIS SECTION*	*COMPLETE THIS SECTION ON DELIVERY*	
■ Complete items 1, 2, and 3. Also complete item 4 if Restricted Delivery is desired. ■ Print your name and address on the reverse so that we can return the card to you. ■ Attach this card to the back of the mailpiece, or on the front if space permits.	A. Signature **X**	☐ Agent ☐ Addressee
	B. Received by (*Printed Name)*	C. Date of Delivery
1. Article Addressed to:	D. Is delivery address different from item 1? ☐ Yes If YES, enter delivery address below: ☐ No	

	3. Service Type
	  ☐ Certified Mail ☐ Express Mail
	  ☐ Registered ☐ Return Receipt for Merchandise
	  ☐ Insured Mail ☐ C.O.D.	

	4. Restricted Delivery? *(Extra Fee)* ☐ Yes	
2. Article Number *(Transfer from service label)*		

PS Form 3811, February 2004   Domestic Return Receipt   102595-02-M-1540

Application Cards

Tear off this page, fill it out, and turn it in to your Post Office™.

Application for Post Office Box or Caller Service – Part 1

Customer: Complete items 1, 3-6, 14-16, and 18-19.   Post Office: Complete items 2, 7-13, 17 and 20.

1. Name(s) to Which Box Number(s) Is (are) Assigned	2. Box or Caller Numbers
	_____ through _____
3. Name of Person Applying, Title *(if representing an organization)*, and Name of Organization *(if Different From Item 1)*	4a. Will This Box Be Used for: ☐ Personal Use ☐ Business Use *(Optional)*
5. Address *(Number, street, apt. no., city, state, and ZIP Code™)*. When address changes, cross out address here and put new address on back.	4b. Email Address *(Optional)*
	6. Telephone Number *(Include area code)*

7. Date Application Received	8. Box Size Needed	9. ID and Physical Address Verified by *(Initials)*	10. Dates of Service
			_____ through _____

11. Two types of identification are required. One must contain a photograph of the adressee(s). Social Security cards, credit cards, and birth certificates are unacceptable as identification. Write in identifiying information. Subject to verification.	12. Check Eligibility for Carrier Delivery ☐ a. City ☐ b. Rural ☐ c. HCR ☐ d. None	13. Service assigned ☐ a. Box ☐ b. Caller ☐ c. Reserve No.
	14. List name(s) of minors or names of other persons **receiving mail** in individual box. Other persons must present two forms of valid ID. If applicant is a firm, name each member **receiving mail**. Each member must have verifiable ID upon request. *(Continue on reverse side.)*	

WARNING: *The furnishing of false or misleading information on this form or omission of information may result in criminal sanctions (including fines and imprisonment) and/or civil sanctions (including multiple damages and civil penalties.) (18 U.S.C. 1001)*	15. Signature of Applicant *(Same as Item 3)*. I agree to comply with all Postal Service® rules regarding Post Office box or caller services.

Use a separate form for each number or consecutive group of numbers, and type of service. File part 1 alphabetically by customer's name.

PS Form **1093,** April 2004 *(Page 1 of 2)* (7530-02-000-7165)

1. Which of these would be a correct entry for Box 7?

A. $3.50

B. April 2, 2005

C. Small

D. 3 p.m.

2. Where would you enter the applicant's address?

A. Box 4b

B. Box 5

C. Box 3

D. Box 6

3. Which of these would be a corrcct entry for Box 8?

A. 12/02/04

B. Medium

C. 2513 Hickory Dr, Farmington Hills, MI 48333

D. $5.00

Application for Post Office™ Box or Caller Service – Part 2

Special Orders

16. Postmaster: The following named persons or representatives of the organization listed below are authorized to **accept** mail addressed to this (these) Post Office box(es) or caller number(s). All names listed must have verifiable ID. *(Continue on reverse side.)*

a. Name of Box Customer *(Same as item 1)*	**Customer Note:**
	The Postal Service® may consider it valid evidence that a person is authorized to remove mail from the box if that person possesses a key or combination to the box.
b. Name(s) of Applicant(s) *(Same as item 3)*	

c. Other Authorized Representative	d. Other Authorized Representative	20. Post Office Date Stamp

17. Box or Caller Number to Which This Card Applies

18. Will this box be used for Express Mail® reshipment? *(Check one)*

   a. Yes ☐   b. No ☐

WARNING: *The furnishing of false or misleading information on this form or omission of material may result in criminal sanctions (including fines and imprisonment) and/or civil sanctions (including multiple damages and civil penalties.)* (18 U.S.C. 1001)

19. Signature of Applicant *(Same as Item 3)*. I agree to comply with all Postal Service® rules regarding Post Office box or caller services.

Use a separate form for each number or consecutive group of numbers, and type of service. File part 2 by box or caller number.

PS Form **1093,** April 2004 *(Detached from Page 1 of 2)* (7530-02-000-7165)

The above is Part II of an Application for Post Office Box or Caller Service. Here are some questions to be answered.

1. Which of these would require a check mark?

A. Box C

B. Box 20.

C. Box 18

D. Box D

2. Where would you enter the names of persons authorized to remove or get mail from the box?

A. Box 17

B. Box a

C. Box b

D. Boxes c and d

3. Which of these would be a correct entry for Box 18?

A. 2 p.m.

B. 05/29/04

C. 2

D. A check mark

Postal Test 473

Part C: Coding and Memory

Postal Test 473 is similar in some ways to the old **470 Battery Test**. The **Memory-for-Address Test** of the old **470 Test** consisted of two Parts: Part A, Practice Test, and Part B: The Actual Test.

Now, **Part C** of the new Test 473 consists of two parts or sections: the **Coding Section** which contains 36 items to be answered or completed in 6 minutes. On the other hand, the **Memory Section** contains 36 items to be answered in 7 minutes.

During the test, you will be presented with a **Coding Guide**, the first column of which consists of **Address Range** and the second column, **Delivery Route**, represented by letters **A, B, C,** and **D.** You must decide which correct code (or route lettered A, B, C, D, and C), is assigned to each item or address range (containing numbers and names of streets, cities, and states.).

You must work on the items as fast and as accurate as you can. But the most important thing to remember is to be able to memorize address ranges containing numbers and names of streets and the delivery routes.

During the first section **(Coding)** of the Part C Test, you will be allowed to look at the coding guide while you are assigning codes, (A,B, C, and D, to each item of the addresses. But you won't be allowed to look at the coding guide while doing the second section **(Memory)** of the Part C Test.

Actually, the Coding section (Part C) may be considered as a practice test. It's because you are allowed to look at the Coding Guide. Since the Coding part of the test is only a practice test, then you can use most of the time allowed to it (3 1/2 minutes studying the test, and then another 6 minutes) in answering the questions. You may use some of the 6-minute time to memorize the coding guide so that you will have an easy time in completing the items (36) of the **Memory Section** test which is to be completed in 7 minutes. You are not allowed to look at the coding guide on the **Memory** section test.

The Post Office, in its Test 473 pamphlet, says that during the actual test, "You are NOT permitted to look at the codes when answering the items in the Memory section."

In view of the above, just do complete such practice items, for example, for 2 or 3 minutes, and then stop doing them. Then allocate the remaining 3 minutes in memorizing the code. As the Post Office, in its Test 473 pamphlet says, "Fully use the practice opportunities and memorization periods you are given to practice memorizing the codes." (The time allowed to memorization of the code is 3 minutes while the time allowed to completing the 36 items in the Memory section is 7 minutes. Before this, there are 2 and 1-1/2 minutes for studying.

At first, you'll have a 2-minute study period. Use this time to memorize the Coding Guide. Then you will have another 1-1/2 minutes to study it. Just answer a few questions, marking some answers. Then stop doing them. Memorize the coding guide instead. You will be given 6 minutes to answer the 36 **coding** questions.

Here's a sample coding guide.

Coding Guide	
Address Range	Delivery Route
200 - 4999 Mayfair Rd 61 - 498 Seaweed St 400 - 1399 Oakwood Dr	A
5000 - 6599 Mayfair Rd 500 - 1699 Seaweed St	B
1 - 199 Oven Hill 1400- 7998 Oakwood Dr 200 - 499 Lebanon Blvd	C
All mail matters that don't fall in one of the address ranges listed above.	D

The coding guide that the Post Office will give you will be used during the **Coding** section test and the **Memory** section test. So you must memorize the address ranges to be aassigned to a delivery route. In the above example, all numbers ranging from 200- 4999 Mayfair Rd are assigned to Delivery Route "A." Another example, all numbers ranging from 500 - 1699 Seaweed St, are assigned to "B" (Delivery Route).

How to Memorize the Codes

There are different ways you can do to memorize the codes. Remember, there's a limited time in remembering the codes and completing the items or questions.

Again, devote most of the 2 minutes and 1-1/2 minutes alloted to the practice test. Then you will also be given 3 minutes to memorize the coding guide. You will be given 7 minutes to complete the 36 items in the Memory Section part of the Part C test.

Here's a short cut to memorizing the codes.

■ From top to bottom, first memorize the names of the streets (excluding the word "Rd" or "St." or the letter "S" (for South).

Address Range	Delivery Route
200 - 4999 Mayfair 61 - 498 Seaweed 400 - 1399 Oakwood	A
5000 - 6599 Mayfair 500 - 1500 Seaweed	B
1 - 199 Oven 1400 - 7998 Oakwood 200 - 499 Lebanon	C
Numbers not covered by the above numbers go to this delivery route.	D
(Mayfair mentioned 2 timesl; Seaweed - 2 times; Oakwood - 2 times.)	

■ In remembering the names, associate *Mayfair, Seaweed,* and *Oakwood* to things or objects you know. For instance, imagine some things such as you saw the Broadway show *Mayfair*, then you went to get a string of *seaweeds*, after which you proceeded to your *Oakwood* Hospital. You can do the same with the other names of streets. Things, objects, or happenings or situations that are stored in the imagination are easily remembered or recalled.

■ You may also combine *Mayfair, Seaweed* and *Oakwood* as one word *"Mayseaoak"* combining the three names into one, just using the first syllable of each word. You can do the same thing with the other addresses.

■ In remembering the some long numbers, such as 500 - 1500 Seaweed, they may be remembered as 5 and 15 Seaweed, excluding the two 0s (zeroes), but not forgetting that there are two zeroes after the numbers 5 and 15 (500 - 1500 Seaweed).

■ In remembering the short numbers, such as the numbers 1 - 199 Oven, memorize 1 - 199 as one string of numbers, 1199. Recall the name Oven by thinking of the oven in your kitchen.

■ It's common that the last number of the first address range of a street ends with a 9 or 99; for instance 1,299. So the last 2 numbers of the first string of numbers of address range (same street) will naturally end with zeroes (00), for instance 1300 - 2599.

Of course, during the exam, you will be given some names of streets, roads, avenues, etc. that you have not heard of in your life. It's up to you how you would would associate them with things, dates, or happenings, to be imagined so that they will stay long in your memory (especially during the test.)

In seeing the increasing numbers with regard to address ranges, let's have the following example:

200 - 4999 Mayfair Rd
5000 - 6599 Mayfair Rd

In this case, we should only memorize the numbers 200, 5000 and 6599 or maybe you can shorten that to 2, 50, and 65(99), remembering that there are two zeroes (00) after 2 and 50. Remember that mail from from numbers 200 to 4999 will be assigned to a Delivery Route "A". That is, numbers below 5000 belong to the first Delivery Route. Then numbers from 5000 to 6599 Mayfair Rd, will be served by another Delivery Route "B".

For instance, when there's address range, such as 840 - 940 Mayfair Rd, (between the numbers 800 - 999 Mayfair Rd, see Coding Guide), all the mail to the address range 840 - 940 Mayfair Rd) will go to Delivery Route A. (In this case, A, is the answer.) Below is a new Coding Guide for your practice tests.

Part C: Coding & Memory

Coding Section Practice Test

Coding Guide	
Address Range	Delivery Route
1 - 299 Mercury Blvd 300 - 1599 St Joseph Pkwy 500 - 1999 Henderson St	A
1600 - 2399 St Joseph Pkwy 300 - 4998 Mercury Blvd	B
100 - 1099 W 12th St 1 - 599 Clinton Springs Ave 2000 - 2598 Henderson St	C
All mail with numbers that don't fall in any of the address ranges listed above go to this route.	D

Go to the next page for your Coding practice test.

Part C: Coding Section - Practice Test

You'll have the time to memorize the Coding Guide on Page 346 for a total of 3 1/2 minutes. (Two minutes and 1 1/2 minutes are alloted to studying the Coding Code.) You are allowed to look at the Coding Guide as you work on the questions.

Use some minutes during the studying time to memorization answering only a few of the questions. Remember our strategies for memorization. You have to work on the Coding's 36 items for 6 minutes.

Questions

	Address	Delivery Route			
1.	4700 Mercury Blvd	A	B	C	D
2.	2697 Henderson St	A	B	C	D
3.	199 Mercury Blvd	A	B	C	D
4.	499 Clinton Springs Ave	A	B	C	D
5.	450 St Joseph Pkwy	A	B	C	D
6.	200 W 12th St	A	B	C	D
7.	3999 Mercury Blvd	A	B	C	D
8.	790 St Joseph Pkwy	A	B	C	D
9.	4933 Mercury Blvd	A	B	C	D
10.	390 Clinton Springs Ave	A	B	C	D
11.	2000 W 12th St	A	B	C	D
12.	400 St Joseph Pkwy	A	B	C	D
13.	300 Mercury Blvd	A	B	C	D
14.	24000 St Joseph Pkwy	A	B	C	D
15.	2000 Henderson St	A	B	C	D
16.	1449 St Joseph Pkwy	A	B	C	D
17.	499 W 12th St	A	B	C	D
18.	59 Clinton Springs Ave	A	B	C	D

Part C: Coding and Memory

Coding Section Practice Test

Coding Guide	
Address Range	Delivery Route
1 - 299 Mercury Blvd 300 - 1599 St Joseph Pkwy 500 - 1999 Henderson St	A
1600 - 2399 St Joseph Pkwy 300 - 4998 Mercury Blvd	B
100 - 1099 W 12th St 1 - 599 Clinton Springs Ave 2000 - 2598 Henderson St	C
All mail with numbers that don't fall in any of the address ranges listed above go to this route.	D

Coding Section Practice Test

(Continuation)

Questions

19	2598 Henderson St	A	B	C	D
20.	4798 Mercury Blvd	A	B	C	D
21.	499 Clinton Springs Ave	A	B	C	D
22.	5000 Mercury Blvd	A	B	C	D
23.	150 St Joseph Pkwy	A	B	C	D
24.	480 Clinton Springs Ave	A	B	C	D
25.	350 St Joseph Pkway	A	B	C	D
26.	251 Mercury Blvd	A	B	C	D
27.	485 W 12th St	A	B	C	D
28.	470 Henderson St	A	B	C	D
29.	600 Clinton Springs Ave	A	B	C	D
30	349 St Joseph Pkwy	A	B	C	D
31.	300 Clinton Springs Ave	A	B	C	D
32.	500 Mercury Blvd	A	B	C	D
33.	2549 Henderson St	A	B	C	D
34.	97 Mercury Blvd	A	B	C	D
35.	2400 St Joseph Kwy	A	B	C	D
36.	350 Mercury Blvd	A	B	C	D

For Answers to the above items or questions, see page 352.

Part C: Coding and Memory

Practice Memory Section Test 2

Coding Guide

Address Range	Delivery Route
1 - 299 Mercury Blvd 300 - 1599 St Joseph Pkwy 500 - 1999 Henderson St	A
1600 - 2399 St Joseph Pkwy 300 - 4998 Mercury Blvd	B
100 - 1099 W 12th St 1 - 599 Clinton Springs Ave 2000 - 2598 Henderson St	C
All mail with numbers that don't fall in any of the above address ranges listed above go to this route.	D

Go to the next page for your Memory Test.

Part C: Coding and Memory

Memory Section Practice Test 2

Here's the actual Memory test. Before you take this test, you will be given 3 minutes to memorize the Coding Guide on page 348 to be used on this test.(Earlier, two minutes and 1 1/2 minutes were alloted to you for studying the Coding Code.)

Use the the strategies in this book in answering the questions instantly and accurately. You have to work on the the 36 items or questions to be answered, without looking at the Coding Code, in 7 minutes. But you are not expected to finish completing them.

Questions

	Address	Delivery Route			
1.	14500 Henderson St	A	B	C	D
2.	95 W 12th St	A	B	C	D
3.	978 Henderson St	A	B	C	D
4.	5000 Mercury Blvd	A	B	C	D
5.	75 Clinton Springs Ave	A	B	C	D
6.	50 Mercury Blvd	A	B	C	D
7.	2000 W 12th St	A	B	C	D
8.	250 St Joseph Pkwy	A	B	C	D
9.	3050 Henderson St	A	B	C	D
10.	1500 St Joseph Pkwy	A	B	C	D
11.	275 Mercury Blvd	A	B	C	D
12.	375 Clinton Springs Ave	A	B	C	D
13.	500 St Joseph Pkwy	A	B	C	D
14.	95 W 12th St	A	B	C	D
15.	98 Clinton Springs Ave	A	B	C	D
16.	980 Henderson St	A	B	C	D
17.	270 Mercury Blvd	A	B	C	D
18.	95 W 12th St	A	B	C	D

Memory Section Practice Test

(Continuation)

Questions

19.	249 Mercury Blvd	A	B	C	D
20.	400 Clinton Springs Ave	A	B	C	D
21.	1499 Henderson St	A	B	C	D
22.	4885 Mercury Blvd	A	B	C	D
23.	150 W 12th St	A	B	C	D
24.	600 Henderson St	A	B	C	D
25.	350 St Joseph Pkwy	A	B	C	D
26.	2499 Henderson St	A	B	C	D
27.	150 Mercury Blvd	A	B	C	D
28.	1700 St Joseph Pkwy	A	B	C	D
29.	600 Clinton Springs Ave	A	B	C	D
30.	700 St Joseph Pkwy	A	B	C	D
31.	499 W 12th St	A	B	C	D
32.	2548 Henderson St	A	B	C	D
33.	5000 Mercury Blvd	A	B	C	D
34.	350 Clinton Springs Ave	A	B	C	D
35.	1600 St Joseph Pkwy	A	B	C	D
36.	700 W 12th St	A	B	C	D

For answers to the above items or questions, see page 352.

Answers to Questions

Part A: Address Checking Section Tests

Answers to Questions on Page 331

1. C	16. D		
2. B	17. A		
3. C	18. C		
4. B	19. A		
5. B	20. D		
6. C	21. C		
7. B	22. B		
8. B	23. B		
9. D	24. C		
10. A	25. B		
11. D	26. B		
12. C	27. A		
13. B	28. C		
14. B	29. A		
15. D.	30 C.		

Answers to Question on Page 333

1. B	16. C
2. C	17. A
3. B	18. D
4. B	19. C
5. B	20. A
6. C	21. D
7. D	22. D
8. A	23. D
9. B	24. C
10. A	25. A
11. D	26. A
12. D	27. D
13. D	28. A
14. B	29. D
15. A	30. C

Answers to Questions on page 335)

1. A	16. A
2. B	17. D
3. B	18. B
4. B	19. C
5. C	20. D
6. A	21. C
7. C	22. B
8. B	23. B
9. A	24. C
10. D	25. A
11. B	26. D
12. B	27. D
13. B	28. D
14. D	29. D
15. C	30. A

Answers to Questions

Part C: Coding and Memory Section Tests

Coding Section		Memory Section	
Answers to Questions on page 345-347.		Answers to Questions on page 349-350.	
1. B	19. C	1. D	19. A
2. D	20. B	2. D	20. C
3. A	21. C	3. A	21. A
4. C	22. D	4. D	22. B
5. A	23. D	5. C	23. C
6. C	24. C	6. A	24. A
7. B	25. A	7. D	25. A
8. A	26. A	8. D	26. C
9. B.	27. C	9. D	27. A
10. C	28. D	10. A	28. B
11. D	29. D	11. A	29. D
12. A	30. A	12. C	30. A
13 B.	31. C	13. A	31. C
14. D	32. B	14. D	32. C
15. C	33. C	15. C	33. D
16. A	34. A	16. A	34. C
17. C	35. D	17. A	35. B
18. C	36. B	18. D	36. C

## 39

Postal Test 473

Inventory of Personal Experiences and Characteristics

Part D that involves **inventory of of personal experiences and characteristics** contains 236 test items to be finished in 90 minutes. That's one and a half hours of evaluating personal characteristics, experiences, tendencies or feelings as related to doing work as an employee of the United States Postal Service.

This portion of the test is divided into three sections. Each section contains several items with response choices. For instance, the **first section** may contain items with response choices, such as "Strongly Agree" to "Strongly Disagree". The **second section** may have items with four response choices, from "Very often" to "Rarely or Never". And the **third section** may consist of items with four to nine response choices.

Here's are some sample questions:

I. Agree/Disagree Section

1. You do not like other workers to intervene in your work.

A. Strongly Agree

B. Agree

C. Disagree

D. Strongly Disagree

2. Family problems should not be discussed in work place.

A. Strongly Agree

B. Agree

C. Disagree

Strongly Disagree

II. Frequency Section

1. You schedule your work ahead of time.

A. Very often

B. Often

C. Sometimes

D. Rarely

2. There should be a division of labor in the work place, doing your own things.

A. Very often

B. Often

C. Sometimes

D. Rarely

III. Experience Section

1. What type of work do you like best?

A. Work that requires physical efforts.

B. Work that needs stretching of hands and feet.

C. Work that requires you doing your job while sitting or standing

D. Doing the same work every day

E. Would not mind doing any of these

F. Not sure"

2. What type of work do you like the least?

A. Work that requires a lot of time of standing

B. Work that requires a lot time sitting down

C. Work that needs too much concentration

D. Doing the same tasks every day

E. Doesn't care doing any of these

F. Not sure

## 40

Test 916 - Custodial Maintenance

(Sample Questions)

The purpose of this section is to illustrate the types of questions that will be used in Test 916. The samples will also show how the questions in the test are to be answered.

The test questions are designed to evaluate the following subject areas:

VOCABULARY AND READING: These questions test your ability to read and understand written materials as used in reading product label instructions and warnings, material safety data sheets (MSDS), equipment operating instructions, and cleaning route sheets.

BASIC SAFETY: These questions test your knowledge of basic safety principles and practices such as proper lifting techniques, use of personal protective equipment, and awareness of electrical, chemical, and other health hazards in the area of cleaning and building maintenance.

GENERAL CLEANING: These questions test your knowledge of general cleaning and disinfecting materials, techniques, equipment, and tools commonly used by custodians.

FOLLOWING WRITTEN INSTRUCTIONS: These questions test your ability to understand and carry out instructions similar to those you might receive on the job.

The suggested answers to each question are lettered A, B, C, D, and E. Select the BEST answer and make a heavy pencil mark in the corresponding space on the Sample Answer Sheet. Each mark must be dense black. Each mark must cover more than half the space and must not extend into neighboring spaces. If the answer to Sample 1 is B, you would mark the Sample Answers Sheet like this:

After recording your answers below, compare them with those in the Correct Answers to Sample Questions on Page 11. If they do not agree, carefully re-read the questions that were missed to get a clear understanding of what each question is asking.

Sample Answer Sheet

1	Ⓐ Ⓑ Ⓒ Ⓓ Ⓔ	5	Ⓐ Ⓑ Ⓒ Ⓓ Ⓔ	9	Ⓐ Ⓑ Ⓒ Ⓓ Ⓔ	13	Ⓐ Ⓑ Ⓒ Ⓓ Ⓔ
2	Ⓐ Ⓑ Ⓒ Ⓓ Ⓔ	6	Ⓐ Ⓑ Ⓒ Ⓓ Ⓔ	10	Ⓐ Ⓑ Ⓒ Ⓓ Ⓔ	14	Ⓐ Ⓑ Ⓒ Ⓓ Ⓔ
3	Ⓐ Ⓑ Ⓒ Ⓓ Ⓔ	7	Ⓐ Ⓑ Ⓒ Ⓓ Ⓔ	11	Ⓐ Ⓑ Ⓒ Ⓓ Ⓔ	15	Ⓐ Ⓑ Ⓒ Ⓓ Ⓔ
4	Ⓐ Ⓑ Ⓒ Ⓓ Ⓔ	8	Ⓐ Ⓑ Ⓒ Ⓓ Ⓔ	12	Ⓐ Ⓑ Ⓒ Ⓓ Ⓔ	16	Ⓐ Ⓑ Ⓒ Ⓓ Ⓔ

DIRECTIONS AND SAMPLE QUESTIONS

Study sample questions 1 through 12 carefully. Each question has several alternative responses. Decide from among the alternatives which is the best response. Find the question number on the Sample Answer Sheet on Page 7 and mark your answer to the question by completely darkening the space corresponding to the letter you have chosen.

VOCABULARY AND READING

1. Avoid **inhaling** the fumes from this product. Inhaling most nearly means:

A) Diluting
B) Expelling
C) Breathing
D) Vaporizing
E) Ventilating

2. The contents of this load are **fragile** and require special handling. Fragile most nearly means:

A) Durable
B) Delicate
C) Valuable
D) Jagged
E) Greasy

3. Safety goggles are **mandatory** when handling corrosive chemicals. Mandatory most nearly means:

A) Essential
B) Awkward
C) Optional
D) Useless
E) Foolproof

4. "Although mixing cleaners can be risky, there are many products that can be harmful on their own. They range from window cleaners to all-purpose scrubs. Even liquid soap containing ammonia can be toxic. Ammonia can cause dizziness, and mixed with certain types of bleach, can create deadly fumes."

The quotation best supports the statement that:

A) Gases can be detected by their color
B) All-purpose cleaners are rarely effective
C) Chemicals should never be mixed with water
D) Cleaners can be toxic even when used alone
E) Combining products will improve air quality

BASIC SAFETY

5. Which of the following lists information on the health hazards of cleaning products?

A) Lockout/tagout fact sheet
B) National Electrical Code (NEC)
C) National Building Code (NBC)
D) Better Business Bureau (BBB)
E) Material Safety Data Sheet (MSDS)

6. What should be done if an electrical cord is defective, damaged, or frayed?

A) Splice to a one-pronged plug
B) Apply finish to maintain appearance
C) Use only when working near water
D) Have the cord replaced at once
E) Run the electrical cord under a rug

7. Which of the following is a general rule of safe manual lifting?

A) Use the back to bear the entire load
B) Bend the back with knees straight
C) Keep the load close to one's body
D) Lift alone, no matter how heavy the load
E) Twist at the waist while carrying loads

8. Which of the following makes it unsafe to stand directly under ladders, lifts, and scaffolds?

A) Radiant energy
B) Falling tools or debris
C) Dog and insect bites
D) Cross-breeze venting
E) Stiff neck syndrome

9. Which of the following is used to apply cleaning solution to a painted wall?

A) Sponge
B) Spatula
C) Scraper
D) Wire brush
E) Drop cloth

10. Which of the following is used to clean inside a toilet?

A) Treated dust cloth
B) Bowl brush
C) Chamois cloth
D) Feather duster
E) HEPA vacuum

11. What is the primary purpose of a disinfectant?

A) Freshen air
B) Prevent fires
C) Flavor foods
D) Stain fabrics
E) Destroy germs

12. Which of the following is used to sweep dust and dirt from smooth floors?

A) Push broom
B) Sponge cloth
C) Floor stripper
D) Counter brush
E) Pressure washer

GENERAL CLEANING

FOLLOWING INSTRUCTIONS

Sample items 13 through 16 below test your ability to follow instructions.

Read each item carefully. Following the instructions in each item will lead you to identify or create a letter-number combination (e.g., P1, S4, Q10, T6). Next, go to the "Look-Up Table" to find the specific letter ("P" through "T") and number (1 through 10) from the combination you identified or created. Locate the intersection of this letter-number combination on the table to find your answer of A, B, C, D, or E. After you have found an answer, darken the corresponding space on your Sample Answer Sheet on Page 7.

For example, if you came up with P1 for Item 1, then your answer from the Look-Up Table would be "A", and you would darken "A" for question 1 on your Sample Answer Sheet. If you came up with T4 as the letter-number combination, then your answer would be "C" and you would darken "C" on your answer sheet, and so on. Apply these instructions when answering sample items 13 through 16.

LOOK-UP TABLE

	P	Q	R	S	T
1	A	B	C	D	E
2	B	C	D	E	A
3	C	D	E	A	B
4	D	E	A	B	C
5	E	A	B	C	D
6	A	B	C	D	E
7	B	C	D	E	A
8	C	D	E	A	B
9	D	E	A	B	C
10	E	A	B	C	D

13. Look at the letter-number combinations below. Draw a line under the second letter-number combination from the left. Write the letter-number combination you drew a line under here: __ __.

Q4   P3   R4   S9   T5

14. Draw a line under each letter in the line below that is <u>not</u> a "P" or "S". Write the letter under which you drew the lines and the number of lines you drew here: __ __.

P S Q P S S P Q P S P Q

15. Look at the circles below. The number inside each circle represents the number of light bulbs in a container. Write the letter "Q" below the container with the most bulbs.

⑤   ⑧   ④   ⑥   ⑦
___   ___   ___   ___   ___

16. Look at the list of hand tools below. Circle the tool with the fewest letters. Count the number of letters in that word. Now write that number and the first letter of that tool here: __ __.

SHOVEL   EDGER   RAKE   SCRAPER   SHEARS

## 41

Test 410 - Postal Center Technician Exam

(Sample Test)

The following samples show the types of questions you will see in the written test. They also show how the questions in the test are to be answered. Test 410 contains questions which test the ability to read and understand technical information, questions on mechanical and electrical principals and applications, and questions on arithmetic. The sample questions illustrate these types of questions.

The suggested answers to each question are lettered A, B, C, D, and E. Select the BEST answer and make a heavy pencil mark in the corresponding space on the Sample Question Answer Sheet. Each mark must be dense black. Each mark must cover more than half the space and must not extend into neighboring spaces. If the answer to Sample 1 is B, you would mark the Sample Question Answer Sheet like this:

After recording your answers compare them with those in the Correct Answers to sample questions.

SAMPLE QUESTIONS

USE THE FOLLOWING PASSAGE TO ANSWER QUESTION 1.

Coins inserted into the machine are registered by the recorder and are in the escrow area of the coin unit. When the coin return lever (scavenger bar) is depressed, the upper cancel switch is moved to the N.O. position, thereby removing the selector switch series from the circuit. This prevents simultaneous vend and coin return.

1. When a customer wants his money back, he pushes the coin return lever. What protection is there against his also getting merchandise as well as return of his money?

   A) The scavenger bar is also depressed
   B) The escrow area prevents vending
   C) The coin return is registered by the recorder
   D) The selector switches are cut out of the circuit
   E) All of the above

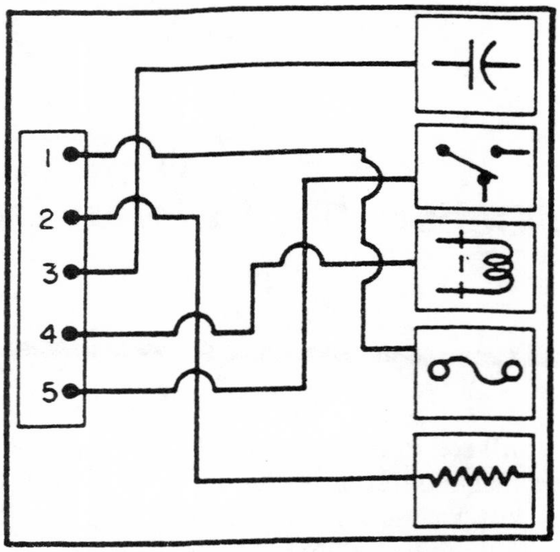

Figure 1

2. Wire 1 connects to which of the following in the diagram shown in Figure 1?

   A) Transformer
   B) Fuse
   C) Switch
   D) Battery
   E) Resistor

3. What is the total cost of a coil of 29-cent stamps, a coil of 8-cent stamps, and a coil of 1-cent stamps, if there are 500 stamps to a coil?

   A) $ 59.50
   B) $180.00
   C) $190.00
   D) $595.00
   E) None of these

4. A Technician paid $25.50 for 3 boxes of envelopes. Each box contained 25 envelopes. What was the cost for each envelope?

   A) $ .34
   B) $ .35
   C) $1.02
   D) $3.40
   E) None of these

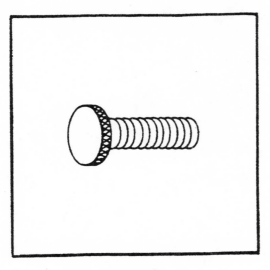

Figure 2

5. The proper method to tighten the item shown in Figure 2 is to use

   A) slip-joint pliers
   B) spanner wrench
   C) thumb and forefinger
   D) spin-type socket
   E) mechanical finger

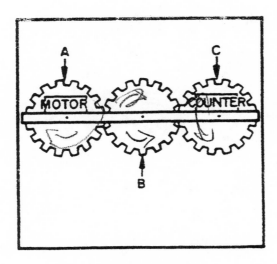

Figure 3

6. In Figure 3, gears A, B, and C are the same size. If gear A is moving in a clockwise direction, which of the following describes the action of gear C?

   A) Turns counterclockwise slower than gear A
   B) Turns clockwise slower than gear A
   C) Turns counterclockwise at the same speed as gear A
   D) Turns clockwise faster than gear A
   E) Turns clockwise at the same speed as gear A

Examination 932
(For Electronics Group)

## 42

United States Postal Service
Sample Questions

The following positions use Examination 932:

Electronics Technician 8 (Register Number M26)
Electronics Technician 9 (Register Number M27)
Electronics Technician 10 (Register Number M28)

The examination, which is known as Examination 932, is given to applicants for the above positions. This exam consists of Part I, *Following Oral Instructions,* and Part II - *Multiple Choice Test,* which involves basic mechanics, basic electricity, and basic electronics and with the use of hand and portable power tools and test equipment. Study books on basic mechanics, basic electricity, and basic electronics in your local library. **(See Who Is Qualified to Apply for Exams,** pages 5-10; **Vocabulary, Spelling, & Reading Comprehension,** pages 169-180; **Analyzing Examination 710,** pages 155-163; and **Strategies for Standardized Tests,** *multiple choice, vocabulary, and solving mathematics problems,* pages 253-258.) An applicant's total qualifications will be evaluated based on the results of the written test and the review panel evaluation.

(For job descriptions of the above positions, see page 211.)

The purpose of this booklet is to illustrate the types of questions that will be used in Test 932. The samples will show how the questions in the test are to be answered.

Test M/N 932 measures 16 Knowledge, Skills, and Abilities (KSAs) used by a variety of maintenance positions. Exhibit A lists the actual KSAs that are measured, and Exhibit B lists the positions that use this examination. However, not all KSAs that are measured in this test are scored for every position listed. The qualification standard for each position lists the KSAs required for the position. Only those questions that measure KSAs required for the position(s) for which you are applying will be scored for the position(s).

The suggested answers to each question are lettered A, B, C, etc. Select the BEST answer and make a heavy pencil mark in the corresponding space on the Sample Answer Sheet. Each mark must be dense black. Each mark must cover more than half the space and must not extend into neighboring spaces. If the answer to Sample 1 is B, you would mark the Sample Answer Sheet like this:

After recording your answers, compare them with those in the Correct Answers to Sample Questions. If they do not agree, carefully re-read the questions that were missed to get a clear understanding of what each question is asking.

During the test, directions for answering questions in Part I will be given orally, either by a cassette tape or by the examiner. You are to listen closely to the directions and follow them. To practice for this part of the test you might have a friend read the direction to you while you mark your answers on the Sample Answer Sheet. Directions for answering questions in Part II will be completely described in the test booklet.

STUDY CAREFULLY BEFORE YOU GO TO THE EXAMINATION ROOM

PART I

In Part I of the test, you will be told to follow directions by writing in a test booklet and then on an answer sheet. The test booklet will have lines of material like the following five samples:

SAMPLE QUESTIONS

SAMPLE 1.   5 _____

SAMPLE 2.   1 6 4 3 7

SAMPLE 3.   D B A E C

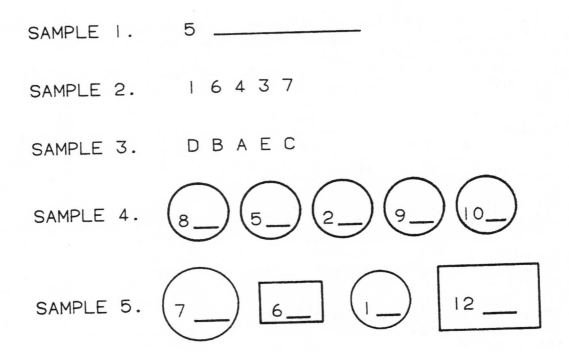

SAMPLE 4.

SAMPLE 5.

To practice this test, have someone read the instructions on the next page to you and you follow the instructions. When they tell you to darken the space on the Sample Answer Sheet, use the one on this page.

SAMPLE ANSWER SHEET

1 Ⓐ Ⓑ Ⓒ Ⓓ Ⓔ   5 Ⓐ Ⓑ Ⓒ Ⓓ Ⓔ   9 Ⓐ Ⓑ Ⓒ Ⓓ Ⓔ
2 Ⓐ Ⓑ Ⓒ Ⓓ Ⓔ   6 Ⓐ Ⓑ Ⓒ Ⓓ Ⓔ   10 Ⓐ Ⓑ Ⓒ Ⓓ Ⓔ
3 Ⓐ Ⓑ Ⓒ Ⓓ Ⓔ   7 Ⓐ Ⓑ Ⓒ Ⓓ Ⓔ   11 Ⓐ Ⓑ Ⓒ Ⓓ Ⓔ
4 Ⓐ Ⓑ Ⓒ Ⓓ Ⓔ   8 Ⓐ Ⓑ Ⓒ Ⓓ Ⓔ   12 Ⓐ Ⓑ Ⓒ Ⓓ Ⓔ

<u>Instructions to be read</u> (the words in parentheses should not be read aloud).

You are to follow the instructions that I shall read to you. I cannot repeat them.

Look at the samples. Sample 1 has a number and a line beside it. On the line write an A. (Pause 2 seconds.) Now on the Sample Answer Sheet, find number 5 (pause 2 seconds) and darken the space for the letter you just wrote on the line. (Pause 2 seconds.)

Look at Sample 2. (Pause slightly.) Draw a line under the third number. (Pause 2 seconds.) Now look on the Sample Answer Sheet, find the number under which you just drew a line and darken space B as in baker for that number. (Pause 5 seconds.)

Look at Sample 3. (Pause slightly.) Draw a line under the third letter in the line. (Pause 2 seconds.) Now on your Sample Answer Sheet, find number 9 (pause 2 seconds) and darken the space for the letter under which you drew a line. (Pause 5 seconds.)

Look at the five circles in Sample 4. (Pause slightly.) Each circle has a number and a line in it. Write D as in dog on the blank in the last circle. (Pause 2 seconds.) Now on the Sample Answer Sheet, darken the space for the number-letter combination that is in the circle you just wrote in. (Pause 5 seconds.)

Look at Sample 5. (Pause slightly.) There are two circles and two boxes of different sizes with numbers in them. (Pause slightly.) If 4 is more than 2 and if 5 is less than 3, write A in the smaller circle. (Pause slightly.) Otherwise write C in the larger box. (Pause 2 seconds.) Now on the Sample Answer Sheet, darken the space for the number-letter combination in the circle or box in which you just wrote. (Pause 5 seconds.)

Now look at the Sample Answer Sheet. (Pause slightly.) You should have darkened spaces 4B, 5A, 9A, 10D, and 12C on the Sample Answer Sheet. (If the person preparing to take the examination made any mistakes, try to help him or her understand why the mistakes are wrong.)

SAMPLE ANSWER QUESTIONS

1 Ⓐ Ⓑ Ⓒ Ⓓ Ⓔ

2 Ⓐ Ⓑ Ⓒ Ⓓ Ⓔ

3 Ⓐ Ⓑ Ⓒ Ⓓ Ⓔ

4 Ⓐ Ⓑ Ⓒ Ⓓ Ⓔ

5 Ⓐ Ⓑ Ⓒ Ⓓ Ⓔ

6 Ⓐ Ⓑ Ⓒ Ⓓ Ⓔ

7 Ⓐ Ⓑ Ⓒ Ⓓ Ⓔ

8 Ⓐ Ⓑ Ⓒ Ⓓ Ⓔ

9 Ⓐ Ⓑ Ⓒ Ⓓ Ⓔ

10 Ⓐ Ⓑ Ⓒ Ⓓ Ⓔ

11 Ⓐ Ⓑ Ⓒ Ⓓ Ⓔ

12 Ⓐ Ⓑ Ⓒ Ⓓ Ⓔ

13 Ⓐ Ⓑ Ⓒ Ⓓ Ⓔ

14 Ⓐ Ⓑ Ⓒ Ⓓ Ⓔ

15 Ⓐ Ⓑ Ⓒ Ⓓ Ⓔ

16 Ⓐ Ⓑ Ⓒ Ⓓ Ⓔ

17 Ⓐ Ⓑ Ⓒ Ⓓ Ⓔ

18 Ⓐ Ⓑ Ⓒ Ⓓ Ⓔ

19 Ⓐ Ⓑ Ⓒ Ⓓ Ⓔ

20 Ⓐ Ⓑ Ⓒ Ⓓ Ⓔ

21 Ⓐ Ⓑ Ⓒ Ⓓ Ⓔ

22 Ⓐ Ⓑ Ⓒ Ⓓ Ⓔ

23 Ⓐ Ⓑ Ⓒ Ⓓ Ⓔ

24 Ⓐ Ⓑ Ⓒ Ⓓ Ⓔ

25 Ⓐ Ⓑ Ⓒ Ⓓ Ⓔ

26 Ⓐ Ⓑ Ⓒ Ⓓ Ⓔ

27 Ⓐ Ⓑ Ⓒ Ⓓ Ⓔ

28 Ⓐ Ⓑ Ⓒ Ⓓ Ⓔ

29 Ⓐ Ⓑ Ⓒ Ⓓ Ⓔ

30 Ⓐ Ⓑ Ⓒ Ⓓ Ⓔ

31 Ⓐ Ⓑ Ⓒ Ⓓ Ⓔ

32 Ⓐ Ⓑ Ⓒ Ⓓ Ⓔ

33 Ⓐ Ⓑ Ⓒ Ⓓ Ⓔ

34 Ⓐ Ⓑ Ⓒ Ⓓ Ⓔ

1. The primary function of a take-up pulley in a belt conveyor is to

    A) carry the belt on the return trip.
    B) track the belt.
    C) maintain proper belt tension
    D) change the direction of the belt

2. Which device is used to transfer power and rotary mechanical motion from one shaft to another?

    A) Bearing
    B) Lever
    C) Idler roller
    D) Gear
    E) Bushing

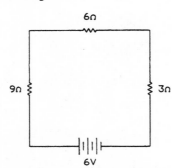

Figure III-A-22

3. Which of the following circuits is shown in Figure III-A-22?

    A) Series circuit
    B) Parallel circuit
    C) Series, parallel circuit
    D) Solid state circuit
    E) None of the above

4. A circuit has two resistors of equal value in series. The voltage and current in the circuit are 20 volts and 2 amps respectively. What is the value of EACH resistor?

    A) 5 ohms
    B) 10 ohms
    C) 20 ohms
    D) Not enough information given

PART II

5. What is the total net capacitance of two 60-farad capacitors connected in series?

    A) 30 farads
    B) 60 farads
    C) 90 farads
    D) 120 farads
    E) 360 farads

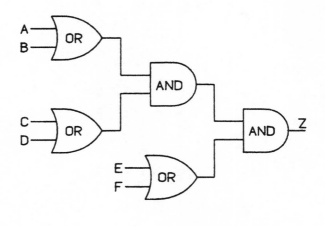

FIGURE 79-4-17B

6. Select the Boolean equation that matches the circuit diagram in Figure 79-4-17B.

    A) Z = AB+CD+EF
    B) Z = (A+B) (C+D) (E+F)
    C) Z = A+B+C+D+EF
    D) Z = ABCD(E+F)

7. If two 30-mH inductors are connected in series, what is the total net inductance of the combination?

    A) 15 mH
    B) 20 mH
    C) 30 mH
    D) 45 mH
    E) 60 mH

8. In pure binary the decimal
   number 6 would be expressed as

   A) 001
   B) 011
   C) 110
   D) 111

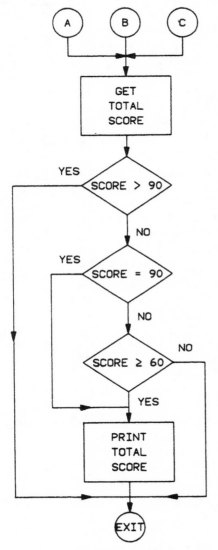

FIGURE 75-8-11

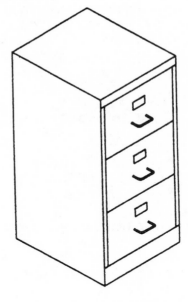

Figure 75-25-1

9. In Figure 75-8-11, which of the
   following scores will be
   printed?

   A) All scores > 90 and < 60

   B) All scores < 90

   C) All scores $\leq$ 90 and $\geq$ 60

   D) All scores < 60

10. Crowbars, light bulbs and
    vacuum bags are to be stored in
    the cabinet shown in Figure
    75-25-1. Considering the
    balance of weight, what would
    be the safest arrangement?

    A) Top Drawer - Crowbars
        Middle Drawer - Light Bulbs
        Bottom Drawer - Vacuum bags
    B) Top Drawer - Crowbars
        Middle Drawer - Vacuum bags
        Bottom Drawer - Light Bulbs
    C) Top Drawer - Vacuum Bags
        Middle Drawer - Crowbars
        Bottom Drawer - Light Bulbs
    D) Top Drawer - Vacuum Bags
        Middle Drawer - Light Bulbs
        Bottom Drawer - Crowbars
    E) Top Drawer - Light Bulbs
        Middle Drawer - Vacuum Bags
        Bottom Drawer - Crowbars

11. Which is most appropriate for
    pulling a heavy load?

    A) Electric lift
    B) Fork lift
    C) Tow Conveyor
    D) Dolly
    E) Pallet truck

12. The electrical circuit term "open circuit" refers to a closed loop being opened. When an ohmmeter is connected into this type of circuit, one can expect the meter to

A)   Read infinity
B)   Read infinity and slowly return to ZERO
C)   Read ZERO
D)   Read ZERO and slowly return to infinity
E)   None of the above

13. Contaminants have caused bearings to fail prematurely. Which pair of the items listed below should be kept away from bearings?

A) Dirt and oil
B) Grease and water
C) Oil and grease
D) Dirt and moisture
E) Water and oil

14. In order to operate a breast drill, which direction should you turn it?

A) Clockwise
B) Counterclockwise
C) Up and down
D) Back and forth
E) Right, then left

15. Which is the correct tool for tightening or loosening a water pipe?

A) Slip joint pliers
B) Household pliers
C) Monkey wrench
D) Water pump pliers
E) Pipe wrench

16. What is one purpose of a chuck key?

A) Open doors
B) Remove drill bits
C) Remove screws
D) Remove set screws
E) Unlock chucks

17. When smoke is generated as a result of using a portable electric drill for cutting holes into a piece of angle iron, one should

A) use a fire watch.
B) cease the drilling operation.
C) use an exhaust fan to remove smoke.
D) use a prescribed coolant solution to reduce friction.
E) call the Fire Department.

18. The primary purpose of soldering is to

A) melt solder to a molten state.
B) heat metal parts to the right temperature to be joined.
C) join metal parts by melting the parts.
D) harden metal.
E) join metal parts.

19. Which of the following statements is correct of a soldering gun?

A) Tip is not replaceable
B) Cannot be used in cramped places
C) Heats only when trigger is pressed
D) Not rated by the number of watts they use
E) Has no light

20. What unit of measurement is read on a dial torque wrench?

A) Pounds
B) Inches
C) Centimeters
D) Foot-pounds
E) Degrees

21. Which instrument is used to test insulation breakdown of a conductor?

A) Ohmmeter
B) Ammeter
C) Megger
D) Wheatstone bridge
E) Voltmeter

22.   1/2 of 1/4 =

A) 1/12
B) 1/8
C) 1/4
D) 1/2
E) 8

23.   2.6 - .5 =

A) 2.0
B) 2.1
C) 3.1
D) 3.3
E) None of the above

24.   Simplify the following
expression in terms of amps:

563×10^{-6}

A)   563,000,000 amps
B)   563,000 amps
C)   .563 amps
D)   .000563 amps
E)   .000000563 amps

25.   Solve the power equation

$P = I^2R$ for R

A) R = EI

B) $R = I^2P$

C) R = PI

D) $R = P/I^2$

E) R = E/I

26.   The product of 3 kilo ohms
times 3 micro ohms is

A) 6×10^{-9} ohms

B) 6×10^{-3} ohms

C) 9×10^3 ohms

D) 9×10^{-6} ohms

E) 9×10^{-3} ohms

In sample question 25 below, select the statement which is most nearly correct according to the paragraph.

"Prior to 1870, a conveyor that made use of rollers was developed for transporting clay. This construction substituted rolling friction at the idler bearing points for the sliding friction of the slider bed. A primitive type of troughing belt conveyor was developed about the same time for the handling of grain. This design was improved during the latter part of the century when the troughing idler was developed."

27.   According to the above paragraph, which of the following statements is most nearly correct?

A)   The troughing belt conveyor was developed about 1870 to handle clay and grain.

B)   Rolling friction construction was replaced by sliding friction construction prior to 1870.

C)   In the late nineteenth century, conveyors were improved with the development of the troughing idler.

D)   The troughing idler, a significant design improvement for conveyors, was developed in the early nineteenth century.

E)   Conveyor belts were invented and developed in the 1800's.

For sample question 28 below, select from the drawings of objects on the right labeled A, B, C, and D, the one that would have the TOP, FRONT, and RIGHT views shown in the drawing at the left

28.

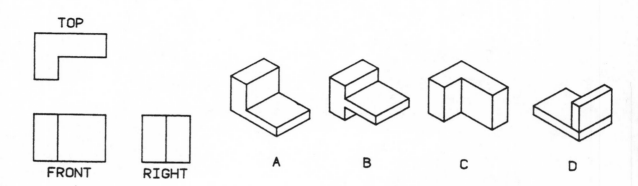

TOP

FRONT   RIGHT

A   B   C   D

In sample question 29 below, there is, on the left, a drawing
of a flat piece of paper and, on the right, four figures
labeled A, B, C, and D. When the paper is bent on the dotted
lines it will form one of the figures on the right. Decide
which alternative can be formed from the flat piece.

29.

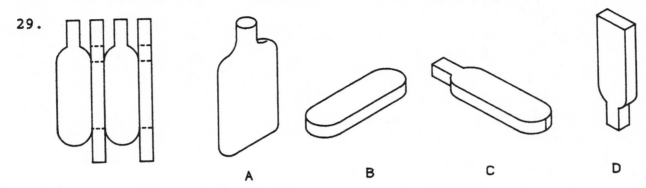

A   B   C   D

In each of the sample questions below, look at the symbols in
the first two boxes. Something about the three symbols in
the first box makes them alike; something about the two
symbols in the other box with the question mark makes them
alike. Look for some characteristic that is common to all
symbols in the same box, yet makes them different from the
symbols in the other box. Among dthe five answer choices,
find the symbol that can best be substituted for the question
mark, because it is like the symbols in the second box, and,
for the same reason, different from those in the first box.

30.

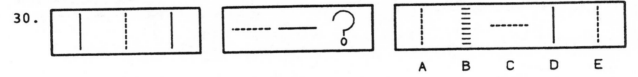

A   B   C   D   E

In sample question 30 above, all the symbols in the first box
are vertical lines. The second box has two lines, one broken
and one solid. Their likeness to each other consists in
their being horizontal; and their being horizontal makes them
different from the vertical lines in the other box. The
answer must be the only one of the five lettered choices that
is a horizontal line, either broken or solid. NOTE: There
is not supposed to be a series or progression in these symbol
questions. If you look for a progression in the first box
and the second box, you will be wasting time. Remember, look
for a likeness within each box and a difference between the
two boxes.

Now do sample questions 31 and 32.

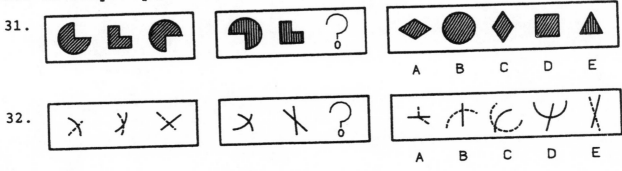

31.   A   B   C   D   E

32.   A   B   C   D   E

33. In Figure 3-8-6 below, what is the measurement of Dimension F? Drawing is not actual size.

A) 1 3/4 inches
B) 2 1/4 inches
C) 2 1/2 inches
D) 3 3/4 inches
E) None of the above

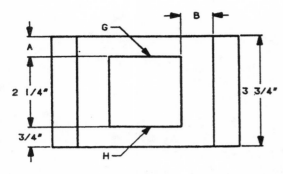

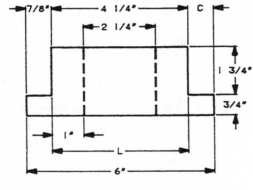

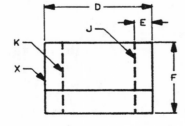

Figure 3-8-6

34. In Figure 160-57 below, what is the current flow through R_3 when:

V = 50 volts

R_1 = 25 ohms

R_2 = 25 ohms

R3 = 50 ohms

R_4 = 50 ohms

R_5 = 50 ohms

and the current through the entire circuit totals one amp?

A) 0.5 amp
B) 5.0 amps
C) 5.0 milliamps
D) 50.0 milliamps
E) None of the above

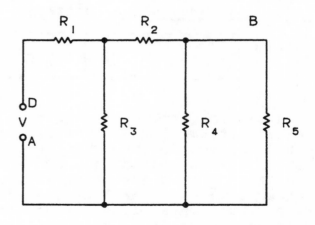

Figure 160-57

CORRECT ANSWERS TO
SAMPLE QUESTIONS

1	Ⓐ Ⓑ ● Ⓓ Ⓔ	18	Ⓐ Ⓑ Ⓒ Ⓓ ●
2	Ⓐ Ⓑ Ⓒ ● Ⓔ	19	Ⓐ Ⓑ ● Ⓓ Ⓔ
3	● Ⓑ Ⓒ Ⓓ Ⓔ	20	Ⓐ Ⓑ Ⓒ ● Ⓔ
4	● Ⓑ Ⓒ Ⓓ Ⓔ	21	Ⓐ Ⓑ ● Ⓓ Ⓔ
5	● Ⓑ Ⓒ Ⓓ Ⓔ	22	Ⓐ ● Ⓒ Ⓓ Ⓔ
6	Ⓐ ● Ⓒ Ⓓ Ⓔ	23	Ⓐ ● Ⓒ Ⓓ Ⓔ
7	Ⓐ Ⓑ Ⓒ Ⓓ ●	24	Ⓐ Ⓑ Ⓒ ● Ⓔ
8	Ⓐ Ⓑ ● Ⓓ Ⓔ	25	Ⓐ Ⓑ Ⓒ ● Ⓔ
9	Ⓐ Ⓑ ● Ⓓ Ⓔ	26	Ⓐ Ⓑ Ⓒ Ⓓ ●
10	Ⓐ Ⓑ Ⓒ Ⓓ ●	27	Ⓐ Ⓑ ● Ⓓ Ⓔ
11	Ⓐ Ⓑ Ⓒ Ⓓ ●	28	Ⓐ Ⓑ ● Ⓓ Ⓔ
12	● Ⓑ Ⓒ Ⓓ Ⓔ	29	Ⓐ Ⓑ ● Ⓓ Ⓔ
13	Ⓐ Ⓑ Ⓒ ● Ⓔ	30	Ⓐ Ⓑ ● Ⓓ Ⓔ
14	● Ⓑ Ⓒ Ⓓ Ⓔ	31	Ⓐ Ⓑ Ⓒ Ⓓ ●
15	Ⓐ Ⓑ Ⓒ Ⓓ ●	32	Ⓐ Ⓑ Ⓒ ● Ⓔ
16	Ⓐ ● Ⓒ Ⓓ Ⓔ	33	Ⓐ Ⓑ ● Ⓓ Ⓔ
17	Ⓐ Ⓑ Ⓒ ● Ⓔ	34	● Ⓑ Ⓒ Ⓓ Ⓔ

EXHIBIT A

Test M/N 932 covers the following Knowledge, Skills and
   Abilities:

(1)   Knowledge of basic mechanics refers to the theory of
      operation, terminology, usage, and characteristics of
      basic mechanical principles as they apply to such
      things as gears, pulleys, cams, pawls, power
      transmissions, linkages, fasteners, chains, sprockets,
      and belts; and including hoisting, rigging, roping,
      pneumatics, and hydraulic devices.

(2)   Knowledge of basic electricity refers to the theory,
      terminology, usage, and characteristics of basic
      electrical principles such as Ohm's Law, Kirchoff's
      Law, and magnetism, as they apply to such things as
      AC-DC circuitry and hardware, relays, switches, and
      circuit breakers.

(3)   Knowledge of basic electronics refers to the theory,
      terminology, usage, and characteristics of basic
      electronic principles concerning such things as solid
      state devices, vacuum tubes, coils, capacitors,
      resistors, and basic logic circuitry.

(4)   Knowledge of digital electronics refers to the
      terminology, characteristics, symbology, and operation
      of digital compo-
      nents as used in such things as logic gates, registers,
      adders, counters, memories, encoders and decoders.

(5)   Knowledge of safety procedures and equipment refers to
      the knowledge of industrial hazards (e.g., mechanical,
      chemical, electrical, electronic) and procedures and
      techniques established to avoid injuries to self and
      others such as lock-out devices, protective clothing,
      and waste disposal techniques.

(6)   Knowledge of basic computer concepts refers to the
      terminology, usage, and characteristics of digital
      memory storage/processing devices such as internal
      memory, input-output peripherals, and familiarity with
      programming concepts.

(19) Ability to perform basic mathematical computations
      refers to the ability to perform basic calculations
      such as addition, subtraction, multiplication and
      division with whole numbers, fractions and decimals.

(20) Ability to perform more complex mathematics refers to
      the ability to perform calculations such as basic
      algebra, geometry, scientific notation, and number
      conversions, as applied to mechanical, electrical and
      electronic applications.

(21)   Ability to apply theoretical knowledge to practical applications refers to mechanical, electrical and electronic maintenance applications such as inspection, troubleshooting equipment repair and modification, preventive maintenance, and installation of electrical equipment.

(22)   Ability to detect patterns refers to the ability to observe and analyze qualitative factors such as number progressions, spatial relationships, and auditory and visual patterns. This includes combining information and determining how a given set of numbers, objects, or sounds are related to each other.

(23)   Ability to use written reference materials refers to the ability to locate, read, and comprehend text material such as handbooks, manuals, bulletins, directives, checklists and route sheets.

(26)   Ability to follow instructions refers to the ability to comprehend and execute written and oral instructions such as work orders, checklists, route sheets, and verbal directions and instructions.

(31)   Ability to use hand tools refers to knowledge of, and proficiency with, various hand tools. This ability involves the safe and efficient use and maintenance of such tools as screwdrivers, wrenches, hammers, pliers, chisels, punches, taps, dies, rules, gauges, and alignment tools.

(35)   Ability to use technical drawings refers to the ability to read and comprehend technical materials such as diagrams, schematics, flow charts, and blueprints.

(36)   Ability to use test equipment refers to the knowledge of, and proficiency with, various types of mechanical, electrical and electronic test equipment such as VOMS, oscilloscopes, circuit tracers, amprobes, and tachometers.

(37)   Ability to solder refers to the knowledge of, and the ability to safely and effectively apply, the appropriate soldering techniques.

EXHIBIT B

The following positions use Test M/N 932:

Position Title	Register Number
Electronic Technician 8	M26
Electronic Technician 9	M27
Electronic Technician 10	M28

Examination 933

(For Mail Processing Equipment Group)

United States Postal Service
Sample Questions

The following positions use Examination 933:

Maintenance Mechanic, MPE 06 (Register Number 32)
Maintenance Mechanic, MPE/07 (Register Number M33))
Overhaul Specialist (Register Number M34)

The examination, which is known as Examination 933, is given to applicants for the above positions. This exam consists of Part I, *Following Oral Instructions,* and Part II - *Multiple Choice Test,* which involves basic mechanics, basic electricity, and basic electronics and with the use of hand and portable power tools and test equipment. Study books on basic mechanics, basic electricity, and basic electronics in your local library. **(See Who Is Qualified to Apply for Exams,** pages 5-10; **Vocabulary, Spelling, & Reading Comprehension,** pages 169-180; **Analyzing Examination 710,** pages 155-163; and **Strategies for Standardized Tests,** *multiple choice, vocabulary, and solving mathematics problems,* pages 253-258.) An applicant's total qualifications will be evaluated based on the results of the written test and the review panel evaluation.

(For job descriptions of the above positions, see page 195.)

The purpose of this booklet is to illustrate the types of questions that will be used in Test 933. The samples will show how the questions in the test are to be answered.

PART I

In Part I of the test, you will be told to follow directions by writing in a test booklet and then on an answer sheet. The test booklet will have lines of material like the following five samples:

SAMPLE QUESTIONS

SAMPLE 1.   5 _____

SAMPLE 2.   1 6 4 3 7

SAMPLE 3.   D B A E C

SAMPLE 4.   (8__) (5__) (2__) (9__) (10__)

SAMPLE 5.   (7__) [6__] (1__) [12__]

To practice this test, have someone read the instructions on the next page to you and you follow the instructions. When they tell you to darken the space on the Sample Answer Sheet, use the one on this page.

```
                    SAMPLE ANSWER SHEET
 1  Ⓐ Ⓑ Ⓒ Ⓓ Ⓔ     5  Ⓐ Ⓑ Ⓒ Ⓓ Ⓔ     9  Ⓐ Ⓑ Ⓒ Ⓓ Ⓔ
 2  Ⓐ Ⓑ Ⓒ Ⓓ Ⓔ     6  Ⓐ Ⓑ Ⓒ Ⓓ Ⓔ    10  Ⓐ Ⓑ Ⓒ Ⓓ Ⓔ
 3  Ⓐ Ⓑ Ⓒ Ⓓ Ⓔ     7  Ⓐ Ⓑ Ⓒ Ⓓ Ⓔ    11  Ⓐ Ⓑ Ⓒ Ⓓ Ⓔ
 4  Ⓐ Ⓑ Ⓒ Ⓓ Ⓔ     8  Ⓐ Ⓑ Ⓒ Ⓓ Ⓔ    12  Ⓐ Ⓑ Ⓒ Ⓓ Ⓔ
```

Instructions to be read (the words in parentheses should not be read aloud).

You are to follow the instructions that I shall read to you. I cannot repeat them.

Look at the samples. Sample 1 has a number and a line beside it. On the line write an A. (Pause 2 seconds.) Now on the Sample Answer Sheet, find number 5 (pause 2 seconds) and darken the space for the letter you just wrote on the line. (Pause 2 seconds.)

Look at Sample 2. (Pause slightly.) Draw a line under the third number. (Pause 2 seconds.) Now look on the Sample Answer Sheet, find the number under which you just drew a line and darken space B as in baker for that number. (Pause 5 seconds.)

Look at Sample 3. (Pause slightly.) Draw a line under the third letter in the line. (Pause 2 seconds.) Now on your Sample Answer Sheet, find number 9 (pause 2 seconds) and darken the space for the letter under which you drew a line. (Pause 5 seconds.)

Look at the five circles in Sample 4. (Pause slightly.) Each circle has a number and a line in it. Write D as in dog on the blank in the last circle. (Pause 2 seconds.) Now on the Sample Answer Sheet, darken the space for the number-letter combination that is in the circle you just wrote in. (Pause 5 seconds.)

Look at Sample 5. (Pause slightly.) There are two circles and two boxes of different sizes with numbers in them. (Pause slightly.) If 4 is more than 2 and if 5 is less than 3, write A in the smaller circle. (Pause slightly.) Otherwise write C in the larger box. (Pause 2 seconds.) Now on the Sample Answer Sheet, darken the space for the number-letter combination in the circle or box in which you just wrote. (Pause 5 seconds.)

Now look at the Sample Answer Sheet. (Pause slightly.) You should have darkened spaces 4B, 5A, 9A, 10D, and 12C on the Sample Answer Sheet. (If the person preparing to take the examination made any mistakes, try to help him or her understand why the mistakes are wrong.)

SAMPLE ANSWER QUESTIONS

1 Ⓐ Ⓑ Ⓒ Ⓓ Ⓔ	18 Ⓐ Ⓑ Ⓒ Ⓓ Ⓔ
2 Ⓐ Ⓑ Ⓒ Ⓓ Ⓔ	19 Ⓐ Ⓑ Ⓒ Ⓓ Ⓔ
3 Ⓐ Ⓑ Ⓒ Ⓓ Ⓔ	20 Ⓐ Ⓑ Ⓒ Ⓓ Ⓔ
4 Ⓐ Ⓑ Ⓒ Ⓓ Ⓔ	21 Ⓐ Ⓑ Ⓒ Ⓓ Ⓔ
5 Ⓐ Ⓑ Ⓒ Ⓓ Ⓔ	22 Ⓐ Ⓑ Ⓒ Ⓓ Ⓔ
6 Ⓐ Ⓑ Ⓒ Ⓓ Ⓔ	23 Ⓐ Ⓑ Ⓒ Ⓓ Ⓔ
7 Ⓐ Ⓑ Ⓒ Ⓓ Ⓔ	24 Ⓐ Ⓑ Ⓒ Ⓓ Ⓔ
8 Ⓐ Ⓑ Ⓒ Ⓓ Ⓔ	25 Ⓐ Ⓑ Ⓒ Ⓓ Ⓔ
9 Ⓐ Ⓑ Ⓒ Ⓓ Ⓔ	26 Ⓐ Ⓑ Ⓒ Ⓓ Ⓔ
10 Ⓐ Ⓑ Ⓒ Ⓓ Ⓔ	27 Ⓐ Ⓑ Ⓒ Ⓓ Ⓔ
11 Ⓐ Ⓑ Ⓒ Ⓓ Ⓔ	28 Ⓐ Ⓑ Ⓒ Ⓓ Ⓔ
12 Ⓐ Ⓑ Ⓒ Ⓓ Ⓔ	29 Ⓐ Ⓑ Ⓒ Ⓓ Ⓔ
13 Ⓐ Ⓑ Ⓒ Ⓓ Ⓔ	30 Ⓐ Ⓑ Ⓒ Ⓓ Ⓔ
14 Ⓐ Ⓑ Ⓒ Ⓓ Ⓔ	31 Ⓐ Ⓑ Ⓒ Ⓓ Ⓔ
15 Ⓐ Ⓑ Ⓒ Ⓓ Ⓔ	32 Ⓐ Ⓑ Ⓒ Ⓓ Ⓔ
16 Ⓐ Ⓑ Ⓒ Ⓓ Ⓔ	33 Ⓐ Ⓑ Ⓒ Ⓓ Ⓔ
17 Ⓐ Ⓑ Ⓒ Ⓓ Ⓔ	34 Ⓐ Ⓑ Ⓒ Ⓓ Ⓔ

PART II

1. The primary function of a take-up pulley in a belt conveyor is to

   A) carry the belt on the return trip.
   B) track the belt.
   C) maintain proper belt tension.
   D) change the direction of the belt.
   E) regulate the speed of the belt.

2. Which device is used to transfer power and rotary mechanical motion from one shaft to another?

   A) Bearing
   B) Lever
   C) Idler roller
   D) Gear
   E) Bushing

3. What special care is required in the storage of hard steel roller bearings? They should be

   A) cleaned and spun dry with compressed air.
   B) oiled once a month.
   C) stored in a humid place.
   D) wrapped in oiled paper.
   E) stored at temperatures below 90 degrees Fahrenheit.

4. Which is the correct method to lubricate a roller chain?

   A) Use brush to apply lubricant while chain is in motion
   B) Use squirt can to apply lubricant while chain is in motion
   C) Use brush to apply lubricant while chain is not in motion
   D) Soak chain in pan of lubricant and hang to allow excess to drain
   E) Chains do not need lubrication

5. A circuit has two resistors of equal value in series. The voltage and current in the circuit are 20 volts and 2 amps respectively. What is the value of EACH resistor?

   A) 5 ohms
   B) 10 ohms
   C) 15 ohms
   D) 20 ohms
   E) Not enough information given

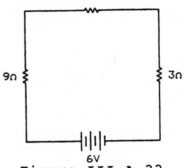

Figure III-A-22

6. Which of the following circuits is shown in Figure III-A-22?

   A) Series circuit
   B) Parallel circuit
   C) Series, parallel circuit
   D) Solid state circuit
   E) None of the above

7. What is the total net capacitance of two 60 farad capacitors connected in series?

   A) 30 F
   B) 60 F
   C) 90 F
   D) 120 F
   E) 360 F

8. If two 30 mH inductors are connected in series, what is the total net inductance of the combination?

   A) 15 mH
   B) 20 mH
   C) 30 mH
   D) 45 mH
   E) 60 mH

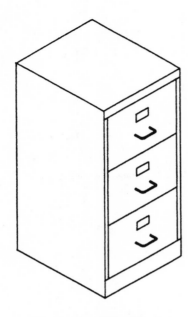

Figure 75-25-1

9. Crowbars, light bulbs and vacuum bags are to be stored in the cabinet shown in Figure 75-25-1. Considering the balance of weight, what would be the safest arrangement?

A) Top drawer - Crowbars
   Middle drawer - Light bulbs
   Bottom drawer - Vacuum bags
B) Top drawer - Crowbars
   Middle drawer - Vacuum bags
   Bottom drawer - Light bulbs
C) Top drawer - Vacuum bags
   Middle drawer - Crowbars
   Bottom drawer - Light bulbs
D) Top drawer - Vacuum bags
   Middle drawer - Light bulbs
   Bottom drawer - Crowbars
E) Top drawer - Light bulbs
   Middle drawer - Vacuum bags
   Bottom drawer - Crowbars

10. Contaminants have caused bearings to fail prematurely. Which pair of the items listed below should be kept away from bearings?

A) Dirt and oil
B) Grease and water
C) Oil and grease
D) Dirt and moisture
E) Water and oil

11. The electrical circuit term "open circuit" refers to a closed loop being opened. When an ohmmeter is connected into this type of circuit, one can expect the meter to

A) read infinity.
B) read infinity and slowly return to ZERO.
C) read ZERO.
D) read ZERO and slowly return to infinity.
E) None of the above

12. Which is most appropriate for pulling a heavy load?

A) Electric lift
B) Fork lift
C) Tow conveyor
D) Dolly
E) Pallet truck

13. In order to operate a breast drill, which direction should you turn it?

A) Clockwise
B) Counterclockwise
C) Up and down
D) Back and forth
E) Right, then left

14. Which is the correct tool for tightening or loosening a water pipe?

A) Slip joint pliers
B) Household pliers
C) Monkey wrench
D) Water pump pliers
E) Pipe wrench

15. What is one purpose of a chuck key?

A) Open doors
B) Remove drill bits
C) Remove screws
D) Remove set screws
E) Unlock chucks

16. When smoke is generated as a result of using a portable electric drill for cutting holes into a piece of angle iron, one should

A) use a fire watch.
B) cease the drilling operation.
C) use an exhaust fan to remove smoke.
D) use a prescribed coolant solution to reduce friction.
E) call the Fire Department.

17. The primary purpose of soldering is to

A) melt solder to a molten state.
B) heat metal parts to the right temperature be be joined.
C) join metal parts by melting the parts.
D) harden metal.
E) join metal parts.

18. Which of the following statements is correct concerning a soldering gun?

A) Tip is not replaceable
B) Cannot be used in cramped places
C) heats only when trigger is pressed
D) Not rated by the number of watts it uses
E) Has no light

19. What unit of measurement is read on a dial torque wrench?

A) Pounds
B) Inches
C) Centimeters
D) Foot-pounds
E) Degrees

20. Which instrument is used to test insulation breakdown of a conductor?

A) Ohmmeter
B) Ammeter
C) Megger
D) Wheatstone bridge
E) Voltmeter

21. 1/2 of 1/4 =

A) 1/12
B) 1/8
C) 1/4
D) 1/2
E) 8

22. 2.6 - .5 =

A) 2.0
B) 2.1
C) 3.1
D) 3.3
E) None of the above

23. Solve the power equation

$P = I^2R$ for R

A) $R = EI$

B) $R = I^2P$

C) $R = PI$

D) $R = P/I^2$

E) $R = E/I$

24. The product of 3 kilo ohms times 3 micro ohms is

A) 6×10^{-9} ohms

B) 6×10^{-3} ohms

C) 9×10^3 ohms

D) 9×10^{-6} ohms

E) 9×10^{-3} ohms

In sample question 25 below, select the statement which is most nearly correct according to the paragraph.

"Prior to 1870, a conveyor that made use of rollers was developed for transporting clay. This construction substituted rolling friction at the idler bearing points for the sliding friction of the slider bed. A primitive type of troughing belt conveyor was developed about the same time for the handling of grain. This design was improved during the latter part of the century when the troughing idler was developed."

25.   According to the above paragraph, which of the following statements is most nearly correct?

A)   The troughing belt conveyor was developed about 1870 to handle clay and grain.

B)   Rolling friction construction was replaced by sliding friction construction prior to 1870.

C)   In the late nineteenth century, conveyors were improved with the development of the troughing idler.

D)   The troughing idler, a significant design improvement for conveyors, was developed in the early nineteenth century.

E)   Conveyor belts were invented and developed in the 1800's.

26. A small crane was used to raise the heavy part. Raise MOST nearly means

A)   lift
B)   drag
C)   drop
D)   deliver
E)   guide

27. Short MOST nearly means

A)   tall
B)   wide
C)   brief
D)   heavy
E)   dark

For sample question 28 below, select from the drawings of objects on the right labeled A, B, C, and D, the one that would have the TOP, FRONT, and RIGHT views shown in the drawing at the left

28.

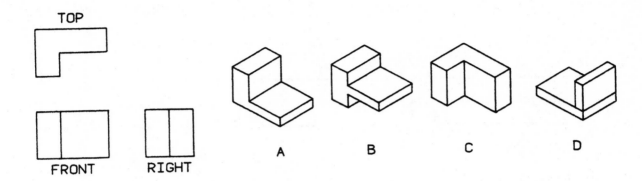

In sample question 29 below, there is, on the left, a drawing of a flat piece of paper and, on the right, four figures labeled A, B, C, and D. When the paper is bent on the dotted lines it will form one of the figures on the right. Decide which alternative can be formed from the flat piece.

29.

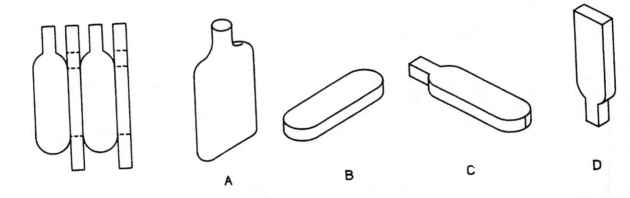

In each of the sample questions below, look at the symbols in the
first two boxes. Something about the three symbols in the first
box makes them alike; something about the two symbols in the other
box with the question mark makes them alike. Look for some
characteristic that is common to all symbols in the same box, yet
makes them different from the symbols in the other box. Among dthe
five answer choices, find the symbol that can best be substituted
for the question mark, because it is <u>like</u> the symbols in the second
box, and, <u>for the same reason</u>, different from those in the first
box.

30.

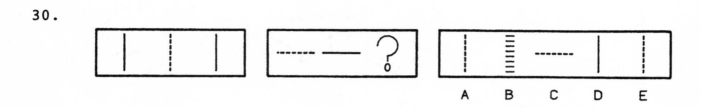

In sample question 30 above, all the symbols in the first box are
vertical lines. The second box has two lines, one broken and one
solid. Their <u>likeness</u> to each other consists in their being
horizontal; and their being horizontal makes them <u>different</u> from
the vertical lines in the other box. The answer must be the only
one of the five lettered choices that is a horizontal line, either
broken or solid. NOTE: There is not supposed to be a series or
progression in these symbol questions. If you look for a
progression in the first box and the second box, you will be
wasting time. Remember, look for a <u>likeness</u> within each box and a
<u>difference</u> between the two boxes.

Now do sample questions 31 and 32.

31.

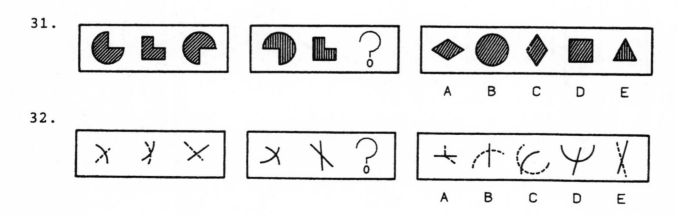

32.

33. In Figure 160-57 below, what is the current flow through R_3 when:

        V = 50 volts

        R_1 = 25 ohms

        R_2 = 25 ohms

        R3 = 50 ohms

        R_4 = 50 ohms

        R_5 = 50 ohms

and the current through the entire circuit totals one amp?

A)   0.5 amp
B)   5.0 amps
C)   5.0 milliamps
D) 50.0 milliamps
E) None of the above

34. In Figure 3-8-6 below, what is the measurement of Dimension F? Drawing is not actual size.

A) 1 3/4 inches
B) 2 1/4 inches
C) 2 1/2 inches
D) 3 3/4 inches
E) None of the above

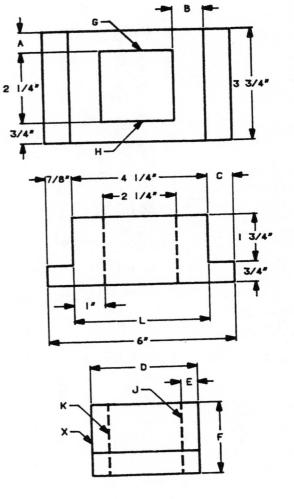

Figure 3-8-6

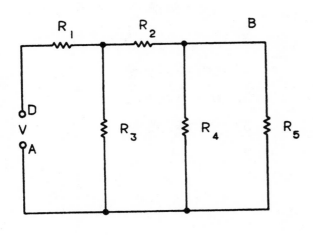

Figure 160-57

CORRECT ANSWERS TO
SAMPLE QUESTIONS

1 Ⓐ Ⓑ ● Ⓓ Ⓔ

2 Ⓐ Ⓑ Ⓒ ● Ⓔ

3 Ⓐ Ⓑ Ⓒ ● Ⓔ

4 Ⓐ Ⓑ Ⓒ ● Ⓔ

5 ● Ⓑ Ⓒ Ⓓ Ⓔ

6 ● Ⓑ Ⓒ Ⓓ Ⓔ

7 ● Ⓑ Ⓒ Ⓓ Ⓔ

8 Ⓐ Ⓑ Ⓒ Ⓓ ●

9 Ⓐ Ⓑ Ⓒ Ⓓ ●

10 Ⓐ Ⓑ Ⓒ ● Ⓔ

11 ● Ⓑ Ⓒ Ⓓ Ⓔ

12 Ⓐ Ⓑ Ⓒ Ⓓ ●

13 ● Ⓑ Ⓒ Ⓓ Ⓔ

14 Ⓐ Ⓑ Ⓒ Ⓓ ●

15 Ⓐ ● Ⓒ Ⓓ Ⓔ

16 Ⓐ Ⓑ Ⓒ ● Ⓔ

17 Ⓐ Ⓑ Ⓒ Ⓓ ●

18 Ⓐ Ⓑ ● Ⓓ Ⓔ

19 Ⓐ Ⓑ Ⓒ ● Ⓔ

20 Ⓐ Ⓑ ● Ⓓ Ⓔ

21 Ⓐ ● Ⓒ Ⓓ Ⓔ

22 Ⓐ ● Ⓒ Ⓓ Ⓔ

23 Ⓐ Ⓑ Ⓒ ● Ⓔ

24 Ⓐ Ⓑ Ⓒ Ⓓ ●

25 Ⓐ Ⓑ ● Ⓓ Ⓔ

26 ● Ⓑ Ⓒ Ⓓ Ⓔ

27 Ⓐ Ⓑ ● Ⓓ Ⓔ

28 Ⓐ Ⓑ ● Ⓓ Ⓔ

29 Ⓐ Ⓑ ● Ⓓ Ⓔ

30 Ⓐ Ⓑ ● Ⓓ Ⓔ

31 Ⓐ Ⓑ Ⓒ Ⓓ ●

32 Ⓐ Ⓑ Ⓒ ● Ⓔ

33 Ⓐ Ⓑ ● Ⓓ Ⓔ

34 ● Ⓑ Ⓒ Ⓓ Ⓔ

EXHIBIT A

Test M/N 933 covers the following Knowledge, Skills and Abilities:

(1) <u>Knowledge of basic mechanics</u> refers to the theory of operation, terminology, usage, and characteristics of basic mechanical principles as they apply to such things as gears, pulleys, cams, pawls, power transmissions, linkages, fasteners, chains, sprockets, and belts; and including hoisting, rigging, roping, pneumatics, and hydraulic devices.

(2) <u>Knowledge of basic electricity</u> refers to the theory, terminology, usage, and characteristics of basic electrical principles such as Ohm's Law, Kirchoff's Law, and magnetism, as they apply to such things as AC-DC circuitry and hardware, relays, switches, and circuit breakers.

(3) <u>Knowledge of basic electronics</u> refers to the theory, terminology, usage, and characteristics of basic electronic principles concerning such things as solid state devices, vacuum tubes, coils, capacitors, resistors, and basic logic circuitry.

(5) <u>Knowledge of safety procedures and equipment</u> refers to the knowledge of industrial hazards (e.g., mechanical, chemical, electrical, electronic) and procedures and techniques established to avoid injuries to self and others such as lock-out devices, protective clothing, and waste disposal techniques.

(8) <u>Knowledge of lubrication materials and procedures</u> refers to the terminology, characteristics, storage, preparation, disposal, and usage techniques involved with lubrication materials such as oils, greases, and other types of lubricants.

(19) <u>Ability to perform basic mathematical computations</u> refers to the ability to perform basic calculations such as addition, subtraction, multiplication and division with whole numbers, fractions and decimals.

(20) <u>Ability to perform more complex mathematics</u> refers to the ability to perform calculations such as basic algebra, geometry, scientific notation, and number conversions, as applied to mechanical, electrical and electronic applications.

(21) <u>Ability to apply theoretical knowledge to practical applications</u> refers to mechanical, electrical and electronic maintenance applications such as inspection, troubleshooting equipment repair and modification, preventive maintenance, and installation of electrical equipment.

(22) <u>Ability to detect patterns</u> refers to the ability to observe and analyze qualitative factors such as number progressions, spatial relationships, and auditory and visual patterns. This includes combining information and determining how a given set of numbers, objects, or sounds are related to each other.

(23) <u>Ability to use written reference materials</u> refers to the ability to locate, read, and comprehend text material such as handbooks, manuals, bulletins, directives, checklists and route sheets.

(26) <u>Ability to follow instructions</u> refers to the ability to comprehend and execute written and oral instructions such as work orders, checklists, route sheets, and verbal directions and instructions.

(31) <u>Ability to use hand tools</u> refers to knowledge of, and proficiency with, various hand tools. This ability involves the safe and efficient use and maintenance of such tools as screwdrivers, wrenches, hammers, pliers, chisels, punches, taps, dies, rules, gauges, and alignment tools.

(32) <u>Ability to use portable power tools</u> refers to the knowledge of, and proficiency with, various power tools. This ability involves the safe and efficient use and maintenance of power tools such as drills, saws, sanders and grinders.

(35) <u>Ability to use technical drawings</u> refers to the ability to read and comprehend technical materials such as diagrams, schematics, flow charts, and blueprints.

(36) <u>Ability to use test equipment</u> refers to the knowledge of, and proficiency with, various types of mechanical, electrical and electronic test equipment such as VOMS, oscilloscopes, circuit tracers, amprobes, and tachometers.

(37) <u>Ability to solder</u> refers to the knowledge of, and the ability to safely and effectively apply, the appropriate soldering techniques.

Wanted: U.S. Postal Inspectors

(Only the exceptional need apply)

Postal inspectors are federal law enforcement officers with investigative jurisdiction in all criminal matters involving the integrity of the mail and the security of the U.S. Postal Service.

U.S. Postal Inspectors

Postal inspectors, among others, investigate criminal and civil violations of postal laws and protect the revenue and assets of the U.S. Postal Service. They are authorized to carry firearms, make arrests, and they testify in court, serve subpoenas, and write comprehensive reports.

It was only January 8, 2003, that the U.S. Postal Inspection Service began recruiting college graduates who don't have previous work experience. Just in case you don't meet one of the special requirements listed in the Application for U.S. Inspectors, but have either a conferred, four-year college degree with a minimum GPA of 3.0 or an advance degree, you may apply for a Postal Inspector job, by submitting the *Application for U.S. Postal Inspector,* with a copy of your college transcript. Or write to: **U.S. Postal Inspection Service,** Office of Recruitment, 9600 Newbridge Drive, Potomac, MD 20854-4436. Or call the office at 301-983-7400.

Other U.S. Postal Inspection Service Jobs

From time to time, the U.S. Postal Inspection Service also recruits for other positions such as:

- Postal Police Officers
- Forensic Scientists
- Information Technology Specialists
- Security Electronic Technicians
- Administration Support Specialists

Excerpted from the U.S. Postal Inspection Service Website:
http://usps.com/postalinspectors/employmt.htm

Requirements for U.S. Postal Inspectors

U.S. Postal Inspectors are federal law enforcement officers. They investigate criminal, civil, and administrative violations of postal laws and are responsible for protecting the revenue and assets of the Postal Service. Inspectors are required to carry firearms, make arrests, testify in court, serve subpoenas, and write comprehensive reports. They must operate motor vehicles and may undergo moderate to arduous physical exertion under unusual environmental conditions. It is essential that Inspectors be in sound physical condition and be capable of performing vigorous physical activities on a sustained basis. The activities may require Inspectors to perform the following: climb ladders; work long and irregular hours; occupy cramped or crowded spaces for extended periods of time; exert physical force in the arrest, search, pursuit, and restraint of another person; and protect themselves and others from imminent danger.

The duties of the position require the ability to communicate with people from all walks of life, be proficient with firearms, have skills in self-defense, and have the ability to exercise good judgment. Inspectors may be relocated according to the needs of the Service.

The recruitment process is extremely thorough, and there is intense competition for relatively few positions. The recruitment and selection process must be completed prior to the applicant's 37th birthday.

This position is exempt from the Fair Labor Standards Act (FLSA) and does not qualify for overtime compensation. Postal Inspector salaries are based on the Inspection Service Law Enforcement (ISLE) pay system. The ISLE pay grades and steps correspond to the General Schedule (GS) pay scale for law enforcement officers.

Selection procedures include the following:

- Completion of this application.
- Written examination, including a business writing test and the 620 Entry Examination (cognitive abilities).
- Language proficiency test, if applicable.
- Completion of the *Comprehensive Application Packet.*
- Assessment Center evaluation of knowledge, skills, and abilities.
- Medical examination
- Polygraph examination.
- Background suitability investigation.
- Management interview.
- Drug screening.
- Residential basic training program at Potomac, Maryland.
- Six-month probation period for nonpostal and nonfederal law enforcement applicants.

Recruiting Standards

Applicants must be U.S. citizen between 21 and 36 years of age and meet all the General Requirements to apply for the position of U.S. Postal Inspector. The Postal Inspection Service is currently seeking individuals who meet the General Requirements, as well as at least one of the Special Requirements, listed below. Applications that do not contain one of the Special Requirements will be kept on file for two years and then purged. If an applicant's skills change during the two-year period, the applicant should contact the Postal Inspection Service.

General Requirements

Applicants must meet the requirements below and undergo a full medical suitability exam to determine fitness to perform the duties of a Postal Inspector, including, but not limited to, the following:

- A conferred-four-year degree from an accredited college or university.
- Binocular vision must test 20/40 (Snellen) without corrective lens. Unconnected vision must test at least 20/100 in each eye. Each eye must be corrected to 20/20, with good color identification and discrimination, depth perception, and normal peripheral vision. Radial keratotomy or orthokeratology are not acceptable.
- Hearing loss, as measured by an audiometer, must not exceed 30 decibels (A.S.A. or equivalent I.S.O.) in either ear in the 500, 1,000, and 2,000 Hz ranges. The applicant must have the ability to perceive normal speech discrimination.
- In good physical condition (weight proportional to height) and possessing emotional and mental stability. Manual dexterity with comparatively free motion of fingers, wrists, elbows, shoulders, hips, and knee joints. Arms, hands, legs, and feet must be sufficiently intact and functioning in order to perform duties satisfactorily.
- No felony convictions (felony charges may also render applicant ineligible.)
- No misdemeanor conviction of domestic violence (other misdemeanor charges or convictions may also render applicant ineligible).
- A current, valid state driver's license, held for at least two years.
- Ability to demonstrate these attributes, as measured by the Assessment Center:

  - Write and speak English clearly.

  - Schedule and complete activities in a logical, timely sequence.
  - Comprehend and execute instructions written and spoken in English.
  - Think clearly and comprehend verbal and nonverbal information.
  - Interact with others to obtain or exchange information or services.
  - Perceive or identify relevant details and associate them with other facts.

Special Requirements

Language Skills

Applicants seeking to enter the recruitment process under the language skills track must have advanced competency in a foreign language deemed as needed by the Postal Inspection Service to meet its investigative mission. The current list is as follows:

Arabic
Czech
French Creole

Hebrew
Italian
Mandarin
Punjabi
Spanish
Thai
Vietnamese
Armenian
Dutch
German
Hindi
Japanese
Norwegian
Russian
Swahili
Turkish
Cambodian
Egyptian
Greek (Modern)
Hmong
Korean
Polish
Serbo-Croatian
Swedish
Ukranian
Cantonese
Farsi (Persian)
Haitian
Indonesian
Lao
Portuguese
Slovak
Tagalog
Urdu

Applicants must pass a formal proficiency test administered by a contractor of the Postal Inspection Service. In addition to the language requirement, applicants in this track must have one year of full-time work experience with the same company or firm within two years of the date of their application.

Specialized Postal Experience

Applicants entering through the specialized postal experience track must be currently employed by the U.S. Postal Service and have at least one year of full-time work experience in one of the postal functional areas designated as critical to the needs of the Postal Inspection Service. Currently, critical needs exist in the following areas:

■ Business Mail Entry
■ Computer Analysis

- EEO Investigation
- Finance/Budget/Revenue Assurance
- Industrial Engineering
- Information/Computer/LAN Systems
- In-Plant Support
- Labor Relations/Workplace Intervention
- Media Relations
- Operations Support
- Safety/Health/Security/Injury Compensation

In addition, Postal Service supervisors in any functional area (including acting supervisors) with at least one year of supervisory experience will also be eligible under this entry track. A letter from he applicant's immediate supervisor must verify that the applicant has been a supervisor for at least one year. Also, Postal Inspection Service employees and/or contract employees with one year of full-time work experience with the Postal Inspection Service would qualify under this skill track.

Specialized Nonpostal Experience

Applicants seeking consideration under the specialized nonpostal skill track must have experience in one of the areas of expertise designated as critical to the needs of the Postal Inspection Service. The areas are as follows:

Law Degree. Candidates must have a Juris Doctorate degree and one year of full-time work experience with the same company or firm within two years of the date of their application.

Certification in auditing or investigations. Candidates with certifications in accounting, such as Certified Public Accountant (CPA), Certified Management Accountant (CMA), Certified Internal Auditor (CIA), and Certified Information Systems examination, such as Certified Protection Professional (CPP) and Certified Fraud Examiner (CFE), are accepted under this skills track. Applicants in this track must have a one year of full-time work experience with the same company or firm within two years of the date of their application. Applicants must also provide proof of certification.

Specialized computer education. Candidates with a four-year degree in one of the following fields: computer science, computer engineering, telecommunications, management information systems, electronic commerce, decision and information science, or computer information systems. Applicants in this track must have one year of full-time work experience with the same company or firm within two years of the date of their application.

Specialized computer expertise. Candidates who are currently employed (and have been employed for at least one year) in a position(s) specialized in one of the following computer forensics, internet investigations, internet security, network security, or information systems security. Applicants in this track must have one year of full-time work experience with the same company or firm within two years of the date of their application.

Certification in computer systems. Candidates with one of the following certifications and one year of work experience with the same firm within two years of the date of their application: Microsoft Certified Systems Engineer (MCSE), Microsoft Certified Professional +_ Internet (MCP+I), Cisco Certified Network Professional (CCNP), Certified Novell Engineer (CNE), A+ Certified Computer Technician, Certified Information Systems Security Professional (CISSP), Linux certification, or Sun Systems Certified Administrator.

Law enforcement. Candidates with at least one year of full-time work experience, within the last two years, in the law enforcement field. This includes detectives, criminalists, and polygraph examiners, and patrol, probation, correction, and parole officers. This track excludes clerical or other technical support personnel. Applicants must provide examples of the type of work conducted.

Diversified Experience

To increase competitiveness and acquire a more diversified candidate pool, applicants may enter the recruitment process along a fourth track, which combines higher education and work experience, including:

■ Bachelor's degree (B.A. or B.S. in any field) plus two years of full-time work experience.

■ Advanced degree (M.A., or Ph.D. in any field) plus one year of full-time work experience.

Applicants entering the recruitment process under the diversified experience entry track must have completed at least one year of full-time work experience with the same company or firm within two years of the date of their application. This includes U.S. Postal Service employees who have a four-year degree and meet the required minimum work experience.

Excerpted from the U.S. Postal Inspection Service Website:
http://usps.com/postalinspectors/employmt.htm

For information on other postal jobs, go to:
tp://usps.com/employment/welcome.htm?from=global&page=employment

U.S. Postal Inspection Service Divisions

Florida Division

3400 Lakeside Dr 6th Flr
Miramar FL 33027-3242
954-436-7200
Fax: 954-436-7282

Gulf Coast Division

PO Box 1276
Houston TX 77251-1276
713-238-4400
Fax: 713-2389-4460

Michigan Division

PO Box 330119
Detroit MI 48232-6119
313-226-8184
Fax: 313-226-8220

Mid-Atlantic Division

PO Box 3000
Charlotte NC 28228-3000
704-329-9120
Fax: 704-357-0039

Midwest Division

1106 Walnut St
St Louis MO 6399-2001
314-539-9300
Fax: 314-539-9306

New York Metro Division

PO Box 555
New York, NY 10116-0555
212-330-3844
Fax: 212-330-2720

North Jersey/Carribean Division

PO Box 509
Newark NJ 07101-0509
973-693-5400
Fax: 973-645-0600

Northeast Division

495 Summer St Ste 600
Boston, MA 02210-2114
617-556-0400

**Northern California
Division**

PO Box 882528
San Francisco CA 94188-2528
415-778-5800
Fax: 415-778-5822

**Northern Illinois
Division**

433 H Harrison St Room 50190
Chicago IL 60669-2201
312-983-7900
Fax: 312-983-6300

Northwest Division

PO Box 400
Seattle WA 9811-4000
206-442-6304
Fax: 206-442-6304

Philadelphia Metro Division

PO Box 7500
Philadelphia PA 19101-9000
215-895-8450
Fax: 215-895-8470

Rocky Mountain Division

1745 Stout St Ste 900
Denver CO 80202-3034
303-313-5320
Fax: 404-608-4500

Southeast Division

PO Box 16489
Atlanta GA 30321-0489
404-608-4500
Fax: 404-608-4505

Southern California Division

PO Box 2000
Pasadena CA 91102-2000
626-405-1200
Fax: 626-317-3430

Southwest Division

PO Box 162929
Ft Worth TX 76161-2929
817-317-3400
Fax: 817-317-4330

Southwest Division

PO Box 162929
Ft Worth TX 76161-2929
817-317-3400
Fax: 817-317-4330

Washington Metro Division

PO Box 96096
Washington DC 20066-6096
202-636-2300
Fax: 202-636-2287

Western Allegheny Division

1001 California Ave Room 2101
Pittsburg PA 15290-9000
412-359-7900
Fax: 412-359-7682

Excerpted from the U.S. Postal Inspection Service website:
http://usps.com/postalinspectors/employmt.htm

Afterword

Now I have revealed all the secrets of how I scored 95 to 100% on post office exams. I didn't hide anything. I even told you about my mistakes....my trial-and-error method.

I have also revealed how the U.S. Postal Service operates, and how it hires people and installs machines. I don't know if it will bring robots into the service, but one thing is sure: robots won't take any written examinations. Whatever happens, I'm sure the Postal Service will hire real people—like you. Why? Because employees die, retire, or change jobs.

When I started to take postal tests, I did not have a system for making high scores. To prove this point, I scored only 78.5% on my first test (Warren, Michigan).

I know that some of you will probably make higher scores than I did. For instance, Pablo R. Abesamis of Glendale, California made scores of 100% on five examinations and 98.80% and 97.00% on two other tests. Many others throughout the United States have done this. Other people will make scores lower than mine. It all depends on how you apply my techniques, and on how much effort you exert to attain your goal.

Just remember, you don't need to finish the exam to make a high score. Go for it!

The Day Before

The night before the test, you should go into a closed, dark room in your home. Close your eyes and visualize yourself as driving your car, going into the examination room, seeing all the people who are to take the test. You look at them and judge yourself: you are better than these people. You can make it. In fact, you are going to top them. Then you see them greeting you, admiring you. Then tell yourself: "*I,* (your name) *do hereby declare that I'm going to make it. I have prepared for this examination and I have mastered it. I have confidence in myself. I know I can do it. Yes, I can do all things.*"

The Day of the Test

When you go to the examination room the next day, repeat the "performance" you gave in your imagination, including the actual taking of the test. Even actors and actresses do this before they perform in front of a large crowd. When a boxer fights an invisible opponent, he isn't crazy. (If he intentionally bumps his head against a cement wall, that's another story.)

While you are taking the test you can concentrate well if you don't imagine that you're swimming with Brooke Shields in the blue lagoon or wrestling with Tom Selleck on the beach in Hawaii. Listen to nothing except the voice of the examiner and, your hearbeat.

The Day After

If you have any comments about exams or about this book, write them and send them to: **Bookhaus Publishers,** P.O. Box 3277, Farmington Hills. MI 48333-3277.

Be patient if no test is being given yet in your area. Call the testing centers in your area or anywhere else, and ask if there's an examination coming up. Call once a week, every week of the year!

We give achievement awards to qualified high scorers on Post Office exams to give examinees added incentives to make high scores. Eligible to receive these awards are top scorers who purchased a copy of this book. To know if you qualify as a high scorer, please write us and tell in a few words how the book has helped you in achieving a top score on the test. Please enclose a photocopy of the test result. Send your letter and photocopy to: **Bookhaus Publishers,** P.O. Box 3277, Farmington Hills, MI 48333-3277.

—Veltisezar B. Bautista
Author

Supplement A

National Directory of U.S. Postal Service Examination Centers

ALABAMA

U.S. Postal Service
351 24th Street N
Birmingham, AL 35203-9998
(205) 521-0251
Job Hotline
(205) 521-0214

ALASKA

U.S. Postal Service
4141 Postmark Drive
Anchorage, AK 99599-9998
(Job Hotline
(907) 564-2962

ARIZONA

U.S. Postal Service
1441 East Buckeye Road
Phoenix, AZ 85026-9998
(602) 223-3631
Job Hotline
(602) 223-3624

ARKANSAS

U.S. Postal Service
4700 E McCain Boulevard
Little Rock, AR 72231-9998
(501) 945-6665

CALIFORNIA

U.S. Postal Service
300 Long Beach Boulevard
Long Beach, CA 90809-9998
(562) 983-3072
Job Hotline
(562) 435-4529

U.S. Postal Service
7001 S Central Avenue
Los Angeles, CA 90052-9998
(323) 586-1340
Job Hotline
(323) 586-1351

U.S. Postal Service
1675 7th Street
Oakland, CA 94615-9998
(510) 874-8344
Job Hotline
(510) 251-3040

U.S. Postal Service
11251 Rancho Carmel Drive
San Diego, CA 92199-9998
(619) 674-0430
Job Hotline
(619) 674-0577
(619) 674-2690

U.S. Postal Service
1300 Evans Avenue
San Francisco, CA 94188-9998
Job Hotline
(415) 550-5534

U.S. Postal Service
1750 Lunday Avenue
San Jose, CA 95101-0086
(408) 437-6925

Job Hotline
(408) 437-6986

U.S. Postal Service
3101 W Sunflower Avenue
Santa Ana, CA 92799-9998
Job Hotline
(714) 662-6375
U.S. Postal Service
28201 Franklin Parkway
Santa Clarita, CA 91383-9461
(661) 775-7040
Job Hotline
(661) 294-7680

U.S. Postal Service
3775 Industrial Boulevard
West Sacramento, CA 95799-0062
(916) 373-8686
Job Hotline
(916) 373-8448

COLORADO

U.S. Postal Service
7500 E 53rd Place Rm 2204
Denver, CO 80266-2204
(303) 853-6132
Job Hotline
(303) 853-6060

CONNECTICUT

U.S. Postal Service
141 Weston Street
Hartford, CT 06101-9998
(860) 524-6110

FLORIDA

U.S. Postal Service
1100 Kings Road
Jacksonville, FL 32203-9998
(904) 359-2921
Job Hotline
(904) 359-2737

U.S. Postal Service
800 Rinehart Road
Lake Mary, FL 32799-9421
(407) 444-2012
Job Hotline
1-888-771-9056
(407) 444-2029

U.S. Postal Service
2200 NW 72nd Avenue
Pembroke Pines, FL 33082-9990
(305) 470-0705
Job Hotline
(305) 470-0412
1-888-725-7295

U.S. Postal Service
5201 W Spruce Street
Tampa, FL 33630-9998
(813) 877-0318
Job Hotline
(813) 877-0381

GEORGIA

U.S. Postal Service
3900 Crown Road Rm. 272
Atlanta, GA 30304-9998
(404) 765-7200

U.S. Postal Service
451 College Street, -9998
(912) 752-8467
Job Hotline
(912) 752-8465

HAWAII

U.S. Postal Service
3600 Aolele Street
Honolulu, HI 96820-9998
Job Hotline
(808) 423-3690

ILLINOIS

U.S. Postal Service
6801 W 73rd Street
Bedford Park, IL 60499-9998
(708) 563-7493

U.S. Postal Service
500 E Fullerton Avenue
Carol Stream, IL 60099-9998
(630) 260-5153
Job Hotline
(630) 260-5200

U.S. Postal Service
433 W Harrison
Chicago, IL 60607-3905
(312) 983-8542

INDIANA

U.S. Postal Service
3939 Bincennes Rd
Indianapolis, IN 46298-9998
(317) 870-8551
Job Hotline

(317) 870-8500

IOWA

U.S. Postal Service
1165 2nd Avenue
Des Moines, IA 50318-7900
(515) 251-2201
Job Hotline
(515) 251-2061

KENTUCKY

U.S. Postal Service
1420 Gardiner Lane, Rm 320
Louisville, KY 40231-9998
(502) 454-1817
Job Hotline
(502) 454-1625

LOUISIANA

U.S. Postal Service
701 Loyola Avenue Rm. T2009
New Orleans, LA 70113-9998
(504) 589-1171
Job Hotline
(504) 589-1660

MAINE

380 Riverside Street
Portland, ME 041013-9998
Job Hotline
(207) 828-8520

MARYLAND

U.S. Postal Service
900 E Fayette Street
Baltimore, MD 21233-9998

(410) 347-4278
Job Hotline
(410) 347-4320

MASACHUSSETTE

U.S. Postal Service
25 Dorchester Avenue
Boston, MA 02205-9998
(617) 654-5500
Job Hotline
 (617) 654-5569

U.S. Postal Service
74 Main Street
North Reading, MA 01889
(978) 664-7079
Job Hotline
(978) 664-7665

U.S. Postal Service
1883 Main St
Springfield, MA 01101
(413) 785-6263
Job Hotline
(413) 731-0425

MICHIGAN

U.S. Postal Service
1401 W Fort Street, Rm 201
Detroit, MI 48233-9998
(313) 226-8259
(313) 226-8490
Job Hotline
1-888-442-5361

U.S. Postal Service
222 Michigan Street, NW
Grand Rapids, MI 49599-9998

(616) 776-1426
Job Hotline
(616) 776-1835

U.S. Postal Service
200 West 2nd Street
Royal Oak, MI 48068-9998
(810) 546-7106
Job Hotline
(810) 546-7104

MINNESOTA

U.S. Postal Service
180 E Kellog Boulevard
St Paul, MN 55101-9997
(651) 293-3036
Job Hotline
(651) 293-3364

U.S. Postal Service
315 W Pershing Road, Rm 572
Kansas City, MO 64108-9998
(816) 374-9310
Job Hotline
(816) 374-9346

MISSOURI

U.S. Postal Service
1720 Market Street, Rm 3027
St Louis, MO 63155-9998
(314) 436-3852
Job Hotline
(314) 436-3855

MISSISSIPPI

U.S. Postal Service
401 E South Street
Jackson, MS 39201-9998

(601) 351-7270
Job Hotline
(601) 351-7099

MONTANA

U.S. Postal Service
841 S 26th Street
Billings, MT 59101-9998
(406) 255-6427
Job Hotline
(406) 657-5763

NEBRASKA

U.S. Postal Service
1124 Pacific Street, Rm 325
Omaha NE 68108-0421
(402) 348-2506
Job Hotline
(402) 348-2523

NEW HAMPSHIRE

U.S. Postal Service
955 Goffs Falls Road
Manchester, NH 03103-9998
Job Hotline
(603) 644-4065

NEW JERSEY

U.S. Postal Service
501 Benigno Boulevard
Bellmawr, NJ 08099-9998
Job Hotline
(609) 933-4314

U.S. Postal Service
21 Kilmer Road

Edison, NJ 08901-9998
(732) 819-3272

U.S. Postal Service
2 Federal Square
Newark, NJ 07102-9998
(973) 693-5200

NEW MEXICO

U.S. Postal Service
1135 Broadway Boulevard, NE, Rm 230
Albuquerque, NM 87101-9998
(505) 245-9518
Job Hotline
(505) 245-9517

NEVADA

U.S. Postal Service
1001 E Sunset Road
Las Vegas, NV 89199-9998
(702) 361-9375
Job Hotline
(702) 361-9564

NEW YORK

U.S. Postal Service
30 Old Karmer Road
Albany, NY 12288-9998
Job Hotline
(518) 452-2445

U.S. Postal Service
1200 William Street
Buffalo, NY 14240-9998
(716) 846-2470
Job Hotline
(716) 846-2478

U.S. Postal Service
142-02 20th Avenue
Flushing, NY 11351-9998
(718) 321-5170
Job Hotline
(718) 529-7000

U.S. Postal Service
1377 Motor Parkway
Hauppauge, NY 11760-9998
(516) 582-7416
Job Hotline
(516) 582-7530

U.S. Postal Service
421 8th Avenue, Rm 3018
New York, NY 10199-9998
(212) 330-3600
(212) 330-2907

U.S. Postal Service
1000 Westchester Avenue
White Plains, NY 10610-9800
(914) 697-7190
(914) 967-8585

NORTH CAROLINA

U.S. Postal Service
2901 S Interstate 85 Service Road
Charlotte, NC 28228-9962
(704) 393-4495
Job Hotline
(704) 393-4490

U.S. Postal Service
900 Market Street, Rm 232
Greensboro, NC 27498-0001
(336) 669-1214
Job Hotline

(336) 271-5573

NORTH DAKOTA

(Same as South Dakota)

OHIO

U.S. Postal Service
675 Wolfledges Parkway
Akron, OH 44309-9998
(330) 996-9501
Job Hotline
(330) 996-9530

U.S. Postal Service
1591 Dalton Avenue, 2nd Floor
Cincinnati, OH 45234-9998
(513) 684-5451
(513) 684-5449

U.S. Postal Service
2200 Orange Avenue
Cleveland, OH 44104-9998
(216) 443-4339

U.S. Postal Service
850 Twin Rivers Drive
Columbus, OH 43216-9998
(614) 469-4357
Job Hotline
(614) 469-4356

OKLAHOMA

U.S. Postal Service
3030 NW Expressway Street, Ste 1042
Oklahoma City, OK 73198-9420
(405) 553-6172

OREGON

U.S. Postal Service
715 NW Hoyt Street
Portland, OR 97208-9999
(503) 294-2277
1-800-275-8777
Job Hotline
(503) 294-2270

PENNSYLVANIA

U.S. Postal Service
2108 E 38th Street
Erie, PA 16515-9998
(814) 898-7031
Job Hotline
(814) 899-0354

U.S. Postal Service
1425 Crooked Hill Road
Harrisburg, PA 17107-9998
(717) 257-2250
Job Hotline
(717) 390-7400

U.S. Postal Service
1400 Harrisburg Pike
Lancaster, PA 17602-9998
(717) 390-7460
Job Hotline
(717) 390-7400

U.S. Postal Service
2970 Market Street
Philadelphia, PA 19104-9422
Job Hotline
(800) 276-5627

U.S. Postal Service
1001 California Avenue
Pittsburgh, PA 15290-9998
(412) 359-7688
Job Hotline
(412) 359-7516
PUERTO RICO

U.S. Postal Service
P O. Box 363367
San Juan, PR 00936-9998
787-767-3351

RHODE ISLAND

U.S. Postal Service
24 Corliss Street
Providence, RI 02904
(401) 276-6845
Job Hotline
(401) 276-6844

SOUTH CAROLINA

U.S. Postal Service
P O. Box 29292
Columbia, SC 29292
(803) 926-6437
Job Hotline
(803) 926-6400

SOUTH DAKOTA

320 S Second Avenue
Sioux Falls, SD 57104-7554
(605) 357-5032

TENNESSEE

U.S. Postal Service
525 Royal Parkway, Rm 207
Nashville, TN 37229-9998
(615) 885-9962
Job Hotline
(615) 885-9190

TEXAS

U.S. Postal Service
951 W Bethel Road
Chappell, TX 75099-9998
Job Hotline
(214) 760-4531

U.S. Postal Service
4600 Mark IV Parkway
Fort Worth, TX 7616-9998
(817) 317-3350
Job Hotline
(817) 317-3366

U.S. Postal Service
1002 Washington Avenue
Houston, TX 77201 -9701
Job Hotline
(713) 226-3872

U.S. Postal Service
10410 Perin Beitel Road
San Antonio, TX 78284-9998
Job Hotline
(210) 368-8400

UTAH
U.S. Postal Service
1760 West 2100, S
Salt Lake City, UT 84199-9998
(801) 974-2210
Job Hotline
(801) 974-2209

VIRGINIA

U.S. Postal Service
8409 Lee Highway
Merrifield, VA 22081-9998
(703) 698-6438
Job Hotline
(703) 698-6561

U.S. Postal Service
1801 Brook Road
Richmond, VA 23232-9998
(804) 775-6196

WASHINGTON

U.S. Postal Service
415 1st Avenue N
Seattle, WA 98109-9998
(206) 442-6236
Job Hotline
(206) 442-6240

U.S. Postal Service
707 W Main Avenue
Spokane, WA 99202-9998
(509) 626-6824
Job Hotline
(509) 626-6896

WASHINGTON, DC

U.S. Postal Service
3300 V Street, NE
Washington, DC 20018-1527
Job Hotline
(202) 636-1537

WEST VIRGINIA

U.S. Postal Service
10002 Lee Street, E
Charleston, WV 25301-9998
Job Hotline
(304) 357-0648

WISCONSIN

U.S. Postal Service
245 W Saint Paul Avenue, 5th Floor
Milwaukee, WI 53203-9998
(414) 287-1834
Job Hotline
(414) 287-1835

APWU National Agreement
Schedule One — Salary and Rates
Effective September 7, 2002

Grade and Step	Full-time Regular Rates				BIWEEKLY DEDUCTIONS										
					CSRS			FERS		FERS — THRIFT SAVINGS PLAN					
	Annual Salary	Biweekly Pay	Straight Time	Night Differential	7% CSRS	1.45% MEDICARE	Maximum 7% TSP	0.80 FERS	7.65% FICA	1% USPS MINIMUM	3% EMPLOYEE	3% USPS	5% EMPLOYEE	5% USPS	12% EMPLOYEE MAXIMUM
2 D	36,678	1,410.69	17.6337	1.37	98.75	20.46	98.75	11.29	107.92	14.11	42.32	56.43	70.53	70.53	169.28
E	36,922	1,420.08	17.7510	1.38	99.41	20.59	99.41	11.36	108.64	14.20	42.60	56.80	71.00	71.00	170.41
F	37,166	1,429.46	17.8683	1.39	100.06	20.73	100.06	11.44	109.35	14.29	42.88	57.18	71.47	71.47	171.54
G	37,411	1,438.88	17.9861	1.40	100.72	20.86	100.72	11.51	110.07	14.39	43.17	57.56	71.94	71.94	172.67
H	37,660	1,448.46	18.1058	1.41	101.39	21.00	101.39	11.59	110.81	14.48	43.45	57.94	72.42	72.42	173.82
3 D	37,270	1,433.46	17.9183	1.39	100.34	20.79	100.34	11.47	109.66	14.33	43.00	57.34	71.67	71.67	172.02
E	37,533	1,443.58	18.0447	1.40	101.05	20.93	101.05	11.55	110.43	14.44	43.31	57.74	72.18	72.18	173.23
F	37,802	1,453.92	18.1740	1.41	101.77	21.08	101.77	11.63	111.23	14.54	43.62	58.16	72.70	72.70	174.47
G	38,063	1,463.96	18.2995	1.42	102.48	21.23	102.48	11.71	111.99	14.64	43.92	58.56	73.20	73.20	175.68
H	38,329	1,474.19	18.4274	1.43	103.19	21.38	103.19	11.79	112.78	14.74	44.23	58.97	73.71	73.71	176.90
4 D	37,912	1,458.15	18.2269	1.42	102.07	21.14	102.07	11.67	111.55	14.58	43.74	58.33	72.91	72.91	174.98
E	38,197	1,469.12	18.3639	1.43	102.84	21.30	102.84	11.75	112.39	14.69	44.07	58.76	73.46	73.46	176.29
F	38,487	1,480.27	18.5034	1.44	103.62	21.46	103.62	11.84	113.24	14.80	44.41	59.21	74.01	74.01	177.63
G	38,772	1,491.23	18.6404	1.45	104.39	21.62	104.39	11.93	114.08	14.91	44.74	59.65	74.56	74.56	178.95
H	39,055	1,502.12	18.7764	1.46	105.15	21.78	105.15	12.02	114.91	15.02	45.06	60.08	75.11	75.11	180.25
5 D	38,608	1,484.92	18.5615	1.45	103.94	21.53	103.94	11.88	113.60	14.85	44.55	59.40	74.25	74.25	178.19
E	38,916	1,496.77	18.7096	1.46	104.77	21.70	104.77	11.97	114.50	14.97	44.90	59.87	74.84	74.84	179.61
F	39,225	1,508.65	18.8582	1.47	105.61	21.88	105.61	12.07	115.41	15.09	45.26	60.35	75.43	75.43	181.04
G	39,530	1,520.38	19.0048	1.48	106.43	22.05	106.43	12.16	116.31	15.20	45.61	60.82	76.02	76.02	182.45
H	39,841	1,532.35	19.1543	1.50	107.26	22.22	107.26	12.26	117.22	15.32	45.97	61.29	76.62	76.62	183.88
6 D	39,358	1,513.77	18.9221	1.48	105.96	21.95	105.96	12.11	115.80	15.14	45.41	60.55	75.69	75.69	181.65
E	39,693	1,526.65	19.0832	1.49	106.87	22.14	106.87	12.21	116.79	15.27	45.80	61.07	76.33	76.33	183.20
F	40,030	1,539.62	19.2452	1.50	107.77	22.32	107.77	12.32	117.78	15.40	46.19	61.58	76.98	76.98	184.75
G	40,361	1,552.35	19.4043	1.52	108.66	22.51	108.66	12.42	118.75	15.52	46.57	62.09	77.62	77.62	186.28
H	40,698	1,565.31	19.5663	1.53	109.57	22.70	109.57	12.52	119.75	15.65	46.96	62.61	78.27	78.27	187.84
7 D	40,172	1,545.08	19.3135	1.51	108.16	22.40	108.16	12.36	118.20	15.45	46.35	61.80	77.25	77.25	185.41
E	40,532	1,558.92	19.4865	1.52	109.12	22.60	109.12	12.47	119.26	15.59	46.77	62.36	77.95	77.95	187.07
F	40,891	1,572.73	19.6591	1.54	110.09	22.80	110.09	12.58	120.31	15.73	47.18	62.91	78.64	78.64	188.73
G	41,252	1,586.62	19.8327	1.55	111.06	23.01	111.06	12.69	121.38	15.87	47.60	63.46	79.33	79.33	190.39
H	41,615	1,600.58	20.0072	1.57	112.04	23.21	112.04	12.80	122.44	16.01	48.02	64.02	80.03	80.03	192.07

PART-TIME FLEXIBLE RATES	Grade	Pay Steps				
		D	E	F	G	H
	2	18.34	18.46	18.58	18.71	18.83
	3	18.64	18.77	18.90	19.03	19.16
	4	18.96	19.10	19.24	19.39	19.53
	5	19.30	19.46	19.61	19.77	19.92
	6	19.68	19.85	20.02	20.18	20.35
	7	20.09	20.27	20.45	20.63	20.81

PART-TIME REGULAR RATES	Grade	Pay Steps				
		D	E	F	G	H
	2	17.63	17.75	17.87	17.99	18.11
	3	17.92	18.04	18.17	18.30	18.43
	4	18.23	18.36	18.50	18.64	18.78
	5	18.56	18.71	18.86	19.00	19.15
	6	18.92	19.08	19.25	19.40	19.57
	7	19.31	19.49	19.66	19.83	20.01

APWU
SALARY AND RATES
Schedule 1 and 2

AMERICAN POSTAL WORKERS UNION, AFL-CIO
1300 L STREET, NW, WASHINGTON, DC 20005

APWU National Agreement
Schedule Two — Salary and Rates
Effective September 7, 2002

Grade and Step	Full-time Regular Rates — Annual Salary	Biweekly Pay	Straight Time	Night Differential	CSRS 7% CSRS	1.45% MEDICARE	Maximum 7% TSP	0.80 FERS	7.65% FICA	1% USPS MINIMUM	3% EMPLOYEE	3% USPS	5% EMPLOYEE	5% USPS	12% EMPLOYEE MAXIMUM
1 BB	23,548	905.69	11.3212	0.84	63.40	13.13	63.40	7.25	69.29	9.06	27.17	36.23	45.28	45.28	108.68
AA	24,473	941.27	11.7659	0.88	65.89	13.65	65.89	7.53	72.01	9.41	28.24	37.65	47.06	47.06	112.95
A	25,398	976.85	12.2106	0.92	68.38	14.16	68.38	7.81	74.73	9.77	29.31	39.07	48.84	48.84	117.22
B	26,323	1,012.42	12.6553	0.95	70.87	14.68	70.87	8.10	77.45	10.12	30.37	40.50	50.62	50.62	121.49
C	27,248	1,048.00	13.1000	0.99	73.36	15.20	73.36	8.38	80.17	10.48	31.44	41.92	52.40	52.40	125.76
D	28,173	1,083.58	13.5447	1.03	75.85	15.71	75.85	8.67	82.89	10.84	32.51	43.34	54.18	54.18	130.03
E	29,098	1,119.15	13.9894	1.07	78.34	16.23	78.34	8.95	85.62	11.19	33.57	44.77	55.96	55.96	134.30
F	30,023	1,154.73	14.4341	1.11	80.83	16.74	80.83	9.24	88.34	11.55	34.64	46.19	57.74	57.74	138.57
G	30,948	1,190.31	14.8788	1.15	83.32	17.26	83.32	9.52	91.06	11.90	35.71	47.61	59.52	59.52	142.84
H	31,873	1,225.88	15.3236	1.18	85.81	17.78	85.81	9.81	93.78	12.26	36.78	49.04	61.29	61.29	147.11
I	32,798	1,261.46	15.7683	1.22	88.30	18.29	88.30	10.09	96.50	12.61	37.84	50.46	63.07	63.07	151.38
J	33,723	1,297.04	16.2130	1.26	90.79	18.81	90.79	10.38	99.22	12.97	38.91	51.88	64.85	64.85	155.64
K	34,648	1,332.62	16.6577	1.30	93.28	19.32	93.28	10.66	101.95	13.33	39.98	53.30	66.63	66.63	159.91
L	35,573	1,368.19	17.1024	1.34	95.77	19.84	95.77	10.95	104.67	13.68	41.05	54.73	68.41	68.41	164.18
M	36,498	1,403.77	17.5471	1.37	98.26	20.35	98.26	11.23	107.39	14.04	42.11	56.15	70.19	70.19	168.45
N	37,423	1,439.35	17.9918	1.41	100.75	20.87	100.75	11.51	110.11	14.39	43.18	57.57	71.97	71.97	172.72
O	38,620	1,485.38	18.5673	1.45	103.98	21.54	103.98	11.88	113.63	14.85	44.56	59.42	74.27	74.27	178.25
RC	39,545	1,520.96	19.0120	1.46	106.47	22.05	106.47	12.17	116.35	15.21	45.63	60.84	76.05	76.05	182.52
2 BB	24,618	946.85	11.8356	0.88	66.28	13.73	66.28	7.57	72.43	9.47	28.41	37.87	47.34	47.34	113.62
AA	25,534	982.08	12.2760	0.92	68.75	14.24	68.75	7.86	75.13	9.82	29.46	39.28	49.10	49.10	117.85
A	26,450	1,017.31	12.7163	0.95	71.21	14.75	71.21	8.14	77.82	10.17	30.52	40.69	50.87	50.87	122.08
B	27,366	1,052.54	13.1567	0.99	73.68	15.26	73.68	8.42	80.52	10.53	31.58	42.10	52.63	52.63	126.30
C	28,282	1,087.77	13.5971	1.03	76.14	15.77	76.14	8.70	83.21	10.88	32.63	43.51	54.39	54.39	130.53
D	29,198	1,123.00	14.0375	1.07	78.61	16.28	78.61	8.98	85.91	11.23	33.69	44.92	56.15	56.15	134.76
E	30,114	1,158.23	14.4779	1.11	81.08	16.79	81.08	9.27	88.60	11.58	34.75	46.33	57.91	57.91	138.99
F	31,030	1,193.46	14.9183	1.14	83.54	17.31	83.54	9.55	91.30	11.93	35.80	47.74	59.67	59.67	143.22
G	31,946	1,228.69	15.3587	1.18	86.01	17.82	86.01	9.83	93.99	12.29	36.86	49.15	61.43	61.43	147.44
H	32,862	1,263.92	15.7990	1.22	88.47	18.33	88.47	10.11	96.69	12.64	37.92	50.56	63.20	63.20	151.67
I	33,778	1,299.15	16.2394	1.26	90.94	18.84	90.94	10.39	99.39	12.99	38.97	51.97	64.96	64.96	155.90
J	34,694	1,334.38	16.6798	1.29	93.41	19.35	93.41	10.68	102.08	13.34	40.03	53.38	66.72	66.72	160.13
K	35,610	1,369.62	17.1202	1.33	95.87	19.86	95.87	10.96	104.78	13.70	41.09	54.78	68.48	68.48	164.35
L	36,526	1,404.85	17.5606	1.37	98.34	20.37	98.34	11.24	107.47	14.05	42.15	56.19	70.24	70.24	168.58
M	37,442	1,440.08	18.0010	1.41	100.81	20.88	100.81	11.52	110.17	14.40	43.20	57.60	72.00	72.00	172.81
N	38,358	1,475.31	18.4413	1.44	103.27	21.39	103.27	11.80	112.86	14.75	44.26	59.01	73.77	73.77	177.04
O	39,374	1,514.38	18.9298	1.48	106.01	21.96	106.01	12.12	115.85	15.14	45.43	60.58	75.72	75.72	181.73
RC	40,290	1,549.62	19.3702	1.49	108.47	22.47	108.47	12.40	118.55	15.50	46.49	61.98	77.48	77.48	185.95
3 BB	25,681	987.73	12.3466	0.93	69.14	14.32	69.14	7.90	75.56	9.88	29.63	39.51	49.39	49.39	118.53
AA	26,588	1,022.62	12.7827	0.97	71.58	14.83	71.58	8.18	78.23	10.23	30.68	40.90	51.13	51.13	122.71
A	27,495	1,057.50	13.2188	1.00	74.03	15.33	74.03	8.46	80.90	10.58	31.73	42.30	52.88	52.88	126.90
B	28,402	1,092.38	13.6548	1.04	76.47	15.84	76.47	8.74	83.57	10.92	32.77	43.70	54.62	54.62	131.09
C	29,309	1,127.27	14.0909	1.08	78.91	16.35	78.91	9.02	86.24	11.27	33.82	45.09	56.36	56.36	135.27
D	30,216	1,162.15	14.5269	1.11	81.35	16.85	81.35	9.30	88.90	11.62	34.86	46.49	58.11	58.11	139.46
E	31,123	1,197.04	14.9630	1.15	83.79	17.36	83.79	9.58	91.57	11.97	35.91	47.88	59.85	59.85	143.64
F	32,030	1,231.92	15.3990	1.18	86.23	17.86	86.23	9.86	94.24	12.32	36.96	49.28	61.60	61.60	147.83
G	32,937	1,266.81	15.8351	1.22	88.68	18.37	88.68	10.13	96.91	12.67	38.00	50.67	63.34	63.34	152.02
H	33,844	1,301.69	16.2712	1.26	91.12	18.87	91.12	10.41	99.58	13.02	39.05	52.07	65.08	65.08	156.20
I	34,751	1,336.58	16.7072	1.29	93.56	19.38	93.56	10.69	102.25	13.37	40.10	53.46	66.83	66.83	160.39
J	35,658	1,371.46	17.1433	1.33	96.00	19.89	96.00	10.97	104.92	13.71	41.14	54.86	68.57	68.57	164.58
K	36,565	1,406.35	17.5793	1.37	98.44	20.39	98.44	11.25	107.59	14.06	42.19	56.25	70.32	70.32	168.76
L	37,472	1,441.23	18.0154	1.40	100.89	20.90	100.89	11.53	110.25	14.41	43.24	57.65	72.06	72.06	172.95
M	38,379	1,476.12	18.4514	1.44	103.33	21.40	103.33	11.81	112.92	14.76	44.28	59.04	73.81	73.81	177.13
N	39,286	1,511.00	18.8875	1.47	105.77	21.91	105.77	12.09	115.59	15.11	45.33	60.44	75.55	75.55	181.32
O	40,193	1,545.88	19.3236	1.51	108.21	22.42	108.21	12.37	118.26	15.46	46.38	61.84	77.29	77.29	185.51
RC	41,100	1,580.77	19.7596	1.52	110.65	22.92	110.65	12.65	120.93	15.81	47.42	63.23	79.04	79.04	189.69
4 A	29,116	1,119.85	13.9981	1.06	78.39	16.24	78.39	8.96	85.67	11.20	33.60	44.79	55.99	55.99	134.38
B	29,969	1,152.65	14.4082	1.10	80.69	16.71	80.69	9.22	88.18	11.53	34.58	46.11	57.63	57.63	138.32
C	30,822	1,185.46	14.8183	1.13	82.98	17.19	82.98	9.48	90.69	11.85	35.56	47.42	59.27	59.27	142.26
D	31,675	1,218.27	15.2284	1.17	85.28	17.66	85.28	9.75	93.20	12.18	36.55	48.73	60.91	60.91	146.19
E	32,528	1,251.08	15.6385	1.20	87.58	18.14	87.58	10.01	95.71	12.51	37.53	50.04	62.55	62.55	150.13
F	33,381	1,283.88	16.0486	1.24	89.87	18.62	89.87	10.27	98.22	12.84	38.52	51.36	64.19	64.19	154.07
G	34,234	1,316.69	16.4587	1.27	92.17	19.09	92.17	10.53	100.73	13.17	39.50	52.67	65.83	65.83	158.00
H	35,087	1,349.50	16.8688	1.31	94.47	19.57	94.47	10.80	103.24	13.50	40.49	53.98	67.48	67.48	161.94
I	35,940	1,382.31	17.2788	1.34	96.76	20.04	96.76	11.06	105.75	13.82	41.47	55.29	69.12	69.12	165.88
J	36,793	1,415.12	17.6889	1.38	99.06	20.52	99.06	11.32	108.26	14.15	42.45	56.60	70.76	70.76	169.81
K	37,646	1,447.92	18.0990	1.41	101.35	20.99	101.35	11.58	110.77	14.48	43.44	57.92	72.40	72.40	173.75
L	38,499	1,480.73	18.5091	1.45	103.65	21.47	103.65	11.85	113.28	14.81	44.42	59.23	74.04	74.04	177.69
M	39,352	1,513.54	18.9192	1.48	105.95	21.95	105.95	12.11	115.79	15.14	45.41	60.54	75.68	75.68	181.62
N	40,205	1,546.35	19.3293	1.52	108.24	22.42	108.24	12.37	118.30	15.46	46.39	61.85	77.32	77.32	185.56
O	41,058	1,579.15	19.7394	1.55	110.54	22.90	110.54	12.63	120.81	15.79	47.37	63.17	78.96	78.96	189.50
RC	41,911	1,611.96	20.1495	1.56	112.84	23.37	112.84	12.90	123.32	16.12	48.36	64.48	80.60	80.60	193.44

APWU National Agreement
Schedule Two — Salary and Rates
Effective September 7, 2002

Grade and Step	Annual Salary	Biweekly Pay	Straight Time	Night Differential	7% CSRS	1.45% MEDICARE	Maximum 7% TSP	0.80 FERS	7.65% FICA	1% USPS MINIMUM	3% EMPLOYEE	3% USPS	5% EMPLOYEE	5% USPS	12% EMPLOYEE MAXIMUM
5 A	30,693	1,180.50	14.7563	1.12	82.64	17.12	82.64	9.44	90.31	11.81	35.42	47.22	59.03	59.03	141.66
B	31,500	1,211.54	15.1442	1.15	84.81	17.57	84.81	9.69	92.68	12.12	36.35	48.46	60.58	60.58	145.38
C	32,307	1,242.58	15.5322	1.19	86.98	18.02	86.98	9.94	95.06	12.43	37.28	49.70	62.13	62.13	149.11
D	33,114	1,273.62	15.9202	1.22	89.15	18.47	89.15	10.19	97.43	12.74	38.21	50.94	63.68	63.68	152.83
E	33,921	1,304.65	16.3082	1.25	91.33	18.92	91.33	10.44	99.81	13.05	39.14	52.19	65.23	65.23	156.56
F	34,728	1,335.69	16.6962	1.28	93.50	19.37	93.50	10.69	102.18	13.36	40.07	53.43	66.78	66.78	160.28
G	35,535	1,366.73	17.0841	1.32	95.67	19.82	95.67	10.93	104.55	13.67	41.00	54.67	68.34	68.34	164.01
H	36,342	1,397.77	17.4721	1.35	97.84	20.27	97.84	11.18	106.93	13.98	41.93	55.91	69.89	69.89	167.73
I	37,149	1,428.81	17.8601	1.38	100.02	20.72	100.02	11.43	109.30	14.29	42.86	57.15	71.44	71.44	171.46
J	37,956	1,459.85	18.2481	1.42	102.19	21.17	102.19	11.68	111.68	14.60	43.80	58.39	72.99	72.99	175.18
K	38,763	1,490.88	18.6361	1.45	104.36	21.62	104.36	11.93	114.05	14.91	44.73	59.64	74.54	74.54	178.91
L	39,570	1,521.92	19.0240	1.48	106.53	22.07	106.53	12.18	116.43	15.22	45.66	60.88	76.10	76.10	182.63
M	40,377	1,552.96	19.4120	1.51	108.71	22.52	108.71	12.42	118.80	15.53	46.59	62.12	77.65	77.65	186.36
N	41,184	1,584.00	19.8000	1.55	110.88	22.97	110.88	12.67	121.18	15.84	47.52	63.36	79.20	79.20	190.08
O	41,991	1,615.04	20.1880	1.58	113.05	23.42	113.05	12.92	123.55	16.15	48.45	64.60	80.75	80.75	193.80
RC	42,798	1,646.08	20.5760	1.60	115.23	23.87	115.23	13.17	125.92	16.46	49.38	65.84	82.30	82.30	197.53
6 A	32,369	1,244.96	15.5620	1.19	87.15	18.05	87.15	9.96	95.24	12.45	37.35	49.80	62.25	62.25	149.40
B	33,131	1,274.27	15.9284	1.22	89.20	18.48	89.20	10.19	97.48	12.74	38.23	50.97	63.71	63.71	152.91
C	33,893	1,303.58	16.2947	1.25	91.25	18.90	91.25	10.43	99.72	13.04	39.11	52.14	65.18	65.18	156.43
D	34,655	1,332.88	16.6611	1.28	93.30	19.33	93.30	10.66	101.97	13.33	39.99	53.32	66.64	66.64	159.95
E	35,417	1,362.19	17.0274	1.32	95.35	19.75	95.35	10.90	104.21	13.62	40.87	54.49	68.11	68.11	163.46
F	36,179	1,391.50	17.3938	1.35	97.41	20.18	97.41	11.13	106.45	13.92	41.75	55.66	69.58	69.58	166.98
G	36,941	1,420.81	17.7601	1.38	99.46	20.60	99.46	11.37	108.69	14.21	42.62	56.83	71.04	71.04	170.50
H	37,703	1,450.12	18.1264	1.41	101.51	21.03	101.51	11.60	110.93	14.50	43.50	58.00	72.51	72.51	174.01
I	38,465	1,479.42	18.4928	1.44	103.56	21.45	103.56	11.84	113.18	14.79	44.38	59.18	73.97	73.97	177.53
J	39,227	1,508.73	18.8591	1.47	105.61	21.88	105.61	12.07	115.42	15.09	45.26	60.35	75.44	75.44	181.05
K	39,989	1,538.04	19.2255	1.50	107.66	22.30	107.66	12.30	117.66	15.38	46.14	61.52	76.90	76.90	184.56
L	40,751	1,567.35	19.5918	1.54	109.71	22.73	109.71	12.54	119.90	15.67	47.02	62.69	78.37	78.37	188.08
M	41,513	1,596.65	19.9582	1.57	111.77	23.15	111.77	12.77	122.14	15.97	47.90	63.87	79.83	79.83	191.60
N	42,275	1,625.96	20.3245	1.60	113.82	23.58	113.82	13.01	124.39	16.26	48.78	65.04	81.30	81.30	195.12
O	43,037	1,655.27	20.6909	1.63	115.87	24.00	115.87	13.24	126.63	16.55	49.66	66.21	82.76	82.76	198.63
RC	43,799	1,684.58	21.0572	1.64	117.92	24.43	117.92	13.48	128.87	16.85	50.54	67.38	84.23	84.23	202.15
7 A	33,144	1,274.77	15.9346	1.22	89.23	18.48	89.23	10.20	97.52	12.75	38.24	50.99	63.74	63.74	152.97
B	33,929	1,304.96	16.3120	1.25	91.35	18.92	91.35	10.44	99.83	13.05	39.15	52.20	65.25	65.25	156.60
C	34,714	1,335.15	16.6894	1.28	93.46	19.36	93.46	10.68	102.14	13.35	40.05	53.41	66.76	66.76	160.22
D	35,499	1,365.35	17.0668	1.32	95.57	19.80	95.57	10.92	104.45	13.65	40.96	54.61	68.27	68.27	163.84
E	36,284	1,395.54	17.4442	1.35	97.69	20.24	97.69	11.16	106.76	13.96	41.87	55.82	69.78	69.78	167.46
F	37,069	1,425.73	17.8216	1.38	99.80	20.67	99.80	11.41	109.07	14.26	42.77	57.03	71.29	71.29	171.09
G	37,854	1,455.92	18.1990	1.41	101.91	21.11	101.91	11.65	111.38	14.56	43.68	58.24	72.80	72.80	174.71
H	38,639	1,486.12	18.5764	1.45	104.03	21.55	104.03	11.89	113.69	14.86	44.58	59.44	74.31	74.31	178.33
I	39,424	1,516.31	18.9538	1.48	106.14	21.99	106.14	12.13	116.00	15.16	45.49	60.65	75.82	75.82	181.96
J	40,209	1,546.50	19.3313	1.51	108.26	22.42	108.26	12.37	118.31	15.47	46.40	61.86	77.33	77.33	185.58
K	40,994	1,576.69	19.7087	1.54	110.37	22.86	110.37	12.61	120.62	15.77	47.30	63.07	78.83	78.83	189.20
L	41,779	1,606.88	20.0861	1.57	112.48	23.30	112.48	12.86	122.93	16.07	48.21	64.28	80.34	80.34	192.83
M	42,564	1,637.08	20.4635	1.61	114.60	23.74	114.60	13.10	125.24	16.37	49.11	65.48	81.85	81.85	196.45
N	43,349	1,667.27	20.8409	1.64	116.71	24.18	116.71	13.34	127.55	16.67	50.02	66.69	83.36	83.36	200.07
O	44,134	1,697.46	21.2183	1.67	118.82	24.61	118.82	13.58	129.86	16.97	50.92	67.90	84.87	84.87	203.70
RC	44,919	1,727.65	21.5957	1.69	120.94	25.05	120.94	13.82	132.17	17.28	51.83	69.11	86.38	86.38	207.32
8 D	38,890	1,495.77	18.6971	1.45	104.70	21.69	104.70	11.97	114.43	14.96	44.87	59.83	74.79	74.79	179.49
E	39,477	1,518.35	18.9793	1.48	106.28	22.02	106.28	12.15	116.15	15.18	45.55	60.73	75.92	75.92	182.20
F	40,064	1,540.92	19.2615	1.50	107.86	22.34	107.86	12.33	117.88	15.41	46.23	61.64	77.05	77.05	184.91
G	40,651	1,563.50	19.5438	1.53	109.45	22.67	109.45	12.51	119.61	15.64	46.91	62.54	78.18	78.18	187.62
H	41,238	1,586.08	19.8260	1.55	111.03	23.00	111.03	12.69	121.33	15.86	47.58	63.44	79.30	79.30	190.33
I	41,825	1,608.65	20.1082	1.58	112.61	23.33	112.61	12.87	123.06	16.09	48.26	64.35	80.43	80.43	193.04
J	42,412	1,631.23	20.3904	1.60	114.19	23.65	114.19	13.05	124.79	16.31	48.94	65.25	81.56	81.56	195.75
K	42,999	1,653.81	20.6726	1.62	115.77	23.98	115.77	13.23	126.52	16.54	49.61	66.15	82.69	82.69	198.46
L	43,586	1,676.38	20.9548	1.65	117.35	24.31	117.35	13.41	128.24	16.76	50.29	67.06	83.82	83.82	201.17
M	44,173	1,698.96	21.2370	1.67	118.93	24.63	118.93	13.59	129.97	16.99	50.97	67.96	84.95	84.95	203.88
N	44,760	1,721.54	21.5192	1.70	120.51	24.96	120.51	13.77	131.70	17.22	51.65	68.86	86.08	86.08	206.58
O	45,347	1,744.12	21.8014	1.72	122.09	25.29	122.09	13.95	133.42	17.44	52.32	69.76	87.21	87.21	209.29
P	45,934	1,766.69	22.0837	1.74	123.67	25.62	123.67	14.13	135.15	17.67	53.00	70.67	88.33	88.33	212.00
RC	46,521	1,789.27	22.3659	1.76	125.25	25.94	125.25	14.31	136.88	17.89	53.68	71.57	89.46	89.46	214.71

NOTES: 1. CSRS. The Civil Service Retirement System requires a 7% deduction from biweekly basic pay. In addition, there is a 1.45% deduction for Medicare. Total deductions is then 8.45%. Basic pay includes all of the COLAs. There are no exclusions from straight-time pay when computing CSRS deductions. However, the CSRS deduction is based on straight-time wages. CSRS deductions are not taken from wages for overtime, night differential, Sunday premium, etc. The Medicare deduction is made on gross wages. Therefore, the actual medicare deduction may be higher than reported here. CSRS participants may contribute to the Thrift Savings Plan; however, contributions are limited to a maximum of 7% of basic wages effective January 12, 2002 (up from 6%). The maximum contribution is reported here. 2. FERS. The Federal Employees Retirement System requires a .8% deduction from biweekly basic pay. In addition, there is a 7.65% deduction for FICA which includes Social Security and Medicare. Total deduction is then 8.45%. The FICA deduction is based on gross pay; therefore, the actual FICA deduction may be higher than reported here. 3. Thrift Savings Plan. CSRS employees may opt to invest in the Thrift Savings Plan as described in Footnote 1. Employees in FERS automatically benefit from the Thrift Savings Plan. The USPS is obligated to contribute a minimum of 1% of an employee's basic pay to TSP. The USPS is also obligated to match an employee's contribution up to 5% of basic pay. FERS participants may contribute up to 12% of basic pay effective January 12, 2002 (up from 11%). The pay chart shows the USPS mandated minimum contribution and how employee investment of 3% and 5% are matched by USPS contributions. The USPS matching figures include the 1% minimum contribution. The chart also shows the employee's maximum 12% investment. The USPS maximum matching amount is found in the 5% column. The USPS matches dollar-for-dollar your voluntary deduction up to 3% in addition to the 1% USPS automatic contribution, so the 3% USPS match column actually shows 4% of basic pay. By electing 3% an employee would have a total of 7% of basic pay invested. Over 3% and up to 5%, the USPS matches 50 cents for every employee dollar.

APWU National Agreement
Schedule Two — Salary and Rates

Effective September 7, 2002

Grade and Step	Annual Salary	Biweekly Pay	Straight Time	Night Differential	7% CSRS	1.45% MEDICARE	Maximum 7% TSP	0.80 FERS	7.65% FICA	1% USPS MINIMUM	3% EMPLOYEE	3% USPS	5% EMPLOYEE	5% USPS	12% EMPLOYEE MAXIMUM
	Full-time Regular Rates				CSRS			FERS		FERS — THRIFT SAVINGS PLAN					
9 D	39,805	1,530.96	19.1370	1.50	107.17	22.20	107.17	12.25	117.12	15.31	45.93	61.24	76.55	76.55	183.72
E	40,426	1,554.85	19.4356	1.52	108.84	22.55	108.84	12.44	118.95	15.55	46.65	62.19	77.74	77.74	186.58
F	41,047	1,578.73	19.7341	1.55	110.51	22.89	110.51	12.63	120.77	15.79	47.36	63.15	78.94	78.94	189.45
G	41,668	1,602.62	20.0327	1.57	112.18	23.24	112.18	12.82	122.60	16.03	48.08	64.10	80.13	80.13	192.31
H	42,289	1,626.50	20.3313	1.60	113.86	23.58	113.86	13.01	124.43	16.27	48.80	65.06	81.33	81.33	195.18
I	42,910	1,650.38	20.6298	1.62	115.53	23.93	115.53	13.20	126.25	16.50	49.51	66.02	82.52	82.52	198.05
J	43,531	1,674.27	20.9284	1.65	117.20	24.28	117.20	13.39	128.08	16.74	50.23	66.97	83.71	83.71	200.91
K	44,152	1,698.15	21.2269	1.67	118.87	24.62	118.87	13.59	129.91	16.98	50.94	67.93	84.91	84.91	203.78
L	44,773	1,722.04	21.5255	1.70	120.54	24.97	120.54	13.78	131.74	17.22	51.66	68.88	86.10	86.10	206.64
M	45,394	1,745.92	21.8240	1.72	122.21	25.32	122.21	13.97	133.56	17.46	52.38	69.84	87.30	87.30	209.51
N	46,015	1,769.81	22.1226	1.75	123.89	25.66	123.89	14.16	135.39	17.70	53.09	70.79	88.49	88.49	212.38
O	46,636	1,793.69	22.4212	1.77	125.56	26.01	125.56	14.35	137.22	17.94	53.81	71.75	89.68	89.68	215.24
P	47,257	1,817.58	22.7197	1.80	127.23	26.35	127.23	14.54	139.04	18.18	54.53	72.70	90.88	90.88	218.11
RC	47,878	1,841.46	23.0183	1.82	128.90	26.70	128.90	14.73	140.87	18.41	55.24	73.66	92.07	92.07	220.98
10 D	40,769	1,568.04	19.6005	1.54	109.76	22.74	109.76	12.54	119.95	15.68	47.04	62.72	78.40	78.40	188.16
E	41,428	1,593.38	19.9173	1.56	111.54	23.10	111.54	12.75	121.89	15.93	47.80	63.74	79.67	79.67	191.21
F	42,087	1,618.73	20.2341	1.59	113.31	23.47	113.31	12.95	123.83	16.19	48.56	64.75	80.94	80.94	194.25
G	42,746	1,644.08	20.5510	1.62	115.09	23.84	115.09	13.15	125.77	16.44	49.32	65.76	82.20	82.20	197.29
H	43,405	1,669.42	20.8678	1.64	116.86	24.21	116.86	13.36	127.71	16.69	50.08	66.78	83.47	83.47	200.33
I	44,064	1,694.77	21.1846	1.67	118.63	24.57	118.63	13.56	129.65	16.95	50.84	67.79	84.74	84.74	203.37
J	44,723	1,720.12	21.5014	1.70	120.41	24.94	120.41	13.76	131.59	17.20	51.60	68.80	86.01	86.01	206.41
K	45,382	1,745.46	21.8183	1.72	122.18	25.31	122.18	13.96	133.53	17.45	52.36	69.82	87.27	87.27	209.46
L	46,041	1,770.81	22.1351	1.75	123.96	25.68	123.96	14.17	135.47	17.71	53.12	70.83	88.54	88.54	212.50
M	46,700	1,796.15	22.4519	1.78	125.73	26.04	125.73	14.37	137.41	17.96	53.88	71.85	89.81	89.81	215.54
N	47,359	1,821.50	22.7688	1.80	127.51	26.41	127.51	14.57	139.34	18.22	54.65	72.86	91.08	91.08	218.58
O	48,018	1,846.85	23.0856	1.83	129.28	26.78	129.28	14.77	141.28	18.47	55.41	73.87	92.34	92.34	221.62
P	48,677	1,872.19	23.4024	1.86	131.05	27.15	131.05	14.98	143.22	18.72	56.17	74.89	93.61	93.61	224.66
RC	49,336	1,897.54	23.7192	1.88	132.83	27.51	132.83	15.18	145.16	18.98	56.93	75.90	94.88	94.88	227.70

PART-TIME FLEXIBLE RATES

Grade	BB	AA	A	B	C	D	E	F	G	H	I	J	K	L	M	N	O	P	RC
1	11.77	12.24	12.70	13.16	13.62	14.09	14.55	15.01	15.47	15.94	16.40	16.86	17.32	17.79	18.25	18.71	19.31		19.77
2	12.31	12.77	13.23	13.68	14.14	14.60	15.06	15.52	15.97	16.43	16.89	17.35	17.81	18.26	18.72	19.18	19.69		20.15
3	12.84	13.29	13.75	14.20	14.65	15.11	15.56	16.02	16.47	16.92	17.38	17.83	18.28	18.74	19.19	19.64	20.10		20.55
4			14.56	14.98	15.41	15.84	16.26	16.69	17.12	17.54	17.97	18.40	18.82	19.25	19.68	20.10	20.53		20.96
5			15.35	15.75	16.15	16.56	16.96	17.36	17.77	18.17	18.57	18.98	19.38	19.79	20.19	20.59	21.00		21.40
6			16.18	16.57	16.95	17.33	17.71	18.09	18.47	18.85	19.23	19.61	19.99	20.38	20.76	21.14	21.52		21.90
7			16.57	16.96	17.36	17.75	18.14	18.53	18.93	19.32	19.71	20.10	20.50	20.89	21.28	21.67	22.07		22.46
8						19.45	19.74	20.03	20.33	20.62	20.91	21.21	21.50	21.79	22.09	22.38	22.67	22.97	23.26
9						19.90	20.21	20.52	20.83	21.14	21.46	21.77	22.08	22.39	22.70	23.01	23.32	23.63	23.94
10						20.38	20.71	21.04	21.37	21.70	22.03	22.36	22.69	23.02	23.35	23.68	24.01	24.34	24.67

PART-TIME REGULAR RATES

Grade	BB	AA	A	B	C	D	E	F	G	H	I	J	K	L	M	N	O	P	RC
1	11.32	11.77	12.21	12.66	13.10	13.54	13.99	14.43	14.88	15.32	15.77	16.21	16.66	17.10	17.55	17.99	18.57		19.01
2	11.84	12.28	12.72	13.16	13.60	14.04	14.48	14.92	15.36	15.80	16.24	16.68	17.12	17.56	18.00	18.44	18.93		19.37
3	12.35	12.78	13.22	13.65	14.09	14.53	14.96	15.40	15.84	16.27	16.71	17.14	17.58	18.02	18.45	18.89	19.32		19.76
4			14.00	14.41	14.82	15.23	15.64	16.05	16.46	16.87	17.28	17.69	18.10	18.51	18.92	19.33	19.74		20.15
5			14.76	15.14	15.53	15.92	16.31	16.70	17.08	17.47	17.86	18.25	18.64	19.02	19.41	19.80	20.19		20.58
6			15.56	15.93	16.29	16.66	17.03	17.39	17.76	18.13	18.49	18.86	19.23	19.59	19.96	20.32	20.69		21.06
7			15.93	16.31	16.69	17.07	17.44	17.82	18.20	18.58	18.95	19.33	19.71	20.09	20.46	20.84	21.22		21.60
8						18.70	18.98	19.26	19.54	19.83	20.11	20.39	20.67	20.95	21.24	21.52	21.80	22.08	22.37
9						19.14	19.44	19.73	20.03	20.33	20.63	20.93	21.23	21.53	21.82	22.12	22.42	22.72	23.02
10						19.60	19.92	20.23	20.55	20.87	21.18	21.50	21.82	22.14	22.45	22.77	23.09	23.40	23.72

Transitional Employee Rates
Effective 11/17/2001

Grade	Rate
1	10.43
2	10.59
3	10.76
4	11.95
5	12.70
6	13.49

AMERICAN POSTAL WORKERS UNION, AFL-CIO

William Burrus, President
1300 L Street, NW
Washington, DC 20005